REPORTING INEQUALITY

Under increasingly intense newsroom demands, reporters often find it difficult to cover the complexity of topics that deal with racial and social inequality. This path-breaking book lays out simple, effective reporting strategies that equip journalists to investigate disparity's root causes.

Chapters discuss how racially disparate outcomes in health, education, wealth/income, housing, and the criminal justice system are often the result of inequity in opportunity and also provide theoretical frameworks for understanding the roots of racial inequity. Examples of model reporting from ProPublica, the Center for Public Integrity, and the San Jose *Mercury News* showcase best practices in writing while emphasizing community-based reporting. Throughout the book, tools and practical techniques such as the Fault Lines framework, the Listening Post, and the editors' Opportunity Index and Upstream-Downstream Framework all help journalists improve their awareness and coverage of structural inequity at a practical level.

For students and journalists alike, *Reporting Inequality* is an ideal resource for understanding how to cover structures of injustice with balance and precision.

Sally Lehrman is an award-winning reporter on medicine and science policy with an emphasis on race, gender, and social diversity. Her byline credits include *Scientific American, Nature, Health*, the *Boston Globe*, the *New York Times*, Salon.com and *The DNA Files*, three public radio series distributed by NPR. Honors include a Peabody Award, a duPont-Columbia Award, and the JSK Fellowship at Stanford University. She started and leads the Trust Project, a global network of newsrooms that is addressing the misinformation crisis through transparency.

Venise Wagner is a professor of journalism at San Francisco State University, where she has taught since 2001. She has a 12-year career as a reporter for several California dailies, including the *Orange County Register*, the *San Francisco Examiner* and *Chronicle*. She has covered border issues, religion and ethics, schools and education, urban issues, and issues in the San Francisco Bay Area's various black communities.

REPORTING INEQUALITY

Tools and Methods for Covering Race and Ethnicity

Edited by Sally Lehrman and Venise Wagner

Routledge
Taylor & Francis Group

NEW YORK AND LONDON

First published 2019
by Routledge
52 Vanderbilt Avenue, New York, NY 10017

and by Routledge
2 Park Square, Milton Park, Abingdon, Oxon, OX14 4RN

Routledge is an imprint of the Taylor & Francis Group, an informa business

© 2019 Taylor & Francis

The right of Sally Lehrman and Venise Wagner to be identified as the
authors of the editorial material, and of the authors for their individual
chapters, has been asserted in accordance with sections 77 and 78 of the
Copyright, Designs and Patents Act 1988.

Library of Congress Cataloging-in-Publication Data
A catalog record for this title has been requested

ISBN: 978-1-138-84987-7 (hbk)
ISBN: 978-1-138-84988-4 (pbk)
ISBN: 978-1-315-72512-3 (ebk)

Typeset in Bembo
by Swales & Willis, Exeter, Devon, UK

Visit the eResource at www.routledge.com/9781138849884

This book grew out of our strong friendship and deep commitment. We dedicate our work to our sister and brother of the heart, the late Dori J. Maynard and Gregory Lewis, who led the way in idea and actions.

We stand on their broad shoulders.

CONTENTS

ILLUSTRATIONS

Figures

Tables

ACKNOWLEDGMENTS

No project like this is possible without a community. We have been blessed with support from so many who have encouraged each of us individually and together. We have been spurred on by friends, colleagues, and even strangers who expressed confidence in the power and potential of the book. Many offered financial support to keep the project afloat. The donation from James Wagstaffe was key to getting our dream off the ground and making sure that writers could get paid. And it was with that money we were able to launch a crowdsourcing campaign to match the initial donation. Thanks for everything, Jim. And Jane Kay, your donation at a crucial moment injected momentum into the campaign. You are a wonderful friend who clearly understands our mission and its vital nature.

Thank you, thank you, thank you Pam Moore and Barbara Rodgers for taking time out of your busy schedules to listen to our pitch and help us refine it. You have broken ground in so many ways and learning from your experience has been invaluable. We are very grateful for your generous contributions to the crowdfunding campaign.

Bob Lehrman, your review of our original proposal provided important insights that continued to inform our work. So many others believed in our cause and generously donated their time or hard-earned funds to it. Thank you Sonny Albarado, Neil Chase, Darolyn Davis (D&A Communications), Laurie Fosner, Jesse Garnier, Ruth Ann Harnisch, Jan Christensen-Heller, Deeana Jang, Kristen and Paul Leathers, Teresa Moore, Annie Nakao, Sharyn Obsatz, and many more.

We are indebted to the scholars and theorists who study structural racism, implicit bias, linguistic theory, news media, and all the various forces that shape the way we perceive our world and interact with it. We especially want to acknowledge Hazel Markus, Amanda Lewis, Chris Bettinger, Patrick Plaisance, Troy Duster, john powell, Anthony Iton, and Zeus Leonardo. Your expertise helped us bolster our theories, methods, and tools. We also thank our many sources over our decades of reporting who sowed the seeds of this book through the knowledge and experiences they shared.

Evelyn Hsu, Martin Reynolds, and the Maynard Institute for Journalism Education, you and former president and chief executive Dori J. Maynard have provided the solid rock upon which rests this and many other efforts to help journalists truly reflect all of America. Thank you for your support and collaboration. As always, it's an honor to be connected with you and your mission.

We each owe a debt of gratitude to our respective institutions, the Markkula Center for Applied Ethics at Santa Clara University, Sally's academic home at the time of writing, and San Francisco State University, including faculty colleagues who have helped us bring race into the classroom more effectively. To Rajiv Bhatia, formerly of the San Francisco Department of Health, the Santa Clara County Department of Public Health, and the excellent community health organizations throughout the Santa Clara region – your assistance to Sally was vital in developing the social determinants model as a reporting tool. A big thank you to Sally's former student and researcher, Anton L. V. Avanceña, who compiled our index with a great deal of thought and care. Much gratitude from Venise also goes out to Columbia University's Graduate School of Journalism for the opportunity to test and refine some of these methods with students during her Laventhol Visiting Professorship.

Sally wants to thank her partner of 33 years, Tom Ballantyne, for picking her up when she fell down. His unwavering optimism and encouragement shined brightly even when things looked dire. A big hug as well to Patricia Westerfield, Lorraine Page, Mark Rosen, and Jane Kay. Your confidence, encouragement, and practical aid keep the pathway lit.

Venise wants to also thank Paul Guess – who has shared the belief that we must always find ways to do good in the world – and her SF State crew, Kitty Millet, Julietta Hua, and Sara Hackenberg. You kept her going with interventions at crucial periods when it seemed the end was far from sight. A big thank you to Laura Savage for the assist with the SFUSD.

To our editor, Erica Wetter, thank you for unfailingly believing in us, our work, and the importance of this book all along the way. Many, many others made important contributions at every stage of this book, from conception to completion. We wish we could name you all, but that would take another book. We are grateful for the community you continue to help create.

NOTE ON TERMINOLOGY

Terms for race and ethnicity – even the categories themselves – are always in flux and evolving, particularly across generations and geography. For that reason and in recognition of people's right to name themselves, we use multiple terms. You will find "black," "African American," and "black American"; "Latino/a" and "Hispanic"; "American Indian" and "Native American"; "Asian American," "Pacific Islander," and "South Asian"; and "white" used in these pages to describe US racial groupings.

INTRODUCTION

Sally Lehrman and Venise Wagner

What's in a Dream?

In 2000 Kareem Ervin was a teenager living in the Hunters Point, a then-pre-dominately poor African American neighborhood in San Francisco. At that time, Kareem was battling both family and personal demons, trying to heal wounds from the trauma of street violence. He wanted to straighten out his life. Luckily he had support from his sister, who was his guardian and wanted to see him soar. When co-editor Venise Wagner first met him, he seemed to be crossing over to the winning side of that fight, but it was unclear where he would ultimately land, for the lure of the streets was strong.

Kareem's story was compelling, but he was one source out of a couple of dozen, a mere anecdote in a story Wagner wrote in the *San Francisco Examiner* reflecting on the continued wealth gap between blacks and whites 37 years after Dr. Martin Luther King Jr. delivered his *I Have a Dream* speech.[1] It was a broad-brush depiction of the problem from the viewpoint of local and national black leaders. Though the story broke down a complicated issue into digestible parts for public consumption, it did not go far enough. It did not examine, for example, why the dream had thus far eluded Kareem. What were the various factors that kept him back? Why were neighborhoods such as his so devastated with unemployment, poor schools, poor health, failing parents, and poor infra-structure? What were the personal decisions that formed his path and what were the outside forces, the invisible yet no less real factors, that shaped those choices and kept opportunity at bay?

In today's political sphere we are hotly debating which policies are most effective to address inequity and, at the same time, the proper role of personal responsibility. Yet in general, journalists fail to equip the public to participate in this debate. Common journalistic practice is to rely on an anecdotal story-telling approach, which rarely illuminates the societal structures that play a role in shaping inequity. As a result, audiences are left with personal responsibility as the sole explanation for disparate outcomes.

Journalists use personal anecdotes to engage and create empathy in readers, working from an enduring journalistic principle that our work serves to call attention to the social problems that may start in one sector but eventually affect all of us. Our first task, editors like to say, is to "make people care." As in Wagner's story, however, this strategy can backfire. News reports are full of stories that try to convey deeper truths about how our society works, but instead become morality tales about poor personal choices.

Why This Book

We wrote, compiled, and edited this book to show journalists how to cover inequity in a more sophisticated, ethical, and ultimately more useful manner: to highlight the public policies, institutional practices, and other structures that shape the opportunities and the choices available to people like Kareem. With such tools, Wagner could have broadened the story of Kareem's internal demons with the external factors that he faced – the very factors that her audiences serve a role in shaping and can address.

In this book, we propose that journalists look beyond the low-hanging fruit of perceived personal, racial, or cultural deficit to explore personal choices and their outcomes from a more sophisticated vantage point. Working within traditional journalism frameworks and values, we show how to uncover the ways in which public policies and institutions shape available choices differently for various sectors of society and precipitate disparity. We offer tools and techniques to accurately and fairly report on who is hurt and how, and also who gains. Such an analysis helps audiences understand not only the forces at play, but also the power dynamics behind them.

The Disparities We All Know

In some sectors, the question of whether racial inequity exists at all has become racialized and politicized. Terms like "identity politics" and "political correctness" have become dismissive epithets suggesting that identity awareness itself is the cause of inequity. To some extent, it's true that identity can be chosen or emphasized to a greater or lesser degree in an individual's life. But focusing on this phenomenon is a distraction from a far more significant reality. Race is not just how people identify themselves, it is how the world identifies and interacts with them. Race – usually perceived by skin color, eye shape, hair texture, and verbal habits – intersects with class, gender, and religious differences to inform an individual's experiences of institutions and systems throughout American society. All too often, racialized policies and practices within those institutions and systems result in hidden, unequal access to opportunity – setting racial and class stratification in motion.

A look at the data reveals a shocking picture of inequity in the United States across race. Consider health.

- African Americans die more often from heart disease and strokes than any other racial or ethnic group.[2]
- Infections of HIV have declined among white men, but increased by 20 percent among Latino gay and bisexual men.[3]
- American Indians and Alaska Natives have faced a lower health status than other Americans for generations. They succumb at higher rates from multiple causes, including unintentional injuries and chronic lower respiratory disease.[4]
- Tuberculosis occurs 30 times more often among Asian Americans than among white people.[5]

We see large gaps in education as well.

- The dropout rate for Latinos is nearly twice that of African Americans and just over three times that of whites. African American students are nearly twice as likely to drop out as white youth.

The United States has the greatest wealth inequality in the world.[6] White Americans benefit most, enjoying more income, wealth, and other resources, too.

- Taken as a whole, white people are more likely to earn more money,[7] own homes, and have a higher net worth,[8] even controlling for a college education. African Americans are the most segregated and isolated racial/ethnic group in the United States and are often relegated to the poorest sectors of our society. Even middle-class African Americans experience more financial vulnerability and typically live in more resource-deprived neighborhoods than low-income white Americans.[9]

Journalists do cover such disparities, but only sporadically and typically failing to explain the deeper causes. Ultimately, we leave readers and viewers with the perception that black people, Latinos, American Indians, and disadvantaged Asian Americans are responsible for their own fate. Stanford University political scientist Shanto Iyengar first revealed this national sentiment clearly in his 1991 study, *Is Anyone Responsible?*, which found that news coverage of the poor and disenfranchised often blamed the victim.[10] His conclusions have significant implications for public policy and politics, but journalists have yet to adjust their work accordingly.

The Race Panic Story

The more common story of race in news today is the "race panic" story. In her book, *Everyday Language of White Racism*, anthropologist and linguist Jane Hill describes society's avoidance of explicit conversations about race except when unavoidably thrust into it.[11] "Race panics," as she calls them, occur when public dialogue about race is suddenly confused, charged, and agitated. People debate whether the event in question was intentionally racist or not. Usually the discussion remains contained with the frameworks of interpersonal acts of racism, explicit and intentional behavior by one person, or the decisions of a small group of people.

Examples include events such as the series of officer-involved deaths that gave rise to the #blacklivesmatter movement. Those publicly discussed over recent years include Michael Brown, 18, in Ferguson, Missouri; Laquan McDonald, 17, in Chicago; Tamir Rice, 12, in Cleveland; Freddie Gray, 25, in Baltimore; Keith Scott, 43, in Charlotte, North Carolina; Mario Woods, 26, and Luis Demetrio Góngora Pat, 45, in San Francisco; and Philando Castile, 32, in Minnesota. Each time, a race panic animates news coverage of the killing through to the verdict.

Beyond police shootings, there are other kinds of "race panic" stories. Throughout the 2016 presidential campaign, for instance, candidate Donald J. Trump frequently made comments about women, immigrants, Muslims, and blacks that were seen by many as derogatory. Weeks into his presidency, he put into motion campaign promises to build a wall between the United States and Mexico and restrict travelers from a number of Muslim-majority countries. Trump's statements and actions prompted a public conversation about whether or not these actions were racially motivated.

The "race panic" discussion often feels high-stakes, with one's political or social integrity potentially in question depending on the position she takes, and in whose company she takes it. Hill argues that such fault-finding debates that speculate about intent are essentially a dead-end. What society fails to explore, she says, are the implicit and structural acts behind a particular event, the ones that are embedded in language, patterned action, and policy. These racialized acts often occur outside of – even in spite of – one's will and intention, because they are rooted in long-standing social practices, institutional policies, and historical legacies.

In this book we are headed in the same direction. We want to move public dialogue to a more productive discussion about race, away from isolated interpersonal interactions to deeply lodged and broadly interacting racial structures.

While most people today believe racism festers primarily via overt interpersonal action, most such clearly definable racial animosity is not the norm. We do see the rise of white racial resentment,[12] which operates at a more subtle and diffuse level. This term describes feelings of hostility and fear against other racial groups perceived as less hard-working and motivated, yet believed to be getting "special favor" and gaining ground to whites' detriment.[13] Analysts increasingly find racial resentment connected to a person's positions on economic and other issues, including climate change, and posit it as a cause of increasing political animosity in the United States.[14,15] We believe journalists must raise awareness about this phenomenon, and also have the potential to offer much more. In recent years, social and political scientists have deepened their understanding of "systemic" and "structural racism" – the interlocking societal structures and institutional policies and practices that lead to racialized outcomes. They seek to understand segregation, for instance, not primarily as an outcome of individual preferences, but of structural racism in lending and real estate practices. Racial resentment can even be seen as structural at root and an outcome of the general lack of awareness of these racialized systems and structures.

Making the Invisible Visible

Returning to young Kareem Ervin, how did opportunity miss his sphere? What were the personal decisions that formed his path and what were the outside forces, the invisible yet no less real factors that shaped those choices and kept opportunity at bay? News stories today typically give audiences a view of the world from the varying perspectives of individual experience, leading the public to believe that individuals largely create their own circumstances. This emphasis perpetuates the dominance of values of individualism[16] and the American Dream, the notion that if any one person puts her mind to it she can achieve anything she wants. Yet individuals, of course, operate within communities, institutions, and society as a whole. Due in part to this imbalance of emphasis in the news, resulting public policy discussions tend to be guided solely by the maxim of personal responsibility rather than the principle of social responsibility.[17]

In this book we are not promoting one principle over the other. We do believe, however, that the public cannot have a productive debate about racial disparities and their roots without all the facts. Journalists have the power and obligation to enlighten the debate and inform the public about the constraints of individual power in the face of structural, institutional, and systemic confines. To do a thorough and ethical job, journalists must report on the ways in which the societal and physical environment affects the individual, including the role that race plays in the construction of that environment.

The Business of Journalism Stands in the Way

Today, effective coverage of inequity is further complicated by painful commercial pressures in mainstream newsrooms and the continuing distribution and revenue disruption online. As news organizations struggle to recreate their business model in the digital environment they have slashed newsroom staff, cut the number and length of stories, and trimmed reporting resources. Recognizing the resulting challenges, this book builds upon a scholarly foundation to make the process of covering inequity manageable. The approach described in these pages can help journalists focus and streamline their efforts, resulting in stories with impact.

This book is organized in four parts. The first part, A New Framework for Covering Race, provides the social science and journalistic foundation underpinning our approach. Following the traditions of muckrakers such as Ida Tarbell, who exposed the systemic workings of oil baron John Rockefeller and the impact of those systems in disenfranchising citizens, we provide conceptual frameworks for journalists to understand the systems of race. The second part, How Opportunity Works, offers journalists approaches to reporting that will help reveal the root causes of disparity. The third section of the book, Best Practices, offers sound journalistic practices that can help reporters address some of the obstacles that arise when writing about racial disparity. Here you will find practical approaches to dealing with stereotypes, interviewing across difference, and cultivating trust in communities that are under-covered in the news. Finally, in the fourth part, we offer case studies from a variety of beats that often deal with racial disparity. Here you will see how journalists have approached reporting projects on health, education, wealth, housing, safety net programs, and immigration.

Finally, we note that venturing into explorations of the root causes of racial inequity can be uncomfortable. It might be painful to learn about your own role in white privilege, or alternatively, the invisible harms that confront you as a person of color. And yet it may be some relief to learn explanations for experiences that seemed limited to your own life, but in fact are widely shared and structurally created. Most people aren't good at talking about race in mixed company. You may feel you are asking impolite questions or worry about saying the wrong thing. You may encounter resistance, even hostility. This type of reporting, while difficult, is powerful because it helps society step beyond accusation, recrimination, and denial to recognize the concrete possibilities for creating more opportunity for everyone. We acknowledge that reporting on unequal opportunity by race is not easy, but it's essential. We hope this book can offer you support and guidance along the way.

Notes

1 Venise Wagner. "The Dream Today: Economic Equality." *San Francisco Examiner,* January 17, 2000. Accessed March 23, 2017 from www.sfgate.com/news/article/ The-dream-today-Economic-equality-3079184.php.

2 Cathleen D. Gillespie, Charles Wigington, and Yuling Hong, MD. "Coronary Heart Disease and Stroke Deaths – 2009." *Morbidity and Mortality Weekly Report* 62, no. 3 (November 22, 2013): 157–160. Accessed July 14, 2018 from www.cdc.gov/ mmwr/preview/mmwrhtml/su6203a26.htm?s_cid=su6203a26_w.

3 Centers for Disease Control Fact Sheet: HIV Incidence: Estimated Annual Infections in the U.S., 2008–2014, February 2017. Accessed July 14, 2018 from www. cdc.gov/nchhstp/newsroom/docs/factsheets/hiv-incidence-fact-sheet_508.pdf.

4 Fact Sheets: Disparities, Indian Health Service, April 2018. Accessed July 14, 2018 from www.ihs.gov/newsroom/factsheets/disparities/.

5 Profile: Asian Americans. U.S. Department of Health and Human Services Office of Minority Health. Accessed December 30, 2018 from https://minorityhealth.hhs. gov/omh/browse.aspx?lvl= 3&lvlid=63.

6 Allianz. *Allianz Global Wealth Map*, 2018. Accessed July 14, 2018 from www.alli anz.com/en/economic_research/research_data/interactive-wealth-map/.

7 Rakesh Kochhar and Anthony Cilluffo. "Key Findings on the Rise in Income Inequality within America's Racial and Ethnic Groups." Pew Research Center, July 12, 2018. Accessed July 15, 2018 from http://www.pewresearch.org/fact-tank/2018/ 07/12/key-findings-on-the-rise-in-income-inequality-within-americas-racial-and-ethnic-groups/.

8 "Demographic Trends and Well-Being," in *On Views of Race and Inequality, Blacks and Whites Are Worlds Apart.* Pew Research Center, July 27, 2016. Accessed July 14, 2018 from www.pewsocialtrends.org/2016/06/27/1-demographic-trends-and-economic-well-being/.

9 John R. Logan and Brian Stults. "The Persistence of Segregation in the Metropolis: New Findings from the 2010 Census." US2010Project, March 24, 2011. Accessed January 15, 2018 from https://s4.ad.brown.edu/Projects/Diversity/Data/Report/ report2.pdf.

10 Shanto Iyengar. *Is Anyone Responsible? How Television Frames Political Issues.* Chicago, IL: University of Chicago Press, 1991.

11 Jane H. Hill. *The Everyday Language of White Racism.* West Sussex: Wiley-Blackwell, 2008.

12 Michael Tesler. *Post-Racial or Most-Racial? Race and Politics in the Obama Era.* Chicago, IL: University of Chicago Press, 2016.

13 Thomas B. Edsall. "The Persistance of Racial Resentment." *New York Times*, February 6, 2013. Accessed July 14, 2018 from https://opinionator.blogs.nytimes.com/2013/ 02/06/the-persistence-of-racial-resentment/.

14 Jeremy Deaton. "Racial Resentment May Be Fueling Climate Denial: New Research Finds a Link between Racial Prejudice and Climate Change Denial." NexusMedia, May 24, 2018. Accessed July 14, 2018 from https://nexusmedianews. com/racial-resentment-could-be-fueling-climate-denial-65d32fbeaa8e.

15 Salil D. Benegal. "The Spillover of Race and Racial Attitudes into Public Opinion about Climate Change." *Environmental Politics* 27, no. 4 (2018): 733–756. doi: 10.1080/09644016.2018.1457287.

16 Herbert Gans. *Democracy and the News.* New York, NY: Oxford University Press, 2003.

17 Iyengar. *Is Anyone Responsible?*

PART I

A New Framework for Covering Race

1

THE INDIVIDUAL IN CONTEXT

Sally Lehrman and Venise Wagner

Every individual makes choices, but she does so in the context of environmental, social and institutional forces – also called the socio-cultural context. Using concepts from the work of social psychologist Hazel Markus, the authors encourage journalists to examine disparity from this framework rather than focus solely on the individual, which can lead audiences to blame the victim for her own circumstances.

Blinded by Sight

A six-year-old black girl, blind since birth, cries inconsolably, refusing to bathe with her friend, who is white. She is afraid her black skin color will rub off on the white girl.

A white teenager, also blind, brings home a picture of a boy she likes at school to show her parents. She feels their disapproval. They explain that she cannot date him because he is black.

A blind white man is certain he can discern a person of Mexican heritage by scent.

Sociologist and law professor Osagie Obasogie interviewed blind people who had never seen another human being.[1] Yet they had strong concepts of race and ethnicity, holding to clear boundaries associated with these. They expressed beliefs about social norms, human difference, and likely behavior based on race. When it came to categorizing others, Obasogie found, the notion of "colorblindness" was meaningless. People who had no sight at all since birth still experienced – and assigned meaning and emotion to – racial distinctions in much the same way as people with sight.

Whatever our attitudes or beliefs about race, we tend to think about racial differences as self-evident, delineated by physical features. We know race, sighted people might say, because we see it. Our sense of real, concrete, and visible distinctions among us is so powerful that even blind people recognize and live by it. As "Jeremy,"[2] one blind person who Obasogie interviewed put it, race is " 'what you learn and then you use your eyes to identify it.' "

When we view race as something so plainly embedded in our bodies, we naturally think of its effects the same way. We look to individual bodies, minds, and behavior to explain the social stratification associated with race, including disparities in health, wealth, educational achievement, and interactions with police. Our commitment to understanding racial boundaries as physical, Obasogie told us in an interview, prevents us from perceiving the ideology and associated practices that bring race into being. Our recognition of race by sound, smell, and sight makes us blind to the multiple social and political commitments built up through US history that shape what race is and how it affects everyday lives.

We're "blinded by sight," as Obasogie puts it – blinded by the idea of race as a natural set of human divisions marked by a set of physical characteristics that signify distinct behavioral tendencies and cultural attributes.

Journalists who want to report accurately on the world and events within it must take into account this visual conditioning. We must learn to look beyond the surfaces of race we have been taught to believe are so important and to uncover the underlying influences that lead to disparate outcomes. To do so, we must step back from our inclination to understand race as "real" because we can see it. Instead we must learn to see the ways in which an individual's behavior and circumstances are shaped by communities and neighborhoods within the boundaries of race. We must examine institutions such as media, laws, finance, and education that constrain or propel lives, and the social systems that contour all of these. And we must help our audiences do the same. We must put the individual in context.

Such an approach is not a natural reflex for journalists because we tell stories. No matter our topic, news is about people who succeed, people who overcome obstacles, and people who are harmed. Nearly every piece of news has some central character or group of people that carries the story and helps others relate to the issue or event we are describing. The words and experiences of individuals help journalists know whether our instincts and assumptions are correct. Using real people's stories to populate our journalism, we believe, supports accuracy and draws the public in.

On their own, tales of individual triumph and woe, however, may not draw the public closer at all. Further, writing about an individual that may seem emblematic of some social concern does not necessarily offer a window into the problem we seek to highlight. Instead, it can activate learned assumptions and biases about race, class, age, or other demographic groupings, according to Mahzarin Banaji, a Harvard social scientist who studies implicit bias (see

Chapter 4 for more on this topic). Just as importantly, it can lead our audience to interpret the problem as individual at root. It can imply that social problems would go away if we all just behaved better. Unless we place our individual in context, we lead our audiences to believe that the inequities across race journalists reveal generally result from personal failings.

How Race Works

Consider that race is not built into our individual bodies by nature. It is not a simple matter of the differing physical features we take in with our eyes and other senses. Race in America, in fact, is a social phenomenon that traces its history to the economic and political forces that formed this country. One powerful institution, slavery, originally victimized people of all shades, then grew to rely upon the brutal maintenance of sharp social divisions. Black skin color as a marker for supposed mental and moral inferiority became a justification for a violent system of ownership and trade of Africans.[3] Similarly, as the colonies expanded, settlers began to look to theories of race to rationalize their attacks and displacement of Indian tribes.[4] The supposed moral weakness and barbaric character of the "Chinese race" helped propel the Chinese Exclusion Act of 1882.[5]

Our nation's earliest institutions and policies were designed to support unequal opportunity. We no longer hold such ideas and most of us have abandoned the racial ideology that conferred special status and benefits to a mythical "Anglo Saxon" elite.[6] We have transformed many economic and social structures designed to keep white-skinned people in power. Yet the harmful legacy of these structures remains. It can be difficult to perceive these enduring inequities built into American systems because we are visually biased toward seeing race as an individual – and biological – phenomenon. What seem to be natural differences, so clearly obvious, actually are a racial system at work, a system that we learn to see in particular ways from birth and that is embedded throughout all aspects of our society.

Individual choices, belief systems, and courage do matter in a person's life course, naturally. We often assert this with variations of the proud claim, "I am the master of my fate" or "I am the captain of my soul." Those lines were written in 1875 by the British poet William Ernest Henley, who lost a leg to tuberculosis and was orphaned at 12.[7] Henley's defiant stance has become a trademark of the American spirit. We spit in the eye of misfortune; we pull ourselves up by our bootstraps. Protagonists in the Horatio Alger stories of the mid 19th century climb from poverty to middle-class respectability, overcoming obstacles by sheer will and self-determination. In the United States, we point out, anyone can become president.

Success stories are a popular journalism standard. With a quick online search, we can find magazines like *Inc., Forbes,* and *Entrepreneur* describe the passion and grit that fueled corporate leaders.[8] Fox News features secrets of success shared by Dallas Mavericks' owner Mark Cuban.[9] In both the *Washington Post* and a local television station in Louisiana, we learn how college students "beat the odds" to graduate.[10] Yet if journalists more deeply probe our success stories, we will discover more than smart choices and a desire to succeed. We'll find a supportive context. And, if we probe individual struggle, we will find structures that make success more difficult.

The Socio-Cultural System

To better understand how individual action and decision-making works within a social context, we sat down with Hazel Markus, a social psychologist at Stanford University. Markus explained that every individual is part of a larger social-cultural ecosystem that includes that person's interactions with others, formal rules dictated by laws, informal rules promulgated by culture or custom, and the policies of institutions like the police, educational systems, or banks. "If you want to understand this individual, you have to understand the world that is embedding that individual," Markus says. "What we call agency, depends on that world." An individual's values, behaviors and attitudes can only be understood within that larger socio-cultural context, a context that ultimately shapes what appear to be choices.

White middle-class people often don't have any awareness of this context because it supports them, according to Markus. They are unlikely to notice the fact that they grew up in a middle-class neighborhood, they had good health care, and they had a family providing for them. Family members likely paid for their college or they received a scholarship, and they could fall back on a financial safety net. They could turn to a helpful network based on family, school, or neighborhood ties when they went out to look for a job or seek funding for an entrepreneurial idea. All these things feed into success – and all these things emerge out of social, institutional, and historical structures that smooth an individual's way. The system around a person enables that person's behavior, informs it, and primes it. "Individuals, their agency, they do what they *can* do in the larger socio-cultural environment," Markus says. "The larger socio environment informs what you can do, the likely courses of action for you."

Of course people can waste opportunities. Some can see good choices where others don't. There's room for the individual, Markus insists. It's the journalist's responsibility, however, to light up the whole system and all the differences along the way that enable and constrain individual choice.

Even the idea of agency itself can differ according to an individual's context. Markus and her colleague, Alana Conner Snibbe, used music preferences and behavioral tests to learn about the ways people think about agency. They found differences among the European American adults by socio-economic status, as indicated by educational attainment. Those who grew up with more resources viewed agency as the ability to express their uniqueness, pursue their individual dreams, exert influence over others, and control their environment and destiny. Those from lower socio-economic backgrounds saw agency as exerting self-control, retaining one's integrity, deflecting influence from others, and having the ability to adjust to circumstances that arise out their control. In general, the researchers concluded, the worlds of high school and college graduates differ in the level of control a person actually has over a given situation in their lives. Thus these differences in perceiving agency are contextually appropriate.[11] They also may shape the way an individual perceives and acts upon the choices in their lives.

It's important to understand here that when we talk about cultural context, we go beyond the customs and values of racial, ethnic, and class groups. We are also including how these groups interact with and are influenced by institutions (such as schools, as one example) and their practices (such as hiring). These symbiotic relationships are in constant interplay and create a foundation for blueprints beyond our individual awareness that inform how we act, think, and feel.[12]

Thus someone with means believes in and values their ability to exert influence on their own environment, the direction of their lives, and their own choices. On the other hand, someone without means may feel quite differently. They must hold true to their ability to stave off influence on their body or mind, and to exert control only within the limits of what's within reach.

Race influences one's sense of agency as well, according to Markus. If you are nonwhite "you have what we call a more interdependent sense of agency," she says.

> You're aware that you are connected with your group and what has happened to your group over history, and the fact that being associated with that group comes into every interaction. So you can't *be* independent, free from history, free from others, doing your own thing.

Along with the choices you wish to make, you live in a context of racial stereotypes, media images of your group, and attitudes about your group in schools, in companies, in other people's heads. W.E.B. DuBois called this double-consciousness the "measuring of one's self by means of a nation that looked back in contempt."[13] In an outrageously misfiring attempt at cultural competence, for example, a nursing textbook released in 2017 noted that "Hispanics may believe that pain is a form of punishment and that suffering must be endured if they are to enter heaven," and "Indians who follow Hindu practices believe that pain must be endured in preparation for a better life in the next cycle."[14] Nurses acting on these stereotypes may discount individuals' own reports about their pain and even attempt to be helpful by withholding adequate medication. Navigating such stereotypes that silently influence how people perceive and treat you can create stress, uncertainty, and anger — as well as self-doubt.

Blaming the Victim

When journalists overlook or misinterpret context, they can do a grave disservice – not just to the individuals involved, but to society as a whole. As journalists we often look at situations from a middle-class lens, even when our subjects may be experiencing things in a completely different context. The same can happen with race. We must resist the temptation to explain individual behavior solely through racial and ethnic culture, when in fact the interaction between culture and the surrounding society is tightly woven together. Socio-cultural context must be fully explained.

The April 2015 riots in Baltimore, unrest that broke out after African American Freddie Gray, 25, died while in police custody, provide a lesson about the complexities of context to all reporters interested in shining a light on inequality. The protesters were black, the police force was more than 40 percent black, the police commissioner was black, the mayor was black, and most of the city council was black, including the council president. This wasn't Ferguson, where the conflict between residents and the police after the shooting of 18-year-old Michael Brown fell neatly along racial lines. Many reporters found understanding the underlying causes of this unrest a challenge.

NPR's *Morning Edition* newscast on April 29, 2015, assessed the cause as class conflict. But this over-simplified explanation missed Baltimore's de facto policy and history of racial segregation, which left sections of black communities socially, politically, and economically isolated. People in these communities had few employment opportunities and poor educational options. Knowing this context would have helped reporters make a more precise assessment of the inequality that had pushed people to the boiling point. Richard Rothstein of the Economic Policy Institute, a nonpartisan, nonprofit think tank, aptly explained the historical and structural roots a week later in an interview on the NPR program, *Fresh Air*. The legacy of segregation informed nonwhite communities' interactions with institutions such as schools, social services, and the police, he said. With the death of Gray, frustrations exploded.

A year later, more protests erupted in cities across the country after the shooting of several African American men, many of them unarmed. But in some cities these protests turned into riots: Milwaukee after the police shooting of 23-year-old Sylville Smith, and in Charlotte, North Carolina, after the police shooting of 43-year-old Keith Lamont Scott. In both of these cities the history and legacy of racial segregation in housing and the schools has had a long reach, with Milwaukee ranking alongside Detroit as the most black/white segregated city in the country.[15] In both cases the shooting police officers were black, as were the victims. To understand the situation, reporters could have examined police interactions with members of these isolated communities. What kind of resources did the police department devote to the community?

Had the execution of the war on drugs created an antagonistic relationship? What was the police department doing to promote trust? What was the homicide rate in these areas and how successful was the police department in solving cases? Had officers undergone implicit bias training?[16]

Such context must be integrated into all the stories we tell about racial disparity. Individual actions and experiences – and in the case of these social uprisings, a group's actions – must be clearly shown within the forces of a larger socio-cultural ecosystem. Residential segregation, as shown above, is a driver behind myriad disparities and inequities, including the education gap, the health gap, and the wealth gap. Residential segregation limits the opportunities available in a neighborhood. As seen in Figure 1.1, white people generally tend to live with other whites and have very low interaction with people of color in their neighborhoods. Most of this racial separation has emerged through policy decisions at the federal and metropolitan level, not through individual choice. Reporters must follow a path of inquiry that reveals these invisible forces at work. Otherwise, readers absorbing an incomplete story fill in the narrative of their choosing. The result is very much the same as when we over-rely on the experience of a central character to tell the story of broader forces at work in the absence of context. Without further information, the public typically blames the victim.[17]

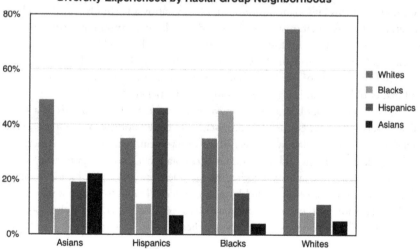

FIGURE 1.1   Diversity Experienced by Racial Group Neighborhoods

Source: US Census Bureau and "The Persistence of Segregation in the Metropolis: New Findings from the 2010 Census" by John R. Logan Brown University, and Brian J. Stults, Florida State University. March 24, 2011. Accessed November 26, 2018 from www.s4.brown.edu/us2010

The rioting protestors, for instance, were often portrayed as being violent, overly emotional, and irrational as they appeared to savage their own communities. The *New York Times, USA Today, Huffington Post*, CNN and others that covered the riots highlighted the angry rhetoric and "chaos" that erupted from what had largely been a peaceful demonstration.[18] One might surmise that the protestors had brought a hostile police presence onto themselves. Equally misplaced, the public may blame unequal outcomes on one bad actor seemingly solely responsible – a biased teacher, a revengeful bureaucrat, or a bully in uniform.[19]

Better Approaches

Showing the individual in context can be done with a few short paragraphs, clear infographics, or deeper investigations. The people of Ferguson, Missouri, erupted in anger and indignation immediately after the fatal shooting of Brown, once again after a grand jury decided not to indict the white police officer who killed the young black man, and yet again one year later. News coverage was slow to recognize the significance of the shooting and then, at first, focused on the confrontations, vandalism, and arrests.

Soon, journalists began to report on context that likely heightened the tensions: the militarized gear, weapons, and vehicles used by the police. Later, journalists – and public interest lawyers – began to unveil the context that may have set the majority black population alight. The *Los Angeles Times* delved into the segregation that followed white flight from the suburbs, the economic devastation caused by subprime loans and plant closures, the deterioration of schools and the lack of government representation that had robbed people in Ferguson and surrounding areas of their dreams.[20] Following a report by the Arch City Defenders,[21] a nonprofit legal group, the *New York Times*, MSNBC, and National Public Radio described the system of escalating traffic fines that the county used to raise funds and that could result in jail time for a simple traffic ticket.[22]

Other news sites looked at the context of US policing. In an analysis of a series of socio-economic indicators, a computational epidemiologist writing in *Wired* found a powerful correlation between the overrepresentation of African Americans in fatal police shootings and their underrepresentation in voter registration rolls.[23] *Vice*, in a series of infographics showing the race, gender, geographic locations, timeline, and outcomes of people killed by police officers, linked to a separate story and graphic that showed the ideological match between the public and police officers, state by state.[24] *Vox* reviewed community policing tactics and implicit bias.[25]

What the Deficit Model Lacks

These data-based stories often applied another important tactic when covering disparity. Instead of emphasizing deficit or loss, the journalists put unequal treatment into context by showing both deficit and advantage. This balance matters because when we cover disparity always as a loss, it once again can trigger unspoken societal expectations. In the flood of bad news about *some* groups, it may begin to seem that *other* groups "naturally" do better, make better decisions, or benefit from more successful cultural attributes.

Oscar Gandy and Zhan Li, while communications professors at the Annenberg School for Communication at the University of Pennsylvania, studied the tendency to use this "deficit model" to cover racial disparity. They reviewed some of the best investigative journalism in the country, examining nearly 800 stories dealing with disparity submitted to Investigative Reporters and Editors journalism competitions between 1978 and 2000.[26] They discovered some harmful trends in the ways journalists framed their stories; that is, what they emphasized as important, why it mattered, and which voices they included.

- Stories about disparity generally compared the position of one group to another, e.g., Latino home ownership is 20 percent lower than of white home ownership.[27]
- When making black/white comparisons, 75 percent of the stories framed the disparity as a loss for blacks, while only 12 percent described it as a gain by whites. In this construction, minorities were described as having a deficit.
- Rarely did stories attribute racism or institutional policies as a factor in the disparity.

Gandy and Li concluded that when reporters take this approach of emphasizing nonwhite loss over white gain, it tends to stigmatize. Such framing, they wrote, activates stereotypes that lead audiences to place responsibility on the victim or her community, rather than on the institutions or policies that reinforce inequity or privilege in various groups.

When journalists cover disparity and they illustrate not only who loses in the system, but also who gains, audiences can then understand the full impact of the systems in play. For example, a story that examines the high rate of diabetes in Native American communities compared to neighboring white communities could delve into the systems that hurt opportunity for good health on Indian reservations (e.g., limited food choices in federal food programs; lack of grocery stores; lack of means to grow one's own healthy foods; lack of mental health services; historical legacies) versus those that offer opportunity to neighboring white communities (e.g., greater access to grocery stores that have healthier food options; means to grow one's own small food garden; historical legacies).

Tricia Rose, who directs the Center for the Study of Race and Ethnicity in America at Brown University, describes the tendency to focus entirely on individual responsibility as an outcome of a "colorblind" ideology, the belief system that asserts that racism was long ago handled through laws such as the Civil Rights Act of 1964. Most people believe in racial equality, the thinking goes, and current laws make discrimination illegal. Without an awareness of the benefits that accrue based on whiteness, the only remaining explanation for disparity is individual behavior, including motivation and discipline, or cultural limitations.

Rose uses unemployment statistics as an example. US unemployment dropped fairly steadily during the Obama administration from 2010 to 2016. For 2015, the unemployment rate by racial and ethnic groups was as follows (see Table 1.1).[28]

TABLE 1.1 Unemployment Rate by Racial and Ethnic Groups, 2015

African Americans	10 percent
American Indian/Alaska Native	10 percent
Asian Americans	4 percent
Hispanic/Latino	7 percent
Native Hawaiian/Pacific Islander	6 percent
White	5 percent

Without further information, it's tempting to ascribe the differences in unemployment to stereotypes about a group's industriousness, cultural values, or "grit." But consider this: In one highly cited study, sociologists found that job applicants with names like Greg and Emily received 50 percent more interview call-backs from employers than applicants with names like Jamal and Lakisha, despite identical résumés.[29] Similar studies using Asian and Arab-sounding names found that "white" names had a significant advantage.[30] In another revealing study, Yale economist Abigail Wozniak studied the use of drug tests in employment and to her surprise, found that testing increased the hiring – and wages – of low-skilled African American workers. Apparently, when lacking the tests' evidence to the contrary, employers typically assumed that drugs would be a problem in this group – and as a result, seemed to gravitate toward hiring white females instead.[31]

Because white people tend to see their successes as individual accomplishments, they are bound to see other groups' disadvantages as individual. When policies, systems, and implicit assumptions are at work, however, journalists can and should portray disproportionate group success as an outcome of systems of privilege. Then audiences are more likely to make a connection between the individual and his or her social and institutional environment.

Context Rather than Culture

Sometimes we have to go beyond conventional thinking to find context. Education writers delving into root causes of the achievement gap between white and minority students might look at parent participation in schools as one element to explore.[32] When Venise covered education for the Hearst-owned *San Francisco Examiner* in the 1990s, she often heard teachers complain that minority parents weren't involved enough in the education of their children. The teachers had concluded that minority parents didn't value education as much as their white counterparts. Education advocates in minority groups argued against this assessment, charging that the district was tone deaf to the concerns of minority parents. Even though they wanted the best for their children, sometimes they were overtaxed with work, didn't know how to advocate effectively for their children, and felt intimidated by or mistrusted the bureaucracy. Much of the current public debate on this topic continues to promote the idea that minority culture fails to rise to the supposedly superior parental involvement of the dominant American culture, that is, white mores. If journalists aren't careful, stories can quickly devolve into an ethnocentric attack on minority values.

In fact, education scholars have identified a variety of parenting styles that influence children's learning. There are racial and ethnic differences in the emphasis of these behaviors in parenting, which has implications for school readiness and achievement. One finding is that black and Latino parents talk less with their children than white parents.[33] A reporter who comes across this study may be inclined to include this piece of evidence in a story about school efforts to improve parent involvement in student learning. But there is more to this story.

Annette Lareau, in her book *Unequal Childhoods: Class, Race and Family Life*, details class differences in parenting, offering some challenges to conventional thinking about the impact of culture. Lareau followed 88 families with children in the fourth grade and found parenting styles fell into two categories: Parents of higher socio-economic status – regardless of race – tended to rely on "concerted cultivation" – highly structured environments filled with an abundance of planned activities, while parents of low socio-economic status – working-class or poor – relied on "natural growth" – long periods of unstructured time.[34] Lareau did not place a higher value on one approach over the other but educators did, rewarding middle-class parents and their children with more approbation and reverence than working-class and poor families. In the end, children from higher socio-economic status families received the most benefit from the educational system, not necessarily because of their parents' behavior, but because the institution valued their parents' behavior.

Additionally, working-class and poor families didn't express the same kind of agency that middle-class parents did. (Remember the Snibbe and Markus study above on expressions of agency.) Rather than make demands of teachers and administrators, these parents deferred to their expertise, believing that educators knew what was best for their children academically. Middle-class to upper-class parents, on the other hand, demanded a lot from teachers and administrators. When things didn't go their way or in their child's favor, they demanded that the schools address their child's individual needs. At the same time, working-class and poor parents often mistrusted education officials, whom they feared in their role as officers of the state could report them to authorities for the smallest of infractions and take their children away. This feeling of vulnerability to institutions meant limiting their interactions with the school.

Race was not the focus of this study, but we know there are significant proportions of Latino, African American, Native American – along with some Asian American and white – children who fall into lower socio-economic groups.[35] Both class and race influence interactions with teachers and administrators.[36] While far from comprehensive, this study helps round out our understanding of the social-cultural context. Armed with this information, education reporters can tell a much fuller and nuanced story about parent involvement in schools in poor and minority communities or any other aspect of the achievement gap.

Explaining, or better still, showing this context through important detail about families and the choices before them, will advance public dialogue about racial and ethnic disparities. Markus suggests a simple reporting solution that contrasts the distinct journeys of two students and their families, highlighting the opportunities and assumptions that surround each one's education. "We want people to see these different experiences through time that have made people who they are," Markus suggests.

Mechanisms of Inequity

As we consider the context that shapes disparate outcomes by race, it's useful to consider the interplay across history, institutions, laws, and social hierarchies. Policies and practices within each of these areas interact and reinforce one another in ways that deepen inequality as a day-to-day experience with repercussions across generations. They form a system of discrimination and privilege – systemic racism – embedded in society so deeply that unequal opportunity becomes entrenched and lasting. The late sociologist Charles Tilly developed a theory to describe the series of mechanisms underlying this hidden system's long-term effects, which he called durable inequality.

Here's how it works. Take female farmworkers harvesting food around the country. Bernice Yeung and Grace Rubenstein, reporters from the Center for Investigative Reporting, looked at a system in the agricultural fields that emboldened and allowed men in positions of authority to sexually harass such workers with impunity. This collaborative investigation with the Investigative Program at the University of California, Berkeley, Graduate School of Journalism, revealed that sexual harassment complaints from workers often went ignored for years. Workers were threatened with and suffered retaliation for complaining.[37] Tilly described four mechanisms that hold such inequality in place: exploitation, opportunity hoarding, emulation, and adaptation.

Exploitation

A well-connected group of people harnesses the labor of others to profit from a resource that they control. The laborers are prevented from receiving the full value that their efforts add.[38] According to the farmworker investigation, more than half of US farmworkers immigrated to the United States illegally, making them vulnerable to deportation. As a result, employers have little incentive to obey labor protections and workers have little to no negotiating power. Many of the companies involved in sexual harassment complaints had no relevant policies in place and no grievance system. Additionally, many laws about workplace conditions don't apply to agriculture.[39]

Opportunity Hoarding

A network of people acquires and maintains access to a valuable resource, restricting access to this resource and creating practices that sustain their control of it.[40] The foremen and field supervisors who abused their power were able to get these positions and keep them because they came from a network of men who had strong connections with growers.

Emulation

The reproduction of unequal and hierarchal structures that already exist.[41] In the farmworkers' case, societal gender hierarchies and power dynamics between employers and laborers were reproduced in the fields. The alleged perpetrators, who were the women's supervisors and often hailed from the same region as their victims, used the threat of retaliation to demand sexual favors.[42]

Adaptation

Everyday practices, policies, and laws codify and bind inequity.[43] When women garnered the courage to complain, they did so through such agencies as the Equal Employment Opportunity Commission, the local Human Rights Commission, or through immigrant advocacy groups. In some instances, local prosecutors did not have enough evidence to file criminal charges – women often had not reported sexual attacks to the police because they feared the potential repercussions to their immigration status and/or jobs. To account for this, some cases tried to hold the companies liable for workplace conditions that fostered sexual harassment. In the end, some juries decided the companies were not at fault and some cases were settled.

Stories about immigration often fall into the category of whether it's good or bad for the country. Is a politician for it or against it? But a story that reveals the workings of durable inequality as described above reveals the layered impact of institutions at work (or not at work), corporate or workplace policies that guide actions, group culture and its influence, and individual choices and opportunities. The public needs to know about this intricate web of connections and interactions in order to interpret events and enter knowledgably into civic debates. Every mechanism of durable inequality need not be detailed. Simply by delving into one or more of them you can provide the context that transforms a story about inequality or harm into a much more informative – and actionable – work of journalism.

Break It Down across Beats

You might consider the workings of race and privilege so complex and so ubiquitous that they are hard to grasp. Fortunately, the newsroom beat structure enables us to look closely at their mechanisms by examining important spheres of social life. These include health, wealth and jobs, housing, education, and criminal justice. Mass media, including journalism, also plays a role.

Rose, who is leading a structural racism project at Brown University, makes the point that all too often, we examine context only through each of these spheres in isolation. To truly understand – and show – the mechanisms of systemic inequity, Rose emphasizes that we must view these spheres as interlocking gears that interact. They reinforce and drive one another along.[44]

Consider the legacy of housing discrimination. We've shown the consequences in neighborhood segregation and the impact on wealth accumulation. Also consider how the resulting pockets of poverty and wealth affect policing practices such as stop-and-frisk. Consider how wealth accumulation in a neighborhood influences zoning laws and local government choices about where to locate public services such as parks, transportation, and hospitals. And now, consider how segregation and neighborhood wealth accumulation affect the resources a family can tap for a health emergency, long-term medical needs, or higher education.

Journalism traditions often point us away from seeing systems because we dive into specific events and issues under debate. We tell individual stories, and rarely help the public connect the dots between those stories and the larger systems that shape them. We rely on our senses and instinct, which in the area of race, can lead us astray.

"Journalists observe something in the world, they write that down, and they interpret that as truth," says Obasogie, the sociologist and law professor who asked blind people about race. "If you're reporting simply what is in front of you, you're missing what's really going on." We tend to assume that race is easily seen and understood – and yet so much of this powerful force operates in ways we must endeavor to notice. We must develop alternate senses and instincts.

Fortunately, we can train ourselves to become more context aware – and make our journalism the same. We can uncover the policies, institutions and expectations that make race and its repercussions so real in society. In the journalist's role of helping society understand itself and make better collective decisions, it's important to put individuals in context. By revealing the hidden systems within society, we can offer the public opportunities to address the roots of unequal outcomes by race, and to choose whether and how to intervene.

Notes

1 Osagie K. Obasogie. *Blinded by Sight: Seeing Race through the Eyes of the Blind*. Stanford, CA: Stanford University Press, 2013.
2 Obasogie used pseudonyms for his interviewees to protect their identity.
3 Audrey Smedley and Brian D. Smedley. *Race in North America: Origin and Evolution of a Worldview*. Third edition. Boulder, CO: Westview Press, 2011, pp. 184–187.
4 Ibid., pp. 73–90.
5 Ronald Takaki. *A Different Mirror: A History of Multicultural America*. New York, NY: Little, Brown and Company, 1993, pp. 204–206.
6 Ibid., pp. 174–177.
7 William Ernest Henley. "Invictus." Accessed August 8, 2017 from www.poetry foundation.org/poems/51642/invictus#poem.
8 For instance: Lauren Ruef. "Sheryl Sandberg's Response to Life's Crushing Blows Is Grit and Resilience – Here Are 5 Ways to Build Both." *Entrepreneur*, September 20, 2017. Accessed February 4, 2018 from www.entrepreneur.com/article/300568.
9 "Mark Cuban on Secret to His Success and the Lure of Politics." *Fox News*, November 5, 2017. Accessed February 4, 2018 from http://video.foxnews.com/v/5636067861001/?#sp=show-clips.
10 Emma Brown. " 'Giving Up Wasn't an Option': How One Man Beat the Odds to Graduate from College." *Washington Post*, July 25, 2017. Accessed February 4, 2018 from www.washingtonpost.com/local/education/giving-up-wasnt-an-option-how-one-man-beat-the-odds-to-graduate-from-college/2017/07/25/3495b6b2-6e4d-11e7-9c15-177740635e83_story.html?utm_term=.526f46cd34f5; Lester Duhé. "Local College Graduate Beats the Odds, Wants to Inspire Others." KLFY.com, December 15, 2017. Accessed February 4, 2018 from www.klfy.com/news/local/local-college-graduate-beats-the-odds-wants-to-inspire-others/933636805.
11 Alana Conner Snibbe and Hazel Rose Markus. "You Can't Always Get What You Want: Educational Attainment, Agency, and Choice." *Journal of Personality and Social Psychology* 88, no. 4 (2005): 703–720. doi:10.1037/00223514.88.4.703.
12 Ibid.
13 W.E.B. Dubois. *Souls of Black Folks*. New York, NY: Penguin Books, 1969, p. 45.

14 Scott Jaschik. "Anger over Stereotypes in Textbook." *Inside Higher Ed*, October 23, 2017. Accessed February 7, 2018 from www.insidehighered.com/news/2017/10/23/nursing-textbook-pulled-over-stereotypes.

15 John R. Logan and Brian J. Stults. "The Persistence of Segregation in the Metropolis: New Findings from the 2010 Census." *US 2010 Project*, March 24, 2011. Accessed March 4, 2018 from https://s4.ad.brown.edu/Projects/Diversity/Data/Report/report2.pdf.

16 See Jill Leovy. *Ghettoside: A True Story of Murder in America*. New York, NY: Spiegel & Grau, 2015, for other structural forces that play out in policing minority communities.

17 Krishna Savani, Nicole M. Stephens, and Hazel Markus. "The Unanticipated Interpersonal and Societal Consequences of Choice: Victim Blaming and Reduced Support for the Public Good." *Psychological Science* 22, no. 6 (2011): 795–802.

18 Sheryl Gay Stolberg and Stephen Babcock. "Scenes of Chaos in Baltimore as Thousands Protest Freddie Gray's Death." *New York Times*, April 25, 2015. Accessed February 3, 2018 from www.nytimes.com/2015/04/26/us/baltimore-crowd-swells-in-protest-of-freddie-grays-death.html; Holly Yan and Dana Ford. "Baltimore Riots: Looting, Fires Engulf City after Freddie Gray's Funeral." CNN, April 28, 2015. Accessed February 3, 2018 from www.cnn.com/2015/04/27/us/baltimore-unrest/index.html; Arthur Delaney and Julia Craven. "Police, Protestors Clash in Baltimore after Freddie Gray Funeral." *Huffington Post*, April 28, 2015. Accessed February 3, 2018 from www.huffingtonpost.com/2015/04/27/freddie-gray-protest-mall_n_7154708.html; Yamiche Alcindor. "Baltimore Police Say Freddie Gray Protest Turns Destructive." *USA Today*, April 25, 2015. Accessed February 3, 2018 from www.usatoday.com/story/news/nation/2015/04/25/baltimore-protests-freddie-gray/26354515/.

19 *The Economist*, for example, examined the context of police officer trust and evaluation in police shootings, but then veered into the "one bad apple" explanation that seemed to place blame on "crazy" cops. "Don't Shoot." *The Economist*, December 11, 2014. Accessed August 2, 2017 from www.economist.com/news/united-states/21636044-americas-police-kill-too-many-people-some-forces-are-showing-how-smarter-less.

20 Tim Logan and Molly Hennessy-Fiske. "Ferguson's Mounting Racial and Economic Stress Set the Stage for Turmoil." *Los Angeles Times*, August 16, 2014. Accessed August 2, 2017 from www.latimes.com/nation/la-na-ferguson-economy-20140817-story.html.

21 Thomas Harvey, John McAnnar, Michael-John Voss, Megan Conn, Sean Janda, and Sophie Keskey. "Arch City Defenders Municipal Courts White Paper." Accessed August 2, 2017 from http://s3.documentcloud.org/documents/1279541/archcity-defenders-report-on-st-louis-county.pdf.

22 NPR had highlighted this issue months before. Joseph Shapiro. "As Court Fees Rise, The Poor Are Paying the Price." National Public Radio, aired May 19, 2014. Accessed August 2, 2017 from www.npr.org/2014/05/19/312158516/increasing-court-fees-punish-the-poor; Frances Robles. "Mistrust Lingers as Ferguson Takes New Tack on Fines." *New York Times*, September 12, 2014. Accessed August 2, 2017 from www.nytimes.com/2014/09/13/us/mistrust-lingers-as-ferguson-takes-new-tack-on-fines.html; Suzy Khimm. "Will the Government Stop Using the Poor as a Piggy Bank?" MSNBC, September 9, 2014. Accessed August 2, 2017 from www.msnbc.com/msnbc/will-the-government-stop-using-the-poor-piggy-bank; Joseph Shapiro. "In Ferguson, Court Fines and Fees Fuel Anger." National Public Radio, aired August 25, 2014. Accessed August 2, 2017 from www.npr.org/2014/08/25/343143937/in-ferguson-court-fines-and-fees-fuel-anger.

23 Maimuna Majumder. "An Intriguing Link between Police Shootings and Black Voter Registration." *Wired*, September 29, 2016. Accessed August 2, 2017 from www. wired.com/2016/09/intriguing-link-police-shootings-black-voter-registration/.
24 Liz Fields. "Police Have Killed at Least 1,083 Americans since Michael Brown's Death." *Vice News*, August 9, 2015. Accessed August 2, 2017 from https://news. vice.com/article/police-have-killed-at-least-1083-americans-since-michael-browns-death.
25 German Lopes, ed. "Police Shootings and Brutality in the US: 9 Things You Should Know." *Vox*, May 6, 2017. Accessed August 2, 2017 from www.vox.com/ cards/police-brutality-shootings-us/community-police-accountability.
26 Oscar Gandy and Zhan Li. "Framing Comparative Risk: A Preliminary Analysis." *Howard Journal of Communications* 16, no. 2 (2005): 71–86.
27 Kelsey Ramirez. "Freddie Mac Breaks down Homeownership Gap in Hispanic Population." *Housing Wire*, June 27, 2017. Accessed August 2, 2017 from www. housingwire.com/articles/40543-freddie-mac-breaks-down-homeownership-gap-in-hispanic-population.
28 US Bureau of Labor Statistics, Current Population Survey, September 2016. Accessed August 2, 2017 from www.bls.gov/opub/reports/race-and-ethnicity/ 2015/home.htm.
29 Marianne Bertrand and Sendhil Mullainathan. "Are Emily and Greg More Employable than Lakisha and Jamal? A Field Experiment on Labor Market Discrimination." *American Economic Review* 94, no. 4 (September 2004): 991–1013.
30 Daniel Widner and Stephen Chicoine. "It's All in the Name: Employment Discrimination Against Arab Americans." *Sociological Forum* 26, no. 4 (2011): 806–823. doi: 10.1111/j.1573–7861.2011.01285.x.
31 Abigail Wozniak. "Discrimination and the Effects of Drug Testing on Black Employment." *Review of Economics and Statistics* 97, no. 3 (2015): 548–566. doi: 10.1162/REST_a_00482.
32 Ronald Ferguson. "Toward Skilled Parenting & Transformed Schools: Inside a National Movement for Excellence with Equity." Wiener Center for Social Policy, John F. Kennedy School of Government, Harvard University, 2005.
33 Jeanne Brooks-Gunn and Lisa B. Markman. "The Contribution of Parenting to Ethnic and Racial Gaps in School Readiness." *The Future of Children* 15, no. 1 (2005): 139–168. Also see Richard E. Nisbett. *Intelligence and How to Get It: Why Schools and Culture Count.* New York, NY: W.W. Norton & Company, 2009.
34 Annette Lareau. *Unequal Childhoods: Class, Race, and Family Life.* Second edition. Berkeley and Los Angeles: University of California Press, 2011.
35 Annie E. Casey Foundation. "Kids Count Data Center, Children in Poverty by Race and Ethnicity, 2012 to 2016." Accessed February 3, 2018 from http://datacen ter.kidscount.org/data/tables/44-children-in-poverty-by-race-and-ethnicity#de tailed/1/any/false/870,573,869,36,868/10,11,9,12,1,185,13/323.
36 Lisa Delpit. *Other People's Children: Cultural Conflict in the Classroom.* New York, NY: The New Press, 2006; Walter S. Gilliam, Angela N. Maupin, Chin R. Reyes, Maria Accavitti, and Frederick Shic. "Do Early Educators' Implicit Biases Regarding Sex and Race Relate to Behavior Expectations and Recommendations of Preschool Expulsions and Suspensions?" Yale Child Study Center, September 28, 2016. Accessed March 4, 2018 from http://ziglercenter. yale.edu/publications/Preschool%20Implicit%20Bias%20Policy%20Brief_final_ 9_26_276766_5379_v1.pdf.
37 Bernice Yeung and Grace Rubenstein. "Female Workers Face Rape, Harassment in US Agricultural Industry." Center for Investigative Reporting, June 25, 2013. Accessed August 8, 2017 from http://cironline.org/reports/female-workers-face-rape-harassment-us-agriculture-industry-4798.

38 Charles Tilly. *Durable Inequality*. Berkeley, CA: University of California Press, 1998, pp. 86–91.
39 Yeung and Rubenstein. "Female Workers Face Rape."
40 Tilly. *Durable Inequality*, pp. 91–95.
41 Ibid., pp. 95–97.
42 Yeung and Rubenstein. "Female Workers Face Rape."
43 Tilly. *Durable Inequality*, pp. 97–98.
44 Tricia Rose. "How Structural Racism Works," presentation for the Center on the Study of Race and Ethnicity in America, Brown University. Published December 21, 2015. Accessed August 8, 2017 from www.youtube.com/watch?v=T5b3DJMBmic.

2

STRUCTURAL AND SYSTEMIC RACISM

Alden Loury

In this chapter, the author uses Chicago as a case study to show the ways in which structures such as law, policies, and practices can lead to inequitable distribution of economic, social, and political resources. The interactions of these policies and practices across institutions create a system of racism.

I spent 12 years working at *The Chicago Reporter*, a small but gritty nonprofit investigative news organization focused on issues of race and poverty. We used data to explain the depths of disparities in the criminal justice system, economics, housing, health care, and other concerns in and around the city. We also used long-form writing to illustrate the ways in which those inequalities played out on the ground and how they affected the lives of real people.

In many of our stories, we used maps to identify the communities most affected by the issues we covered. There was an eerie sameness to our maps. We'd even joke that we could recycle the same map for practically all of our stories.

It didn't matter if we were writing about poverty, homicides, fatal police shootings of civilians, subprime home mortgage lending, the relocation of residents from demolished public housing high-rises, chronic youth unemployment, educational attainment, underfunded schools, lottery ticket sales, or consumer dollars spent outside the neighborhood.

The maps always looked the same.

The most severe conditions almost always were found on Chicago's south and west sides, the heavily segregated areas of the city where most black people lived.

We used graphics in many of our stories to illustrate broad disparities between racial groups, no matter where they lived in the city, county, or state. Those pie charts, line graphs, and bar graphs also took on a similar look: the bars for blacks were typically the highest bars when showing the most severe conditions. They were often the smallest bars when illustrating positive outcomes. For whites, it was the exact opposite.

The gaps in the heights of those bars by race persisted even when they displayed outcomes for subsets of other demographic categories with similar characteristics. For instance, black folks still had the highest bars for unemployment even among individuals who all had the same level of education. Blacks also had the highest bars for prison sentences for drug crimes even among individuals who all had similar criminal histories. And the highest bars for subprime home loans belonged to African Americans even among all people earning six-figure incomes.

No matter how we segmented the universe, the data almost always revealed wide gaps in outcomes – most often between whites and African Americans.

Tale of Two Cities

After 12 years of documenting such disparities across a wide spectrum of data illustrating the human experience in and around Chicago, I was left to conclude that the city was deserving of the "tale of two cities" moniker often ascribed to it. The data clearly showed that people of different racial groups in Chicago truly lived in different communities, faced different circumstances, and led different lives. Those observations were solidified just by driving through the Chicago area, long known for its racial and economic segregation. You don't really need to know the numbers. You can easily see the inequities with your own eyes.

As a native Chicagoan, I've spent practically my entire life witnessing those differences. I've written about their impact on me as a teenager growing up on the city's south side and recognizing how things changed when I crossed the imaginary boundary between the black community of my childhood and the white community to the west. "The houses were bigger, the lawns were prettier, the cars were fancier, and the streets were cleaner. As a result, I presumed that the people there were happier and wealthier," I wrote in 2016 for the online *Social Justice News Nexus*. "The sun even seemed to shine brighter on the other side of that line."

The reasons why such disparities exist are much harder to see.

But they need not be visible to be recognized. The pervasive and persistent presence of inequalities, the fact that they are locked into specific geographic areas and affect specific groups of people, suggest a broader phenomenon at play.

A Web that Locks in Disparity

This phenomenon can be described as structural racism. This is the invisible force of inequality that causes maps and graphics of varied indicators of well-being to look so similar no matter how we slice and dice the data.

"The term structural racism refers to a system in which public policies, institutional practices, cultural representations, and other norms work in various, often reinforcing ways to perpetuate racial group inequity." That's how the Aspen Institute defined structural racism in its June 2004 report, "Structural Racism and Community Building."[1]

For many of us, when we think of racism we think of chattel slavery, the removal of Native Americans during the westward expansion of the United States, the slaughter of millions of European Jews during the Holocaust, the use of racial epithets, and the racial violence endured by those who dared to challenge "whites-only" schools, neighborhoods, and lunch counters.

Because of that history, we may view racism as virulent, hateful, and intentional behavior. But we must divorce our understanding of racism, particularly structural racism, from a time when such beliefs and actions were social norms, displayed often and widely accepted.

In simple terms, structural racism is a complex web of policies and practices that produce and reinforce inequalities by race. Structural racism can exist without the intentionality, hateful rhetoric, and emotional intensity that we associate with past racism.

Even if we can't see how social and institutional structures produce disparities, even if we can't see the racism built into the policies and practices of those structures, we should suspect that structural racism exists because of the persistent presence of pervasive racial inequality. And with deeper examination, we can reveal the seeds of structural racism and explain why the disparities persist.

To understand how this invisible force of structural racism forms, we must examine some of the things that we already understand and acknowledge about racism, as well as some of the things that we don't comprehend.

We're all aware of the history of racism and discrimination in the United States. Most of us don't challenge its existence or its catastrophic impact. For instance, we openly accept the abomination of slavery and Jim Crow.

We're also aware of the many steps taken throughout US history to address racism and discrimination. We're aware of the Emancipation Proclamation that ended slavery, the Supreme Court ruling that declared school segregation unconstitutional, and the turbulent Civil Rights era that culminated in constitutional protections for equal rights and voting rights for all Americans. And we know that the open, hate-filled rhetoric that, at one time, dominated both public and private dialogue about racial minorities has generally subsided. Of course, we still hear such rhetoric, but we're more likely nowadays to be shocked by it.

Still, there are some things about racism and discrimination of which many of us are not aware or that we fail to acknowledge. Many of us fail to comprehend the cumulative impact of racial discrimination coming from multiple sources and the generational impact of past discrimination.

In its 2004 book *Measuring Racial Discrimination*, the National Research Council provides several examples. The authors note that discrimination in one generation may diminish opportunities for later generations. "For instance, parents' poor health or employment status may limit their ability to monitor or support their child's education, which in turn may lower the child's educational success and, subsequently, his or her socioeconomic success as an adult."[2]

The Council also pointed out how discrimination at earlier stages can affect later outcomes within domains such as housing, criminal justice, and education:

> For example, discriminatory behavior in teacher evaluations of racially disadvantaged students in early elementary school may increase the probability of future discrimination in class assignments or tracking in middle school. Similarly, in the labor market, discrimination in hiring or performance evaluations may affect outcomes (and even reinforce discrimination) in promotions and wage growth.[3]

And discrimination in one domain can diminish opportunities in other domains. "Families that live in segregated neighborhoods may have limited access to adequate employment and health care," the authors noted.[4] (See Chapter 3 for a full discussion on the "disaccumulation" of opportunity.)

The difficult conversations we've had about reparations for slavery serve as a prime example of our challenge in understanding that this institution continues to affect the descendants of slaves generations after it was abolished.

Even the more recent internment of nearly 120,000 Japanese Americans during World War II – called "the greatest deprivation of civil liberties by government in this country since slavery" by an official of the American Civil Liberties Union[5] – is rarely recognized for its impact on the families who lost their property and endured that trauma, and on the generations that followed them. Ultimately, after Japanese Americans campaigned more than a decade for reparations, President Ronald Reagan signed the Civil Liberties Act of 1988, which provided $20,000 in redress to each surviving detainee of the internment camps. In 1992, Congress appropriated an additional $400 million to ensure the remaining number of surviving detainees were paid.

Unseen, Unacknowledged Impact

The wrong done by centuries of slavery and discrimination didn't end the moment we signed proclamations, rendered court rulings, and passed laws to end such abhorrent practices. Yet, we often fail to acknowledge this fact when discussing and responding to the racial disparities that are the legacy of those past crimes.

The racial disparities of today's education system are deeply rooted in the legacy of discrimination experienced during slavery and Jim Crow. It was against the law to teach slaves to read, and even after slavery ended, newly emancipated African Americans and subsequent generations were relegated by law to segregated and poorly resourced schools. The modern US education system still resembles the segregated system in place more than 60 years ago when mandated school segregation was struck down by the US Supreme Court. Given that painful history, it's certainly no wonder why African Americans trail their white counterparts on indicators of academic achievement.

However, even if equitable schools had become a reality immediately when slavery ended or upon the *Brown* v. *Board of Education* decision, African Americans would have still been generations behind their white counterparts academically.

With limited connections to formal education, newly freed slaves lacked experiences with and expectations for academic success – factors that would surely affect the manner and ability by which they would pursue such opportunities once they were made available. And those same factors would also influence the degree to which future generations would pursue educational opportunities.

"Several researchers have found that parents' education can influence youths' educational aspirations and attainment," the authors of *Measuring Racial Discrimination* wrote.

> Moreover, knowledge about and expectations of going to college influence not only this generation's college attendance but also the knowledge and expectations of the next generation. Thus, parents who experience discrimination may socialize their children to avoid certain places or situations, or they may have educational and occupational experiences, knowledge, or goals that limit prospects for their children.[6]

Furthermore, while the achievement gap has narrowed since 1940, in recent years that progress has slowed to a halt.[7] The lack of continued progress may be a reflection of the lasting impact of centuries of discriminatory policies and the structural racism that persists in today's education system and in other areas.

Many of us are clueless how that legacy is experienced in the day-to-day lives of people of color in this country. Due in large part to the ways in which we remain segregated in our neighborhoods, schools, workplaces, and social networks, many of us have little awareness of the wide differences in the lived experiences of different racial groups.

Reniqua Allen wrote in a 2013 opinion article that appeared in the US edition of the *Guardian*:[8]

> It's time for us to face the reality that for many Americans, even if we live and work around "diversity," our best friends and spiritual leaders,

the people we invite into our lives and homes, often look like we do, reinforcing a de facto segregation.

As a result of all these factors, many of us simply fail to comprehend how the weight carried by those who suffered past discrimination and exclusion is still felt today by their great-great-grandsons and great-great-granddaughters. We may even question whether racism still exists.

While the open and virulent racism of the first half of the 20th century has mostly subsided, the persistence of racial segregation, particularly in our neighborhoods and schools, should serve as a strong reminder that we still live with the repercussions of that old racism.

Measurements of racial segregation in America are highest among African Americans and whites, and the highest levels of black–white segregation are found in areas where millions of African Americans migrated from Southern states during the first half of the 20th century – a period known as the Great Migration. Those areas include Chicago, Cleveland, Detroit, Los Angeles, Milwaukee, New York City, and Philadelphia.[9]

As black populations grew during the Great Migration, federal, regional, and city policies sought to bar residential integration. Owners and developers placed racial covenants on deeds, preventing current and subsequent owners from selling their homes to black folks and often to other ethnic or religious minorities as well.[10]

Federal and local governments supported these covenants and also implemented policies that segregated public housing and, in some cases, restricted black people from accessing public housing, particularly during World War II when defense workers especially needed it.

During the Depression, the Roosevelt administration sponsored the Home Owners' Loan Corporation to refinance homes headed for foreclosure. Administrators used detailed maps to determine where refinancing was and wasn't allowed. Fully white neighborhoods were designated as green, signaling that residents could take part in this New Deal program. Jews in a neighborhood degraded it to blue or yellow. Neighborhoods with black residents were designated as red and were excluded.[11] Through the 1950s the Federal Housing Administration embraced these maps and used them to determine which commercial mortgages they would guarantee. The practice was called redlining.

In addition to making it hard for black families to secure mortgages and incentivizing white families to keep them away, this practice also affected home values. White people often feared that once black people started moving into the neighborhood, their property values would go down.[12]

Modern racial segregation is often viewed solely as the result of people choosing to live near members of the same racial or ethnic group. As that thinking goes, largely African American communities exist because black people want to live close to other black people. But close observation of racial change in urban areas, like metro Chicago, suggests more nuance.

In Chicago, the hardening of segregation over time has limited both black and white folks' social networks and their perceptions of various parts of the city, making some neighborhoods unimaginable for them to live in.

Residential racial segregation is also the product of white people choosing to live near other white people and fleeing areas when nonwhites, particularly African Americans, become a significant share of the population.[13] An analysis of census demographic data shows that Chicago's south and west sides flipped from nearly all-white to nearly all-black between 1950 and 1980. Many of the white residents who fled the city settled in existing suburban communities or they created new ones.

Since 1990, many of those same suburbs have been experiencing the same racial flipping that dramatically changed neighborhoods decades ago.[14] Suburban white residents are returning to the city or moving to other parts of the region as African Americans, Latinos, and Asians increasingly take up residence in Chicago's suburbs. The analysis found that integrated areas in the Chicago region, with a few exceptions, are largely areas in transition from one racial or ethnic group to another.[15]

Similar racial patterns have been replicated in public schools. While Chicago is nearly one-third white in population, less than one-tenth of students in Chicago Public Schools are white. The share of white students in the city's public schools fell dramatically in the 1950s and 1960s as the black population in the city soared. And white students never returned in large numbers.[16] The same is true in most major American cities with a significant African American population.

Racial minorities are deeply affected by this nation's legacy of racism and discrimination, which leaves an indelible mark on their lives. America's history, institutions, customs, power structure, and wealth are all shaped by that legacy. There's no escaping it. Living in such an environment presents a daily struggle for racial minorities to affirm their worth and value.

In addition, persistent segregation reinforces a lack of familiarity between members of different racial and ethnic groups and an ignorance about their struggles, hopes, and dreams – and how racism, discrimination, and their legacy may still shape them. It's the combination of what we believe and what we don't fully comprehend or acknowledge that serve as the seeds for structural racism.

Those seeds remain viable out of a belief that the sins of the past have been addressed and that the scourge of racism has faded. It is a belief held by many who lack an understanding of the intergenerational impact of past discrimination, the real-life challenges for racial minorities living in a white-dominated society, and the continuing presence of a softer, more subtle and sophisticated form of racism.

Those seeds grow and develop into a sense that today's social conditions are not the result of our nation's history of prejudice, exclusion, and discrimination, but due to a lack of determination, moral character, discipline, or intellect on the part of those at the bottom of various indicators of social and economic well-being. The presence of high test scores, strong employment, and low incarceration rates, among other indicators, serve as assumed proxies for wisdom, work ethic, and trustworthiness among individuals within groups consistently at the top of many variables of well-being.

We've replaced the hate-driven motivations that fueled the old racism of the 20th century with a set of soft stereotypes.

That's the racism.

In response, we've adopted policies and practices meant to address the deficiencies we perceive among the individuals and communities who have the least in our society, creating more barriers and penalties that ultimately exacerbate inequities. We seek to address disparities by "fixing" the people involved, without fully addressing the societal factors that may be a much greater force. In doing so, we overlook the favoritism and exclusion built into so many of our institutions, laws, and customs.

This perpetuates a cycle within our various structures of education, labor, housing, economic, and criminal justice policy, just to name a few. The disparities persist, entrench stereotypes further, and serve as fuel for additional policies and practices that reinforce the inequity.

That's the structural racism.

Two-Tiered Educational System

A closer look at several public policy arenas illustrates the ways in which structural racism maintains itself and deepens racial inequality. As in many urban areas, education has long been a racialized issue in metropolitan Chicago. The Chicago region is home to wide gaps in education funding and academic achievement by race. The funding disparity is rooted in a reliance on property taxes to fund public education in Illinois. Better than 60 percent of public education funding in the state comes from property taxes. The largest gaps in funding can be found in the Chicago region, which includes posh, mostly white suburban school districts where per pupil funding is at least 50 percent higher than it is in metro Chicago and in the smaller, cash-strapped suburban school districts where most students are poor and either black or Latino. While the poorer school districts benefit from additional state and federal resources, these don't close the funding gap. Illinois provides the lowest per-pupil funding for low-income students in the nation, according to a 2018 study by The Education Trust, a nonprofit advocating for education equity.[17]

Researchers disagree on the impact of education spending on academic achievement and studies to assess it have produced varying results.[18] Still, many parents actively seek well-resourced schools with the belief that they will provide children a higher-quality education and the best chances for future success.

Funding could be one reason that, in Illinois, the percentage of low-income students performing at grade level is far lower than that of wealthier students. In 2017, just one-fifth of low-income students met or exceeded expectations on the state's standardized test in elementary schools, placing them on track for college and career readiness, compared with nearly half of students who were not low-income.

Efforts to change the way schools are financed largely have fallen short over the years. Education reform advocates have long fought to dramatically increase spending overall, particularly from the state. They've also argued for more equitable distribution of education dollars, citing the state's heavy reliance on property taxes. The landscape improved with the passage of legislation in 2017 that directed state resources to school districts based on need – resulting in an additional $450 million for Chicago Public Schools, a boost of roughly 8 percent to its $5.5 billion annual budget.

But without further increases in state education spending, inequitable funding is almost guaranteed to continue. Unequal dollars maintain a legacy of unequal education between whites and people of color, particularly African Americans and Latinos. This is a legacy centuries in the making and rooted in deliberate actions. (See Chapter 12, Case Study C for more detail about reporting on school funding.)

Chicago has also become one of the most prominent stages for school-choice policies like the use of selective-enrollment, magnet, and charter schools, which have displayed strong racial overtones as they play out on the ground.

Over the past 40 years, the Chicago Public Schools have developed several world-class, selective-enrollment high schools that routinely rise onto lists of the nation's best public high schools. For instance, the five highest-ranking Illinois high schools to make the 2017 *U.S. News & World Report* Best Public High Schools list are all selective-enrollment schools in Chicago. The competition for these schools is fierce. Students are chosen based on composite scores that reflect their grades, attendance, and performance on standardized tests.

But the city's selective-enrollment public high schools don't reflect the demographic makeup of all public high school students. Among white high school students in Chicago Public Schools during the 2016–2017 school year, nearly 39 percent – about two of every five students – were enrolled at one of those five selective-enrollment schools deemed the best in the state. However, among African American high school students that year, just 3 percent – about one in every 33 students – were enrolled in one.

It's not exactly clear why whites are overrepresented and African Americans (and Latinos to a lesser extent) are underrepresented in those top-five high schools. Those schools are among 11 selective-enrollment high schools in the city. The remaining six schools are overwhelmingly attended by either African American or Latino students and located in largely African American or Latino communities on the city's south, southwest, and west sides.

Some speculate that the lower numbers of African American and Latino students in the top-five high schools is due to their preference for the other selective-enrollment high schools or other well-performing high schools closer to their homes.

Regardless, the result is that a far lower share of African American students attend the very best public high schools in Chicago, effectively continuing a legacy of inequitable education stretching back several decades. The most prominent illustration of that history in Chicago occurred on October 22, 1963 (coined as "Freedom Day"), when African American families boycotted Chicago Public Schools – keeping more than 200,000 students at home – to protest segregationist policies in the city's overcrowded and under-resourced all-black schools.

Some argue that the selective-enrollment model simply rewards the system's best students based on prior academic performance in the form of grades, standardized test scores, and entrance exam results. Students aren't even allowed to take the selective-enrollment entrance exam unless they score at a certain level on routine standardized tests. However, the model's reliance on past academic performance and test scores perpetuates inequity. The students who compete more favorably for seats at the coveted selective-enrollment high schools often have benefited from an inequitable grade school system.

Like many large cities, Chicago has numerous prestigious private elementary schools, including the University of Chicago Laboratory Schools, where elementary school tuition is more than $30,000 a year – a price tag that puts such schools far out of the reach of many families, particularly those in minority groups. For instance, among elementary school students in Chicago during the 2016–2017 school year, just 5 percent of African American students attended private schools compared with 6 percent of Latino students, 10 percent of Native American students, 14 percent of Asian students and nearly 38 percent of white students.

Many public school districts in Chicago's suburbs have seen rapidly growing numbers of Latino students within the past two decades. That growth has forced those school districts to respond to the language needs of some students who are learning English or who are more comfortable speaking Spanish. Those districts, like many others across the country, have employed limited-English-proficiency, or LEP, programs to help those students. But the decision to place a student in an LEP program for some time can have a profound impact on their ability to compete academically. Students in LEP programs in

Illinois score significantly lower on standardized tests. For instance, in 2017, just one in ten English learners met or exceeded expectations on the state's standardized test in elementary schools, compared with one in three students in the state overall.

Several Chicago suburban districts have been cited by the state for not meeting bilingual programming requirements. Those districts' programs are feeling squeezed financially because government funding for bilingual education has declined.[19] The result could be inadequate programs where students simply don't move along fast enough. On top of that, a heavy Spanish accent or struggles with the complexities of English grammar could be misinterpreted as signs of low intelligence. Interestingly, once LEP students leave those programs, typically after a few years and presumably because they have become proficient in English, they perform just as well on standardized tests as students who've never been in LEP. A study of nationwide data found that former LEP students narrowed the achievement gap by as much as 39 percent, depending upon subject and grade level.[20] Considering the lower academic performance in LEP programs and the growth witnessed after completing them, Latino students who are kept in LEP programs longer than they may need see their academic trajectory dampened or delayed.

Unfairness that Replicates

The outcomes of racial disparities in educational attainment in and around Chicago are almost predictable given the historic advantages and disadvantages built into the system. Such structural racism has lifelong implications given that educational attainment is profoundly linked to employment and earning potential. Furthermore, the labor market itself is rife with structural barriers that widen racial gaps that take root in our schools.

Among the nation's 20 largest cities in 2016, Chicago was home to the highest black unemployment rate and the widest gulf between black and white unemployment. That year, the black unemployment rate was 16.8 percent, more than five times higher than the white unemployment rate of 3.2 percent, according to my analysis of US Census Bureau data.[21]

A separate analysis of Census microdata finds that the disparity exists even when examining unemployment among black and white Chicagoans of equal education levels. In fact, whites were more likely to be employed in 2015 than African Americans who had several more years of education. For instance, the unemployment rate for whites with a high school diploma and no college was just 7.5 percent. Only African Americans with an advanced degree were more likely to be employed.[22]

The presence of such wide disparities even when considering education suggests that structural and systemic barriers are present. In 2003, sociologist

Devah Pager reported the results of a matched-pair experiment that offered compelling evidence of such barriers. Male testers, half of them white and half of them black, applied for entry-level jobs posted in Milwaukee newspapers. The applicants presented equal credentials in terms of education and experience. Within each pair of white and black applicants, one tester also indicated that they had committed a non-violent drug possession offense.[23]

Pager's primary objective was to measure the effect of a criminal record in the job market. But her study also found deep racial discrimination. Just 14 percent of black testers who did not indicate a criminal past received a callback. That compared to 17 percent of white testers who indicated that they did have a criminal past. "The persistent effect of race on employment opportunities is painfully clear in these results," Pager wrote.[24]

"When we combine the effects of race and criminal record, the problem grows even more intense," Pager added. "Not only are blacks much more likely to be incarcerated than whites; based on the findings presented here, they may also be more strongly affected by the impact of a criminal record."[25] The percentage of whites who received a callback diminished by one half when they had a criminal record. However, for African Americans, the percentage who received callbacks dropped by nearly two-thirds.

Pager's work was inspired by the rapid growth of America's prison population, which she noted had grown by more than 600 percent during the previous three decades. The prison boom was felt in black communities within the nation's largest metro areas more than anywhere else – and there its impact was devastating. Deeply segregated communities beset by decades of racial discrimination were now dealing with a new enemy: a rapidly growing number of lives, families, and social networks disrupted by prison stays – often brief ones for low-level drug and other offenses. As Pager's study highlighted, the stigma of a criminal record all but sealed the fate of hundreds of thousands of young black men.

Entrenched Injustice

The structural barriers present within the criminal justice system are perhaps the most rigid, long-standing, and unforgiving of any system in our nation's history. Their roots stretch back centuries and the deepening struggles witnessed in modern times between police and African American communities, in particular, suggest that these structural barriers may remain in place for years to come. From the earliest slave rebellions to the modern-day Black Lives Matter protests, racial tensions have intersected with efforts by law-enforcement agencies to exert control. We've been bombarded in recent years with news stories about unarmed African Americans being killed at the hands of police officers. And while such incidents involving Native American victims appear in the news less frequently, they actually die at the hands of police at an even higher rate than African Americans.[26]

The anti-immigrant sentiment and harsh treatment from US immigration enforcement agents experienced by Muslims and Latinos today is actually a resurgence of attitudes and behavior dating back to the mid 19th century when millions of Irish immigrants fled their homeland in the wake of famine, in the late 19th century when millions of Italian immigrants sought refuge from poverty in Southern Italy and Sicily, and in the mid 20th century when nearly all of the 120,000 Japanese Americans and some German and Italian Americans were detained in US concentration camps shortly after Japan's bombing of Pearl Harbor.

For long periods, each of those groups were considered threats, particularly during times when they'd arrived in large numbers among concentrations of native-born white Americans, and when they'd been vocal about barriers to quality schools, decent housing, good-paying jobs, and other aspects of the so-called American Dream.

Widespread suspicion of such "outsiders" has forged the political backing to enact heavy-handed policies to monitor, police, and penalize them in an effort to protect the majority population.[27] In turn, intensive law enforcement of these groups also has served to embolden stereotypes about their supposed violent and criminal tendencies. These perceptions in turn lead to additional punitive policies. Today's criminal justice system offers many examples of such structural racism, especially in the enforcement of drug laws. While data on self-reported drug use surveys, emergency room visits for drug abuse, and drug-related deaths all indicate similar levels of drug use among African Americans and whites in Chicago, blacks are disproportionately stopped, searched, and arrested by police for drug possession.

For years, studies have shown that police were more likely to find guns and drugs when they stopped white drivers than when they stopped black drivers. However, African Americans were three times more likely to be the target of traffic stops by police, according to a 2013 federal study. In Chicago, African Americans were five times more likely to be stopped.[28]

Chicago Police have dubbed Interstate 290 "heroin highway" because of the long-running practice of suburban whites using that roadway to drive into the city, buy drugs at one of more than 200 heroin corners on the city's west side, and then return to I-290 for the trip home. Still, African Americans make up the vast majority of those arrested for drug possession on the west side.

The open-air drug trade is a major engine of the underground economy in the west side's largely poor and disinvested communities. With few job opportunities, there's an ample supply of willing young men to serve those corners, repopulating them as others are arrested, detained, and eventually imprisoned. They are also serving as the raw material for another economic engine of sorts, one that is fueled by tax dollars and supports the middle-class families of police officers, jail guards, probation officers, court clerks, prosecutors, and judges of all racial groups.

The disparities within the criminal justice system often worsen when policymakers seek to stem the flow of illegal drugs or violence by imposing harsh penalties. For years, Chicago's mayor and police superintendent have fought for more stringent penalties for gun crimes. The Illinois General Assembly, led by its legislative black caucus, had resisted such moves for fear that it would lead to longer sentences for African American defendants and further limit future chances.

In the aftermath of national headlines about Chicago's skyrocketing homicide counts in 2016, however, state legislators in Illinois approved a bill that could lead to three- to seven-year sentences for illegal possession of a firearm. Ex-felons in Chicago often live in some of the city's toughest neighborhoods, places where carrying a gun is an attractive method of protection. Even though they're not allowed to carry guns, ex-felons often take the risk. Crime figures posted to the city's public data portal show that Chicago police arrest thousands in the city's black communities each year for unlawful possession of a firearm. What had been a one-year sentence can now lead to three- to seven-year sentences. There's no guarantee that the measure will put a dent in the violence, but it will lead to longer sentences for many black men, further diminishing their prospects and potentially widening racial gaps in employment, earnings, and incarceration.

"In our frenzy of locking people up, our 'crime control' policies may in fact exacerbate the very conditions that lead to crime in the first place," wrote Pager, who referred to research findings that a good, steady job is one of the strongest predictors of crime deterrence.[29]

Geographic Boundaries

Consider that this overlapping system occurs within the same geographic spaces. As mentioned at the outset, many of the disparate outcomes illustrated in *The Chicago Reporter* maps show up in the same residential areas – primarily black communities on Chicago's south and west sides. We've touched on the structural barriers to opportunity within housing, education, labor, and the criminal justice system. These communities also are ground zero for redlining in housing and commerce. Chicago's black communities were turned inside out by rampant subprime mortgage lending in the first decade of the 2000s and the fallout from foreclosures resulting from those high-priced loans as well as the economic downturn during the 2007–2009 Great Recession. Many neighborhoods have yet to recover and property values have plummeted. In addition, mainstream retailers often bypass these communities. Residents must travel great distances to find quality options for food, clothes, and other necessities. They find little nearby in the way of jobs or other economic activity.

In the wake of the housing crisis has sprung another in which African Americans are exiting Chicago at a record pace. The city's black population fell by 180,000 over the decade between 2000 and 2010. The slide has continued, including an estimated reduction of 40,000 in 2016 alone, pushing Chicago's black population below 800,000 for the first time in half a century. The city's black population has fallen below that of Latinos, making African Americans now Chicago's third-largest group after Latinos and whites – a symbolic step down on the city's totem pole. The decline may represent black communities' response to unfavorable living conditions and a desire to seek better options. It also weakens their political and economic power.

Chicago's black communities are in freefall, in large part due to the city's entrenched culture of racial segregation. Hundreds of thousands of African Americans came to Chicago during the Great Migration. They forever changed the city, its culture, and its identity – not only because of their contributions, but also because of the visceral reaction by white people to their presence.

White flight and racial segregation created black spaces in and around Chicago with high walls. Even though they are invisible, these barriers are real and effectively seal in the structural forces described above. Those walls also limit the view from the outside. We can't see the people living inside. We can't see their pain, their pride, their passion, or their power. For through the decades of fighting for equality and human dignity, an elegant community has emerged in impoverished black neighborhoods. It's one that survives off the scraps thrown away by the more fortunate. It's one that finds the will to live a life with little money when others would find such a life not worth living. And it's one that endures through faith even when it can no longer hope for a better future.

Legendary hip-hop artist Talib Kweli describes it as "the beautiful struggle." It's the name of one of his most popular songs, one of several released in his 2004 album of the same name. The second verse concludes, "The struggle is beautiful. I'm too strong for your slavery."

"The beautiful struggle" describes the gritty, street-smart, and regal men and women of urban America who continue to beat the odds. It celebrates the resilience and the achievements of the people and the communities that we often fail to acknowledge. Absent an understanding of the continuing and long-lasting legacy of systemic racism, there's no way a journalist can responsibly convey what's happening in this country. There's no way she or he can offer a true reflection of the struggles, the strengths, the pain, and the beauty of all of America's communities and their inhabitants.

Notes

1 Aspen Institute Roundtable on Community Change. *Structural Racism and Community Building*, 2004. Accessed July 7, 2018 from https://assets.aspeninstitute.org/content/uploads/files/content/docs/rcc/aspen_structural_racism2.pdf.

2 Rebecca M. Blank, Marilyn Dabady, and Constance F. Citro, eds. *Measuring Racial Discrimination*. Panel on Methods for Assessing Discrimination. Committee on National Statistics, Division of Behavioral and Social Sciences and Education. National Research Council. Washington, DC: The National Academies Press, 2004.

3 Ibid.

4 Ibid.

5 Donna K. Nagata. "Intergenerational Effects of the Japanese American Internment," in *International Handbook of Multigenerational Legacies of Trauma*, ed. Yael Danieli. Boston, MA: Springer, The Plenum Series on Stress and Coping, 1998, pp. 125–139.

6 Blank et al. *Measuring Racial Discrimination*.

7 Graziella Bertocchi and Arcangelo Dimico. "Slavery, Education, and Inequality." *European Economic Review* 70 (August 2014): 197–209. doi: 10.1016/j.euroecorev.2014.04.007.

8 Reniqua Allen. "Our 21st Century Segregation: We're Still Divided by Race." *Guardian*, April 3, 2013. Accessed July 7, 2018 from www.theguardian.com/commentisfree/2013/apr/03/21st-century-segregation-divided-race.

9 Gregory Acs, Rolf Pendall, Mark Treskon, and Amy Khare. "The Cost of Segregation: National Trends and the Case of Chicago, 1990–2010." Metropolitan Housing and Communities Policy Center, March 2017.

10 These covenants met with legal challenges in the 1940s, one of which is the famous case out of Chicago, *Lee* v. *Hansberry*, the family of the famed author Lorraine Hansberry. In *Shelley* v. *Kramer* (1948) the US Supreme Court deemed it discriminatory for states to enforce racial covenants, but the decision also allowed private parties to use them if they wished, saying that the covenants themselves were not unconstitutional. The practice became illegal in 1968 with the implementation of the Fair Housing Act.

11 Beryl Satter. *Family Properties: Race, Real Estate, and the Exploitation of Black Urban America*. New York, NY: Henry Holt and Company, 2013. To access the actual maps used by lenders, see Robert K. Nelson, LaDale Winling, Richard Marciano, Nathan Connolly, et al. "Mapping Inequality," in *American Panorama*, ed. Robert K. Nelson and Edward L. Ayers. Accessed November 24, 2018 from https://dsl.richmond.edu/panorama/redlining/#loc=4/36.74/-96.90&opacity=0.8.

12 For a full history of such practices and their impact on current segregation patterns see Arnold R. Hirsch. *Making the Second Ghetto: Race and Housing in Chicago, 1940–1960*. Chicago, IL: University of Chicago Press, 1983; Douglas S. Massey and Nancy A. Denton. *American Apartheid: Segregation and the Making of the Underclass*. Cambridge, MA: Harvard University Press, 1993; Richard Rothstein. *The Color of Law: A Forgotten History of How Our Government Segregated America*. New York, NY: Liveright Publishing Corporation, 2017.

13 Maria Krysan and Kyle Crowder. *Cycle of Segregation: Social Processes and Residential Stratification*. New York, NY: Russell Sage Foundation, 2017.

14 Alden Loury. "Data Points: Chicago's Segregation Isn't Just in the City." *Metropolitan Planning Council*, 2016. Accessed July 8, 2018 from www.metroplanning.org/news/7324/Data-Points-Chicagos-segregation-isnt-just-in-the-city.

15 Marisa Novara et al. "Our Equitable Future: A Roadmap for the Chicago Region." Metropolitan Planning Council, 2018. Accessed July 8, 2018 from www.metroplanning.org/costofsegregation/roadmap.aspx?utm_source=%2froadmap&utm_medium=web&utm_campaign=redirect.

16 Alden Loury. "The Persistent Problem of Segregation in Chicago's Public Schools." Metropolitan Planning Council, 2017. Accessed July 8, 2018 from www.metroplan ning.org/costofsegregation/roadmap.aspx.

17 Ivy Morgan and Ary Amerikaner. "Funding Gaps 2018: An Analysis of School Funding Equity across the U.S. and Within Each State." The Education Trust. February 27, 2018. Accessed July 14, 2018 from https://edtrust.org/resource/fund ing-gaps-2018/.

18 Charlene Tow. *The Effects of School Funding on Student Academic Achievement: A Study of California School Districts 2000–2004.* Undergraduate Economic Honors Thesis, University of California, Berkeley. Spring, 2006. Accessed July 8, 2018 from https://pdfs. semanticscholar.org/c5ac/56ccc2f172cdcee48ec468f3041bb5c91794.pdf.

19 Rebecca Harris. "Suburban Chicago Schools Lag as Bilingual Needs Grow." *Chicago News Cooperative, New York Times,* February 9, 2012. Accessed July 8, 2018 from www.nytimes.com/2012/02/10/education/suburban-chicago-schools-lag-as-bilingual-needs-grow.html.

20 Tala Salem. "Are Schools Measuring the Progress of English-Language Learners All Wrong?" *U.S. News & World Report,* June 12, 2018. Accessed July 8, 2018 from www.usnews.com/news/education-news/articles/2018-06-12/are-schools-measur ing-the-progress-of-english-language-learners-all-wrong.

21 Even as unemployment hit an all-time low in the second quarter of 2018, according to the Bureau of Labor Statistics, African American unemployment still outpaced that of other racial and ethnic groups. See Bureau of Labor Statistics. "Household Data Not Seasonally Adjusted Quarterly Averages, E16, Unemployment Rates by Age Sex Race, and Hispanic or Latino Ethnicity." Accessed July 9, 2018 from www.bls.gov/web/empsit/cpsee_e16.htm. For example, CNN reported that in December 2017, black unemployment hit the lowest level since 1972, at 6.8 percent. For whites it was 3.7 percent. See Patrick Gallespie. "Black Unemployment Hits All-Time Low." CNN Money, January 5, 2018. Accessed July 9, 2018 from http://money.cnn.com/2018/01/05/news/economy/black-unemployment/index.html.

22 Blacks with a bachelor's degree had a 9 percent unemployment rate, according to my analysis.

23 Devah Pager. "Mark of a Criminal Record." *American Journal of Sociology* 108, no. 5 (March 2003): 937–975. Accessed July 9, 2018 from http://s3.amazonaws.com/fiel dexperiments-papers2/papers/00319.pdf.

24 Ibid.

25 Ibid.

26 See Stephanie Woodard. "The Police Killings No One Is Talking about." *In These Times,* October 17, 2016. Accessed July 9, 2018 from http://inthesetimes.com/fea tures/native_american_police_killings_native_lives_matter.html. and see A. J. Vicens. "Native Americans Get Shot by Cops at an Astonishing Rate." *Mother Jones,* July 15, 2015. Accessed July 9, 2018 from www.motherjones.com/politics/2015/07/native-americans-getting-shot-police/.

27 Ryan D. King, Steven F. Messner, and Robert D. Baller. "Contemporary Hate Crimes, Law Enforcement, and the Legacy of Racial Violence." *American Sociological Review* 72, no. 2 (April 2009): 291–315.

28 Jeff Guo. "Police Are Searching Black Drivers More Often, but Finding More Illegal Stuff with White Drivers." *The Washington Post,* October 27, 2015. Accessed July 9, 2018 from www.washingtonpost.com/news/wonk/wp/2015/10/27/police-are-searching-black-drivers-more-often-but-finding-more-illegal-stuff-with-white-drivers-2/?noredirect=on&utm_term=.86b12e13bc13.

29 Pager. "Mark of a Criminal Record," p. 961.

3

THE ACCUMULATION AND DISACCUMULATION OF OPPORTUNITY

Michael K. Brown, Martin Carnoy, Elliot Currie, Troy Duster, David B. Oppenheimer, Majorie M. Shultz, and David Wellman

This chapter is excerpted from the book Whitewashing Race: The Myth of a Color-Blind Society. *The book was originally published in 2003, and yet it remains relevant today. Here the authors explain how years of economic and social isolation limit opportunity by race. Over time, they show, this disinvestment compounds. We have updated statistics and removed some dated language from the original text. While the authors discuss racial power structures mainly through a black/white paradigm, we hope readers can recognize similar power dynamics between whites and other minorities.*

The Emerging Racial Paradigm

A number of books have appeared that elaborate and refine the popular understanding of race and racial inequality in America.[1] The most important of these is Stephen and Abigail Thernstrom's *America in Black and White: One Nation Indivisible* (1997). These books have been promoted as reasoned and factually informed discussions of race in America. All of the authors give the understanding of race and racism the appearance of scholarly heft and intellectual legitimacy. And they represent a diverse set of political positions. Yet all might be identified as "racial realists," as Alan Wolfe calls the proponents of this perspective.[2]

Although each of these authors has written a very different book about race, all set out to demolish the claims of color-conscious policy advocates and anyone who suggests that racial discrimination is a persistent American problem. Racial realists make three related claims. First, they say that America has made great progress in rectifying racial injustice. The economic divide between whites and blacks, in their view, is exaggerated, and white Americans have been receptive to demands for racial equality.[3] Thus, racism is a thing of the past.

The racial realists' second claim is that persistent racial inequalities in income, employment, residence, and political representation cannot be explained by white racism, even though a small percentage of whites remain intransigent racists.

The racial realists' final assertion is that the civil rights movement's political failures are caused by the manipulative, expedient behavior of black nationalists and the civil rights establishment.

Although racial realists do not claim that racism has ended completely, they want race to disappear. For them, colorblindness is not simply a legal standard; it is a particular kind of social order, one where racial identity is irrelevant. They believe a colorblind society can uncouple individual behavior from group identification, allowing genuine inclusion of all people. In their view, were this allowed to happen, individuals who refused to follow common moral standards would be stigmatized as individuals, not as members of a particular group.[4]

In the following analysis, we assume people bear certain responsibility for the outcomes of their lives. We do not ignore or make excuses when broadly accepted moral and legal standards are violated. Nor do we attribute every problem and failure in communities of color to persistent racism. But we cannot accept the proposition that racial inequality does not matter and that racism has all but disappeared from American life. In our judgment, the new public understanding subscribes to a false dichotomy: either we have racial prejudice or we have black failure. We think this view is deeply flawed.

The Persistence of Durable Racial Inequality

Racial realists pose the wrong question. The real issue, so far as they are concerned, is whether the United States has made progress in reducing racial inequality. But every serious student of contemporary racial inequality concedes there has been progress. The Thernstroms remind us repeatedly that the good news "regarding the emergence of a strong black middle class has not received the attention it deserves."[5] Good tidings, they assert, are neglected because of a volatile mixture of "black anger" and "white guilt." This is hardly true. Every gain the black middle class has made, every uptick in black employment, is trumpeted from the rooftops. There is no gainsaying the progress of the black middle class, but to dwell on this amounts to celebrating economic gains while ignoring the large and persistent gaps in economic and social well-being between blacks and whites.

An abundance of evidence documents persistently large gaps between blacks and whites in family income, wages, and wealth since the economic boom of the post-World War II years and after the civil rights revolution. (See Appendix 3A on racial disparities.) Black families have clearly gained relative to whites over the last 68 years, but the absolute income gap between them has widened. The gap began to narrow in the early 1990s, but during the Great Recession, it began to widen again to pre-1990 levels. By 2015, the real median income of black families was 62 percent of that of whites, only 10 points higher than it was in 1947 when the ratio was 52 percent. Over the same period, however, the absolute real median income gap nearly tripled, rising from $10,386 to $28,510.[6] (If one compares black family income to that of non-Hispanic whites, a more accurate measure, the ratio is 57 percent, a gap that is largely unchanged since the early 1970s.[7])

Relative to non-Hispanic white men, black men made income gains between 1972 and 2015. Their real median income rose from 60 percent to 69.4 percent of white median income. The absolute gap dipped between 1972 and 2001 from $11,624 to $10,325, but rose again in 2015 to $12,087. The absolute gap in annual income between black and white women is much smaller than the one for the men – a reflection of the wage discrimination experienced by all women.[8]

Just as important is the startling persistence of racial inequality in other areas of American life, despite laws passed to address the disparities. Housing and health care are two matters vital to the well-being of individuals and their families, and both illustrate the limits of the civil rights revolution. The 1968 Civil Rights Act outlawed housing discrimination, yet African Americans continue to be the most residentially segregated group in the United States. They are far more likely to live in segregated neighborhoods than either Asian Americans or Latinos.[9] Blacks are much less likely to own a home, and when they can get a mortgage, they receive far less favorable terms than do comparable whites. For example, between 1993 and 1998, subprime lending – loans with higher interest rates and predatory foreclosure practices – grew by 30 times in Chicago's black neighborhoods, but by only two-and-a-half times in white residential areas. Race, not social class, explains this difference: in 1998, subprime lenders made 53 percent of the home-equity loans in middle-income black areas but only 12 percent of the loans in middle-income white areas.[10] During the mortgage crisis, black and Latino neighborhoods were hit especially hard with toxic subprime loans. In Cleveland, Ohio, for example, between 2005 and 2009, the depths of the collapse, white households lost 16 percent of their net worth, while black households lost 53 percent and Latino households lost 66 percent of their net worth.[11]

Medicare and Medicaid succeeded in expanding access to health care to many people, a clear example of progress. Racial and income differences in the use of health care facilities, including hospital stays as well as visits to doctors' offices, diminished substantially after these two laws were enacted. These laws made a difference; largely because of Medicaid, black infant mortality rates dropped by half between 1960 and 1980. Yet racial differences for many health indicators remained unchanged or in some cases widened. The white infant mortality rate has remained more than twice as low as the black rate.[12] In other words, neither the civil rights revolution nor diminishing prejudice have made much difference to racial disparities in mortality, the most fundamental matter of health. Neither income nor poverty status alone can explain these racial differences.[13]

One reason for these disparities is that blacks and Latinos are still much less likely to have access to primary care physicians than whites. Limited access to primary care shows up in many basic health statistics. David Smith reports that "the proportion of blacks receiving adequate prenatal care, up-to-date childhood immunizations, flu shots as seniors, and cancer screenings lags significantly behind whites, even though most of the financial barriers to such preventive services have been eliminated."[14] Even when blacks have equal access to medical care, evidence indicates that significant racial disparities in treatment and care remain. For example, among Medicare beneficiaries of similar age, gender, and income, blacks are 25 percent less likely to have mammography screening for breast cancer and 57 percent less likely to have reduction of hip fracture.[15] (See Chapter 4 on a discussion of implicit bias on physician care of patients.)

Any credible analysis of race in America must confront and account for these durable and persistent inequalities between blacks and whites. Many proponents of racial realism as well as those Americans who subscribe to the new explanation for racial inequality fail to do this for two reasons. First, they ignore or obscure dramatic and persistent facts of racial inequality. Second, the methodological assumptions that guide their investigation of race in America lead them to ignore alternative explanations that more closely "fit" the evidence they do cite. In the following analysis, we address each of these concerns.

The Minimal Relevance of Individual Choice to Durable Racial Inequality

Today the predominant approach to understanding racial stratification in American life assumes that "social life results chiefly or exclusively from the actions of self-motivated, interest-seeking persons."[16] For those promulgating this view, it is solely the stated intentions and choices of individuals that explain discrimination. It leads writers to focus on individual whites' beliefs about African Americans and civil rights. Persistent racial inequality is attributed to blacks' individual choices of lifestyles and attitudes.

By focusing on the stated intentions and choices of individuals, these writers ignore the systemic and routine practices of white Americans and the consequences of their behavior. Whether actions are motivated by group values and interests or operate through private and public institutions, the inescapable results are harmful to African Americans and other people of color.

When social scientists analyze income, employment, or occupational disparities between categorical groups – blacks–whites, men–women – they assume these gaps in material well-being are due mostly to differences in education and job skills that would affect an individual's productivity and thus that person's ability to succeed in competitive labor markets. Studies of wage discrimination, for example, typically proceed by removing the effects of individual characteristics such as education or experience that might explain wage differences between men and women or between racial groups. Any remaining gap in wages is then attributed to (individual) discrimination. Yet as Ruth Milkman and Eleanor Townsley explain:

> This approach ... fails to capture the depth with which gender discrim-
> ination and the norms associated with it are embedded in the economic
> order – in fact, they are embedded so deeply that a willful act of discrim-
> ination is not really necessary to maintain gender inequality.[17]

By focusing only on individuals and the skills they bring to the labor market, moreover, analysts obscure the relationship between racial groups, a fundamental element in the development of durable racial inequality. One cannot assume that individuals are the only appropriate unit of analysis. By making this assumption, racial realists neglect the collective actions of groups, the role of intermediary institutions, and the cumulative effects of durable racial inequality.

Group Hoarding and the Economic Theory of Discrimination

As we indicated earlier, the economic theory of labor market discrimination is a theory of individual choice. This one-dimensional theory, however, is empirically flawed. Because it assumes that economic competition drives out discrimination, the theory cannot explain why racial inequality persists once education, training, and experience are taken into account. Nor can it explain historical patterns of labor market segregation in both the North and the South. And attempts to rescue the theory by attributing differences in the economic success of African Americans and immigrants to cultural values have failed miserably.[18]

While individuals can and do discriminate, labor market discrimination is better understood as a group phenomenon. It is an instance of what Charles Tilly calls opportunity hoarding. This occurs when members of a group acquire and monopolize access to valuable resources or privileges. Most people know that informal networks of family, extended kinship, friendships, and associates are the typical routes to employment. Employers commonly recruit new workers through informal ties and word-of-mouth suggestions; current employees typically identify job candidates.[19] Because workers tend to be friends and acquaintances of members of the same race and sex, a bias toward re-creating a homogeneous workforce is overwhelming. Discrimination, therefore, can be passive and unobtrusive. One need not be a racist to use one's position to benefit friends and acquaintances, even if it means awarding jobs to whites rather than blacks.[20]

But the process of labor market discrimination is not always so passive. Once members of a group acquire access to resources, they may hoard the resources by denying access to outsiders. Tilly suggests that hoarding can be found in a variety of groups, including immigrants, criminal conspiracies, and even elite military units.[21] Once a group of employees acquire the best jobs and perks, they can make it difficult for employers to hire outsiders. Insiders can harass unwanted workers by disrupting their work and reducing their value to employers, which can eventually exclude outsiders. Intimidation is a way for insiders to discourage outsiders from even applying for a job. Justifying exclusionary practices with beliefs that denigrate the work habits and skills of excluded workers is the final step in this process. For a long time white workers used the "myth of the machine" – the idea that black workers were incapable of working with machines – to exclude African American workers from skilled, higher paying work.[22]

The Thernstroms assume that changing attitudes toward blacks is the key to reducing racial inequalities in wages, income, and employment. It makes more sense, however, to examine racial labor market competition – a prime example of opportunity hoarding – to get a better handle on a critical determinant of racial inequality. Simple models of discrimination that assume that unequal rewards to otherwise identical workers are motivated by prejudice do not capture the complexity and depth of racially divided labor markets in the 20th century. When white workers compete for jobs, they use their advantages to exclude or subordinate black or Latino workers. Two prominent labor market economists, William Darity Jr. and Samuel Myers Jr, write that discrimination is "endogenously linked to the employment needs of nonblack males." Competition between black and white workers intensifies when blacks threaten the status of white workers, either because the blacks have acquired the education and job skills to be competitive or because the job opportunities for whites diminish.[23] Employers' evaluations of the skills and talents of black workers are often based on negative stereotypes of their productivity rather than on independent assessments of their work. These stereotypes are the residue of racial labor market competition and push black workers to the bottom of the employment queue.[24]

Racial labor market competition is obviously affected by the state of the economy. When economic growth is sluggish or depressed, labor markets are slack and competition for jobs unleashes white racism. Robust economic growth produces tight labor markets as demand for workers rises, and typically has a greater impact on black unemployment rates than on white unemployment rates. Similarly, as high-wage manufacturing jobs are eliminated and whites are displaced, competition intensifies between blacks and whites for low- and moderate-wage service jobs. Job competition based on race can be modified by public policies that regulate wages and access to jobs through full employment or affirmative action policies. But unless or until a third party steps in to demand or induce employers to pursue a different recruitment strategy, a homogeneous racial and gendered workforce will almost inevitably be reproduced.

Institutions and the Routine, Ordinary Generation of Inequality

Because the realist analysis of racial inequality assumes that racism is produced exclusively by the intentions and choices of individuals, intermediate institutions that play a crucial part in generating and maintaining racial inequality are rarely analyzed. The routine practices of corporations, law firms, banks, athletic teams, labor unions, the military, and educational institutions tend to be ignored or minimized. These institutions are neither scrutinized nor analyzed unless or until they institute strategies that redress past social grievances. Accordingly, advocates of this approach to racial inequality believe that individual access to previously segregated institutions is all that is necessary to redress past racial injustice. They never discuss the ways in which these institutions might be transformed to accommodate or better engage the groups they formerly excluded.

Any analysis of racial inequality that routinely neglects organizations and practices that, intentionally or unintentionally, generate or maintain racial inequalities over long periods of time is incomplete and misleading. Such an analysis will be unable, for example, to detect the ways in which real estate and mortgage lending industries routinely sustain segregated housing markets and discriminate against would-be black homeowners. It will also not notice that discrimination in the criminal justice system is produced by a large number of small decisions by the police that single out young black men, the results of which then extend to their treatment in adult courts.

Nowhere is the folly of neglecting institutional practices more apparent than in the case of racial disparities in health care and mortality. Many health care institutions remain partially segregated despite the end of Jim Crow and federal laws that prohibit distribution of federal funds to institutions that discriminate. The private nursing home industry, for example, has continued to be segregated, largely because for-profit nursing homes are reluctant to accept Medicaid patients, particularly elderly blacks, and state governments have little incentive to enforce civil rights laws. Elderly blacks are therefore less likely to use private nursing homes even though they have a greater need for such care. In Pennsylvania the segregation index for nursing homes is almost as high as the indexes for housing in metropolitan areas.[25] Moreover, nonwhites are almost twice as likely as whites to be admitted to a nursing home sanctioned by state officials for serious deficiencies in care and facilities.[26]

Segregated and unequal treatment in health care is an endemic problem, though not one that is attributable to the actions of prejudiced individuals. David Barton Smith concludes that at least some of the reported differences in rates of drug addiction, sexually transmitted diseases, and possibly even infant mortality reflect differences in the screening and reporting practices of the setting in which care is provided to blacks, as opposed to those catering to whites.[27]

While there are numerous examples of how economic, educational, and governmental organizations unintentionally produce unequal racial outcomes, it is also the case that certain institutions do better than others in reducing racial inequalities. These practices will not be discovered, however, when one looks for racism in individual motivations.

Cumulative Inequalities

Inequalities are cumulative, a fact adherents of the new public wisdom on race ignore in their rush to celebrate progress.

Focusing on individual motivations for discrimination neglects how the past has shaped contemporary patterns of racial inequality, or how it continues to constrain the choices of African Americans and other groups. Thus, racial realists ignore how the accumulation of wealth – economic, cultural, social, and political capital – molds economic opportunities for all Americans over time. Wealth matters. At the conclusion of his book on race, wealth, and social policy in the United States, Dalton Conley writes:

> One may conclude that the locus of racial inequality no longer lies in the labor market, but rather in class and property relations that, in turn, affect other outcomes. While young African American men may have the opportunity to obtain the same education, income, and wealth as whites, in actuality, they are on a slippery slope, for the discrimination their parents faced in the housing and credit markets sets the stage for perpetual economic disadvantage.[28]

When the economy falters, privileged members of society are able to help themselves over the difficult bumps and fluctuations of a market economy. Their net worth, not wages, provides the necessary reserves to ride out cyclical downturns in the economy or other disasters. Differences in the accumulation of wealth between different racial groups are not solely the result of age, family structure, or the inclination to save – blacks and whites save about the same proportions of their income.[29] Further, African Americans lost much of the wealth they acquired after the Civil War to white thievery and discrimination. A study by the Associated Press found that more than 400 blacks were dispossessed of more than 24,000 acres of farm and timber land in the South, worth millions of dollars today, through fraud, discrimination by lenders, and other illegal means.[30]

Since inequalities accumulate over generations, an analysis of racial inequalities in the distribution of wealth explodes any distinction between past and present racism. Today's racial disparities in wealth reflect the legacies of slavery, Jim Crow, and labor market discrimination.

The Origins of Durable Racial Inequality

Discussions of racial inequality commonly dwell on only one side of the color line. We talk about black poverty, black unemployment, black crime, and public policies for blacks. We rarely, however, talk about the gains whites receive from the troubles experienced by blacks. Only when the diverging fates of black and white Americans are considered together – within the same analytic framework – will it be possible to move beyond the current stale debate over how to transform the American color line.

In our view, the persistence of racial inequality stems from the long-term effects of labor market discrimination and institutional practices that have created cumulative inequalities by race. The result is a durable pattern of racial stratification. Whites have gained or accumulated opportunities, while African Americans and other racial groups have lost opportunities – they suffer from disaccumulation of the accoutrements of economic opportunity.

Accumulation versus Disaccumulation

The idea of accumulation is straightforward and can be illustrated with a simple example. Investment counselors routinely explain to their clients the importance of long-term investments. For example, a young couple that set aside just $40 a month beginning in 1970 and simply let it sit in an account paying 5 percent interest would accumulate about $34,000, or more than double the amount invested, by the year 2000. Rolling over modest investments of capital produces an impressive accumulation. Similarly, very small economic and social advantages can have large cumulative effects over many generations.

While accumulation is relatively well understood, there is a parallel and symmetrical idea that is usually ignored. This is the idea of disinvestment and, over time, what might be called disaccumulation. Just as a positive investment of $40 can accumulate over time, so too can a negative investment produce a downward spiral. Consider what happens if one owes the Internal Revenue Service a few hundred dollars but allows that debt to go unpaid for a decade. The amount of that debt can increase dramatically and can lead to a debt of several thousand dollars. The amount owed can increase fivefold. From the point of view of the debtor, this is negative accumulation, or for purposes of this discussion, disaccumulation. Just as economic advantages (for example access to skilled trades) can accumulate, economic disadvantages (such as exclusion from well-paying jobs) can also be compounded over time.

Home ownership is a good example of how the principle of accumulation and disaccumulation works in a racial context. Today's very large gap in median net worth between whites and African Americans is mostly due to the discrepancy in the value of the equity in their respective homes. Blacks experience more difficulty obtaining mortgage loans, and when they do purchase a house, it is usually worth less than a comparable white-owned home. White flight and residential segregation lower the value of black homes. As blacks move into a neighborhood, whites move out, fearing that property values will decline. As whites leave, the fear becomes a reality and housing prices decline. The refusal of white Americans to live in neighborhoods with more than 20 percent blacks means that white-owned housing is implicitly more highly valued than black-owned housing. Redlining completes the circle: banks refuse to underwrite mortgage loans, or they rate them as a higher risk. As a consequence, when black homeowners can get a loan, they pay higher interest rates for less valuable property. This results in disinvestment in black neighborhoods and translates into fewer amenities, abandoned buildings, and a lower property tax base. Because white communities do not suffer the consequences of residential disaccumulation, they receive advantages denied to black homeowners; the value of their housing increases and they accumulate wealth. In this way interlocking patterns of racialized accumulation and disaccumulation create durable inequality.[31]

The distribution of economic wealth is central to any account of racial inequality, but it is not the only dimension of racial accumulation and disaccumulation. For example, inadequate access to health care contributes to disaccumulation in communities of color. Health is fundamental to every aspect of life: without health, a student cannot do well in school; a worker cannot hold a job, much less excel at one; a family member cannot be an effective parent or spouse. Health crises and the staggering costs they impose are critical underlying causes of poverty, homelessness, and bankruptcy. Housing, employment, and education are vital, but without health, and the care necessary to maintain it, the quality of life, indeed life itself, is uncertain. The effect is cumulative. Inadequate prenatal care results in low birth-weight babies, which in turn leads to infant mortality and to severe physical and mental disabilities among those who survive.[32] One-fifth to one-third of African American children are anemic, and they account for a disproportionate number of children exposed to lead poisoning. Both problems impair intellectual functions and school performance.[33]

Accumulation also includes cultural and social advantages – meeting "the right people" at Harvard, Yale, and Princeton (who can and often do provide a substantial boost to one's career), for example. A symmetrical process operates in the criminal justice system, with the opposite consequences: judges frequently incarcerate black juveniles rather than sending them home because the court believes these youngsters have fewer outside resources to help them. However well-intentioned, these decisions then become part of the juvenile's record, counting against him or her in future scrapes with the criminal justice system. Diverting black youth to state institutions rather than sending them home is analogous to acquiring a small debt that can be compounded. Similarly, critics of affirmative action are correct when they tell black, Latino or Native American students who have been denied admission to the University of California at Berkeley that "there is nothing wrong with attending UC Riverside." But that is only half the story. Elite institutions are saturated with an accumulated legacy of power and privilege along lines of race and gender. The advice to attend Riverside ignores that "who you meet" at Harvard, Yale, or Princeton – or at Berkeley, Ann Arbor, or Madison – is an important aspect of the accumulation of economic and social advantage.

Many Americans, but particularly conservatives, object to the idea that past discrimination matters in the present. Racial realists believe that the accumulation of wealth and power by white Americans over the past 360 years is irrelevant to current patterns of racial stratification, and the use of race-conscious remedies to redress past racial injustices is therefore unnecessary and unfair. As they see it, basing current policies on past practices is wallowing in the past. The main impediment to racial equality, they feel, is state-sponsored discrimination, and the civil rights movement put an end to that. Thus, past discrimination should not matter. Ironically, adherents of this point of view ignore a different form of state-sponsored racial inequality – the use of public policy to advantage whites. Racism is not simply a matter of legal segregation; it is also policies that favor whites.

The Origins of Modern State-Sponsored Racial Inequality

One need not go back 300 years to find the antecedents of contemporary white advantage. The New Deal is the most recent benchmark for the accumulation of white privilege and the generation of black disadvantage. Franklin D. Roosevelt's policies were instrumental to both the cause of racial equality and the perpetuation of racial inequality. New Deal agricultural policies paved the way for the mechanization of southern agriculture and precipitated black (and white) migration to the North and the entry of blacks into manufacturing jobs. The Wagner Act legalized unions; minimum wage laws put an economic floor under all workers; the Social Security Act gave workers a measure of security; and the Employment Act of 1946 codified the government's responsibility for aggregate employment and price levels. These policies, combined with postwar economic growth, undermined the prewar northern racial order, set in motion changes that would dismantle Jim Crow, and reduced black as well as white poverty.

African Americans benefited from New Deal policies. They gained from the growth of public employment and governmental transfers like social security and welfare. The Great Society went further, reducing racial inequality, ameliorating poverty among the black poor, and helping to build a new black middle class. But if federal social policy promoted racial equality, it also created and sustained racial hierarchies. Welfare states are as much instruments of stratification as they are of equality. The New Deal's class-based, or race-neutral, social policies did not affect blacks and whites in identical ways. Federal social policy contributed disproportionately to the prosperity of the white middle class from the 1940s on. Whites received more from the New Deal than old-age protection and insurance against the business cycle. Housing subsidies paved the way for a white exodus to the suburbs; federal tax breaks secured union-bargained health and pension benefits and lowered the cost to workers; veterans' benefits were an avenue of upward mobility for many white men. To assume that government policies benefited only blacks or were colorblind, as many white Americans commonly believe, is like looking at the world with one eye.

Three laws passed by Congress in the mid 1930s were instrumental in generating the pattern of racial stratification that emerged during the New Deal: the Social Security Act, the Wagner Act, and the Federal Housing Act. These laws contributed to the accumulation of wealth in white households, and they did more than any other combination of factors to sow and nurture the seeds of the future urban ghetto and produce a welfare system in which recipients would be disproportionately black. It is commonly assumed that the New Deal was based on broad and inclusive policies. While there is some truth to the claim that Roosevelt's New Deal was designed, as Jill Quadagno states it, to provide a "floor of protection for the industrial working class," it was riddled with discrimination. Brokered compromises over New Deal labor and social policies also reinforced racial segregation through social welfare programs, labor policy, and housing policy.[34] How and why did this happen?

Although the Social Security Act created a work-related social right to an old-age pension and unemployment compensation, Congress defied the Roosevelt administration and explicitly excluded domestic and agricultural workers from coverage. It also exempted public employees as well as workers in nonprofit, voluntary organizations. Only 53 percent of all workers, about 26 million people, were initially covered by the old-age insurance title of the Social Security Act, and less than half of all workers were covered by unemployment compensation. Congress subsequently excluded these exempt workers from the Wagner Act and the 1938 Fair Labor Standards Act as well.[35]

Congress's rejection of universal coverage was not a race-neutral decision undertaken because, as some people claimed at the time, it was difficult to collect payroll taxes from agricultural and domestic workers. As Charles Houston, Dean of the Howard University Law School, told the Senate Finance committee, "It [the Social Security bill] looks like a sieve with the holes just big enough for the majority of Negroes to fall through." Almost three-fifths of the black labor force was denied coverage. When self-employed black sharecroppers are added to the list of excluded workers, it is likely that three-quarters or more of African Americans were denied benefits and the protection of federal law. Black women, of whom 90 percent were domestic workers, were especially disadvantaged by these occupational exclusions.[36]

Agricultural and domestic workers were excluded largely because southern legislators refused to allow implementation of any national social welfare policies that included black workers. Roosevelt presided over a fragile coalition of northern industrial workers and southern whites bound to an agrarian economic order. Although blacks began to leave the party of Lincoln for the party of Roosevelt, three-quarters of the African American population still lived in the South, where they could not vote. Southerners feared that federal social policies would raise the pay of southern black workers and sharecroppers and that this in turn would undermine their system of racial apartheid. Black criticisms of the legislation were ignored as Roosevelt acquiesced to southern demands, believing he could not defy powerful southern committee chairmen and still pass needed social welfare legislation.

As black workers moved north into industrial jobs, they were eventually included under the Social Security Act, and Congress ultimately extended coverage of old-age insurance to agricultural workers in 1950 and 1954. Although the Social Security Administration made every effort to treat black and white workers equally, black workers were nevertheless severely disadvantaged by the work-related eligibility provisions of the Social Security Act. Both old-age insurance and unemployment compensation rewarded stable, long-term employment and penalized intermittent employment regardless of the reason. In the name of fiscal integrity, the architects of social insurance in the 1930s were adamant that malingerers, those on relief, or those weakly attached to the labor market be excluded from eligibility and their benefits limited. Due to labor market discrimination and the seasonal nature of agricultural labor, many blacks (and Latinos) have not had stable, long-term employment records. Thus, they have had only limited eligibility for old-age and unemployment benefits.

The racial consequences of wage-related eligibility provisions were already apparent in the 1930s. Because labor market discrimination lowers the wages of black workers relative to white workers or denies them employment altogether, blacks receive lower benefits than whites from old-age insurance and unemployment compensation or are denied access at all. By 1939, for example, only 20 percent of white workers who worked in industries covered by social insurance and who paid payroll taxes for old-age insurance were uninsured, but more than twice as many black workers (42 percent) were uninsured.[37] From the outset, social security transferred income from African American workers to white workers. This disparity continues today. Even though most black workers are currently covered by social security, on average they still receive lower benefits than whites and pay a higher proportion of their income in social security taxes.[38] Like old-age insurance, there is little evidence of overt discrimination in unemployment compensation – eligible black workers are almost as likely as white workers are to receive benefits. But because states imposed strict eligibility requirements during the 1940s and 1950s, black workers were disproportionately excluded.[39] Social insurance is neither universal nor race-neutral.

In combination, labor market discrimination and work-related eligibility requirements excluded blacks from work and social insurance programs in the 1930s, forcing many to go on relief and later on welfare, Aid to Dependent Children (ADC). In fact, most black women were excluded from the unemployment compensation system until the late 1960s. This is because domestic workers were statutorily excluded from unemployment compensation, and as late as the 1950s more than half of all black women in the civilian labor force still worked as domestics. Unemployed black women typically had nowhere to turn but welfare, and this is exactly what they did. By 1960, African Americans accounted for two-fifths of all welfare recipients, a participation rate that did not change much even when the welfare rolls expanded in the 1960s. It is labor market discrimination and New Deal social policies, not welfare, as the conservatives believe, that has harmed black families. The problem cannot be explained by a pathological black family structure.[40]

Social insurance in the United States has operated much like a sieve, just as Charles Houston predicted, and blacks have fallen through the holes. The Wagner Act and the 1937 Housing Act compounded the problem, enlarging the holes in the sieve. Sometimes labeled the Magna Charta of the labor movement, the 1935 Wagner Act was, upon closer inspection, the Magna Charta of white labor. Black leaders tried to add an antidiscrimination amendment to the law, but the American Federation of Labor and the white southerners who controlled key congressional committees fought it. As a result, the final version excluded black workers. The law legalized the closed shop, which, as Roy Wilkins of the NAACP pointed out, would empower "organized labor to exclude from employment in any industry those who do not belong to a union." The law also outlawed strikebreaking, a weapon black workers had used successfully to force their way into northern industries. Preventing blacks from entering into newly protected labor unions meant that black workers were subject to the racist inclinations of white workers.[41] One of the consequences of the Wagner Act's failure to protect black workers was that union rules confined them to low-wage unskilled jobs. When these jobs were eliminated as businesses modernized after World War II, black unskilled workers were replaced by automated manufacturing technologies.[42] Thus, the current high levels of black unemployment can be traced directly to New Deal legislation that allowed white workers to deny job opportunities to blacks.

State-sponsored racial inequality was also augmented by a third set of New Deal policies: federal housing and urban renewal legislation. These policies, including those policies before the New Deal, which primarily benefitted whites,[43] sealed the fate of America's cities by establishing "apartheid without walls." Contrary to the commonly held notion that white flight is responsible for creating ghettos and barrios, it was actually the federal government's explicit racial policy that created these enclaves.

Each of these policies, routinely hailed as major progressive government interventions to boost the economy and place a safety net under all citizens, was instrumental in creating long-run patterns of accumulation and disaccumulation based on race. These policies, along with others, institutionalized white advantage over blacks and other people of color.

Race Equality and the Possessive Investment in Whiteness after the Civil Rights Revolution

In the post-civil rights era, formal equality before the law coexists with de facto white privilege and whites' resentment of race-conscious remedies. Whites' resentment reflects their "possessive investment in whiteness."[44] Historically, white Americans have accumulated advantages in housing, work, education, and security based solely on the color of their skin. Being white, as a consequence, literally has value. Though race may be a cultural and biological fiction, whiteness, like blackness, is a very real social and legal identity. Both identities are crucial in determining one's social and economic status. This is why, when Professor Andrew Hacker asked his white students how much money they would demand if they were changed from white to black, they felt it was reasonable to ask for $50 million if they were to be black for the rest of their lives, or $1 million a year for each year they were black.[45] That was the financial value they placed on being white. It was, to use W.E. B. DuBois's phrase, the dollar amount they attached to their "wages of whiteness." The idea of a possessive investment in whiteness helps to explain the structures of durable racial inequality and the color-coded community processes of accumulation and disaccumulation. The formation of racial identity, in turn, connects interests to attitudes toward public issues that have racial consequences and color-conscious remedies.

Americans still face the question of what racial inequality means and what the nation is obligated to do about it. We think it makes the most sense to consider carefully how labor market discrimination, private institutional practices, and public policies have generated the accumulation of economic and social advantages in white communities, and the concomitant disaccumulation

APPENDIX 3A Disparity in Economic, Health, and Social Indicators by Race in the United States

Indicator Type	Statistic	Asian	Latino	Native American	African American	White
Economic	Median Income (2016)	$80,720	46,882	39,719	38, 555	63,165
	Per Capita Income (2016)	$36,350	18,389	18,961	21,452	36,938
	Home Ownership (2016)	57.9 percent	45.8 percent	53.7 percent	41.9 percent	71.4 percent
	Poverty Rate (2016)	11.8 percent	21.0 percent	26.2 percent	23.9 percent	10.6 percent
	Unemployment (2016)	4.5 percent	6.7 percent	12.0 percent	10.1 percent	4.6 percent
Health	Infant Mortality (2015)	4.2/1,000	4.7/1,000	8.3/1,000	11.3/1,000	4.9/1,000
	Life Expectancy (2015)	N/A	82.0	N/A	75.1	78.7
	Health Insurance **Uninsured** (2016)	10.8 percent	23.4 percent	23.3 percent	13.7 percent	8.1 percent
Social	High School Degree (2016)	86.6 percent	67.1 percent	79.9 percent	85.2 percent	92.5 percent
	Bachelor's Degree (2016)	53.2 percent	15.3 percent	14.5 percent	20.9 percent	35.0 percent
	Incarceration per 100,000 (2015)	N/A	584.5	N/A	1,322.9	252.6

Sources: US Census Bureau
Median Income: Table S1903
Per Capita Income: Tables B19301B, B19301C, B19301D, B19301H, B19301I
Homeownership: Tables B25003B, B25003C, B25003H, B25003D, B25003I
Poverty: Tables B17001B, B17001C, B17001D, B17001H, B17001I
Unemployment: Table S2301
Health Insurance: Table S2701
Educational Attainment: Table S1501

Infant Mortality: User Guide to the 2015 Period Linked Birth Infant Death Public File, Centers for Disease Control and Prevention, Table 2
Life Expectancy: Health United States 2016, with Chartbook on Long-term Trends in Health, pp.44 and 45, Centers for Disease Control and Prevention
Incarceration: Prisoners in 2015, Table 3, Bureau of Justice Statistics and US Census population tables.

of social and economic capital in communities of color. By comparing the assumptions, arguments, and evidence articulated by racial realists to an alternative framework, we think it is possible to see the major differences between these two perspectives and the remedies that follow from a theory that focuses on cumulative inequalities.

Notes

1 Jim Sleeper. *Liberal Racism*. New York: Penguin Books, 1997; Tamar Jacoby. *Someone Else's House: America's Unfinished Struggle for Integration*. New York: The Free Press, 1998; Dinesh D'Souza. *The End of Racism: Principles for a Multiracial Society*. New York: The Free Press, 1995; Shelby Steele. *A Dream Deferred*. New York: Harper Perennial, 1999.
2 Alan Wolfe. "Enough Blame to Go Around." *New York Times Book Review*, June 21, 1998, p. 12.
3 Stephen Thernstrom and Abigail Thernstrom. *America in Black and White: One Nation, Indivisible*. New York: Simon & Schuster, 1997.
4 Sleeper. *Liberal Racism*, p. 178.
5 Thernstrom and Thernstrom. *America in Black and White*, p. 183.
6 US Bureau of the Census. "Race and Hispanic Origin of Householder – Families by Median and Mean Income: 1947 to 2015." (Table F-5), Historical Income Tables – Families. Accessed September 17, 2017 from www.census.gov/data/tables/time-series/demo/income-poverty/historical-income-families.html.
7 Ibid. See also Sheldon Danziger and Peter Gottschalk. *America Unequal*. New York: Russell Sage Foundation, 1995, pp. 71–73. Using a measure of income that adjusts for family size and unrelated individuals, Danziger and Gottschalk show that in 1991 the real median income of black families was 1.85 times the poverty line, compared to 3.54 times for white families. Not until 1991 did black family income reach a level comparable to 1959 family income for the total population. Among nonelderly, two-parent families the ratio rose from 44 percent to 71 percent in 1991, still a large gap. In 2001, after the economic expansion, black married couples' income was 80 percent of white married couples'. However, this measure is not comparable to Danziger and Gottschalk's and may overstate the ratio.
8 US Bureau of the Census. "Race and Hispanic Origin of People by Median Income and Sex: 1947 to 2015." (Table P-2), Historical Income Tables – People. Accessed September 17, 2017 from www.census.gov/data/tables/time-series/demo/income-poverty/historical-income-people.html.
9 Douglas Massey and Nancy Denton. *American Apartheid: Segregation and the Making of the Underclass*. Cambridge, MA: Harvard University Press, 1993, pp. 77, 87–88. Also see a series of studies and papers from John Logan and Brian Stults, among them, "The Persistence of Segregation in the Metropolis: New Findings from the 2010 Census." US2010 Project, March 24, 2011. Accessed September 17, 2017 from https://s4.ad.brown.edu/Projects/Diversity/Data/Report/report2.pdf.
10 Preliminary studies conducted by the National Fair Housing Alliance reveal how this gap is created. The Alliance found that when creditworthy whites approach subprime lenders, they are systematically referred to prime lenders, who make loans on more favorable terms, with lower interest rates and less predatory foreclosure practices.
11 National Fair Housing Alliance. The Case for Fair Housing, 2017 Fair Housing Trends Report. Accessed September 18, 2017 from http://nationalfairhousing.org/wp-content/uploads/2017/07/TRENDS-REPORT-2017-FINAL.pdf.

12 The ratio of black–white infant mortality rate rose from 2.07 in 1983 to 2.22 in 2014. National Center for Health Statistics. "Infant Mortality Rates, Fetal Mortality Rates, and Perinatal Mortality Rates, according to Race: United States, Selected Years 1983–2014" (Table 10), Centers for Disease Control. Accessed September 17, 2017 from www.cdc.gov/nchs/products/pubs/pubd/hus/tables/2001/ 01hus023.pdf; Additional information came from Centers for Disease Control and Prevention. User Guide to 2015 Period Linked Birth/Infant Death Public Use File. Accessed September 17, 2017 from ftp://ftp.cdc.gov/pub/Health_Statistics/NCHS/ Dataset_Documentation/DVS/periodlinked/LinkPE15Guide.pdf.

13 In 1986, for example, among males under 65, those with the highest educational attainment showed the largest relative racial discrepancies in mortality rates. For adult females, the largest relative racial disparity in mortality rates is found in the highest income category. Gregory Pappas et al. "The Increasing Disparity in Mortality between Socioeconomic Groups in the United States, 1960 and 1986." *New England Journal of Medicine* 329 (1987): 103–109.

14 David Barton Smith. *Health Care Divided: Race and Healing a Nation.* Ann Arbor, MI: University of Michigan Press, 1999, p. 201.

15 Ibid, p. 208, Table 6.8. Also see Irene V. Blair, Edward P. Havranek, David W. Price, Rebecca Hanratty, Diane L. Fairclough, Tillman Farley ... John F. Steiner. "Assessment of Biases against Latinos and African Americans among Primary Care Providers and Community Members." *American Journal of Public Health* 103, no. 1 (2013a): 92–98; Same authors, "Clinicians' Implicit Ethnic/Racial Bias and Perceptions of Care among Black and Latino Patients." *Annals of Family Medicine* 11, no. 1 (2013b): 43–52. doi: 10.1370/afm.1442.

16 Charles Tilly. *Durable Inequality.* Berkeley and Los Angeles: University of California Press, 1998, p. 17.

17 Ruth Milkman and Eleanor Townsend, "Gender and the Economy," in *Handbook of Economic Sociology*, ed. Neil J. Smelser and Richard Swedberg. Princeton, NJ: Princeton University Press, 1994, p. 611; cited in Tilly. *Durable Inequality*, p. 31.

18 William Darity Jr. "What's Left of the Economic Theory of Discrimination," in *The Question of Discrimination*, ed. Steven Shulman and William Darity Jr. Middletown, CT: Wesleyan University Press, 1989, pp. 335–374. Economists have advanced a variety of ingenious explanations for the persistence of racial discrimination; all of these assume (at least implicitly) that discrimination is temporary and all are based on individual-level explanations. See Darity, W.A. and Mason, P. "Evidence of Discrimination in Employment: Codes of Color Codes of Gender." *Journal of Economic Perspectives* 12, no. 2 (1998): 81–87 for a summary. However, James Heckman points out that a bigoted employer can "indulge that taste so long as income is received from entrepreneurial activity" – so long, that is, as there is a willingness to pay the price. See James Heckman. "Detecting Discrimination." *Journal of Economic Perspectives* 12 (1998): 112.

19 Peter V. Marsden. "The Hiring Process: Recruitment Methods." *American Behavioral Scientist* 7 (1994): 979–991; Shazia R. Miller and James E. Rosenbaum. "Hiring in a Hobbesian World." *Work and Occupations* 24 (1997): 498–523.

20 Philip Kasinitz and Jay Rosenberg. "Missing the Connection: Social Isolation and Employment on the Brooklyn Waterfront." *Social Problems* 43 (1996): 180–196; for a description see Thomas Sugrue. *The Origins of the Urban Crisis.* Princeton, NJ: Princeton University Press, 1996, Chapter 4.

21 Tilly. *Durable Inequality*, p. 91.

22 Economists have developed a very similar theory to Tilly's idea of opportunity hoarding. See Derek Leslie. *An Investigation of Racial Disadvantage.* Manchester, England: Manchester University Press, 1998, pp. 33–37.

23 Darity and Myers. *Persistent Disparity: Race and Economic Inequality in the United States Since 1945*. Northampton, MA: Edward Elgar, 1998, p. 58.

24 See Reynolds Farley and Walter Allen. *The Color Line and the Quality of Life in America*. New York: Oxford University Press, 1989, p. 247; Stanley Lieberson. *A Piece of the Pie: Blacks and White Immigrants since 1880*. Berkeley and Los Angeles: University of California Press, 1980, pp. 294–313. Richard Epstein assumes that at least one employer will be motivated by the bottom line and not by negative stereotypes. But this neglects the pressure that white workers may bring to bear on employers to exclude blacks. *Forbidden Grounds: The Case against Employment Discrimination Laws*. Cambridge, MA: Harvard University Press, 1992.

25 Pennsylvania nursing homes have a segregation index of 0.68, which means that 68 percent of nursing home residents would have to move in order to equalize the distribution of blacks and whites across all homes. The 1990 average segregation index for northern cities was 0.78. Some of the segregation in nursing homes is an artifact of residential segregation, but not all of it – the segregation index for Philadelphia nursing homes is 0.63. Smith. *Health Care Divided*, pp. 264–265, 267; Massey and Denton. *American Apartheid*, p. 222.

26 Smith. *Health Care Divided*, p. 267.

27 Ibid., pp. 319–320.

28 Dalton Conley. *Being Black, Living in the Red*. Berkeley: University of California Press, 1999, p. 152.

29 Blacks save 11 percent of their income; whites save 10 percent. Ibid., p. 29.

30 Todd Lewan and Delores Barcal. "Torn from the Land: AP Documents Land Taken from Blacks through Trickery, Violence and Murder." Associated Press, December 2001. Accessed September 17, 2017 from http://nuweb9.neu.edu/civil rights/wp-content/uploads/AP-Investigation-Article.pdf.

31 Conley. *Being Black, Living in the Red*, pp. 38–39; Massey and Denton. *American Apartheid*, pp. 54–55.

32 Black babies are one and one-third times as likely as whites to suffer from low birth weight and more than three times as likely to suffer very low birth weight. See W. Michael Byrd and Linda A. Clayton. *An American Health Dilemma, Vol. 1: A Medical History of African Americans and the Problem of Race: Beginnings to 1900*. New York, NY: Routledge, 2000, p. 30.

33 Among black children one to six years of age, 11.5 percent had elevated blood lead levels in 1991–1994, compared to 2.6 percent of white children of the same age. US Department of Health and Human Services. *Healthy People 2010: Understanding and Improving Health*, Second ed. Washington, DC: US Government Printing Office, 2000, pp. 8–21.

34 Jill Quadagno. *The Color of Welfare*. New York: Oxford University Press, 1994, pp. 19–24.

35 Michael K. Brown. *Race, Money, and the American Welfare State*. Ithaca, NY: Cornell University Press, 1999, p. 71.

36 Ibid., p. 82. And US Congress, Senate, Committee on Finance. Economic Security Act Hearings on S. 1130, 74th Congress, 1st Session, 1935, p. 641.

37 Brown. *Race, Money, and the American Welfare State*, p. 82.

38 Quadagno. *The Color of Welfare*, pp. 160–161.

39 Robert Lieberman. *Shifting the Color Line: Race and the American Welfare State*. Cambridge, MA: Harvard University Press, 1998, pp. 198–199, 210.

40 Brown. *Race, Money, and the American Welfare State*, Chapters 2 and 5.

41 Herbert Hill. *Black Labor and the American Legal System*. Madison: University of Wisconsin Press, 1985, p. 105; Quadagno. *The Color of Welfare*, p. 23; Brown. *Race, Money, and the American Welfare State*, p. 68.

42 Irving Bernstein. *Promises Kept: John F. Kennedy's New Frontier*. New York, NY: Oxford University Press, 1991, pp. 165–167.

43 See George Fredrickson. *The Arrogance of Race*. Middletown, CT: Wesleyan University Press, 1988 and *White Supremacy*. New York: Oxford University Press, 1981; and Leon A. Higginbotham. *In the Matter of Color: Race and the American Legal Process*. New York: Oxford University Press, 1978.
44 George Lipsitz. *The Possessive Investment in Whiteness: How White People Profit from Identity Politics*. Philadelphia: Temple University Press, 1998.
45 Andrew Hacker. *Two Nations*. New York: Ballantine Books, 1992, p. 32.

4

EXAMINING IMPLICIT RACIAL BIAS IN JOURNALISM

Satia A. Marotta, Simon Howard, and Samuel R. Sommers

The authors of this chapter are three social psychologists with expertise in stereotyping, prejudice, and discrimination. Here they discuss research in their field that addresses the various ways implicit bias can emerge in the reporting and writing process. In addition, they provide methods journalists can use to reduce the impact of implicit bias in professional practice.

Journalists strive to deliver truth to the public, unbiased and without favor.[1] Behavioral science research, however, suggests that even people most motivated to remain objective may be influenced by unconscious, automatic attitudes that operate outside their awareness. These attitudes, referred to as implicit attitudes, can color our perceptions and behaviors, resulting in bias against others. In the domain of journalism, we might consider such bias as being much like binoculars through which stories and sources are seen. Implicit bias can limit a journalist's field of vision and lead them to focus on certain stories as opposed to others; it can distort their perception and influence how they see sources; and implicit bias can create distance between journalists and their sources, harming interactions. Thus, implicit bias can have a significant influence on the types of stories journalists choose to cover, the sources they select, how interviews are interpreted, and how these findings are ultimately reported.

This chapter explains what implicit bias is and how it can influence many stages of the pursuit for journalistic truth. We end with strategies that journalists can use to identify their implicit biases and attempt to counter them. While implicit bias can affect attitudes and perceptions of any social group (e.g., people who are overweight, individuals of lower social economic status, those with disabilities), our current focus will be on implicit *racial* bias in journalism, reflecting the unique historical legacy of racial bias in the United States.[2]

What Is Implicit Bias?

Implicit bias refers to the unconscious and relatively automatic associations we have towards people based on a number of characteristics including age, ethnicity, gender, race, religion, sexual orientation, and socio-economic status.[3] These associations influence our perceptions, actions, and decision-making in ways that often contribute to the maintenance of disparities and structural inequities. Explicit biases are the attitudes and beliefs we have about a person or group on a conscious level, whereas implicit biases operate in an unintentional and unconscious manner.

Imagine Joan, a white female who harbors an overt dislike of Latino people. Joan's explicit bias toward Latinos likely influences her conscious decisions when interacting with members of this group. For example, if Joan is the manager of a department store she may deliberately avoid promoting Latinos because she believes they are lazy.

In contrast, imagine Rachel, a white female who has no explicit bias against Latinos and endorses an egalitarian, anti-prejudice mindset. Rachel's exposure to direct and indirect messages associating people of color with negativity may create, for her, an unconscious association of Latinos with negative attributes such as criminality, a lack of intelligence, or laziness. If Rachel was also a department store manager she too might prevent Latinos from being promoted, though in her case it would be without the intent to discriminate. Though Rachel explicitly holds egalitarian beliefs, implicit racial bias may lead her to act in ways that subtly discriminate against minorities. While this harm is unintentional, its impact is no less significant. For this reason, implicit bias must be addressed as early and conclusively as possible, because even when we intend to avoid being prejudiced, implicit bias can still affect our perceptions and behaviors.

Origins of Implicit Bias

We are frequently exposed to direct and indirect messages from our parents, religious doctrines, the media, and other sources that associate particular individuals or groups with positivity or negativity. For example, in the United States, Christian iconography generally depicts Jesus and other important religious figures as white, explicitly and implicitly creating the association between whiteness and godliness.[4] Alternatively, despite the fact that terrorists' attacks in the US are more likely to be carried out by white right-wing extremists relative to other groups, Muslims are dramatically overrepresented in the news media as the perpetrators of terrorism. This overrepresentation contributes to the association many Americans have between Muslims and terrorism, religious extremism, and fear.[5]

The presentation of out-group members in a negative light, whether intentionally or unintentionally, can have real and severe consequences for race relations. President Trump's travel ban was presented as protecting Americans from terrorists who planned to come to the United States to do them harm.[6,7] On multiple occasions, it was stated that 72 individuals from the seven countries identified in the ban had been implicated in terrorism-related activities. However, none of these people were actually involved in terrorism-related deaths in the United States, and while many were investigated for charges related to terrorism, most did not actually face terrorism-related charges or convictions. The statements suggesting that banning individuals from entire countries would prevent terrorist attacks perpetuated negative stereotypes associating people from majority Muslim countries, or those with Arabic names, with terrorism. Decades of scientific research demonstrate that chronic exposure to stereotype-laden messages such as these can strengthen automatic negative associations, which can lead to stigmatized groups.

Implicit racial bias has been linked to a number of disparities, such as those along racial and ethnic lines in economic and educational outcomes.[8,9] The Department of Education reports that black students are three-and-a-half times more likely to be suspended than their white counterparts for identical offenses.[10] Social psychologists Jason Okonofua at the University of California at Berkeley and Jennifer Eberhardt at Stanford University have found evidence that implicit bias in perceptions of student behavior may be partly to blame for this disparity.[11] Kindergarten through twelfth grade teachers were asked to review a school record for a student who was either white or black and had either one or two infractions. They then made judgments about their perceptions of the student's behavior and how severe his punishment should be. The results suggest that while perceptions and recommended punishments after the first infraction were similar, after the second infraction, teachers were more troubled, recommended more severe disciplinary action, and were more likely to view the behavior as indicative of a pattern when viewing a black versus white student's record.

Teachers were also more likely to label a black student as a troublemaker and to imagine suspending him for these infractions. The extent to which a teacher believed the infractions were indicative of a pattern of behavior, which varied by student race, explained much of the variation in imagined suspensions. Most educators are appalled at the suggestion that they could be treating their students differently based on race. In other words, teachers are not consciously aware that race influences their disciplinary actions. However, due to the strong cultural association between black and bad behavior, black students' behavior is often perceived to be more problematic relative to their white counterparts, resulting in racial disparities in suspensions.

In the legal domain, ethnic minority children are more likely to be placed in foster care than with a parent or guardian when compared to white children, though bias training and the use of informational materials have helped to curtail this trend.[12]

While much existing research focuses on implicit racial bias against black people, implicit bias against other racial groups is also prevalent. For example, one study found that the more implicit racial bias a participant harbored against American Indians, the more likely the participant expected an American Indian student to enjoy completing a test of stereotype-consistent knowledge (e.g., general culture and environmental issues), as opposed to a test of stereotype-inconsistent knowledge (e.g., math and science).[13]

How Is Implicit Bias Measured?

Social psychologists and their collaborators have developed multiple ways to assess implicit attitudes. The computer-based Implicit Association Test (IAT) is the most well-known and widely used test to measure an individual's unconscious attitudes.[14] The standard race-based IAT works by measuring the strength of associations between racial groups (e.g., blacks, American Indians) and adjectives or categories (e.g., good, bad). Participants must quickly categorize faces, objects, or words into provided categories.

In the trials, faces flash on the computer screen along with words or objects. Participants are instructed to quickly pair the two in a particular fashion by using keys on their computer keyboard. Faster correct categorizations indicate stronger associations between members of a social group (represented by the faces) and the presented objects or words. For example, if a respondent is slower to categorize darker skin tones with pleasant words than with negative words over the course of the trial, or if they more quickly associate black faces with guns than with harmless objects during the test period, then they are described as having an implicit bias.

Because the IAT combines speed with accuracy, researchers believe that the test can address problems that confound other measures of bias. For example, people generally wish to avoid appearing prejudiced and so, given more time for deliberation, may adjust their responses accordingly. Results from more than 57,500 unique participants who completed the Asian American/European American and American/Foreign IAT indicate that 61 percent of respondents more quickly associated Asian American faces with "foreign" and European American faces with "American" than the reverse.[15,16]

Extensive studies using the IAT have found that implicit bias, in all forms, is pervasive. While the majority of journalists are likely successful in reporting newsworthy events and incidents without intentional bias, even journalists with the best intentions may fall victim to implicit biases. These cognitive slips can affect all facets of decision-making.

Selecting Stories

Several factors determine which stories are covered in the news: current events, assignments from editors, and journalists pursuing their own interests. When editors or journalists select stories, implicit bias can shape their focus.

For example, crime stories that dominate media platforms, particularly the most violent ones, tend to rely on the frame of a nonwhite offender and a white victim.[17,18,19] These incidents are consistent with stereotypes of nonwhites being criminals, and of whites being law-abiding citizens.

It is unlikely that journalists consciously decide to cover stories with nonwhite victims less often. In fact, in one study examining news coverage of missing person cases in Louisiana from 2009 to 2013, white and nonwhite missing person cases were equally likely to receive news media attention.[20] However, the depth and breadth of that attention differed, with white missing persons receiving three times as much total media attention, including more articles and articles with higher word counts than nonwhite missing persons. These findings are supported by a comprehensive analysis comparing the coverage of missing persons in four major news outlets to data in the Federal Bureau of Investigation's Active Missing Person File, which is a list of all missing persons in the United States.[21] The results of this analysis suggest that black individuals were less often represented in media coverage compared to their proportion in the Active Missing Person File, while white missing persons were more intensely covered than would be expected based on their proportion in the Active Missing Person File. Thus, perhaps subconsciously, white missing persons were perceived as more newsworthy and deserving of coverage.

Further, many journalists investigate stories to expose the wrongs that have been committed against ordinary citizens. But implicit bias may influence how journalists perceive the severity of a wrong and determine whether they pursue a story. Extrapolating from a study on juror perceptions of victims and perpetrators,[22] journalists may view nonwhite victims as more responsible for the crimes committed against them, and see white perpetrators of crimes against nonwhite victims as less blameworthy. In this study, Arabic victims of violent crime were more often seen as responsible for their own assault than black or white victims. Similarly, white assailants who attacked Arabic individuals were seen as less blameworthy than those who attacked black or white individuals.

Journalists may cover incidents in which racial minorities are victims less often because they perceive the wrong they have suffered as less severe and as more of their own making. Journalists may want to actively reflect on why one story seems more compelling than another. This exercise may help address disparate coverage and offer a means to identify stories that may not have been previously considered newsworthy.

Perception of Sources

In addition to influencing which stories to cover, implicit bias may also influence how journalists perceive potential sources or interviewees. When quickly assessing a source's reliability and usefulness, a reporter may draw on reactive assumptions rather than objective observations. If implicit bias acts as a pair of binoculars, sometimes they can distort our vision and we misperceive people and situations.

For example, one study found that participants who had higher levels of pro-white implicit bias were more likely to perceive white faces as being more trustworthy than black faces, even though they had no other information about the people in the photos they were evaluating.[23] In addition to social markers like skin color, we may rely on other cues like perceived engagement and question response time to assess trustworthiness, credibility, and intelligence. However, these markers may also be influenced by implicit racial bias.

In one study, psychologists at Lehigh University and a neuroscientist at Temple University discovered that participants who were highly motivated to avoid acting in prejudiced ways tended to perceive the passage of time differently when viewing white and black faces.[24] Specifically, participants perceived that a picture of a black face had appeared on the screen for longer than it actually had. For these participants, time seemed to slow when they viewed a black as opposed to white face. This finding has implications for a journalist's perceptions about how "quick-witted," engaged, or helpful a potential interviewee may be. Although the interviewee may be responding appropriately and thoughtfully, the journalist may experience that person as taking longer to react to questions. The perceived delay could in turn influence her assessment as to whether the source was telling the truth.

The factor driving this perceptual distortion seems to be the physiological arousal caused by concerns about appearing prejudiced.[25] One way to reduce susceptibility to this distortion would be to train journalists in strategies to counter bias so that they might be more at ease when interacting with sources of other races.

Skin color may also influence how journalists perceive a source's intelligence and reliability. A sociologist at Villanova University conducted an archival analysis of the American National Election Survey (2012), revealing that when an interviewee had darker skin, an interviewer tended to perceive this individual as less intelligent, regardless of actual level of education and vocabulary.[26] Taken together, race and skin color can lead someone to view people of color as less trustworthy, less persuasive, and less intelligent, which may reduce the chance that they are interviewed and the amount of credibility they are afforded.

During the widely covered trial of George Zimmerman for the fatal shooting of the unarmed black teenager, Trayvon Martin, one of the witnesses, Rachel Jeantel, a dark-skinned, full-figured black woman, faced derision and disdain from the defense attorney and the media.[27] At one point during her cross-examination, the defense attorney went as far as to ask her if she had difficulty understanding English. Jeantel spoke what is considered black English. The defense and news media portrayed her as being less intelligent, less credible, and as having little respect for the court proceedings. Being aware of the ways in which implicit bias can influence perceptions of others can help journalists take active measures to curb those biases in decisions about who to interview and how to interview and characterize them.

Interacting with Sources

Our review of the published psychological research revealed that there has been no research specifically on how implicit racial bias can affect interactions between journalists and their sources. However, there has been extensive research on implicit racial bias and its influence in professional interactions in other domains, including, for example, between doctors and patients. There are parallels between physicians and journalists in that both interact with an individual from whom they seek information, often in a time-compressed context.

In both professions, the interviews aim to identify supporting evidence and decide upon a proper course of action. Both professions rely on creating a safe environment in which the people being interviewed feel at ease and able to disclose personal information. Unfortunately, implicit bias can create distance between interviewers and interviewees, harming the success of interactions.

Research in the health-care domain suggests that implicit racial bias may hinder positive professional interactions and trust. One study compared the implicit racial bias of physicians and community members and found that while physicians tended to demonstrate lower levels of implicit bias toward blacks and Latinos than found in the larger community, implicit bias was still substantial.[28] This bias was perceptible to patients. Irene Blair and her colleagues at Denver Health reviewed evaluations of care and found that as the pro-white implicit bias of physicians increased, nonwhite patients described the interaction more negatively.[29] University of Michigan social psychologist Louis Penner and his colleague found that averse racism is sometimes at play.[30] This is a phenomenon where racial minorities are attuned to contradictions between what physicians explicitly express and the implicit attitudes they telegraph.

Black patient evaluations of physicians were the most positive when physicians were either low in both implicit and explicit bias, or high in both implicit and explicit bias.[31] The most negative evaluations were toward physicians who were low in explicit bias but high in implicit bias. The more authentic a physician seems – that is when explicit and implicit attitudes align – the more nonwhite patients view the experience positively.[32]

Although journalists and physicians aim to be unbiased, implicit bias can harm their interactions with sources and patients. Once we have determined which implicit biases we hold, we can begin to take precautions against exhibiting them in interactions and ensuring that our nonverbal behaviors are reinforcing the attitudes we explicitly express. Implicit bias may be expressed in various ways, for example, how much we choose to listen versus speak in interview settings. In the health-care domain, when physicians harbored stronger implicit racial biases, they were more likely to talk during a patient interaction.[33] By dominating the conversation during these interactions, doctors prompted patients to feel less involved in their own treatment and less receptive to instructions.

If the same pattern occurs in news interviews, sources who are the targets of the implicit bias may feel the journalist is uninterested in their story or devaluing their experience, which could lead them to withdraw from the process. Based on these findings, journalists should consider how long they speak to sources, how well they appear to engage with the source, and how they pose questions. All of these factors may influence how sources perceive implicit bias in the journalist.

Additionally, when interviewing more than one person, journalists should consider whether they are asking the right person the most relevant questions. In a study investigating doctor–patient interactions between pediatricians and children, researchers at the Max Planck Institute for Psycholinguistics discovered that as the implicit racial bias harbored by pediatricians increased, they were more likely to address questions to black and Latino children's parents, rather than the children themselves.[34] The same pattern was not observed when addressing white children. In all cases the children were competent, and likely best able to describe their own symptoms.

As is outlined in the Society of Professional Journalists' Code of Ethics, journalists should try to talk directly to original sources whenever possible to obtain accurate information.[35] However, implicit bias may make them feel more comfortable or confident asking questions of a source who is similar to themselves, even though someone who is dissimilar may provide a more informed account. If the objective is to discover and reveal truth, journalists must ensure that they consult sources with primary knowledge, not more familiar representatives, whenever possible.

While we have outlined several findings that can be extrapolated to journalism, there are notable differences between physicians and journalists. Most significant is that a physician must determine a course of action after interacting with patients and that action directly impacts the well-being of their patients. In contrast, while journalists must decide what to do with the information they collect and how to convey it to others, they do not act directly to address the issue their source is facing. Despite this, the choices journalists make in which stories to cover and who to consult for information can have profound effects on the lives of others.

Reporting to the Public

While journalists strive to provide objective assessments of truth, this is not always easy to achieve. Our own group memberships can influence how we perceive the behaviors of others.

Researchers have been examining the impact group membership has on the motives people attribute to behavior. For example, psychologists at Northwestern University and the Humboldt University of Berlin examined whether German participants would perceive ambiguous behaviors differently when they were performed by either a German or a Turk.[36] They found that participants who held stronger negative implicit attitudes toward Turkish people saw behaviors as more negative when committed by a Turk as opposed to a German. However, participants with minimal implicit bias perceived behaviors by the two groups in the same way.

As previously addressed, racial minorities tend to be overrepresented in the news media as perpetrators of crime. Researchers have also widely observed that there are dramatic variations in how the parties involved in these crimes are portrayed.[37] For one, journalists tend to emphasize the redeeming qualities of white suspects and offenders, while emphasizing the negative qualities of black victims. In recent years, police shootings of unarmed black civilians have been highly publicized. Many of these victims were subsequently denigrated in the media. In response, three black women, Alicia Garza, Opel Tometi, and Patrisse Cullors, started the hashtag and movement Black Lives Matter to protest excessive use of force and to address systemic and institutional bias against black people.[38] Though these protests have largely been peaceful, the individuals involved are often described by opponents as being anti-police and hostile, prompting reactionary declarations that "All Lives Matter" and "Blue Lives Matter." Implicit bias research suggests that observers more easily associate anger or hostility with black faces.[39] When white participants viewed a racially ambiguous face, they were more likely to categorize it as black when it had an angry versus happy expression. In the same vein, it is likely that peaceful black protesters will be seen as more threatening than they really are. Journalists should consider whether implicit biases are influencing how they describe events to the public. Word choice has an impact. Whether individuals are described as activists or rabble-rousers, passionate or angry, the label can have real, unintended consequences for the ways in which the public perceives and reacts to events. Journalists should consider whether they would describe a group the same way if they looked more like themselves or shared a similar worldview. This may be one way to determine if they are reporting information in an unbiased manner.

Confronting bias is uncomfortable, but this discomfort is what makes for fair coverage.

Journalists have the ability to shape public discourse and, sometimes, opinion. One way to encourage constructive dialogue is to avoid using generalizations and to portray individuals of all group memberships as they are: neither entirely good nor entirely bad. One study conducted by psychologists at Université Clermont Auvergne in France and York University in Canada attempted to reduce implicit bias by exposing French participants to posters that described Middle Easterners in only positive terms, or in both positive and negative terms.[40] These researchers found that attempting to modify attitudes by portraying stigmatized groups only in positive terms elicited negative reactions and was less acceptable to participants, while portraying these groups in both positive and negative terms reduced implicit bias.

One of the easiest ways to help audiences see racial and ethnic minorities as individuals, not stereotypes, is to portray them as accurately and completely as possible. In addition to what we explicitly communicate, it is also necessary to consider the nonverbal signals we might be conveying, particularly when communicating via video. Implicit bias may be "contagious."[41] Harvard University social psychologist Greg Willard and his colleagues found that participants who held more explicit and implicit pro-white bias exhibited more negative nonverbal behaviors toward black interaction partners. These negative behaviors included less smiling and affirmative head nods, among other behaviors. When naive participants viewed the video-recorded interactions between black and white individuals, their liking toward the black interaction partner decreased when the white partner exhibited more pro-white implicit bias.[42] The participants watching the recordings seemed to adopt the nonverbal cues from the white partner, even though the partner did not speak in a biased manner. This pattern was observed even when participants could not see the reactions of the black partners. This has important implications for broadcast journalists. It is even more noteworthy given that in all cases, this effect was driven by the non-verbal behavior of the partners.

Though it takes work, being mindful of body language in interactions with sources, particularly those of stigmatized groups, is needed to avoid unintentionally communicating disdain or dislike for someone as a result of implicit bias.

Addressing and Reducing Implicit Racial Bias

There are a number of studies examining the types of interventions that can reduce implicit bias or limit its consequences, allowing individuals to see others clearly and accurately. Strategies to reduce implicit bias include attempting to empathize with sources, engaging in meaningful interactions with people who are different from ourselves, and being intentional and mindful in how we interact with others.

The first step in addressing our own implicit biases is to determine which implicit biases we hold.[43] To do this, we recommend visiting the Project Implicit website[44] and taking an IAT. This can help to illuminate biases and empower journalists to address them with the strategies we outline in the following paragraphs.

Some of these interventions are more easily implemented than others. Here we present strategies you can implement on your own as well as a few training activities that your organization may wish to implement in coordination with scholars at a local university or research institution.

While it is unclear whether or not these strategies are as effective when individuals are aware of their intended purpose, in general there is evidence that just being motivated to control prejudice can reduce implicit bias.[45] Being interested in these interventions may already be a positive indicator that you are both aware of your bias and aim to control its effects. It is worth noting, however, that merely being motivated to act in non-prejudiced ways can backfire.[46] To address this, here we present actionable strategies that can be implemented in everyday interactions to counter the unintended consequences of wanting to act in unbiased ways.

Building Empathy

Many of the interventions that show promise in reducing implicit racial bias rely on empathizing with targets.[47] While we cannot always fully understand what it is like to be the target of implicit bias, we can build empathy by imagining ourselves in someone else's shoes and trying to understand their experiences.[48] Fostering this empathy may be as simple as reading about the experiences of out-group members in their blog posts and articles. The internet has provided many previously silenced individuals with a voice and an audience. Similarly, viewing movies and films featuring racial minorities may increase empathy.[49]

In one study, participants who watched a three-minute video with the aim of understanding what a female, Asian protagonist was experiencing showed reduced implicit in-group bias in general, not just reduced bias toward Asians. While it is not necessary to agree with every post or resonate with every movie, they can still be used to try to understand the experiences of racial and other minorities.

Widening Your Circle

Expanding how we conceptualize our in-group can also reduce implicit bias.[50] For example, having a close friend who is a racial minority also predicts reduced implicit racial bias.[51] Consider being more outgoing toward those with whom you assume you have little in common. Engaging in more frequent, positive, interracial interactions may also reduce implicit bias.

We often have more in common with each other than we expect, and implicit bias can lead us to focus on superficial differences when we are not always all that different. Researchers found that implicit bias decreased when participants were trained to categorize pictures of racial out-group members as being part of their own group, as opposed to part of another group.[52] Further, when participants listed traits and group memberships that they likely shared with racial out-group members, their implicit racial bias was also reduced.[53] Similarly, researchers discovered that administering a modified IAT in which participants saw out-group members as also having a shared group membership (e.g., alma mater) reduced implicit bias.[54]

Be Intentional and Mindful

Many of the strategies outlined above require the active confrontation of our implicit biases. However, new research suggests that there may be other, more indirect ways to reduce bias. For example, one study conducted at Central Michigan University by psychologists Adam Lueke and Bryan Gibson found that white college participants who practiced mindfulness mediation tended to have reduced implicit racial and age bias.[55] In their experiment, practicing mindfulness seemed to reduce the association between "black" and "bad," and "old" and "bad," without impacting positive associations between "white" and "good," and "young" and "good."

Workshops and Trainings

A news organization can also implement many types of training to reduce implicit racial bias. One such training involves re-conceptualizing prejudice as a habit that we are able to break.[56] In this training, researchers found long-term reductions in implicit racial bias when their participants were first taught about their own implicit biases and learned that implicit bias in general can be thought of as a bad habit. Participants were then given a series of five strategies, including perspective-taking or imagining yourself in someone else's shoes, and looking for the individuating characteristics of out-group members to reduce tendencies to generalize. These training sessions may work most effectively as seminars with several individuals in your organization and can be coordinated with scholars (e.g., psychologists, diversity scientists) from local universities, although individuals could request them as well.

Conclusion

Throughout this chapter, we have provided evidence that implicit bias, and implicit racial bias in particular, is pervasive and can influence our attitudes and behaviors. This is not an accusation. Instead it is an acknowledgment that even with the best intentions we must be vigilant in order to ensure that the principles of fairness and transparency in journalism, and in general, are being upheld.

Access to information, whether local, national, or global, is one of the cornerstones of democracy. Finding and delivering that information to the public is a noble and necessary pursuit that often carries with it consequences and challenges. Implicit bias is yet another challenge to overcome and it will take conscious effort to counter the biases many of us are just discovering we have.

Mistakes are likely, but when they happen, take responsibility quickly and sincerely to limit their negative consequences. The more we employ strategies to reduce implicit bias, the more proficient we become at countering bias. While effort is needed at the outset, over time these strategies and remedies will become second nature. As these implicit biases have developed over time it will also take time to hone strategies to counter them, but with diligence and motivation we can further ensure that the public receives the news free from bias in its many forms.

Notes

1 Society of Professional Journalists' Code of Ethics, Society of Professional Journalists, Revised September 6, 2014. Accessed September 20, 2017 from www.spj.org/ethicscode.asp.
2 Jennifer A. Coleman, Kathleen M. Ingram, Annalucia Bays, Jennifer A. Joy-Gaba, and Edward L. Boone. "Disability and Assistance Dog Implicit Association Test: A Novel IAT." *Rehabilitation Psychology* 60, no. 1 (2015): 17–26. doi: 10.1037/rep0000025; Milan Dragović, Johanna C. Badcock, Milenković Sanja, Margareta Gregurović, and Zlatko Šram. "Social Stereotyping of Left-Handers in Serbia." *Laterality: Asymmetries of Body, Brain and Cognition* 18, no. 6 (2013): 719–729. doi: 10.1080/1357650X.2012.755993; Bethany A. Teachman, Kathrine D. Gapinski, Kelly D. Brownell, Melissa Rawlins, and Subathra Jeyaram. "Demonstrations of Implicit Anti-Fat Bias: The Impact of Providing Causal Information and Evoking Empathy." *Health Psychology* 22, no. 1 (2003): 68–78. doi: 10.1037/0278-6133.22.1.68; Jennifer A. Richeson and Samuel R. Sommers. "Toward a Social Psychology of Race and Race Relations for the 21st Century." *Annual Review of Psychology* 67 (2016): 439–463.
3 Dolores Albarracín and Patrick Vargas. *Attitudes and Persuasion: From Biology to Social Responses to Persuasive Intent.* Hoboken, NJ: John Wiley & Sons Inc., 2010.
4 Simon Howard and Samuel R. Sommers. "Exploring the Enigmatic Link between Religion and Anti-Black Attitudes." *Social and Personality Psychology Compass* 9, no. 9 (2015): 495–510. doi: 10.1111/spc3.12195; Simon Howard and Samuel R. Sommers. "Exposure to White Religious Iconography Influences Black Individuals' Intragroup and Intergroup Attitudes." *Cultural Diversity and Ethnic Minority Psychology* 23, no. 4 (2017): 508–514. doi: 10.1037/cdp0000152.
5 Erin Kearns, Allison Betus, and Anthony Lemieux. "Why Do Some Terrorist Attacks Receive More Media Attention than Others?" Social Science Research Network (March 5, 2017). Accessed February 23, 2018 from https://ssrn.com/abstract=2928138.
6 Eugene Kiely. "Terrorism and Trump's Travel Ban." FactCheck.org, February 26, 2017. Accessed April 21, 2017 from www.factcheck.org/2017/02/terrorism-and-trumps-travel-ban/.
7 David Neiwert. "Trump's Fixation on Demonizing Islam Hides True Homegrown US Terror Threat." Center for Investigative Reporting, Revealnews.org, June 21, 2017. Accessed January 22, 2018 from www.revealnews.org/article/home-is-where-the-hate-is/.
8 Elizabeth R. Peterson, C. Rubie-Davies, Danny Osborne, and C. Sibley. "Teachers' Explicit Expectations and Implicit Prejudiced Attitudes to Educational Achievement: Relations with Student Achievement and the Ethnic Achievement Gap." *Learning and Instruction*, 42 (2016): 123–140. doi: 10.1016/j.learninstruc.2016.01.010.
9 Marianne Bertrand and Sendhil Mullainathan. "Are Emily and Greg more Employable than Lakisha and Jamal? A Field Experiment on Labor Market Discrimination."

National Bureau of Economic Research Working Paper Series, no. 9873 (2003). Accessed September 20, 2017 from www.nber.org/papers/w9873.pdf.

10 U.S. Department of Education, Office for Civil Rights. Civil Rights Data Collection: Data Snapshot (School Discipline). [Fact Sheet] 2014. Accessed September 20, 2017 from www2.ed.gov/about/offices/list/ocr/docs/crdc-discipline-snapshot.pdf.

11 Jason A. Okonofua and Jennifer L. Eberhardt. "Two Strikes: Race and the Disciplining of Young Students." *Psychological Science* 26, no. 5 (2015): 617–624. doi: 10.1177/0956797615570365.

12 Jesse Russell and Alicia Summers. "Reflective Decision-Making and Foster Care Placements." *Psychology, Public Policy, and Law* 19, no. 2 (2013): 127–136. doi: 10.1037/a0031582.

13 John Chaney, Amanda Burke, and Edward Burkley. "Do American Indian Mascots = American Indian People? Examining Implicit Bias towards American Indian People and American Indian Mascots." *American Indian and Alaska Native Mental Health Research: The Journal of the National Center* 18, no. 1 (2011): 42–62.

14 William A. Cunningham, Kristopher J. Preacher, and Mahzarin R. Banaji. "Implicit Attitude Measures: Consistency, Stability, and Convergent Validity." *Psychological Science* 12, no. 2 (2001): 163–170. doi: 10.1111/1467-9280.00328.

15 Anthony G. Greenwald, Debbie E. McGhee, and Jordan L.K. Schwartz. "Measuring Individual Differences in Implicit Cognition: The Implicit Association Test." *Journal of Personality and Social Psychology* 74, no. 6 (1998): 1464–1480. doi: 10.1037/0022-3514.74.6.1464.

16 Brian A. Nosek, Frederick L. Smyth, Jeffrey J. Hansen, Thierry Devos, Nicole M. Lindner, Kate A. Ranganath, and Mahzarin R. Banaji. "Pervasiveness and Correlates of Implicit Attitudes and Stereotypes." *European Review of Social Psychology* 18 (2007): 36–88. doi: 10.1080/10463280701489053.

17 Steven Chermak and Nicole M. Chapman. "Predicting Crime Story Salience: A Replication." *Journal of Criminal Justice* 35, no. 4 (2007): 351–363. doi: 10.1016/j.jcrimjus.2007.05.001.

18 Jeff Gruenewald, Jesenia Pizarro, and Steven M. Chermak. "Race, Gender, and the Newsworthiness of Homicide Incidents." *Journal of Criminal Justice* 37, no. 3 (2009): 262–272. doi: 10.1016/j.jcrimjus.2009.04.006.

19 Richard J. Lundman. "The Newsworthiness and Selection Bias in News About Murder: Comparative and Relative Effects of Novelty and Race and Gender Typifications on Newspaper Coverage of Homicide." *Sociological Forum* 18, no. 3 (2003): 357–386. doi: 10.1023/A:1025713518156.

20 Michelle N. Jeanis and Ráchael A. Powers. "Newsworthiness of Missing Persons Cases: An Analysis of Selection Bias, Disparities in Coverage, and the Narrative Framework of News Reports." *Deviant Behavior* 38, no. 6 (June 2017): 668–683. doi: 10.1080/01639625.2016.1197618. Social Science Premium Collection, 1884887133.

21 Zach Sommers. "Missing White Woman Syndrome: An Empirical Analysis of Race and Gender Disparities in Online News Coverage of Missing Persons." *Journal of Criminal Law and Criminology* 106, no. 2 (Spring 2016): 275–314.

22 John W. Clark, Robert J. Cramer, Amy Percosky, Katrina A. Rufino, Rowland S. Miller, and Shara M. Johnson. "Juror Perceptions of African American and Arabic-Named Victims." *Psychiatry, Psychology and Law* 20, no. 5 (2013): 781–794. doi: 10.1080/13218719.2012.736283.

23 Damian A. Stanley, Peter Sokol-Hessner, Mahzarin R. Banaji, and Elizabeth A. Phelps. "Implicit Race Attitudes Predict Trustworthiness Judgments and Economic Trust Decisions." *PNAS Proceedings of the National Academy of Sciences of the United States of America* 108, no. 19 (2011): 7710–7775. doi: 10.1073/pnas.1014345108.

24 Gordon B. Moskowitz, Irmak Olcaysoy Okten, and Cynthia M. Gooch. "On Race and Time." *Psychological Science* 26, no. 11 (2015): 1783–1794. doi: 10.1177/0956797615599547.

25 Ibid.

26 Lance Hannon. "Hispanic Respondent Intelligence Level and Skin Tone: Interviewer Perceptions from the American National Election Study." *Hispanic Journal of Behavioral Sciences* 36, no. 3 (2014): 265–283.

27 John McWhorter. "Rachel Jeantel Explained, Linguistically: Trayvon Martin's Friend and a Key Witness in the Trial of George Zimmerman Made a Lot More Sense than You Think." *Time*, June 28, 2013. Accessed February 23, 2018 from http://ideas.time.com/2013/06/28/rachel-jeantel-explained-linguistically/.

28 Irene V. Blair, Edward P. Havranek, David W. Price, Rebecca Hanratty, Diane L. Fairclough, Tillman Farley, ... John F. Steiner. "Assessment of Biases against Latinos and African Americans among Primary Care Providers and Community Members." *American Journal of Public Health* 103, no. 1 (2013a): 92–98.

29 Irene V. Blair, John F. Steiner, Diane L. Fairclough, Rebecca Hanratty, David W. Price, Holen K. Hirsh, ... Edward P. Havranek. "Clinicians Implicit Ethnic/Racial Bias and Perceptions of Care among Black and Latino Patients." *Annals of Family Medicine* 11, no. 1 (2013b): 43–52. doi: 10.1370/afm.1442.

30 Louis A. Penner, John F. Dovidio, Tessa V. West, Samuel L. Gaertner, Terrance L. Albrecht, Rhonda K. Dailey, and Tsveti Markova. "Aversive Racism and Medical Interactions with Black Patients: A Field Study." *Journal of Experimental Social Psychology* 46, no. 2 (2010): 436–440. doi: 10.1016/j.jesp.2009.11.004.

31 Ibid.

32 Ibid.

33 Nao Hagiwara, Louis A. Penner, Richard Gonzalez, Susan Eggly, John F. Dovidio, Samuel L. Gaertner, ... Terrance L. Albrecht. "Racial Attitudes, Physician–Patient Talk Time Ratio, and Adherence in Racially Discordant Medical Interactions." *Social Science & Medicine* 87 (2013): 123–131. doi: 10.1016/j.socscimed.2013.03.016.

34 Tanya Stivers and Asifa Majid. "Questioning Children: Interactional Evidence of Implicit Bias in Medical Interviews." *Social Psychology Quarterly* 70, no. 4 (2007): 424–441. doi: 10.1177/019027250707000410.

35 SPJ Code of Ethics.

36 Bertram Gawronski, Daniel Geschke, and Rainer Banse. "Implicit Bias in Impression Formation: Associations Influence the Construal of Individuating Information." *European Journal of Social Psychology* 33, no. 5 (2003): 573–589. doi: 10.1002/ejsp.166.

37 Joanna R. Pepin. "Nobody's Business? White Male Privilege in Media Coverage of Intimate Partner Violence." *Sociological Spectrum* 36, no. 3 (2016): 123–141. doi: 10.1080/02732173.2015.1108886; Nick Wing. "When the Media Treats White Suspects Better than Black Victims." *The Huffington Post*, August 14, 2014. Accessed February 23, 2018 from www.huffingtonpost.com/2014/08/14/media-black-victims_n_5673291.html.

38 #BlackLivesMatter. "Black Lives Matter: Freedom and Justice for All Black Lives," April 2017. Accessed September 21, 2017 from http://blacklivesmatter.com/.

39 Kurt Hugenberg and Galen V. Bodenhausen. "Ambiguity in Social Categorization: The Role of Prejudice and Facial Affect in Race Categorization." *Psychological Science* 15, no. 5 (2004): 342–345. doi: 10.1111/j.0956-7976.2004.00680.x; Jennifer T. Kubota and Tiffany A. Ito. "The Role of Expression and Race in Weapons Identification." *Emotion* 14, no. 6 (2014): 1115–1124. doi: 10.1037/a0038214.

40 Markus Brauer, Abdelatif Er-rafiy, Kerry Kawakami, and Curtis E. Phills. "Describing a Group in Positive Terms Reduces Prejudice Less Effectively than Describing

It in Positive and Negative Terms." *Journal of Experimental Social Psychology* 48, no. 3 (2012): 757–761. doi: 10.1016/j.jesp.2011.11.002.

41 Greg Willard, Kyonne-Joy Isaac, and Dana R. Carney. "Some Evidence for the Nonverbal Contagion of Racial Bias." *Organizational Behavior and Human Decision Processes* 128 (2015): 96–107. doi: 10.1016/j.obhdp.2015.04.002.

42 Ibid.

43 Laurie A. Rudman. "Social Justice in Our Minds, Homes, and Society: The Nature, Causes, and Consequences of Implicit Bias." *Social Justice Research* 17, no. 2 (2004): 129–142. doi: 10.1023/B:SORE.0000027406.32604.f6.

44 Project Implicit. Accessed September 21, 2017 from https://implicit.harvard.edu/implicit/.

45 Thomas J. Allen, Jeffrey W. Sherman, and Karl Christoph Klauer. "Social Context and the Self-Regulation of Implicit Bias." *Group Processes & Intergroup Relations* 13, no. 2 (2010): 137–149. doi: 10.1177/1368430209353635.

46 Moskowitz et al. "On Race and Time."

47 Belinda Gutierrez, Anna Kaatz, Sarah Chu, Denis Ramirez, Clem Samson-Samuel, and Molly Carnes. "'Fair Play': A Videogame Designed to Address Implicit Race Bias through Active Perspective Taking." *Games for Health* 3, no. 6 (2014): 371–378. doi: 10.1089/g4h.2013.0071; Anna Woodcock and Margo J. Monteith. "Forging Links with the Self to Combat Implicit Bias." *Group Processes & Intergroup Relations* 16, no. 4 (2013): 445–461.

48 Gutierrez et al. "'Fair Play'."

49 Margaret J. Shih, Rebecca Stotzer, and Angélica S. Gutiérrez. "Perspective-Taking and Empathy: Generalizing the Reduction of Group Bias Towards Asian Americans to General Outgroups." *Asian American Journal of Psychology* 4, no. 2 (2013): 79–83. doi: 10.1037/a0029790.

50 Natalie R. Hall, Richard J. Crisp, and Mein-woei Suen. "Reducing Implicit Prejudice by Blurring Intergroup Boundaries." *Basic and Applied Social Psychology* 31, no. 3 (2009): 244–254. doi: 10.1080/01973530903058474; W. Anthony Scroggins, Diane M. Mackie, Thomas J. Allen, and Jeffrey W. Sherman. "Reducing Prejudice with Labels: Shared Group Memberships Attenuate Implicit Bias and Expand Implicit Group Boundaries." *Personality and Social Psychology Bulletin* 42, no. 2 (2016): 219–229. doi: 10.1177/0146167215621048.

51 Christopher L. Aberson, Carl Shoemaker, and Christina Tomolillo. "Implicit Bias and Contact: The Role of Interethnic Friendships." *The Journal of Social Psychology* 144, no. 3 (2004): 335–347. doi: 10.3200/SOCP.144.3.335–347.

52 Woodcock and Monteith. "Forging Links."

53 Hall et al. "Reducing Implicit Prejudice."

54 Scroggins et al. "Reducing Prejudice with Labels."

55 Adam Lueke and Bryan Gibson. "Mindfulness Meditation Reduces Implicit Age and Race Bias: The Role of Reduced Automaticity of Responding." *Social Psychological and Personality Science* 6, no. 3 (2015): 284–291. doi: 10.1177/1948550614559651.

56 Patricia G. Devine, Patrick S. Forscher, Anthony J. Austin, and William T.L. Cox. "Long-Term Reduction in Implicit Race Bias: A Prejudice Habit-Breaking Intervention." *Journal of Experimental Social Psychology* 48, no. 6 (2012): 1267–1278. doi: 10.1016/j.jesp.2012.06.003.

5

THE COLORBLIND CONUNDRUM

Sally Lehrman and Venise Wagner

In this chapter the authors discuss the ethical underpinnings of journalism that compel reporters to look at the racial implications of policies and institutional practices. While some reporters believe that colorblindness is the best way to maintain impartiality, the authors argue that the colorblind approach prevents journalists from unearthing the invisible forces of race. Instead, they say, journalists must be willing to put on racial and ethnic lenses.

Journalists play a powerful role as shapers of public discourse. As we document the story of the nation and the world, we have a duty to be more racially inclusive in our choices about what to cover and who to consult. We must recognize the forces of implicit bias and guard against their interference in our interpretation of events and possible distortion of the facts we learn. We also must seek out and speak truth about the workings of our society. School choice, neighborhood schools, the diabetes epidemic, drug sentencing laws, housing affordability and access, income inequality and unemployment – all bear the repercussions of America's history as a racially stratified society.

In the past decade, especially after the election of Barack Obama to the presidency, many adopted the belief that we live in a post-racial society with race just a casual feature. Then, during the candidacy of President Donald J. Trump and after his election, race again came to the forefront in debates over a border wall, immigration law, and the white supremacists among his supporters. The president's name even became a provocative racial jeer, used against nonwhites and immigrants in schoolrooms and sports arenas.[1] Yet some people continue to see race as a matter of acceptance or prejudice, of behavior and attitudes toward one another, denying the structural aspects of life experience based on skin color.

How do we decide when race should become a consideration in reporting? And how do we include it well? What's the line between exposing injustice and taking a stance? Race can be an obvious element in news stories, such as in the Native American voting rights movement in the West and Midwest.[2] It also can be hidden or unrecognized, as in the immense effect that a Supreme Court decision on car rental searches and privacy had on black and Hispanic drivers, who are frequent car renters and also more likely to get pulled over and searched.[3,4] How do we pull back layers of meaning within public discourse and reveal the racial belief systems and structures at their heart, while still maintaining balance and fairness? In this chapter we will address these questions and provide journalists with tools to address race when it's a factor, whether apparent or not.

We begin with the traditional mission and ethics of journalism, along with historic examinations of the role of the press. Journalism's foundational tenets include giving voice to the voiceless and shining light on injustice. The Society of Professional Journalists' Code of Ethics spells out these journalism ideals in its preamble and several sections of the code itself. Journalism exists, the preamble states, to serve public enlightenment, which leads to justice and democracy. Ethical news gatherers strive for "free exchange of information that is accurate, fair and thorough."[5] We follow basic principles of impartiality, giving the accused an opportunity to respond and exploring alternate explanations for supposed wrongdoing. And we go further. The tenets of justice, fairness, and accuracy underpin all we do.

In his book, *Media Ethics: Key Principles for Responsible Practice*, former journalist and communications theorist Patrick Lee Plaisance devotes a chapter to describing the importance of justice as a central value of journalism.[6] More than a reference to standards of fairness and balance, he writes, "justice" refers to social values that underpin a successful, functioning society. Journalists serve the public interest and, in doing so, must pursue justice.

This idea of justice can be split into two dimensions, Plaisance explains.[7] "Conservative" justice strives to preserve stability in order to ensure that social institutions can address competing interests. As a result, everyone benefits. "Reformative" justice addresses social wrongs and embraces marginalized groups in the interest of promoting fairness and expanding the social system to include all. Journalism straddles the tension between the two. We report impartially on the workings of government, police and health agencies, business and other powerful entities – that's conservative justice. We also hold such institutions accountable to the public, shine light on problems, and reveal the everyday lives, frustrations, and dreams of people outside of the mainstream – that's reformative justice. In serving these two kinds of justice, it is important for journalists to explore the ways in which race is embedded in our institutions and examine both positive and negative repercussions that flow from our society's racial structuring. And, as part of this effort, we must examine discourse about race, whether implicit or overt. We must understand the ways we speak and write about race as a society, and also cover the implications of the language we choose.

Reporters serve conservative justice when we work within a beat structure that reflects a stable social order. We serve it when we cover the problems that government and other institutions seek to remedy. In reporting inequity strictly through the social-order lens, however, journalists can be complicit in perpetuating beliefs about minority groups. Uncovering the disproportionate rates of incarceration of Native American youth,[8] describing the ravages of hepatitis C in Appalachia, and even showing the sordid quality of public housing in some cities can activate preconceptions about group behavior and culture. As we discussed in Chapter 1, without further information about the reasons behind inequality, readers and viewers turn to their own belief systems for explanations.

That's one reason journalists also highlight ways in which social institutions may be organized to give favor to some demographic groups over others. In doing so, we are serving reformative justice. Journalists attend to all segments of society, pointing to issues and concerns that involve competing interests and require an airing in order to achieve institutions, policies, and practices that are fair to all. This is fundamental to the process of seeking "truth," a process that "sets journalism apart from all other forms of communication," Plaisance writes.[9]

While some may argue that this practice constitutes advocacy journalism because it requires active awareness of race, they are overlooking the racial structuring of our social system and its subtle influence in every area of our lives. We believe that applying a variety of racial lenses to our work gives journalists a more robust understanding of people's various lived realities. This is true journalism of inclusiveness, a practice grounded in sound journalism ethics.

The SPJ Ethics Code specifically addresses the question of covering race and promoting dialogue about race in its four core principles: "seek truth and report it, minimize harm, act independently, and be accountable and transparent."[10] The code advises journalists to avoid stereotyping, and to "examine the ways their values and experiences may shape their reporting." Journalists should "boldly tell the story of the diversity and magnitude of the human experience" and "seek sources whose voices we seldom hear."

Journalists should "support the open and civil exchange of views, even views they find repugnant," the code says. As a result, journalists should even report hate speech, although with care and caution. Hate speech is designed to intimidate marginalized groups and hinder their full participation in society. Journalists must avoid becoming unwitting tools in the effort.[11]

Similar to SPJ's ethics code, several other journalism organizations also ask journalists to be conscious of their role in shaping the perceptions of one group by another. These ethics fundamentals ask journalists to reach beyond our own experiences and into what may be uncomfortable territory. This requirement includes noticing and covering the workings of race.

Fairness and Accuracy

Fairness requires deepening our awareness, including recognizing and correcting our habits as journalists. Without care, our reporting can indirectly justify the very social organization and institutions that lead to unequal opportunities and outcomes. When we fail to explore the currents of race and ethnicity in our stories, we perpetuate misunderstandings and mistaken beliefs. For example, when we report on basic health questions through profiles of individuals taking steps to get regular exercise, good sleep, and eat well, and yet no people of color are present in our stories, we are perpetuating the view that only white people consciously care for their health. When we report on innovations at a federally funded hospital without checking into their translation services, which are legally required, we are ignoring unequal access. When we cover higher education and any mention of Latinos involves stories about undocumented immigrants, we are perpetuating ignorance of this population's deep roots in this land. When we report on a school's remarkable test scores without looking into its population, resources, and treatment of non-English proficient speakers, we are ignoring the privileges afforded white students in our schools.

Over the years, civic leaders have examined the role of journalism in a multicultural society and spelled out its duty to address the undercurrents of race and ethnicity. One of the first calls for inclusive coverage came from the Hutchins Commission, officially titled Commission on the Freedom of the Press, which convened for four years starting in 1943. The commission was created when *Time* magazine publisher Henry Luce asked former Yale classmate and University of Chicago professor Robert Hutchins to assemble a blue ribbon panel to examine increasing problems with the press. Of growing concern was the perception that journalists behaved badly, appealing to the basest human interests and focusing on celebrity and vice. If the press didn't do something, Luce and other media owners worried, the government would intervene.

In its report, the commission called for a more socially responsible media that maintains freedom from government intervention, and that serves the public interest. It established five standards by which news media should operate: (1) provide a truthful account of the day's events in context that explains the events' meaning; (2) serve as a forum for an exchange of ideas; (3) portray representative images of constituent groups in society; (4) present and clarify society's goals and values; (5) offer access to the day's intelligence.[12]

The third standard speaks directly to the need for improved coverage of minority communities, whose representation in the news up until then had been primarily negative.[13] The report states:

> The truth about any social group, though it should not exclude its weaknesses and vice, includes also recognition of its values, its aspiration, and its common humanity. The Commission holds to the faith that if people are exposed to the inner truth of the life of a particular group, they will gradually build up respect for and understanding of it.[14]

The other standards emphasize the importance of offering historical context, providing a forum for an exchange of ideas from a variety of society's segments, and facilitating the hashing out of society's values and goals in an inclusive public square.

Nearly 20 years later, the Kerner Commission Report from the National Advisory Commission on Civil Disorders, led by Illinois Governor Otto Kerner, examined the role of the press in the public's understanding of the string of riots that had plagued several cities in the 1960s. In addition to declaring the United States a nation divided, it also laid the responsibility on mainstream media to improve coverage of marginalized communities, in this case black urban communities. It concluded that the media had inadequately explained the plight of African Americans, the discrimination and indignities they faced daily. "The media report and write from the standpoint of a white man's world. The ills of the ghetto, the difficulties of life there, the Negro's burning sense of grievance, are seldom conveyed,"[15] the report said. The commission called upon the media to improve relations with minority communities and cover them more accurately and fully.

Many news organizations responded by attempting to increase the ranks of minority journalists in their newsrooms. This push started modestly, only beginning in earnest in 1978 when the American Society of Newspaper Editors (ASNE) board adopted a goal that the staff of American newsrooms should reach racial and gender parity with the national population by the year 2000. ASNE tracked progress and reported it in a newsroom census each year. A high point was reached in 2006 with newsrooms employing 14 percent minorities, although the country's minority population continued to rise and had reached 33 percent at the time. Then the recession and the expansion of the internet began to disrupt traditional business models and newsrooms began laying off staff. From 2008 to 2009, newsrooms suffered the largest employment decline in the history of the ASNE census, losing 5,900 newsroom jobs. The goal of parity was pushed to 2025. According to the most recent census in 2017, minorities made up just under 17 percent of newsrooms, compared to 39 percent of the US population.[16]

"It's more important than ever for newsrooms to properly reflect and authentically cover communities of color," ASNE Diversity Committee Co-Chair Karen Magnuson, executive editor of the Rochester (New York) *Democrat & Chronicle*, said in the 2017 ASNE announcement. And yet parity, we must remember, is merely a means to an end. That end is more accurate minority representation in news content overall.

All journalists carry the responsibility to broaden their own perspectives and assess their reporting for accuracy. The first step to challenging our own buried biases is humility. We must recognize that our entire upbringing has shaped the world in a particular way for us, and that we must seek out and listen more closely to other versions of the world.

Habits of the Eyes

Journalists often will defend their commitment to fairness and accuracy by saying, "I write what I see." But what we notice and "see" differs person-to-person, based on our own identity and what assumptions or ideas we bring to the situation. To take a gender-based example, one journalist covering a technology conference might "see" that there are very few women in the room and notice that speakers are peppering their comments with sexual innuendo. Another may "see" the powerful male leaders in the room and notice their dynamic calls for creativity and entrepreneurship. Both accounts are true.[17] Neither is neutral.

Our varied perceptions, including the differences in what we literally see, affect how journalists think about and understand a developing story. They result in a particular interpretation of an event or issue, its relevance, and the key ideas or characters involved. Even as journalists adhere firmly to facts and accuracy, what they notice and what they miss shapes the story.

In his renowned book *Public Opinion*, published in 1922 the American social critic, social scientist, and journalist Walter Lippmann examined the ways in which public opinion forms through propaganda and the news media. The world is too complex for any one individual to experience and understand it fully, Lippmann wrote. Thus we develop habits of seeing what we want and what we expect to see. This tendency, combined with the world created for us through the media we consume, result in a fractured and incomplete understanding of issues and events.

Because of these limitations Lippmann went so far as to challenge the ideal of journalism as a way to build a competent, enlightened citizenry that can make rational governance decisions. To the contrary, we believe that journalists can train themselves to see the world more fully and accurately and can play this role well. We also believe that, given a full and fair picture by the press, the public is fully competent to govern itself.

Nevertheless, Lippmann offers a very important proposal about widening the ways we see the world. Much of his astute assessment of our limited perceptions – and of journalists and their reporting – is now supported by research in social psychology (see Chapter 3). Lippmann understood that selective perception often interferes with a reporter's interpretation and chronicling of news events.

> A report is the joint product of the knower and the known, in which the role of the observer is always selective and usually creative. The facts we see depend on where we are placed and the habits of our eyes.[18]

Lippmann pointed out in *Public Opinion* that we define the world according to our own experience, and *then* we see it. What we see, in other words, is based on the images in our minds acquired over time based on our personal experiences. He applied the word "stereotype" to describe the phenomenon:

> In the great blooming, buzzing confusion of the outer world we pick out what our culture has already defined for us, and we tend to perceive that which we have picked out in the form stereotyped for us by our culture.[19]

Today, we understand "stereotype" to describe a set of fixed and over-simplified characteristics imposed on a person based on assumptions about their social group. Race is no exception. Nor religion. Nor gender.

The Perception Cycle

It's key to recognize that the news media work within a social system and also serve as a force that helps shape this system. This system can affect the way individual journalists "see" events and make decisions about whether race, gender, or class are relevant, and how to incorporate them. It can affect how we interpret an individual or community's actions, depending on their role within the social system.

As journalists' stereotypes make their way into the news, these in turn reinforce and influence audience adoption of stereotypes. We all engage in a perception cycle that links what we see and notice, what we think and what we say. Journalists' words, visuals, and text deeply influence the perception cycle for others. Figure 5.1 illustrates the process.

Mass media and mass communication scholars have studied this phenomenon. In ground-breaking research in 2000, political scientist Robert Entman and communication scholar Andrew Rojecki found that news media portrayals of black people were generally limited to crime and sports, separating blacks from the core of society.[20] In multiple studies that followed, black people were found to be overrepresented as perpetrators in crime reports, while whites were disproportionately shown as police officers and victims.

In more recent research, the misrepresentation by race remains, but the colors have shifted somewhat. Whites remain in sympathetic or "hero" roles, while Latinos have become the dominant perpetrator. In 2015, Travis Dixon studied portrayals of violent crime on local television news in Los Angeles. He found that depictions of black people had improved. They appeared true to

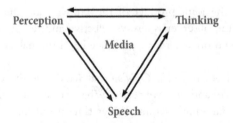

FIGURE 5.1 The Perception Cycle Affects the Stories Journalists See

their real-world proportions as perpetrators, victims, and officers. Latinos were now proportionately depicted as perpetrators, but absent in more sympathetic roles. Whites were overrepresented as victims and officers, and Asians were overrepresented as victims.[21]

Dixon, working with Charlotte Williams, also studied network and cable news coverage from 2008 to 2012. They found that white people were accurately represented true to their proportions as both violent crime perpetrators and homicide victims. Black people, however, were greatly underreported in both roles. In addition, when Latinos were included as crime suspects and perpetrators, they were greatly overrepresented as both legal and undocumented immigrants. Muslims were disproportionately shown as terrorism suspects.[22] Such distortion isn't limited to criminal justice stories. In a 2017 study of local and national news and opinion media, Dixon found that black families were disproportionately described as poor, associated with criminality and dependent on welfare. White families were severely underrepresented as having these characteristics in their lives.[23]

Such skewed portrayals both stem from and feed into the implicit biases that social psychologists Mahzarin Banaji, Anthony Greenwald, and their colleagues have studied for decades (see Chapter 4). They also reflect what Dixon describes as "ethnic blame" discourse, an ethnocentric framing of the "other" as causing problems for whites. Structural economic interests help keep these portrayals in place, Dixon suggests, because the audience is assumed to be mainly white. Unusual and attractive victims, depicted as white, would hold audience interest. In addition, covering Latinos more inclusively might require translators and other additional resources.[24]

Critically, Dixon and others have found that our distorted portrayals reinforce the way our audiences see the world. In one study, news viewers tended to associate Afrocentric physical features with characters recalled from violent local news stories,[25] for example, and misidentified perpetrators as black in another.[26] Heavy news users were more likely to consider a defendant guilty,[27] and to favor punitive remedies including the three-strikes law and the death penalty.[28]

Journalists can help correct these tendencies by being deliberate in our reporting and language, aiming for a well-rounded portrait of the world in which we live. For some journalists, focusing on race, gender, sexual orientation, or other identities might seem contrary to fairness. But in truth, being conscious of our own identities and those of the people we are covering leads to greater fairness. That's because being "identity-blind" requires ignoring the experiences that people without historical power live with, every day.

Fairness requires particular attention to race. While white people may experience stigma based on their other identities, most don't have to live with racial stigma. Instead they are judged on their individual traits and characteristics. As we discussed in Chapter 1, people of color with obvious markings, however, are often seen via group characteristics before their individual characteristics are taken into account and put in context.

Scholars Peggy McIntosh and Robert Jensen highlight the repercussions of the hidden hierarchy of skin color built into society in their writings on white privilege.[29] In her essay, "White Privilege: Unpacking the Invisible Knapsack," McIntosh lists the many unnoticed privileges afforded to her because her skin color is white, from small things like the color of Band-Aids to major concerns like her ability to buy or rent a home.[30] Journalists must recognize such racial realities, how they came to be through law and practice, and how they play out in various domains of our society – also working to shed their own privilege[31] and recognize their own role in its maintenance.[32]

Abandoning a colorblind stance may be uncomfortable for some journalists. They may feel such an approach creates racial discord and divisiveness, and want to avoid that role. But consider Dr. Martin Luther King, Jr.'s thoughts on the *semblance* of racial harmony. On March 18, 1956, King delivered a sermon at the Dexter Avenue Baptist Church in Montgomery during the bus boycott, and talked about a conversation he had with a white man who said that he felt the boycotters were disrupting peace in the community.

> He discussed the peace being destroyed in the community, the destroying of good race relations. I agree that there is more tension now. But peace is not merely the absence of this tension, but the presence of justice. And even if we didn't have this tension, we still wouldn't have positive peace. Yes, it is true that if the Negro accepts his place, accepts exploitation and injustice, there will be peace. But it would be a peace boiled down to stagnant complacency, deadening passivity, and if peace means this, I don't want peace.[33]

How Race Takes Shape

Most people recognize that race is socially constructed. Race may be marked by features such as skin color, hair texture, and eye shape, but our categories are cultural at root and malleable. Over time, the social meanings around them may change. An easy way to see this is to look across national boundaries. Brazil's census, for instance, uses five racial categories by color: blanco (white), pardo (brown), preto (black), amarelo (yellow), and indigenous.[34] Brazilians themselves use as many as 136.[35] In the United States, our four categories have morphed over time. In the late 19th and early 20th centuries, there was much debate over who qualified as "white." In 1908, a US district attorney attempted to bar 16 radical Finns from naturalization, for instance, claiming that they were "Mongolian" in origin.[36]

Sociologists Michael Omi and Howard Winant call this process racial formation – that is, the "socio-historical process by which racial categories are created, inhabited, transformed, and destroyed."[37] Racial formation is an ongoing process, always in flux, with racial meanings asserted and contested. Racial projects shape this process, serving as a means to assign meaning to race and then structure resources around it. Omi and Winant write, "A racial project is simultaneously an interpretation, representation, or explanation of racial dynamics, and an effort to reorganize and redistribute resources along particular racial lines." Racial projects can manifest in many ways – through laws, social movements, and cultural representations.[38]

These projects can be at the macro-level of a policy such as affirmative action and sentencing laws, or the micro-level of everyday experiences, such as the nature of our interactions with police or the racially themed costumes we may see at Halloween parties. Racial projects flip back and forth between public discourse and practice, which in many ways inform and sustain each other symbiotically.

Journalists must awaken ourselves to these racial projects – both macro and micro – in order to more fully understand and report on society's changing racial structures and their impact on everything from personal interactions to national, local, and institutional policies and practices. And as party to and often hosts of public dialogue about these policies and practices, journalists have a duty to help audiences untangle racialized webs of meaning.

The Power of Race in Speech

One way journalists can use the concept of racial formation to improve reporting is to explore and analyze language that reveals, justifies, or masks racial dynamics in our society. Critical discourse analysis is a tool to examine written, oral, or nonverbal forms of public speech that cause or exacerbate social problems and to uncover the power dynamics embedded in language that engender these problems.[39] Racial discourse analysis focuses specifically on the area of language that reproduces or intensifies racial social problems. It's not just language *about* race that can be revealing. Language can sometimes obscure racial meaning in an issue, thus allowing the problem to grow worse without attention. Language can also be used to maintain racial hierarchies and privilege. And, of course, the terms "discourse" and "language" reach beyond the confines of words.

Several studies have analyzed language employed in public dialogue and in the defense of policies that lead to disparate racial outcomes in education, health, housing, and the criminal justice system.[40] The use of the term "preferential treatment," for example, in discussions of affirmative action policies creates the perception that people of color gain an unfair advantage over whites from these policies, even though they were designed to correct a history of unequal opportunity.[41] "Identity politics" is often used to trivialize race and other forms of identity as mere artifacts that can be donned or removed at whim like a mask. The term suggests that people of color pull on the mask when they want to gain an unfair advantage over whites or make them feel guilty. The word, "entitlements" for programs such as Medicare, Medicaid, and welfare suggests undeserving people getting privileges they have not earned. Journalists must notice how and when these loaded terms are used and recognize the power dynamics contained within them. And we should avoid adopting them in our own reports.

Critical theorists have pleaded with journalists to become more aware and judicious in use of language and in chronicling discourse that either explicitly or implicitly addresses racial stratifications.[42,43] Below we offer an example of using racial discourse analysis to unpack the racial projects under way in a developing news story.

The Racial Discourse Analysis Approach: The Trayvon Martin Case

All too often men of color are demonized in the news and even though journalists are increasingly aware of this stereotype, the narrow portrayal persists. To broaden our understanding and improve our coverage, we can methodically examine the racial underpinnings of stories involving this population in the speech of sources and in policy statements and goals. Such an analysis must also consider the unsaid, which can be as important as what is said.

We don't suggest that journalists guess what people mean. But we can learn to look for the subtle gestures in language, code words and nonverbal expressions that convey meaning beyond the surface. It is the journalist's responsibility to reconcile that meaning, to press the source to explicitly state their intentions. But to do that, the journalist has to identify the subtext and be prepared to ask a direct question.

We propose a four-part model adapted from Teun Van Dijk's discourse analysis model for such an examination of speech and images in a given situation. You can address these any order and keep these in your mind as you consider a debate, speech, images, and the elements of a story as it unfolds: (1) Analyze racial categories and assess their power dynamics; (2) Identify any racial subtext – that is, the unspoken thoughts, understandings and meanings; (3) Examine the structural and contextual elements, noticing the impact one's environment has on individual or group behavior; (4) Unveil the signifiers and code words.

Here is how it can work.

In February 2012, a 17-year-old black teenager was fatally shot by a neighborhood watch volunteer. The self-appointed neighborhood sentinel, George Zimmerman, 26, saw Trayvon Martin walking down the street with his hoodie on and immediately thought him suspicious. For his part, Martin, returning to a family friend's home after a trip to a nearby 7-Eleven store for snacks, told his girlfriend on his cell phone that he was being followed by a strange man. Although Martin increased his gait, Zimmerman caught up with him and confronted him. Ultimately, Zimmerman shot and killed Martin. He claimed that he was acting in self-defense. Martin, however, carried no weapon, only a bag of Skittles he had just purchased. Five months later in July, Zimmerman was acquitted of all charges.

Using Proquest we did a keyword search for print stories about the Martin–Zimmerman case and found 33 news and opinion stories between February and July of 2012. We also used LexisNexis to find articles about the coverage in professional news and media watchdog publications, as well as in the scholarly literature. Our review found that most news stories initially stuck with the facts of the case, focusing on details such as where Martin was walking and how Zimmerman responded. They tended to steer away from overt discussions of racism. Most of that was left for opinion writers and columnists. The debate remained fairly superficial, however, because the opinion pieces relied on news reports, which came up short in any analysis of the role of race.[44]

As time went on, both the news stories and opinion pieces we analyzed took on one of two news frames: questions about stand-your-ground laws and questions about the practice of racial profiling.

Racial Power Dynamics

Between February and July 2012 after Zimmerman shot Martin, most news stories framed the event as an encounter between two individuals. Journalists tried to learn more about Zimmerman to understand his possible motives. As reporters examined Zimmerman's past behavior toward minority groups, the narrative quickly developed into a story about individual racism. News outlets also began to shift focus to Martin's behavior, both that evening and in the years before he died. For example, CNN, ABC News, and other broadcasters ran photos and texts from Martin's cell phone about drug use, marijuana plants, and a gun.[45]

As they gathered details, journalists fit each person into a larger social category. Martin was stereotyped as a budding thug, and Zimmerman, as a flagrant racist and ne'er-do-well. The likely motives of each person that evening were important and interesting, but reporters had to speculate broadly. Zimmerman did not consent to interviews, and Martin was dead.

In order to tell a coherent story, reporters reached reflexively toward a black/white paradigm, in which all racial interaction in the United States is reduced to those two groups. A common tendency, this binary approach overlooks the more complex dynamics of race and ethnicity in America. Zimmerman's father reacted by writing to the *Orlando Sentinel* to complain that his son was actually a "Spanish-speaking minority." His mother was Peruvian and father, white. As reporters learned that Zimmerman was half Latino, they struggled. Some commentators began to argue that Zimmerman couldn't be racist because he wasn't white. He self-identified as Hispanic on his voter's registration and driver's license, reported a Lafayette, Indiana, *Journal & Courier* columnist. Later, NPR, the *New York Times*, and NBC Nightly News called him a "white Hispanic."[46] While this new approach drew criticism, it agreed with US Census categories, which separate race (Asian, American Indian, Pacific Islanders, blacks and whites), from ethnicity (Hispanic). The shift allowed journalists to fall back into the comfort of framing the story around individual behavior and black/white conflict.

Their narrow approach obscured broader processes within society that deserve our attention. For instance, the confusion over Zimmerman's "race" provided ample opportunity to explore racial categories and their social significance. What are the power relations embedded in US racial and ethnic categories and how did they shape this incident, including the public's response? How do racial categories play out in the instant of person-to-person interaction – through assessments of skin color, hair texture, clothing, or other characteristics? How might racial categorizations have interacted with individual power struggles in that moment? Rather than focusing on Zimmerman's explicit racial attitudes, reporters could have explored more important questions about the interplay between stereotypes about criminality, the resulting cognitive shortcuts we rely upon, and the likelihood of honest – but mistaken – judgments about the need for self-defense.[47]

Zimmerman was engaged in a "racial project" of defending property against intrusion by the foreign presence represented by Martin, argues political scientist Michael Hanchard at Johns Hopkins University.[48] Being multiracial or Latino did not inoculate Zimmerman from bigotry against a young man perceived as black and male, Hanchard says. In his view, the incident should be understood as an example of the power dynamics often embedded in volunteer policing, citizen defense organizations and militias throughout US history and expressed through racial violence. A better story might have addressed that history and shown its reverberations today.

Some news stories did look at the police decision not to make an arrest or file charges right away in the context of racial profiling of black youth – the assumption that Martin was likely dangerous – and the parallel exceptionalism that can benefit white, middle-class perpetrators. But they relied on the assumption that this dynamic could only function if Zimmerman himself was white.

Subtext

In covering the Zimmerman case, it also would have been useful to look at the racial subtext already present in so many parts of American life, particularly the implicit association of black youth with criminality threaded through entertainment, news media and other influences. How might this subtext have influenced Zimmerman's decision to pursue Martin? What are the social forces that sustain the connection of young black men to crime in the popular mind? Who benefits from this persistent association? What are its concrete repercussions for both the young men affected and broader society?

Stanford psychology professor Jennifer Eberhardt studies the consequences of the association between race and crime. She and Phillip Goff, now at John Jay College of Criminal Justice, built upon previous implicit association research that has linked people's perceptions of black people to crime and criminal objects. They wanted to find out whether the reverse was true. Could a concept, such as crime or sports, trigger thoughts of black people? She and Goff found that activating ideas about crime (and sports) then led people, including police officers, to pay more attention to black male faces.[49] Black faces – but not white ones – prompted them to more quickly visually process crime-relevant objects. Research such as this gives insight into the effects of attention and visual processing that may have shaped Zimmerman's encounter with Martin and the police's response. Not only might unarmed black people become the undeserved target of suspicion and be placed in danger, but police officers may be slow to respond to armed white suspects and be more likely to get hurt or killed. Journalists can ask, how might these visual processing shortcuts affect all sorts of everyday encounters? How might they unfold across the criminal justice and juvenile justice systems?

Some journalists described the fear that parents of black young men feel every time they walk out the door, and conversely, how the world perceives such youth once they leave the safety of their homes. Journalists also could have explored the racialized reality experienced by men of color. At what point in their childhood must they set aside their carefree ways and come to grips with society's views about them as dangerous? How does this affect their interactions in the world?

Structure, Context, and Environment

To truly draw out the significance and meaning of a racialized encounter like that between Zimmerman and Martin, we suggest that journalists consider the structural elements at play. A group of young activists in Florida who call themselves the Dream Defenders raised these structural issues in their reaction to the trial and the verdict that set George Zimmerman free. To them, Martin's death and the aftermath symbolized the historical inequities threaded throughout American educational and economic systems, and our collective refusal to face them. "If we were to truly reflect on the America in the Mirror, we would realize that we are **all** [*original emphasis*] complicit in death of Trayvon Martin," reads the original Dream Defender blog post.[50] The activists, who began a 31-day sit-in in the Florida State Capitol three days after Zimmerman was acquitted, said they were not protesting one man's actions or his trial. Instead they focused on the structural racial inequity they see built into policies such as "stand your ground" laws in Florida and other states,[51] racial profiling in policing and in schools, and the uneven application of justice by race.

The group cited the example of Marissa Alexander – an African American mother of three who served nearly seven years of a 20-year prison sentence for firing what she called a "warning shot" at her husband, who was not injured. He had been under a protective order because of previous violence against her. Alexander declined a plea bargain and came under the rules of a Florida minimum-sentencing law.[52] The case offers a useful opportunity to consider the interplay of race and law enforcement when a woman is at the center.

Despite the Dream Defenders' unusually long, peaceful action and the involvement of civil rights leaders and celebrities, their focus on structural inequities got very little national news media attention. Nor did their call for reconciliation across race, sexual orientation, national origin, and other differences.

Some stories did attempt to understand the larger social/cultural context in which Zimmerman and Martin were operating, and we applaud them. A March 2012 story in the *Tampa Bay Times*,[53] for instance, examined the sociological and psychological outcomes of the rise of the gated community during the housing boom of the 2000s and its subsequent decline. Now we gain insight into Zimmerman's actions not as a lone reactionary, but as part of the larger forces around him that affect all of our lives.

Signifiers and Code Words

Especially in a story so racially charged, reporters and editors must go beyond what sources say directly. It's helpful to take note of nonverbal gestures, code words, the absence of certain information, and even the role of an object or piece of clothing. A March 2012 opinion piece in the *Tampa Bay Times*[54] examined the social meaning assigned to hoodies. A great example of racial discourse analysis, the story called attention to the changing meaning of a single garment depending on the race, age, and class of the person who wears it – and who is looking.

Racial discourse analysis helps us see that language and approaches that seem "neutral" often instead give favor to groups that hold the most power in society. We must actively interrogate and explore the racial meaning in stories, even when it may seem obvious. You can use this tool to find hidden racial meaning, develop incisive questions for policymakers and those who influence policy, and more effectively frame your stories. It will help you notice the power of language choices that have consequences for all.

For those who believe this approach is too tedious for today's journalists who are buckling under demands to produce more content more quickly, much of this work boils down to changing our awareness and the habits of our thinking. Once we begin applying this approach, it can become second nature. Put simply, it is an essential element of critical thinking.

The Journalist's Role

The job of a journalist is to synthesize facts, observations, and stakeholders' perspectives in a context that illuminates their meaning. Journalists have a duty to uncover what is invisible to society, to shine light on the hidden or overlooked. All this is done for a greater purpose – to provide a foundation for the shared understandings people need in order to make decisions about their everyday lives, their communities, and their government. As set out in the SPJ Code of Ethics and supported by both the Hutchins and Kerner Commissions, journalists work to help people understand one another, listen to one another, and strengthen the democratic process overall.

The reporting and editing strategy described in this book builds upon an awareness of the hidden structures and systems of race within society. To uncover the ways in which language props these up, we apply scholarship about the perception cycle and also incorporate racial discourse analysis. Our approach moves beyond a call to qualitatively and quantitatively improve representations of people of color in coverage. It nudges reporters beyond the passive desire to heighten one's racial awareness. Instead it asks journalists to actively engage with a variety of socio-racial realities. It proposes that we broaden our personal worldview and wear racial lenses for an extended period of time, including through analyzing the racialized speech of sources, including policymakers, influential power-brokers, politicians, and people on the street. Our strategy also requires examination of our own ideologies and paradigms – our habits of seeing – that can distort the direction our reporting takes us.

Developing a stronger sense of the racial structuring of society and building this into our stories may seem to make journalists vulnerable to the charge of "liberal bias." Race, however, is an undeniable facet of American life. Journalists must cover it honestly. By doing so in a way that deepens understanding beyond simple accusations and grievances, we ultimately can help bridge the partisan divide. Uncovering the forces behind unequal outcomes is not itself a stance, other than against racism itself. And this stance we encourage, because it is empowering to society and contributes to our collective betterment. As Omi and Winant state:

> By noticing race we begin to challenge racism, with its ever-more-absurd reduction of human experience to an essence attributed to all without regard for historical or social context. By noticing race, we can challenge

the state, the institutions of civil society, and ourselves as individuals to combat the legacy of inequality and injustice inherited from the past.[55]

Journalists covering racism provide a foundation for effective intervention – enabling informed decision-making without advocating particular solutions. On the other hand, the anecdotal and isolated treatment of race in the news, together with implicit stereotyping and racial subtexts, is also a stance and in fact a form of bias. It even cultivates further bias. Such an approach, which is common throughout news media, harmfully activates well-worn belief systems and divisions.

Addressing the inequities embedded in race and the racial projects that keep it in place is our duty as we seek truth and report it. It is part and parcel of our pursuit of justice. The most enterprising journalists highlight ways in which social institutions themselves are organized to give favor to some demographic groups over others. They follow the money, uncovering funding and other policy decisions – those racial projects – that have eased the path of the white majority for generations and continue to do so. They also recognize that race is not monolithic – that many white rural and blue-collar residents feel marginalized by the global transitions the country is experiencing. These journalists not only portray victims of discrimination, they also explain the policies, practices, and cultural imagery that give rise to it – and the hidden, even unwanted benefits that many white people may reap. Finally, they avoid the habit of participating in racial formation themselves by attending to nonwhites or women only as victims or problem people, instead showing members of these groups as part of the norm, including acting positively on their own behalf. They make a conscious effort to include all segments of society and present their voices as equal. They shine light on issues and events in a manner that seeks to achieve institutions, policies and practices that are fair to everyone. They take the stance of both conservative and reformative justice.

Notes

1 Dan Barry and John Eligon. "'Trump, Trump, Trump!' How a President's Name Became a Racial Jeer." *New York Times*, December 16, 2017. Accessed December 29, 2017 from www.nytimes.com/2017/12/16/us/trump-racial-jeers. html?_r=0. A White House spokesman condemned the use of Trump's name in such a manner.
2 Julie Turkewitz. "For Native Americans, 'Historic Moment' on the Path to Power at the Ballot Box." *New York Times*, January 4, 2018. Accessed January 4, 2017 from www. nytimes.com/2018/01/04/us/native-american-voting-rights.html?rref=collection%2Fti mestopic%2FNative%20Americans&action=click&contentCollection=timestopics&re gion=stream&module=stream_unit&version=latest&contentPlacement=1&pgtype=col lection&_r=0.
3 Adam Liptak. "Pulled over in a Rental Car, with Heroin in the Trunk." *New York Times*, January 1, 2018. Accessed February 21, 2018 from www.nytimes.com/ 2018/01/01/us/politics/rental-car-privacy-supreme-court.html.

4 Richard Wolf. "From Heroin in Rental Car Trunk to Stolen Motorcycle, Supreme Court Defends Privacy Rights." *USA Today*, June 1, 2018. Accessed July 15, 2018 from www.usatoday.com/story/news/politics/2018/06/01/heroin-motorcycle-supreme-court-privacy-rights/660586002/. The court decided in June 2018 that Terrance Byrd's absence from the rental agreement did not give police the right to search the car.

5 Society of Professional Journalists. Preamble to the SPJ Code of Ethics. Accessed February 21, 2018 from www.spj.org/pdf/spj-code-of-ethics.pdf.

6 Patrick Lee Plaisance. *Media Ethics: Key Principles for Responsible Practice*. Los Angeles, CA: Sage Publications, 2009, pp. 73–104.

7 Ibid., p. 78.

8 "Stemming the Rising Tide: Racial & Ethnic Disparities in Youth Incarceration & Strategies for Change," W. Haywood Burns Institute, May 2016. Accessed February 10, 2018 from www.burnsinstitute.org/wp-content/uploads/2016/05/Stemming-the-Rising-Tide_FINAL.pdf.

9 Ibid., p. xviii.

10 SPJ Code of Ethics.

11 For a detailed discussion on the ethics of handling hate speech and "hate spin," the violent response to perceived religious offense by a community, see Cherian George. "Journalism and the Politics of Hate: Charting Ethical Responses to Religious Intolerance." *Journal of Mass Media Ethics* 29, no. 2 (2014): 74–90. doi: 10.1080/08900523.2014.893771.

12 Robert M. Hutchins et al. *A Free and Responsible Press*. Report by the Commission on the Freedom of the Press. Chicago, IL: University of Chicago Press, 1947. Accessed February 11, 2017 from www.archive.org/stream/freeandrespon sib029216mbp#page/n5/mode/1up.

13 Juan Gonzalez and Joseph Torres. *News for All the People*. London: Verso, 2011.

14 Hutchins et al. *A Free and Responsible Press*.

15 Otto Kerner et al. *Report of the National Advisory Committee on Civil Disorders*. The New York Times edition. New York, NY: E.P. Dutton & Co., 1968, 366.

16 American Society of News Editors, *The ASNE Diversity Survey, 2017*. Accessed December 8, 2017 from http://asne.org/diversity-survey-2017.

17 Kashmir Hill. "'Sexism' Public-Shaming via Twitter Leads to Two People Getting Fired (Including the Shamer)." *Forbes*, March 21, 2013. Accessed February 11, 2017 from www.forbes.com/sites/kashmirhill/2013/03/21/sexism-public-shaming-via-twitter-leads-to-two-people-getting-fired-including-the-shamer/#359c27 bb3eb3.

18 Walter Lippmann. "The Habits of Our Eyes: Toward a Critique of Public Opinion." *The Century Magazine*, December, 1921, 243–252. Accessed February 11, 2017 from www.unz.org/Pub/Century-1921dec-00243.

19 Ibid., p. 81.

20 Robert M. Entman and Andrew Rojecki. *The Black Image in the White Mind*. Chicago, IL: University of Chicago Press, 2000.

21 Travis L. Dixon. "Good Guys Are Still Always in White? Positive Change and Continued Misrepresentation of Race and Crime on Local Television News." *Communication Research* 44, no. 6 (2015): 775–792. doi: 10.1177/0093650215579223.

22 Travis L. Dixon and Charlotte L. Williams. "The Changing Misrepresentation of Race and Crime on Network and Cable News." *Journal of Communication* 65, no. 1 (February 2015): 24–39. doi: 10.1111/jcom.12133.

23 Travis L. Dixon. "A Dangerous Distortion of Our Families: Representations, by Race, of Families in News and Opinion Media." Co-commissioned by Family Story and Color of Change, December 2017. Accessed December 31, 2017 from https://s3.amazonaws.com/coc-dangerousdisruption/full-report.pdf.

24 Dixon. "Good Guys Are Still Always in White?" pp. 775–792.
25 Mary Beth Oliver, Ronald L. Jackson, Ndidi N. Moses, and Celnisha L. Dangerfield. "The Face of Crime: Viewers' Memory of Race-Related Facial Features of Individuals Pictured in the News." *Journal of Communication* 54, no. 1 (2004): 88–104. doi: 10.1111/j.1460–2466.2004.tb02615.x.
26 Travis L. Dixon. "Black Criminals and White Officers: The Effects of Racially Misrepresent-ing Law Breakers and Law Defenders on Television News." *Media Psychology* 10, no. 2 (2009): 270–291. doi: 10.1080/15213260701375660.
27 Travis L. Dixon. "Psychological Reactions to Crime News Portrayals of Black Criminals: Understanding the Moderating Roles of Prior News Viewing and Stereotype Endorsement." *Communication Monographs* 73, no. 2 (2006): 162–187. doi: 10.1080/03637750600690643.
28 Frank D. Gilliam and Shanto S. Iyengar. "Prime Suspects: The Influence of Local Television News on the Viewing Public." *American Journal of Political Science* 44, no. 3 (July 1, 2000): 560–573.
29 Peggy McIntosh. "White Privilege: Unpacking the Invisible Knapsack." National SEED Project on Inclusive Curriculum, 1989. Accessed February 11, 2017 from www.nationalseedproject.org/white-privilege-unpacking-the-invisible-knapsack; Robert Jensen. *The Heart of Whiteness: Confronting Race, Racism, and White Privilege.* San Francisco, CA: City Lights, 2005.
30 A report from the Center for Investigative Reporting and aired on the PBS New Hour shows the difficulty blacks and Latinos have in obtaining home mortgages. Aaron Glantz. "Struggle for Black and Latino Mortgage Applicants Suggests Modern-Day Redlining." PBS News Hour, aired February 15, 2018. Accessed February 21, 2018 from www.pbs.org/newshour/show/struggle-for-black-and-latino-mortgage-applicants-suggests-modern-day-redlining.
31 Geneva Smitherman-Donaldson and Teun Van Dijk, eds. *Discourse and Discrimination.* Detroit, MI: Wayne State University Press, 1988.
32 Zeus Leonardo. "The Color of Supremacy: Beyond the Discourse of 'White Privilege.'" *Educational Philosophy and Theory* 36, no. 2 (2004): 137–152.
33 Clayborne Carson, ed. *The Papers of Martin Luther King, Jr. Vol. III: Birth of a New Age, December 1955 – December 1956.* Berkeley, CA: University of California Press, 1997, pp. 207–208.
34 Stanley R. Bailey and Edward E. Telles. "Multiracial versus Collective Black Categories: Examining Census Classification Debates in Brazil." *Ethnicities* 6, no. 1 (2006): 74–101. doi: 10.1177/1468796806061080.
35 Stephanie Nolen. "Brazil's Colour Bind," July 31, 2015. *The Globe and Mail.* Accessed January 5, 2018 from www.theglobeandmail.com/news/world/brazils-colour-bind/article25779474/.
36 Peter Kivisto and Johanna Leinonen. "Representing Race: Ongoing Uncertainties about Finnish American Racial Identity." *Journal of American Ethnic History* 31, no. 1 (2011): 11–33.
37 Michael Omi and Howard Winant. *Racial Formation in the United States from the 1960s to the 1990s,* Second edition. New York, NY: Routledge, 1994, pp. 55–56.
38 Ibid.
39 Teun van Dijk. "Critical Discourse Studies: A Sociocognitive Approach," in *Methods of Critical Discourse Analysis,* ed. Ruth Wodak and Michael Meyer, Second edition. London: Sage Publications, 2010, p. 63.
40 Zeus Leonardo. *Race, Whiteness, and Education.* New York, NY: Routledge, 2009, pp. 127–142; Gloria Ladson-Billings. "Just What Is Critical Race Theory and What's It Doing in a Nice Field Like Education?" in *Foundations of Critical Race Theory in Education,* ed. Edward Taylor, David Gillborn and Gloria Ladson-Billings. New York, NY: Routledge, 2009, 2016, pp. 15–30; Michelle Alexander. Revised

Edition *The New Jim Crow: Mass Incarceration in the Age of Colorblindness*. New York, NY: The New Press, 2012, p. 43; Brentin Mock. "The Meaning of Blight." *City Lab*, February 16, 2017. Accessed March 4, 2018 from www.citylab.com/equity/2017/02/the-meaning-of-blight/516801/.
41 Ladson-Billings. "Just What Is Critical Race Theory," p. 24.
42 Jane H. Hill. *The Everyday Language of White Racism*. Malden, MA: Wiley-Blackwell, 2008.
43 In an email conversation Wagner had with van Dijk, he lamented his failed efforts at convincing journalists in Denmark and other parts of the world to use the discourse analysis approach. Email conversation with Teun van Dijk, March 12, 2012.
44 The Pew Research Center analyzed coverage on social media, cable TV, and talk radio. It found that Twitter focused on outrage at Zimmerman's actions, cable and talk radio focused on gun control and Florida's Stand Your Ground law, while blogs examined the role of race. Certainly, the delineation of subjects by platform suggests the fragmentation of news audiences. The study also found that conservative shows focused on Martin's character and the defense of Zimmerman, while liberal shows focused on gun control. See "How Blogs, Twitter and the Mainstream Media Have Handled the Trayvon Martin Case." Pew Research Center, March 30, 2012. Accessed February 18, 2018 from www.journalism.org/2012/03/30/special-report-how-blogs-twitter-and-mainstream-media-have-handled-trayvon-m/.
45 Michael Pearson and David Mattingly. "Gun, Drug Texts Feature in New Trayvon Martin Shooting Evidence." CNN, May 26, 2013. Accessed February 11, 2017 from www.cnn.com/2013/05/23/justice/florida-zimmerman-defense/; Russell Goldman. "Trayvon Martin Drug Photos Can't Be Mentioned, Says Judge." ABC News, May 28, 2013. Accessed February 11, 2017 from http://abcnews.go.com/US/trayvon-martin-drug-photos-mentioned-judge/story?id=19271093.
46 "Was Trayvon Martin Targeted for Being Black?" NPR's Tell Me More program, March 20, 2012. Accessed February 22, 2018 from http://wamc.org/post/was-trayvon-martin-targeted-being-black; Lizette Alvarez. "A Florida Law Gets Scrutiny after a Teenager's Killing." *New York Times*, March 20, 2012. Accessed February 22, 2018 from www.nytimes.com/2012/03/21/us/justice-department-opens-inquiry-in-killing-of-trayvon-martin.html; "Florida Police Question Whether the Shooting of a 17-Year-Old Was Self-Defense or Unjustified Over-Reaction." *NBC Nightly News*. Aired March 17, 2012. Accessed through The Internet Archive February 22, 2018 from https://archive.org/details/WBAL_20120317_223000_NBC_Nightly_News/start/1260/end/1320.
47 L. Song Richardson and Phillip A. Goff. "Self-Defense and the Suspicion Heuristic." *Iowa Law Review* 98, no. 1 (2012): 293–336.
48 Michael Hanchard. "You Shall Have the Body: On Trayvon Martin's Slaughter." *Theory & Event* 15, no. 3 Accessed November 29, 2018 from *https://muse-jhu-edu.jpllnet.sfsu.edu/article/484426*. (2012).
49 Jennifer L. Eberhardt, Phillip A. Goff, Valerie J. Purdie, and Paul G. Davies. "Seeing Black: Race, Crime, and Visual Processing." *Journal of Personality and Social Psychology* 87, no. 6 (2004): 876–893. doi: 10.1037/0022-3514.87.6.876.
50 Dream Defenders (blog), July 9, 2013. Accessed February 11, 2017 from www.dreamdefenders.org/blog?page=1.
51 These laws were incorporated in jury instructions in the trial and discussed by the jury. For a discussion of their significance in the Zimmerman case, see Ta Nehisi-Coates. "How Stand Your Ground Relates to George Zimmerman." *The Atlantic*, July 16, 2013. Accessed February 11, 2018 from www.theatlantic.com/national/archive/2013/07/how-stand-your-ground-relates-to-george-zimmerman/277829/.

52 Christine Hauser. "Florida Woman Whose 'Stand Your Ground' Defense Was Rejected Is Released." *New York Times*, February 7, 2017. Accessed February 11, 2017 from www.nytimes.com/2017/02/07/us/marissa-alexander-released-stand-your-ground.html?_r=0.

53 Lane Degregory. "The Retreat." *Tampa Bay Times*, March 25, 2012, p. 1A.

54 Stephanie Hayes. "The Hoodie's Many Personas." *The Tampa Bay Times*, March 25, 2012, p. 1P. Accessed February 22, 2018 from www.tampabay.com/opinion/essays/hoodies-have-a-complicated-fashion-story/1221529.

55 Omi and Winant. *Racial Formation*.

PART II
How Opportunity Works

6

REPORTING THE STORY UPSTREAM

Sally Lehrman and Venise Wagner

With less time to report and tell stories, how can journalists immerse themselves in the challenging realm of racial inequity? It's easy to be overwhelmed by the immensity and complexity of the subject. In this chapter the authors introduce a metaphor and framework that makes reporting about inequity easier to understand and approach. By adopting analytical models used in the field of public health, reporters can follow important lines of inquiry that reveal the structural roots of disparity. The authors call it upstream reporting.

The Ideal and the Practical

Imagine writing a story with impact. A story that changes the way government agencies or institutions operate. A story that holds policymakers accountable. That places readers in the shoes of people who are generally seen as "other." That empowers the public to make well-informed decisions about how society should work.

Most journalists got into the business because they wanted to make a difference. They understood the power of uncovering untold stories, including the stories of those who couldn't tell their own. They became journalists because they knew that to expose corruption, hidden issues, and the seeds of a problem makes our democracy stronger. Idealistic? Yes. But journalistic aspirations generally start with the ideal.

Then the reality of the news business sets in.

The daily life of a reporter has transformed dramatically in the last decade. In addition to keeping up with a beat, many reporters now have to write for multiple spaces: online as news breaks, a print version, various updates, and in some cases, video and audio versions. They have to craft tweets and post on Facebook to attract readers to the brand's website. They may keep up a blog that gives readers behind-the-scenes insights, or appear on television or radio to promote their work. Local television reporters are under extreme pressure to produce several packages a day. If the station is poorly resourced, then the reporter may also be responsible for doing his or her own camera work. Many TV and radio journalists do not have the luxury of focusing on one particular beat. They must cover a variety of stories in the course of the week, making it difficult for them to develop expertise in any one area. With less time to report and delve deeply into a subject, how can journalists immerse themselves into the heady realm of racial inequity? It's easy to get overwhelmed by the immensity and complexity of the topic. Where does one start?

Upstream Reporting

The framework we offer in this chapter can make reporting about inequity easier to achieve. Used as a flexible, idea-generating tool, this framework can help you develop long-term ideas or smaller, more manageable stories with more impact than usual.

As an example, let's start with the comparatively low rates of disease and death among whites compared to nonwhites, and the way this disparity is usually covered. African Americans and Latinos disproportionately live with the debilitating effects of diabetes.[1] Among new cases of full-blown AIDS, both groups carry the highest burden.[2] Asian Americans have a higher prevalence of tuberculosis than any other group[3] and also the highest number of cases of chronic hepatitis B.[4] The list goes on. Most mainstream news organizations only occasionally touch on aspects of the health gap. When they do, the take-away message often seems to be that nonwhites have a predisposition to poor health, consistently make poor choices that lead to medical problems, or simply lack resources. When those explanations seem insufficient, reporters often point to potential biological differences without any further support.

Consider infant survival, one of the best ways to understand health and well-being across populations. As mentioned in Chapter 3, white and Asian American infant mortality rates are lower than any others. More than twice as many African American babies die before their first birthday than in these groups. American Indian and Alaska Native families, too, bear an especially high burden of Sudden Infant Death Syndrome (SIDS).[5] A story in *U.S. News & World Report* took a common approach to this disparity. The reporter noted the high rates of SIDS among American Indian, Alaskan Native and African American infants, explaining that "varying smoking rates, along with racial and ethnic differences, may be at play."[6]

Let's step back. What "differences" could these be? To start, a more informative story would have clarified the lack of evidence of any cultural norms or biological susceptibility to blame.[7] And what about those smoking rates or exposure to smoke? Why might they vary? Tobacco companies disproportionately market their products to racial and ethnic minorities through advertisements, scholarship programs, and cultural support.[8] We also find more tobacco retailers in lower-income or minority neighborhoods,[9] a trend associated with higher smoking rates.[10] Tobacco sellers don't end up there by chance. Licensing, zone, and board of health rules play a role. In addition, state and local policies about smoking affect exposure to second-hand smoke in apartment buildings and outdoor areas.

When new health statistics come out, we often see a report like one from Sonoma County, California, noting leading causes of death by race and ethnicity. A news story in the local *Press Democrat* mentioned that unintentional injury deaths, such as overdoses, falls, car crashes, or other accidents, were among the top five causes of death for Latinos, Native Americans and Asians.[11] Only substance abuse was noted as an important risk factor. Rather than stopping there, an enterprising reporter might ask some questions. In regard to overdoses, what sort of substance abuse treatment is available to Latinos, Native Americans, and Asians, relative to whites? Accidents also were a major cause of death. Are these often farm machinery or other heavy equipment accidents, considering that Sonoma County's Latino workforce is concentrated in food service, farm labor, construction, and maintenance?[12]

For Asian Americans, news reports often focus on what seems to be a surprising rise in incidence of disease. This population is generally assumed to be healthy, often based on poor data or data that groups all Asians together. The *San Jose Mercury News* and the *Chicago Tribune*, for example, both ran a story about rising breast cancer rates among Asian Americans, characterizing the rate among Korean Americans as "astonishing" and pointing to behavioral risk factors as a possible cause.[13] A more illuminating story in NBC News explained that the groups most affected, such as Pakistanis, Cambodians, and Hmong, had recently immigrated. Longer established populations such as Japanese Americans showed patterns similar to non–Hispanic white women. Late detection, stigma, and the assumption that Asian American women don't get breast cancer were all described as potentially relevant. An even better story might have explored the structural and institutional factors behind late detection, such as physicians that underestimate risk and some immigrant women's role as primary breadwinners, which may limit their ability to take time to address their own health needs.[14]

These stories do raise awareness about the health gap. They even strive to highlight the fundamental causes. But there's much more to the story. You can use your regular reporting to give audiences a deeper understanding of the structural factors that drive health inequity. All you have to do is shift your thinking a bit, build your knowledge step-by-step, and look for opportunities in daily coverage.

Social Determinants of Health

Let's take a look at a diagram (Figure 6.1) called the Responsibility Continuum, which lays out the forces and players responsible for an individual's or

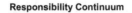

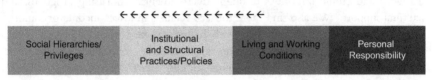

FIGURE 6.1 Responsibility Continuum

family's health. This continuum illustrates the hierarchy of influence that ultimately leads to disparate social outcomes. The Personal Responsibility box is farthest to the right because individual decisions are not made in a vacuum. They are influenced by Living and Working Conditions, which in turn are directly influenced by Institutional and Structural Practices or Policies. These, in turn, are directly affected by Social Hierarchies and Privileges.

So, for instance, we know that some foods that reflect Mexican American cultural tradition, like flour tortillas, fried foods, and rice, when consumed in large portions or without additional vegetables and fruits, may contribute to high rates of diabetes in that population.[15] Since food ways are central to social cohesion (also important to good health), it takes skillful balancing to negotiate cultural and family expectations. More generally, we each must make a decision whether to allocate time to exercise and cook up a meal at home, rather than stop by a fast-food outlet or order pizza. That's the far-right box. But as you can see, cultural traditions and personal choices are just one part of the story. Public health experts have developed a way of understanding the rest of the continuum – the forces behind individual decision-making and health inequities overall – by studying the relevant structural components of society. They call these "social determinants" of health.[16]

Social determinants are the interacting economic and social conditions built into society that affect how we grow up, live, work, and play. These include our social and physical environment, health care structures, and the resources we can access. They are shaped by the distribution of wealth and power throughout society. Looking at the Living and Working Conditions box in Figure 6.1, consider how the physical surroundings and working conditions of families influence the choices they make. For example, families in urban areas that rely on public transportation may have to travel an hour or more by bus to get to the grocery store. How does that affect their decisions about the foods they buy and the meals they eat? In other communities, cracked sidewalks and speeding cars make walking along the street unsafe. If there are any parks nearby, they are decaying and dark. How likely are residents to exercise?

Moving further up the continuum, we see that institutional policies directly affect living and working conditions. Along with market forces, zoning laws dictate the types of businesses established in communities. Poor African American and Latino communities have a greater density of liquor stores than in affluent communities,[17] and fewer full-service groceries and farmers' markets.[18] Some big employers run their own private buses for workers, potentially weakening community support for expanded public transportation. Local governments decide where to place high-speed traffic routes and how to allocate resources to maintain parks and safety within neighborhoods.

Going further up the continuum, we see that Social Hierarchies and Privileges directly affect policies. Many predominately nonwhite neighborhoods suffer the effects of long-forgotten decisions and other legacies that at one time may have been deliberately intended to steer resources to whites. While the origins of such policies may not win favor today, the people who experience their continuing repercussions often lack the socio-political clout to push agencies to change. More recent policies, even without any intention to harm, also reflect political influence and social hierarchies in the deployment of resources. Communities of color may have little say over funds for transportation, decisions about zoning, or the distribution of resources to parks and recreation programs. In a powerful, in-depth series, *Environmental Health News* reporters described the historical and political forces that have placed people of color in the most polluted neighborhoods of the country. They detailed the biological repercussions, including high levels of asthma, diabetes, and other disorders.[19] The reporters carefully identified historical patterns of segregation that have led to the establishment of polluting factories and high-speed transportation corridors in neighborhoods where African Americans, Latinos, or immigrant Asians often live. The stories in the series linked health outcomes to the years of unequal practices and policies that help shape them.

As the Responsibility Continuum illustrates, while our reporting on disparity often begins with individual choices and personal responsibility, it shouldn't end there.

Applying the Framework to Health Stories

You can deepen your understanding of the Responsibility Continuum by studying the Upstream-Downstream Framework that public health experts have developed. This framework, illustrated in Figure 6.2, offers a means to better visualize the social determinants that shape health inequity.

We tend to focus our attention in the far-right boxes – reporting on fundamental measures such as infant mortality and longevity, or calling attention to stark inequities across populations in mortality, disease, and injury. We might cover specific disparities such as those mentioned previously, like the distressingly high death rates of Mexican Americans with high blood pressure or the unusually high prevalence of tuberculosis among Asian Americans. Health stories also often focus on remedies associated with behavior – campaigns that raise awareness about the need for regular mammograms or other tests, for instance, community projects that aim to improve exercise, or education programs to encourage healthy eating. If journalists report only about this part of the stream, though, we leave the public without moorings.

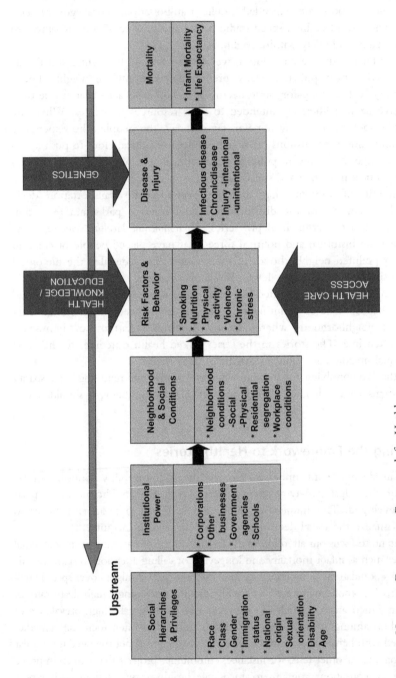

FIGURE 6.2 Upstream–Downstream Framework for Health
Modified with permission from the Bay Area Regional Health Inequities Framework

From Risk Factors to Surrounding Conditions

Going back to the infant mortality story in *U.S. News and World Report*, recall that the story vaguely referred to smoking rates and unnamed racial and ethnic differences.[20] Audiences are left to understand that African Americans, American Indians, and Native Alaskans essentially bring high infant death rates upon themselves through their behavior. People might wonder, do pregnant mothers protect themselves and their babies from second-hand smoke? Take advantage of prenatal doctor visits? These choices matter a great deal, of course. But we can get more answers further upstream by exploring the impact of neighborhoods and living conditions on a mother's options. Are there apartment rules that protect families from enduring the smoke of a chain smoker in the next unit – or from a courtyard that is being used as a smoking room? Is the neighborhood doused with traffic exhaust twice a day during peak commutes? Do neighbors know one another and benefit from civic gatherings, such as events in parks or community centers, which provide opportunities for social support?

The Upstream-Downstream Framework invites us to pursue the story further by thinking of these outcomes as the toxic debris washed downstream. How did this debris get here? Why? These questions will take you upstream. Consider an insightful story in the *Los Angeles Times* that moves from outcomes to the conditions that shape them. Reporter Ann Simmons looked at the 10-year gap in life expectancy between African Americans who dwell in the Antelope Valley and everyone else in Los Angeles County.[21] Poor access to health care, she wrote, was at root. The story then listed some of the neighborhood and social conditions at play, particularly the lack of medical specialists in the area, including dentists and psychiatrists. It cited social environment, level of education and jobs, and the walkability of the community as constraints to good health. Naming these factors helps audiences understand why unhealthy behaviors may take shape. At the same time, there's an even richer story that can be told, one that offers useful fodder to imagine potential solutions. Without more information, a reader might assume that these social and neighborhood conditions are inevitable or perhaps created by the community itself. By looking into more deeply into the "why?" however, a reporter can begin to explore the institutional practices and policies that shape neighborhood and social conditions. Are there any incentives to draw medical specialists to the area? Are schools adequately funded and equipped to address unique population needs? What are the primary factors limiting access to jobs? What has been the impact of the decline of the aerospace industry, once a major employer in the area?

Institutional Power

By continuing upstream, we can examine the impact of institutional policies and practices that create systemic barriers to both individual and neighborhood health – or can work to explode such barriers. We can compare institutions across locales for clues.

When neighborhood safety hampers residents from exercising, for instance, what institutional support systems are in place elsewhere that might highlight potential solutions? The city of San Antonio offers free exercise classes in parks, libraries, and community centers.[22] Are there incentives for grocery stores to build in the neighborhood, or for corner markets to provide fresh fruits and vegetables? In New York City, the Food Retail Expansion to Support Health Program uses zoning incentives and tax cuts to encourage neighborhood stores to offer fresh meat, fruit, and vegetables.[23] In Maryland, the state government took steps to address the lack of medical specialists in poor black communities by creating "Health Enterprise Zones" to counter historical neglect. Funds were provided to bring physicians into these areas and enable them to connect residents to primary care and preventive services.[24]

Practices by individual employers, schools, and agencies also play an important role. Is it difficult, for instance, to get time off from work to visit the doctor? Are sick days frowned upon? Does the workplace provide walkways through attractive, landscaped areas to invite exercise and support psychological well-being, or offer amenities like shaded picnic tables so workers can eat a nutritious bag lunch brought from home?

Social Hierarchies and Privileges

Finally, furthest upstream we see the impact of hierarchies and privileges organized around race, immigration status, class, disability status, and other social categories that directly inform institutional decision-making. Here, we can ask why policies and practices are in place. Do they stem from historical factors such as segregation? Unequal distribution of resources today? Political or social networks that tend to leave out some populations? Implicit bias?

The *New York Times* did a great job highlighting the importance of living conditions in a story that highlighted the poor health of residents in an impoverished Baltimore neighborhood. The piece delved into industrial decline and the resulting lack of job opportunities, as well as poverty, as the reasons for poor health.[25] The reporter described tragic conditions that directly harm health and also block people's chances to avoid disease and violence. Yet the story led to multiple dead ends. Why are most jobs so far away? Why are so many buildings left vacant? What policies enable the proliferation of liquor stores? Going to specific health dangers in the neighborhood, why are asthma intubation rates so high? What are the policies or practices that might lead to poor air quality? Why are lead paint violations left unaddressed? The story ends with a resident's commitment to lose weight and eat more broccoli. Her efforts are empowering and worthy. Yet the story does a disservice by emphasizing individual choice in light of such conditions. Instead, a look at the power structures that shape political and institutional decisions about that area would have been enlightening.

In contrast, a story in the *Oregonian* went all the way upstream. Reporter Bill Graves described the high health risks faced by Native Americans, particularly urban Indians who live far from the health and social services available on reservations. He explained historical trauma and the ongoing assaults on American Indian identity and culture that are root causes, using the diabetes epidemic in the community as an example of the harm done.[26] Institutional factors at play include the misclassification and underreporting of disease and death, which limit the availability of funds and services. Then there are the inadequate health care funds and services available through the Indian Health Service, which was originally established as compensation for taking Native land. Graves also pointed to the boarding schools, relocations and other legacies that not only had sown distrust of government promises, but also had undermined community identity and self-efficacy. The piece highlighted innovative health organizations that Portland's urban Indians have created in response.

Graves addressed power structures and their impact on Native Americans by outlining historical factors and an ongoing skew in the provision of attention and resources. We also can probe the interpersonal impact of power structures and social ideologies – both outright and implicit. When we look at infant mortality rates, we might ask: Is a mother's care affected by implicit racism at the clinic where she receives prenatal support? Is her day at work peppered by remarks or assumptions associated with her race or class? Does she have access to culturally appropriate guidance and treatment by caregivers who speak her language? As with other aspects of health, lifelong experiences also play a role. In a study among African American women in Chicago, pediatricians and public health experts found that the effects of exposure to interpersonal racial discrimination accumulated over their lives, adding up to an independent risk factor for preterm delivery.[27]

The Time Factor

By reporting upstream you can show how unequal health outcomes develop and give your audiences a more complete picture of the disparities we see every day. Don't fall into the trap of considering upstream factors a luxury reserved for the long series or takeout. It's important to recognize that you need not address every level of the stream in every story. You can use the framework to develop stories within one level or show connections between a couple of them. Even though we've become accustomed to focusing our efforts downstream at the lowest three levels of behavior, disease, and mortality, we can shift more reporting to each of the upper levels. Use this framework as a prompt that helps you target new areas for potential stories. It can also give you ideas for charts and graphics that can show the roots of inequities and the underlying relationships visually.

Using the Framework for Education

Our upstream framework can be applied to other beats and areas of coverage. Let's look at education. Latinos have the highest high school dropout rate of all other racial and ethnic groups. According to the National Center for Education Statistics, in 2014 the Latino dropout rate was 10.6 percent; for African Americans, 7.4; for whites, 5.2.[28]

Many stories, including examples we found in the *Chicago Tribune, Houston Chronicle,* and the ABC news affiliate website in Salt Lake City, have reported on the dropout rate among Latinos and in various forms looked at student behavior and choices.[29] In some cases these are same-day stories that reporters had to cover, such as meetings. But each could have provided at least one line pointing to the structural factors that lead to these dropout rates. If we use the framework in Figure 6.3, we see that there is a much richer story to be told.

First, note that educational outcomes as outlined in the second box to the right in Figure 6.3 have direct social consequences such as income, wealth, employment, and health later in life. Moving left to the educational box, let's home in on dropout rates. We see that behavior plays an important role in student attendance, study habits, and disciplinary actions such as suspensions and expulsions. Even here, the red arrow points to other influences on behavior that lead to dropping out. Peer influence is key. If a student hangs out with people who are cutting class, she will likely be persuaded to follow. And if the student had poor schooling prior to high school, then of course it will be difficult for her to catch up to grade-level work. Additionally, if the student moved around frequently with her family, her chances of staying on track will be low. Most of the news reports cited above stay in this box and leave the public to understand that all we need to do is change student behavior to improve the situation. But there are more solutions further upstream.

School Conditions and Institutional Power

The *Los Angeles Times* ran a series of articles – "The Vanishing Class" – that explored the high dropout rate in the Los Angeles Unified School District in depth. Six *Los Angeles Times* reporters spent eight months at a school, Birmingham High School, in Van Nuys, California, getting to know teachers and students. The articles did an excellent job detailing student pressures that carry them down the path of dropping out. For example, a beautiful narrative described the four-year journey of 11 boys. Only three graduated and the story touched on some of the factors that contributed to their decisions.[30] The series took the issue of dropout rates a bit further upstream from the focus of most news stories and features. But more often than not, readers were given little to understand the policy factors, practices, and social hierarchies beneath the surface.

Most of the untold story revolves around race, ethnicity, and class. Latinos, African Americans, and Native Americans are more likely to attend

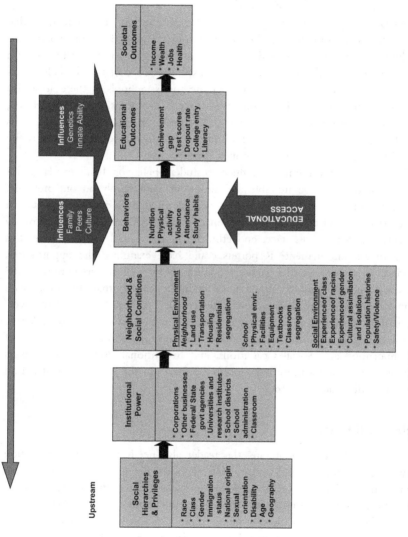

FIGURE 6.3 Upstream–Downstream Framework for Education

Modified with permission from the Bay Area Regional Health Inequities Framework

low-performing schools.[31] Because Birmingham High School is predominately Latino and segregated,[32] the series might have explored the repercussions of segregated environments. According to researcher Robert Balfanz,
about 15 percent of the nation's high schools produce half of its dropouts.
He calls them dropout factories and most of them can be found in urban
centers that serve people of color.[33]

Racial segregation is strongly tied to the distribution of resources, in that
most schools of color tend to be poorly resourced with the least experienced
teachers, fewer counselors, and fewer course materials.[34] If the school is in a
high-poverty area, the series could have explored some of the difficult environments that lure students away from their books. Schools in these areas also
are more likely to experience under-resourced classrooms, bullying, fighting,
high teacher turnover, and vacancies.[35] A school's priorities are revealed in its
spending priorities. What kind of resources did the school get? What is the
school's budget and how is that money spent?

The size of the campus also influences student behavior. If it's too large, it's
easy for students to be invisible and drop out with hardly anyone noticing.
Other structural questions emerge. For example, is there a connection between
the curriculum and the real-life experiences or goals of these students? How do
students experience class, race, and ethnicity in the school and how does this
affect student engagement? Reporters could have examined the opportunities
provided to students in their earlier schooling. How well-prepared are students?
Minority students tend to attend poor grammar schools that do not prepare
them for the academic challenges of high school.[36] A story looking at the cycle
of social promotion at all levels might also be an important element to explore.

All of these questions push the story further upstream to the boxes of
Neighborhood and Social Conditions, and Institutional Power. The answers
help audiences gain a more informed perspective on the influence of structure
on racially disparate outcomes.

Policy and Practice

To understand the dropout rate, the reader also needs to see the connection
between the institution itself and student outcomes. For example, the number of
counselors and the size of their caseloads can have a direct effect on student success. Other institutional issues involve language and communication between the
school and parents. Was there someone there who could reach out to parents
who spoke only Spanish, not just about attendance, but also about academic progress? How about teacher experience? Schools in poor communities often have
higher rates of teacher turnover and a larger percentage of teachers with less than
five years of experience. What was the relationship between the school and the
surrounding neighborhood? If residents in the surrounding neighborhood feel dis-
connected from the school, how can they support the school's mission?

One article in the *Los Angeles Times* series, "A Formula for Failure in Los Angeles Schools," by Duke Helfand, detailed students' difficulty in passing algebra, which the state of California requires to receive a high school diploma.[37] Though lofty, the article stated, the local board's policy did not take into account the resources necessary to prepare students. A policy that was meant to help more students get to college ended up leaving students stranded. If the school board had paid attention to the large number of students failing basic math in Van Nuys, a San Fernando Valley neighborhood, Helfand wrote, perhaps they would have implemented a policy that was more responsive to student academic needs. With this article the reader can't help but see the connection between policy and educational outcomes.

As much as this article addressed the connection between policy and educational outcomes – in this case, the dropout rate – it missed an opportunity to explore any unequal racial impact. Was there a disparate impact on nonwhite or poor students? Were there structural factors beyond the general availability of resources that drove racial inequity, such as unequal distribution of those resources? How experienced are teachers who teach math in minority schools versus white schools? Here a reporter could explore remediation in poor minority schools versus affluent white schools.

Criminal Justice Upstream

National Public Radio ran a special series on the heavy burden the bail bond system places on poor people.[38] The reporter, Laura Sullivan, found that two-thirds of inmates in US jails were there for petty, non-violent crimes, yet many were too poor to cover the cost of bail. They were in jail awaiting trial, so they hadn't been convicted of crimes. When inmates had jobs, they often lost them because they couldn't get to work. Some ended up pleading guilty just so they could get out faster. Sullivan made important connections between policies and the limited choices poor people had. By going upstream, she demonstrated the power dynamic that might have gotten lost in a trend story or an individual narrative about the bail burden. The series started by using data to show the overall trend. Part 2 told the individual story of a man who had to make the difficult choice of pleading guilty to a small crime he said he didn't commit, or fighting the charge and languishing in jail. Finally, in the third story, Sullivan examined the power of the bail lobby, which pressured a local commission in Florida to gut a successful Broward County pretrial release program designed to keep people out of jail and at work.

This exceptional piece of journalism walked up the disparity ladder to show how power and business influences are sometimes used to limit poor people's options. Yet, while all of these connections were well made, Sullivan's reports would have been strengthened if she had exposed the disparate racial impact of bail bonds policies. US Justice Department data shows that African Americans,

American Indians, and, in some cases, Latinos are disproportionately dragged into the criminal justice system for nonviolent crimes.[39] Such numbers would help the public understand that bail policies can have a disproportionate impact on people of color, even when race is not explicitly addressed. Nationally, even though African Americans in 2015 made up about 12 percent of the total population, they made up 35 percent of the jail population. Native Americans were 0.8 percent of the population and 1.2 percent of the jail population. Whites, on the other hand, made up 61 percent of the general population and 48 percent of those jailed. Latinos were 17 percent of the population and 14 percent of those jailed; Asians, 5.4 percent of the population and 0.8 percent of those jailed. Local data, of course, might show even greater disparities. In addition, Sullivan's reporting helps show that prison population demographics are not simply evidence of cultural decline, neglectful families, or something genetic. Oft-overlooked policies such as bail rules can radically skew the jail population.

An enterprising reporter can examine many such systems that exist throughout the United States. In California, for example, many counties charge the parents of incarcerated juveniles daily fees that can add up to tens of thousands of dollars. A KQED public radio story correctly made clear that this policy disproportionately affects young people of color and their families.[40]

The public won't know about the disparate impact of policies like these unless the press reveals it to them. Use the technique of reporting upstream to examine nearly any beat or topic area, including courts, sports, real estate, and business. Economics, small business, banking, and employment all lend themselves to exploring racially unequal outcomes.

B Matter and B Roll

One of the comments we often get from journalists when we show them this framework is, "That's all well and good, but journalists are on tight deadlines. How can we get all that reporting done in a day?" It's a good point. Fortunately, there are ways to work these reporting ideas around and within the demands of daily journalism – both in print and broadcast. Make it a point to find slivers of time to explore the Upstream-Downstream Framework and gather material to provide context for stories on your beat. This will serve as your B matter or B roll, the content you've prepared on a topic in anticipation of a breaking news story. You can gather B matter for any story that would benefit from showing the structural forces involved.

When covering an election, reporters don't know the results, so they report a story that can go either way. They report on the substantive issues related to each potential outcome and create material that can be plugged into news about which candidate wins, or what measure gains favor. Or, when anticipating the end of a trial or a decision by the city council, reporters do the same thing – gather material on the issue so they are prepared with context, background, and relevant perspectives. You can follow the same practice as you report on disparity. If you are on the police beat, for example, gather census data so you know the demographic makeup of the community you're covering, neighborhood by neighborhood. Look for policies that have led to the demographic trends and the physical spaces that help or hinder safety. The types of housing, businesses, open space, and other features of a neighborhood result not from isolated decisions, but from land use and other policies. The maintenance of streets, provision of lighting, and safety of parks reflect budget and staffing priorities. Take time to look at patterns of neighborhood segregation, police arrests by race and class, the allocation of police resources, and the potentially unintended consequences of police practices. The next time you get a story about crime trends or a police shooting, you can incorporate this B matter into your story, helping the audience understand the larger structural forces at play.

Other beats can benefit from the same treatment. Health reporters can gather local data about health outcomes by race and build their knowledge about upstream causes. Studies about unequal clinical care, the impact of stress on health outcomes, and the connection between health behaviors and transportation, land use, housing, or other policies can prepare you to pop in an explanatory statement or paragraph on short notice. Conversations with public health specialists about upstream factors in your coverage area will keep you up to date. You can even prepare some explanatory material in advance, ready to adapt and incorporate. Such practices are simply an extension of the work any beat reporter does to keep up with issues, events, and people, readying to pounce when the right moment comes.

Small Chunks

Again, it doesn't require months of reporting and thousands of words to bring structural inequities to light. You can use the Upstream-Downstream Framework to identify structure and easily manage what might seem like an overwhelming area. Instead of attempting to cover all facets and causes of disparity head on and in a broad fashion, you can address them in individual stories.

Let's go back to the typical health story that emphasizes the role of exercise in good health. You might select one issue in one box in the upstream portion of the chart to pursue. If a person wants to exercise without having to travel to a gym, pay health club fees, or buy expensive equipment, for instance, then he or she might go out in the neighborhood for a walk or run. Focusing a feature on neighborhood conditions would shed light on the real possibilities of such a choice. And rather than allowing blighted or verdant conditions to seem random, the story can show the impact of zoning laws and maintenance on the proportion of asphalt to greenery. To bring such a story to life, a reporter could map a three-mile walk that a resident might take to get in shape. Is there greenery on the walk? Do the sidewalks connect to one another and are they in good condition?

Do smokers hover about? Is there noxious smoke from fireplaces or factories? What about neighborhood safety? Do traffic and congestion create pedestrian hazard? What are the businesses or stores like? Consider the resources available. Is there a park? If so, is the park well-maintained, with an exercise course, ball courts, events, and supervised activities?[41]

After exploring these questions, find out who and what is responsible. What policies are in place that lead to this environment? Now you can make a connection between the racial makeup of the neighborhood, the burden of chronic disease among residents, and opportunities and incentives for residents to exercise. Similarly, a reporter could do a story tracing a kid's journey to school and the environment he has to navigate.

Cross Pollination

Reporting upstream on structural inequity also allows you to make connections between beats. This may lead to more collaboration and more powerful insights. Former WNYC public radio reporter Alisa Chang reported a story about New York's stop-and-frisk policy, analyzing police data to find that one in five people stopped in 2011 was a teenager. Eighty-six percent of those stopped were black or Hispanic. Chang wrote:

> Last year, there were more than 120,000 stops of black and Latino kids between 14 and 18. The total number of black and Latino boys that age in the entire city isn't much more than that – about 177,000 – which strongly suggests a teen male with dark skin in New York City will probably get stopped and frisked by the time he's graduated from high school.[42]

Chang asked Brooklyn students from both low-income and affluent neighborhoods to describe their experiences with the policy. She found that in white and Asian neighborhoods, students were rarely targeted, but in black and Latino neighborhoods, students of color were stopped frequently. Not surprisingly, the most heavily targeted neighborhood was one that experienced high levels of violent crime. But for junior high and high school students in that area, this meant that they might not be able to get through a day without being stopped several times – sometimes much more. Officers were brusque and dumped students' books on the ground. One student described his feelings: "It made me feel, I dunno, retarded." The online piece included a map detailing where stops were most and least concentrated, and a video of interviews of the kids, many of them smiling broadly in their school uniforms. Chang's story advances the discussion about crime policy in our country and raises questions about its effects on education. It pushes us to question whether our policies reflect our values as a society. Furthermore, educational attainment correlates highly with civic engagement – so the people most harmed by these policies are unlikely to play a role in their for-mation or change.[43] Journalists can draw the lines between these various points and guide audiences to do the same.

A reporter can make many natural connections across beats. Most of us know that where a family lives determines which schools children attend, for instance, so housing policies also affect educational opportunities. But have you considered how policies about multi-family housing maintenance and garbage collection also flow into students' health and thus their educational opportunities? Poor housing quality can also exacerbate asthma. In turn, researchers have found, asthma symp-toms are associated with lower grades, quality of schoolwork, and a difficulty focusing.[44]

Perhaps the next school story you write will be within the context of hous-ing or policing. Or the next health story you write will be in the context of schools. Here are three story ideas to get you started.

- *Explore the impact of neighborhood violence or incarceration rates on student mental health and therefore academic performance.*

Public health experts are exploring the effect of neighborhood violence on mental health. They are finding that many residents of communities with high rates of violent crime suffer from post-traumatic stress.[45] What are the effects of this dis-order on school-age children and does it affect their academic performance? You can also explore whether school resources are used to address the problem. Does the school have trained counselors who can treat or address mental health?

- *What does the prevalence of childhood obesity look like through the lens of race? Explore the ways in which school structures play a role in the rise of the epidemic.*

Many stories have looked at school lunches and the prevalence of unhealthy snack vending machines in schools. But is there a difference between the lunches at a poor minority school and those at an affluent school? You can examine the issue from the perspective of the student and his routines. What does he eat for lunch? Is his lunch from the school cafeteria, a fast-food outlet or from home? Why? Many students from poor neighborhoods get free or reduced-cost lunch. So the lunch menu will say a lot. Does the student have gym class? What kinds of activ-ities are available during recess? Collect data from two different schools, one, a poor minority school, the other, a white affluent school.

- *The Poverty Tax. Look at all the fees, fines and extra costs that people pay because their economic resources don't match their needs.*

Start with check cashing fees, fees for paying a bill late, interest rates on sub-prime credit cards, payday lending fees, and traffic fines that escalate over time.

Rent-to-own stores charge high rates not only for furniture and television sets, but also school necessities like computers. If you miss your payments, you lose your investment. You can look into costs stemming from the safety and nature of the neighborhood, too: bars on windows or chain link fences, high auto insurance rates, cab fare to go to the grocery store. There are many ways costs are higher for those with fewer resources, making it even more difficult to stay afloat, let alone get ahead. Explore how these costs tend to hit minorities hardest and show the impact in areas such as health, education, or employment.

Conclusion

In recent years, journalists have made great strides in highlighting disparity and covering unequal racial outcomes in society across education, health, criminal justice, and other areas. This is core to our role of shining light on injustice and serving as a watchdog over public affairs and government. While such reporting is a good first step, however, it can leave major gaps in public under-standing. As we've shown, focusing primarily on outcomes data, illustrated through individual experience, can create a sense of inevitability and even point audiences toward blaming the people harmed.

The Upstream-Downstream Framework offers a route to more accurate, informed and useful coverage. With more awareness of the various layers of social hierarchy, the conditions that shape disparities, and the policies and prac-tices involved, more opportunities for possible intervention come to light. Whatever your audience's political persuasion, your story can open up insights and suggest possibilities for an effective response.

Use the Upstream-Downstream Framework as a flexible tool to deepen your reporting. As you report on an event or issue, you can use the model to briefly add the context of historical legacies, for instance. Or you may take more time and space to fully elaborate on structures that stubbornly block opportunity for some and enable others. You may choose to look at a policy that limits oppor-tunity downstream, or when reporting on a particular disparity, point to some of the upstream conditions that shape it, along with the institutional practices that create those conditions. The Upstream-Downstream Framework offers a flexible tool to deepen your reporting, no matter your time or space constraints.

One of our country's central values is the idea that opportunity is to be equally distributed, as long as you are willing to work for it. We should all have the chance to pursue our dreams. But it's easy to let this ideal become a morality tale about personal responsibility unless you see how laws, policies, and practices shape how opportunities work. The reality is that opportunities are made available to some groups more often than others.

In the next chapter we offer a tool to help reporters identify and quantify opportunity within communities – and the lack thereof – and recognize the many factors that go into molding opportunity. We call it the Opportunity Index.

Notes

1 Centers for Disease Control and Prevention. Table 40 (page 1 of 3). "Diabetes Prevalence and Glycemic Control among Adults Aged 20 and Over, by Sex, Age, and Race and Hispanic Origin: United States, Selected Years 1988–1994 through 2011–2014," in "Health, United States, 2016." Accessed February 19, 2018 from www.cdc.gov/nchs/data/hus/hus16.pdf#040.
2 Centers for Disease Control and Prevention. *HIV Surveillance Report* 28 (2016). Published November 2017. Accessed March 9, 2018 from www.cdc.gov/hiv/library/reports/hiv-surveillance.html.
3 Centers for Disease Control and Prevention. "Reported Cases of Tuberculosis in the United States, 2015." Accessed March 9, 2018 from www.cdc.gov/tb/statistics/reports/2015/table2.htm.
4 Centers for Disease Control and Prevention. "Health Disparities in HIV/AIDS, Viral Hepatitis, STDs and TB, 2017." Accessed March 9, 2018 from www.cdc.gov/nchhstp/healthdisparities/asians.html.
5 T.J. Mathews and Anne K. Driscoll. "Data Brief 279: Trends in Infant Mortality in the United States, 2005–2014." National Center for Health Statistics, Centers for Disease Control and Prevention. Accessed February 19, 2018 from www.cdc.gov/nchs/data/databriefs/db279_table.pdf#1.
6 Steven Reinberg. "Babies Face Higher SIDS Risk in Certain States." *U.S. News & World Report*, February 12, 2018. Accessed February 19, 2018 from https://health.usnews.com/health-care/articles/2018-02-12/babies-face-higher-sids-risk-in-certain-states.
7 Abdulrahman M. El-Sayed, Magdalena Paczkowski, Caroline G. Rutherford, Katherine M. Keyes, and Sandro Galea. "Social Environments, Genetics and Black-White Disparities in Infant Mortality." *Paediatric & Perinatal Epidemiology* 29, no. 6 (2015): 546–551. doi: 10.1111/ppe.12227.
8 See Centers for Disease Control and Prevention. "Hispanics/Latinos and Tobacco Use." September 28, 2017. Accessed February 24, 2018 from www.cdc.gov/tobacco/disparities/hispanics-latinos/index.htm.
9 Daniel Rodriguez, Heather A. Carlos, Anna M. Adachi-Mejia, Ethan M. Burke, and James D. Sargent. "Predictors of Tobacco Outlet Density Nationwide: A Geographic Analysis." *Tobacco Control* 22 (2013): 34–355.
10 Nina C. Schleicher et al. "Tobacco Outlet Density Near Home and School: Associations With Smoking and Norms among U.S. Teens." *Preventive Medicine* 91 (2016): 287–293.
11 Martin Espinoza. "New Report Details Life Expectancy, Leading Causes of Death in Sonoma County." The *Press Democrat*, February 16, 2018. Accessed February 19, 2018 from www.pressdemocrat.com/news/7997819-181/new-report-details-life-expectancy.
12 Sonoma County Economic Development Board. *Hispanic Demographic Trends*, 2017. Accessed March 13, 2018 from www.sonomaedb.org/Data-Center/Demographics/.
13 Tracy Seipel. "Breast Cancer on the Rise among Asian Americans." *Chicago Tribune*, April 27, 2017. Accessed February 19, 2018 from www.chicagotribune.com/lifestyles/health/ct-breast-cancer-rise-among-asian-americans-20170427-story.html.
14 Grace Hwang Lynch. "Breast Cancer Rates Rise among Asian-American Women as Others Stay Stable." *NBC News*, April 21, 2017. Accessed February 24, 2017 from www.nbcnews.com/news/asian-america/breast-cancer-rates-rise-among-asian-american-women-others-stay-n749366.
15 Sandra Benavides-Vaello and Sharon A. Brown. "Sociocultural Construction of Food Ways in Low-Income Mexican-American Women with Diabetes: A Qualitative

Study." *Journal of Clinical Nursing* 25, no. 15–16 (2016): 2367–2377. doi: 10.1111/jocn.13291/full.

16 Richard Hofrichter and Rajiv Bhatia, eds. *Tackling Health Inequities through Public Health Practice: Theory to Action.* New York, NY: Oxford University Press, 2010.

17 Ethan M. Berke, Susanne E. Tanski, Eugene Demidenko, Jennifer Alford-Teaster, Xun Shi, and James D. Sargent. "Alcohol Retail Density and Demographic Predictors of Health Disparities: A Geographic Analysis." *American Journal of Public Health* 100, no. 10 (October 2010): 1967–1971. doi: 10.2105/AJPH.2009.170464.

18 Renee Walker, Christopher R. Keane, and Jessica G. Burke. "Disparities and Access to Healthy Foods in the United States: A Review of Food Deserts Literature." *Health and Place* 16, no. 5 (2010): 876–884.

19 "Pollution, Poverty, and People of Color." A nine-part series with various authors. *Environmental Health News*, June 4, 2012 – June 20, 2012. Accessed February 28, 2017 from www.environmentalhealthnews.org/ehs/news/2012/pollution-poverty-people-of-color-series-summary.

20 Reinberg. "Babies Face Higher SIDS Risk in Certain States."

21 Ann M. Simmons. "For Antelope Valley African Americans, a Lower Life Expectancy." *Los Angeles Times*, May 29, 2012. Accessed February 28, 2017 from http://articles.latimes.com/2012/may/29/local/la-me-av-black-health-20120529.

22 San Antonio Parks and Recreation. *Fitness in the Park.* Accessed March 2, 2018 from www.sanantonio.gov/ParksAndRec/Programs-Classes-Fun/Programs-Classes/Fitness/Fitness-in-the-Park.

23 Department of City Planning. *NYC Planning, FRESH Food Stores.* Accessed February 25, 2018 from www1.nyc.gov/site/planning/zoning/districts-tools/fresh-food-stores.page.

24 Michael Dresser. "State Designates Five 'Health Enterprise Zones.'" *The Baltimore Sun*, January 24, 2013. Accessed February 25, 2018, from www.baltimoresun.com/health/bs-md-health-enterprise-20130124-story.html.

25 Sabrina Tavernise. "Health Problems Take Root in a West Baltimore Neighborhood that is Sick of Neglect." *New York Times*, April 29, 2015. Accessed February 28, 2017 from www.nytimes.com/2015/04/30/us/health-problems-take-root-in-a-west-baltimore-neighborhood-that-is-sick-of-neglect.html?hp&action=click&pgtype=Homepage&module=b-lede-package-region&region=top-news&WT.nav=top-news&_r=0.

26 Bill Graves. "Portland-Area Native Americans Burdened by Health Hurdles Generation after Generation." *The Oregonian*, May 2, 2013. Accessed February 28, 2017 from www.oregonlive.com/health/index.ssf/2012/05/portlands_native_americans_wag.html.

27 James W. Collins Jr., Richard J. David, Arden Handler, Stephen Wall, and Steven Andes. "Very Low Birthweight in African American Infants: The Role of Maternal Exposure to Interpersonal Racial Discrimination." *American Journal of Public Health* 94, no. 12 (2004): 2132–2138.

28 National Center for Education Statistics. Table 219.70 "Percentage of High School Dropout among Persons 16 to 24 Years Old (Status Dropout Rate), by Sex, Race/Ethnicity: Selected Years, 1960 through 2014." *Digest of Education Statistics.* Accessed March 2, 2017 from https://nces.ed.gov/programs/digest/d15/tables/dt15_219.70.asp.

29 See Ana Beatriz Cholo. "Latino Dropout Rate Called 'Crisis.'" *Chicago Tribune*, January 8, 2004. Accessed March 17, 2018 from http://articles.chicagotribune.com/2004-01-08/news/0401080381_1_dropout-rate-dropout-problem-hispanic-dropout; Antonio Lujan. "Rise in Latino Dropout Rate." ABC News Salt Lake City, November 15, 2011; Silvia Struthers. "Hispanic Dropout Rate Raises Concern in Houston." *Houston Chronicle*, May 26, 2012. Accessed March 2, 2017 from www.chron.com/news/houston-texas/article/Houston-s-Hispanics-dropping-out-of-school-at-3587972.php.

30 Erika Hayasaki. "'It's Like You're Climbing Everest': Eleven Boys thought They'd Leave High School as They Entered It – Together – on Graduation Day. It Wasn't That Simple." Series: The Vanishing Class, Third of Four Parts. *Los Angeles Times*, February 3, 2006. Accessed March 13, 2018 from http://articles.latimes.com/2006/feb/03/local/me-dropout3.

31 John Logan. "Whose Schools Are Failing?" Russell Sage Foundation and Brown University, July 25, 2011. Accessed March 17, 2018 from https://s4.ad.brown.edu/Projects/Diversity/Data/Report/report5.pdf.

32 Jonathan Kozol. *The Shame of the Nation: The Restoration of Apartheid Schooling in America*. New York, NY: Crown Publishing, 2005.

33 Robert Balfanz and Nettie Legters. "Graduation Rate Crisis: We Know What Can Be Done About It." *Education Week*, July 12, 2006.

34 Ibid.; Gary Orfield, John T. Yun, and Civil Rights Project (Harvard University). *Resegregation in American Schools*. Cambridge, MA: Civil Rights Project, Harvard University, 1999.

35 Robert Balfanz, Liza Herzog, and Douglas J. Mac Iver. "Preventing Student Disengagement and Keeping Students on the Graduation Path in Urban Middle-Grade Schools: Early Identification and Effective Interventions." *Educational Psychologist* 42, no. 4 (2007): 223–235.

36 Kozol, *The Shame of the Nation*; Logan, "Whose Schools Are Failing?".

37 Duke Helfand. "A Formula for Failure in L. A. Public Schools." Series: Vanishing Class, Fourth of Four Parts. *Los Angeles Times*, January 30, 2006. Accessed March 13, 2018 from www.latimes.com/local/la-me-dropout30jan30-story.html.

38 Laura Sullivan. "Behind the Bail Bond System." National Public Radio. Three-part series. Aired January 21–22, 2010. Accessed March 8, 2017 from www.npr.org/series/122954677/behind-the-bail-bond-system.

39 Bureau of Justice Statistics. Table 3. "Number of Confirmed Inmates in Local Jails, by Characteristics, Midyear 2000, 2005 and 2010–2014; Yearend 2015." December 2016. Accessed March 9, 2017 from www.bjs.gov/content/pub/pdf/ji15.pdf.

40 Sukey Lewis. "New Bill Aims to Stop Charging Parents of Incarcerated Kids." KQED Radio, aired March 8, 2017. Accessed March 9, 2017 from https://ww2.kqed.org/news/2017/03/09/new-bill-aims-to-stop-charging-parents-of-incarcerated-kids/.

41 Deborah A. Cohen et al. "The Paradox of Parks in Low-Income Areas: Park Use and Perceived Threats." *Environmental Behavior* 48, no. 1 (January 2016): 230–245.

42 Alisa Chang. "For City Teens, Stop-and-Frisk is Black and White." WNYC News, Aired May 29, 2012. Accessed March 7, 2017 from www.wnyc.org/story/212460-city-teenagers-say-stop-and-frisk-all-about-race-and-class/.

43 Cindy D. Kam and Carl. L. Palmer. "Reconsidering the Effects of Education on Political Participation." *The Journal of Politics* 70, no. 3 (2008): 612–631.

44 Daphne Koinis Mitchell. "Asthma and School Functioning in Children: Still More Work to Do." *Brown University Child and Adolescent Behavior Letter*, September 1, 2015.

45 Emily Goldmann, Allison Aiello, Monica Uddin, Jorge Delva, Karestan Koenen, Larry M. Gant, and Sandro Galea. "Pervasive Exposure to Violence and Posttraumatic Stress Disorder in a Predominantly African American Urban Community: The Detroit Neighborhood Health Study." *Journal of Traumatic Stress* 24, no. 6 (December 2011): 747–751. doi: 10.1002/jts.20705.

7

THE OPPORTUNITY INDEX

Sally Lehrman and Venise Wagner

This chapter provides journalists with tools to quantify disparity and deepen their under-standing of the ways in which opportunity emerges and grows in some communities, while it declines in others. The authors discuss how to use various online sites and tools for in-depth reporting. They also provide a detailed guide to calculating an independent Opportunity Index by neighborhood.

Soon after the collapse of the housing market in 2007, the *New York Times* ran an article based on a study from NYU's Furman Center for Real Estate and Urban Policy that showed a disparity in the types of mortgage loans that black people and Latinos received compared to whites.[1] People living in predominately black and Latino neighborhoods were more likely to get subprime mortgage loans – that is, with less favorable terms and higher interest rates – than those living in predominately white neighborhoods. Such loans are designed for those less likely to qualify for better loans due to unemployment, bankruptcy, or other financial problems, yet these subprime loans often went to people in areas with comparable median incomes and who could have qualified for better terms.

This excellent piece of reporting made an important link between race and banking policy. In one of many follow-ups, the author, Manny Fernandez, showed the real-life consequences by going to a neighborhood in Jamaica, Queens that had experienced the highest rate of foreclosure in New York.[2] Before the housing bubble burst, it was an up-and-coming working-class neighborhood. As foreclosures mounted, gains in areas such as neighborhood safety began to reverse.

The reporter wrote powerful stories by quantifying the disparity in mortgage lending, then demonstrating the impact on real people's lives. In this chapter we offer some examples of indices that you can use to unpack disparity and the contributing factors in a particular geographic location and compare it to other areas. We also introduce you to our Opportunity Index method, which will allow you to quantify disparity, place the numbers in context, and clearly show the human impact. By using these tools, a reporter can discover and illuminate the interacting forces behind disparity on any beat.

Accumulation/Disaccumulation

The authors of Chapter 3 explain durable inequality – that is, the uneven social and financial investment that has been placed in racialized, segregated communities and that compounds, both positively and negatively, over the years. White people, they show, generally have had a wide range of economic, social, and political opportunities made available to them in their communities. African Americans and other racial minority groups, however, historically have had far fewer. Examples include unequal spending allocations to public transportation, discriminatory labor markets, and favoritism in access to home loans. These gaps in opportunity interact and worsen over time. The lack of investment in isolated neighborhoods reaps further inattention: the city neglects maintenance of streets and parks, business investment declines, and local taxes fail to provide adequate school funding. Over time, segregation confers a lasting, harmful legacy. Quantifying this process can help audiences understand why some minority neighborhoods never recover from decades of disenfranchisement.

We propose three approaches to strengthening your reporting on such disparity. One is to use individual indicators within a metropolitan area or community, such as access to neighborhood grocery stores that sell fresh fruits and vegetables. Another method, which can provide a richer picture, would be to use existing indices that have been developed to highlight a particular area of opportunity, such as health, education, or jobs. Many times an index designed to shine light on one topic has broader uses because of the interacting nature of social and living conditions. The third method involves constructing your own index by using a combination of indicators to compare neighborhoods within a community.

Great Tools for Finding Indicators

Journalists are lucky because, today, social scientists and think tanks across the country are quantifying the link between opportunity and outcomes. Many of the tools they've created provide reporters with important insights that help reveal the impact of disparity within specific communities. Some, like Census Reporter,[3] are designed specifically for journalists and provide a means to slice and dice data from a single source – in this case, the rich resources of the US Census. Others, such as the Equity Atlas and Justice Atlas, offer data on a select set of indicators or integrate that data to help users gain insights on a particular problem. Below is a sampling of tools you can use, with more listed in the Resources chapter.

Toolbox

Census Reporter: http://censusreporter.org/

Created by and for journalists, this site serves as a how-to guide and tool for using the American Community Survey (ACS), collected by the US Census Bureau. The ACS is gathered every year from US households on a rotating basis, covering a small percentage of households overall and hitting each one no more than once every five years. It contains richly detailed socio-economic information – much more than the basic 10-year census. The Census Bureau aggregates results in one-year and five-year estimates of community characteristics across demographic, economic, social, and housing features, providing them at many geographic levels. Census Reporter will hold your hand through the maze. Once you choose the geographic area, Census Reporter automatically serves up the best data to use, taking into account a balance of accuracy and currency. For smaller communities, the longer period estimates are more accurate even though they are less current.

As you use this data, it's important to remember that the ACS reflects responses from each day of the year, rather than a single point in time such as a day, period, or year. As a result, you need to be careful with the data. The estimates won't reveal seasonal fluctuations in populations in a college community, for instance, or one that draws summer residents from colder climes. For the five-year estimate, you won't be able to see the impact of a big, point-in-time event such as a hurricane or earthquake. In deciding whether to go with short- or long-term estimates, decide whether you want currency (one-year) or precision (longer).

This tool gives you a warning when you should be cautious with the data because of a large potential for error. You can also search by topic or ACS table, such as this one on commute data, "B08013: Aggregate Travel Time to Work (In Minutes) of Workers by Sex," and see examples of the questions asked.[4] With Census Reporter, you can compare the lived experiences, demographics, and other aspects of one community to another, or look for patterns in an individual community.

Community Commons: www.communitycommons.org/maps-data/

Community Commons is designed to help nonprofits, government agencies, and community members investigate health disparities and share their work. Despite the health emphasis, any reporter will likely find the tools useful because they focus on the social determinants of health, which encompass all aspects of well-being. "You can't lead a healthy life if these things around you are broken," explains Andrea Waner, communications manager for the Institute for People, Place and Possibility, a nonprofit that founded the site. Waner suggests that you start by creating a report on disparities at the county level through their Community Health Needs Assessment tool. Then you can break the results down by demographic subcategories such as race or education, and also by indicators such as environmental factors or clinical outcomes.

You also might pull up a Location Opportunity or Vulnerable Populations Footprint Map to identify geographic areas of particular opportunity or vulnerability, then run an indicator report to investigate further. You can use the site to explore questions or build new insights. One reporter, for instance, used the tool to understand why so many people in her area, which was replete with hospitals, medical schools, and other medical services, did not have access to a primary care provider. The site incorporates 300 topics and more than 20,000 data layers, many going down to the zip code level, with county data the most robust. Topics run across multiple dimensions of social and living conditions, such as climate, completed streets, food production, the gender pay gap, opioids, education, internet access, migration, and so on. The data comes from more than 100 sources including the Behavioral Risk Factor Surveillance System, Center for Agriculture, and the IRS. You can build your own reports and maps, and look at materials others have built.

Diversity Data: http://diversitydata.org/anddiversitydatakids.org

Created by the Heller School for Social Policy and Engagement at Brandeis University, this tool focuses on the intersection of health equity with education, employment, and housing opportunities. It uses over 100 measures within eight topic areas that describe quality of life overall: demographics, education, economic opportunity, housing, neighborhoods, crime, physical environment, and health. There's even a measure of the concentration of power wielded by governments within a metro region. You can view rankings or maps by topic, or pull up a profile of a particular metro area and compare it to others. The site is robust, allowing you to create maps and tables and pull down data to crunch on your own. Reports provided on the data may suggest avenues for further exploration, such as one on changing racial segregation for black and Latino children and its impact on educational and health opportunities. Diversitydatakids.org, created by the Heller School in collaboration with the Kirwan Institute at Ohio State University, provides similar data with a focus on children. You can search at a variety of levels: state, metropolitan area, county, large city, and large school district. Data is from multiple sources, include federal agencies, the US Census, state agencies, and academic analyses of agency data.

Justice Atlas for Sentencing and Corrections: www.justiceatlas.org/

This atlas describes the residential distribution of people who have entered prison, re-entered their communities from prison, or are living under parole or probation. Maps, with underlying data, show spatial patterns at state, county, municipal, zip code, and census tract levels. US Census data-based charts give context in areas including median household income, race and ethnicity, single-parent households, and unemployment. You can click on a region and compare it to others across each dimension. For example, in Florida, Gadsden County has the highest parolee rate of the state (0.97 people per 1,000 adults), the third-highest prison releases rate (8.26) and the fourth-highest probationer rate (19.13). Also in Gadsden, nearly a third of the population lives with income under $25,000, 67 percent are nonwhite, and 24 percent are single-parent households. A reporter could look closely at high-incarceration neighborhoods within the county and the associated challenges in schools, health-care delivery, employment, and safety. Criminal justice data for this tool was provided by relevant departments of corrections, parole, and probations. Be sure to consult the "About the Data" section to understand both the value and the limitations of the results you see. Also understand that not all regions are covered.

National Equity Atlas: http://nationalequityatlas.org/

Built by a partnership between PolicyLink and the USC Program for Environmental and Regional Equity, the National Equity Atlas serves up data from a mix of public and private sources with the goal of showing economic opportunity in a community by race, ethnicity, ancestry, and nativity. The database uses three categories of indicators: "economic vitality," including wages, unemployment, income inequality; "readiness," including a skilled workforce and an educated, healthy population; and "connectedness," which describes affordable housing, commute times and access to a car, and neighborhood poverty. You'll find data for the 100 largest US cities, 150 largest metro regions, 50 states and the United States as a whole. Poke around and test out some of the indicators in your area and see if the results spark story ideas. For instance, a search on schools in Atlanta, Georgia, will show that more than one-quarter of white and Asian/Pacific Island children attend public schools with low levels of poverty, compared with about 13 percent of Native Americans and 10 percent of black children, according to the National Center for Education Statistics. On the other hand, 62 percent of black students and 23 percent of Native Americans attend public schools with high levels of poverty, compared to 2.5 percent of whites. How might such racial and economic isolation across schools affect students' abilities to succeed in a diverse workforce? What supports do the low-poverty schools provide that elude children from lesser-resourced institutions? Review the Atlas's policy suggestions to get started on reporting about the policies and practices that lead to the data you see. Don't be put off by the advocacy bent of this site – instead, set aside the strong perspective it takes and rely on your own analysis. Do be careful about citing the data, however, because even though methods are carefully described, there is no margin of error shown and neither are actual population numbers or proportions. The Equity Atlas shows data from both public and private entities, with the Integrated Public Use Microdata Series from the US Census as its primary source.

Opportunity Index: http://opportunitynation.org

This interactive tool allows you to assess conditions that underlie economic and educational opportunity in your county and compare these to conditions in other counties, including a cluster of peers, or those in the state and nation. It includes indicators across four dimensions: economy (e.g., median household income, access to banking services, broadband internet subscription); education (e.g., children in preschool, on-time high school graduation); community (e.g., volunteering, voter registration, access to primary health care, grocery stores, incarceration rate); and health (e.g., health insurance coverage, deaths related to alcohol, drugs, or suicide). There are aggregate scores for each dimension, plus data on each individual indicator. The tool also provides other indices, including business diversity, industry growth rate, and the probability of automation across local industries. Graphs show job skills in demand, those in supply, and themes in news coverage associated with the four opportunity dimensions, including positive or negative sentiment. In McKinley County, New Mexico, for example, the overall opportunity score is 25. Its health score is 17.5, compared with 40.1 for the entire state. One-third of the population lacks health insurance and the age-adjusted rate of deaths due to alcohol, drugs, or suicide is 50.9 per 100,000 people. This compares to Los Alamos County, which has an opportunity score of 65.2 and a health score of 56.4. In Los Alamos, only 5.8 percent of the population lacks health insurance and the death rate from alcohol poisoning, drug abuse, or suicide is 29.3. In McKinley County, home to a portion of the Navajo Nation, three-quarters of the population is Native American. In Los Alamos, the same portion is white.

The site also delivers maps of opportunity by county, based on each indicator. You can quickly spot the counties across the nation with the best access to broadband internet, for example, or with high numbers of youth not in school and not working. Data is drawn from the US Census Bureau, US Bureau of Labor Statistics, US Department of Justice, and the Centers for Disease Control and Prevention, as well as the consulting firm PwC and Monster.com, and covers 2016 and 2017. Check out the technical supplement for an excellent description of each indicator and the methodology overall. Opportunity Nation is a bipartisan coalition of more than 350 organizations such as the American Association of Community Colleges, AARP, Boys and Girls Club of America, Points of Light, and Year Up. The group focuses on educational opportunity and economic mobility for young people, no matter their zip code.

Other Sites to Explore

There are also advocacy-oriented sites that provide data on racial equity indicators, usually by state (www.racecounts.org/issues/). They can be helpful resources to track such indicators and gather story ideas. Check the source of the data and confirm the numbers for yourself before using it. Foundations and states also produce targeted data resources, such as the Annie E. Casey Foundation's Kids Count Data Center (https://datacenter.kidscount.org/), the California Healthy Places Index (http://healthyplacesindex.org/map/), Connecticut Health Equity Index (www.cadh.org/health-equity-index/), and the multiple data sources provided by Minneapolis agencies on areas such as environmental public health and child well-being (www.health.state.mn.us/divs/chs/genstats/heda/Demographics.html).

Statistics Basics

Apply a few cautions when using these or similar tools. First, look very closely at the origin of the data you're using. Is it a reliable source? Use the same skepticism about a source of data as you would any other source of information. Second, consider how reliable the data itself may be. Check the margin of error. If you're comparing two numbers with an overlapping margin of error, then you're looking at two numbers that may be exactly the same. Say you are reporting on student achievement. Based on a sampling of student report cards in a large school, a study finds that the average GPA of Latino students is 3.8, while the average GPA of white students is 4.0. You learn that the margin of error for both numbers is 0.2. There's no reason to report that there is any difference at all. The smaller the sample size, the larger the margin of error is likely to be.

Correlation

In another common misstep, when we see a trend or pattern among community measures, we may tend to jump to the conclusion that they are related. Instead, we must investigate further to understand what is causing that pattern, if anything. Tyler Vigen, a consultant at Boston Consulting and former military analyst, wrote a program to spot spurious correlations in public data and came up with some examples that should give you pause. For example, between 1999 and 2009, the period in which he did his analysis, trends in US spending on science, space, and technology correlated nearly perfectly with the number of suicides by hanging, strangulation, and suffocation. The divorce rate in Maine correlated with per capita consumption of margarine. The up-and-down trend of the number of letters in the Scripps National Spelling Bee's winning word rose and fell in near-perfect tandem with the number of people killed by venomous spiders.[5] As you can see, just because two things often occur simultaneously, or one occurs before the other, doesn't mean that one *caused* the other.

On the other hand, correlations are an important tool used in science in order to explore potential causality. For example, a study in the highly regarded journal *Environmental Health Perspectives* investigated connections between the quality of the built environment and birth outcomes.[6] Environmental health scientists examined more than 50 variables on residential tax parcels in Durham, North Carolina, compiling them into seven indices of built environment features including housing damage, crime, and property disorder such as high weeds, garbage, and discarded furniture. They found that five of the indices – housing damage, property disorder, tenure, vacancies, and nuisance count – were associated with poor outcomes such as preterm births and low birth weight. After statistically adjusting for race, age, education, and other factors, housing damage stood out in statistically significant association with poor birth outcomes.

While it doesn't prove causation, this study indeed "suggests a robust relationship between the quality of the built environment and birth outcomes," as the authors wrote. When looking at apparent relationships or links between data, rule out other possible explanations for the connection, as these scientists did. Check the strength of the relationship. Are there multiple correlations that point in the same direction? A plausible biological or behavioral route to the outcome?

Check the Context

Reporters who want to write with accuracy and impact also should be very clear on context before applying single indicators to a community. Offer information to show the complexity of the situation and preclude stereotyping and stigma. For example, black unemployment in 2018 reached an all-time low. Yet one could still find 10 percent unemployment – more than twice the national average – in some majority Latino or Asian American communities. This might prompt some to assume hopeless circumstances or even a lack of ambition. In fact, it's likely an outcome of many things such as a lack of job training, few companies opening businesses, few tax incentives for job creation, or poor transportation links to major employers and business and service centers.[7] Or the explanation might simply be that most residents are college students or retirees. Similarly, if a reporter describes a white or Asian American community as highly educated without providing further context, she risks perpetuating the belief that these racial groups are somehow smarter or more diligent than others. It would be misleading simply to use high unemployment or high education levels as shorthand to describe any community and its characteristics. Use the indicators as avenues to explore in reporting, not as labels.

Here's a concrete example. In the city of Berkeley, California, we find high rates of poverty in the west part of the city and near the University of California. We also see high rates of unemployment and underemployment in those same areas. In the area near the university, these community characteristics are associated with student populations. But in pockets further from the university, these high rates of unemployment and underemployment are experienced by adults who have less education than students striving for college degrees. Despite showing high measures of poverty, these students have great opportunity. As we can see, then, a high-poverty rate in some pockets of West Berkeley means a different thing than a high-poverty rate in others. A closer look also might reveal rich bus routes and student-serving businesses close to the university, with a paucity of transportation and other community-enhancing features further away.

Creating Your Own Index of Opportunity

You might find it especially fruitful to develop your own index. While the tools created by the organizations above can offer a particular lens through which to understand disparity, often their indicators are limited to the organization's area of concern, or to metropolitan areas rather than neighborhoods within an area. Creating your own index could provide you with a deeper understanding of the negative accumulative effects of a lack of opportunity at the neighborhood level. It could also help you see how these individual indicators interact with each other.

Below we walk you through the steps needed to develop your own index, based primarily on US Census data. We'll use other sources as well. As we described, the Census Bureau collects different types of data. In the Decennial Census, census takers go to each home and even on the street, recording the names of individuals living there and some basic information about them. This is a direct head count of all the people in the United States, regardless of housing or immigration status.[8] In addition, the bureau collects data every day of the year as part of the ACS. This data, which includes far more questions than the Census,[9] is released in estimates for one-year and five-year periods, and also in supplemental estimates (the three-year estimate was discontinued in 2015).[10] The ACS gives you a random sampling of people living in a particular geographic area. The five-year dataset, of course, is a larger sampling than the one-year dataset. And for this reason, the one-year dataset has a higher margin of error for smaller geographic areas.[11,12]

Each of these datasets – the five-year and one-year community surveys – can be analyzed at various geographic levels: US, state, county, Congressional districts, zip codes, census tract levels, block levels, and school districts. If you want to look at and compare opportunity in specific neighborhoods, census tracts and zip codes are the best geographic spaces to use. We'll use both for the index. Some neighborhoods have more than one census tract and other neighborhoods include a fraction of a census tract. If your neighborhood is a fraction of a census tract, then use the corresponding proportion for your total numbers. For example, if a quarter of your census tract is included in your neighborhood, only take a quarter of that corresponding number. Also, some zip codes encompass more than one neighborhood. But for now, we'll move forward with the census tracts.

When creating your own index for a neighborhood, it is best to use the five-year ACS dataset. It will be more current than the Decennial Census, and also have the lowest margin of error for the census tracts, which are relatively small geographic areas. To find the ACS go to www.factfinder.census.gov

Your index will consist of 20 indicators categorized under four areas: Wealth/Income/Employment; Community; Voice; Second Chances/Safety Net. These areas represent social determinants that are often interwoven and influence each other, and when looked at together can paint a full picture of what's happening to a geographic area. You can organize it this way in an Excel file. See Figure 7.1.

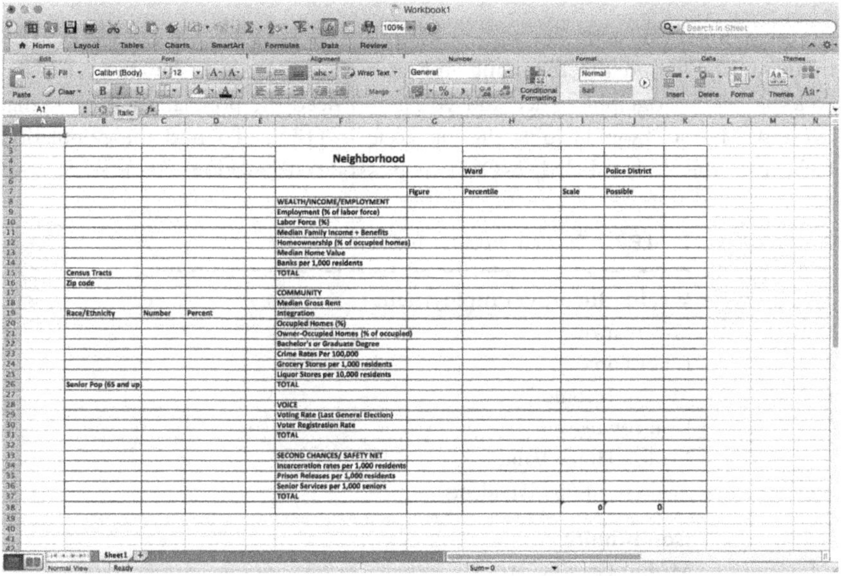

FIGURE 7.1 Excel File for Data Collection

For now we'll start the process with a simple table, which you can start on an Excel file. See Table 7.1.

Notice that we are counting homeownership twice, once each in two different categories, therefore we're weighting it more heavily than other indicators. We see homeownership as a significant indicator that demonstrates individual and community wealth *and* community and social cohesion. Homeownership helps provide the glue – the stability – that keeps communities strong.[13]

To build our index, let's use Jackson Heights in Queens, New York. Go to the American FactFinder site (www.factfinder.census.gov) to begin our search for our core indicators at the neighborhood level. Use data from the latest five-year ACS.

The census tracts for Jackson Heights are 281, 283, and 285. The following indicators will be easily found there:

- Employment
- Labor Force
- Median Income
- Homeownership
- Median Home Value
- Median Gross Rents
- Occupied Homes
- Owner-Occupied Homes
- Bachelor's or Graduate Degrees.

By using AmericanFactfinder and clicking on INDUSTRY CODES – NAICS Industry, you'll find the following indicators. For this data, you must use zip codes as your geographic space and you'll also need the population size for that zip code. For Jackson Heights the zip code is 11372. To find the population we'll use the link labeled 5-Digit Zip Code Tabulation Area – 860 of

TABLE 7.1 20 Indicators for Index

Wealth/Income/Employment
Employment
Labor Force
Median Income
Homeownership
Median Home Value
Banks per 1,000 Residents

Community
Median Gross Rent
Integration
Occupied Homes
Owner-Occupied Homes
Bachelor's or Graduate Degree
Crime Rates per 100,000 Residents
Grocery Stores per 1,000 Residents
Liquor Stores per 10,000 Residents

Voice
Voting Rate (Last General Election)
Voter Registration Rate

Second Chances/Safety Net
Incarceration Rates per 1,000 Residents
Prison Release per 1,000 Residents
Senior Services per 1,000 Seniors
Child and Youth Services per 1,000 Youth

geographic areas on the census. If your neighborhood has more than one zip code and is a fraction of each, you'll need to adjust the population size by taking the correct proportion of the zip code area. For example, if your neighborhood is one quarter of the zip code area, then you would divide the population size by a quarter. The same follows with the number of banking institutions, senior centers, etc. For the industry codes we'll use the link labeled 5-Digit Zip Code – 861 to find the number of businesses in each commercial code. The population in Jackson Heights' zip code is 66,636. The following are the industry codes that we'll use in the index.

- Banking – Commercial Banking, Code: 522110
- Grocery Stores – Supermarkets and other grocery, Code: 445110
- Liquor Stores – Retail Trade – Beer, wine and liquor stores, Code: 445310
- Senior Services – Services for elderly and persons with disabilities, Code: 624120
- Child and Youth Services – Code: 624110.

Banking, grocery stores, senior services, youth services are measured per 1,000 residents. Liquor store density is measured per 10,000 residents. There are 19 banks in this zip code. To calculate per 1,000 we're going to first divide the population in this zip code by 1,000.

$$\textbf{(number of banks} \div \textbf{population)} \times \textbf{1,000}$$
$$19/66,636 = 0.000286 \times 1,000 = 0.29$$

This is the rate of the presence of these institutions in the neighborhood. Insert the number in the index. Using the same formula, calculate the number for grocery stores, senior services, youth services. For liquor stores, instead of dividing the population total by 1,000, you will now divide by 10,000. For Jackson Heights, there are 12 liquor stores. So here's the math.

$$\textbf{(liquor stores} \div \textbf{population)} \times \textbf{10,000}$$
$$(12 \div 66,636) \times 10,000 = 1.80$$

Now let's calculate youth services. For this we need the population of youth under 25 in our census tracts. Follow the same formula we used for senior services.

Violent crime rates, which are measured per 100,000 residents, can be found locally through your police department by precinct, ward, or parish. Jackson Heights is the 115th precinct, where the violent crime rate at the time the stat was pulled was 550.78 per 100,000 residents. When pulling this stat make sure to use total violent crime, which consists of murder, rape, robbery, and aggravated assault.

Voting rates and the voting registration rates can be gathered from the local office of elections. Some offices may have the voting rate of the last general election, while others may not have it. At the time this index was done, New

York did not have voting rates available for the last general election. It did have the voting registration rate, though. You can collect updated incarceration rates and parole or release rates at the county level from your state department of corrections.

So now your index should look like this in a spreadsheet such as Excel. (See Table 7.2.)

TABLE 7.2 Indicators for Jackson Heights, Queens, New York

WEALTH/INCOME/EMPLOYMENT	
Employment (% of labor force)	93.92
Labor Force (%)	71.23
Median Family Income + Benefits	61,111.00
Homeownership (% of occupied homes)	37.50
Median Home Value	270,400.00
Banks per 1,000 residents	0.29
COMMUNITY	
Median Gross Rent	1,149.00
Integration	74
Occupied Homes (%)	94.00
Owner-Occupied Homes (% of occupied)	37.50
Bachelor's or Graduate Degree	34.59
Violent Crime Rates per 100,000 Residents	550.78
Grocery Stores per 1,000 Residents	0.95
Liquor Stores per 10,000 Residents	1.80
VOICE	
Voting Rate (Last General Election)	N/A
Voter Registration Rate	39.57
SECOND CHANCES/SAFETY NET	
Incarceration Rates per 1,000 Residents	0.58
Prison Releases per 1,000 Residents	0.24
Senior Services per 1,000 Seniors	0.12
Youth Services per 1,000 Youth	0.07

Measuring Segregation/Integration

The final number to include in the index measures integration. Before we explain how to calculate that number, you need to first understand how sociologists assess residential segregation. The dissimilarity index is the most common tool to measure segregation within a metropolitan community. If you are in a metropolitan area with a variety of racial and ethnic groups, then you will only be able to measure dissimilarity by looking at two groups at a time, say whites and Asians, whites and blacks, or whites and Latinos, etc. We'll walk through this option, then show how you can pull it all together.

To measure dissimilarity between blacks and whites in a metropolitan area, we first have to identify the population of blacks and whites by ward or district. To illustrate this, we'll look at the fictional metropolitan area of Winston. Winston has four wards with a total population of 240.

This is the calculation we'll be using to measure the dissimilarity in the metropolitan area.

$$D = 0.5 \; SUM \, | \; (b_i \div B) - (w_i \div W) \, |$$

We'll start with Ward 1.

b_i = black population in ward 1 = 5
B = total black population in all wards = 115
w_i = white population in ward 1 = 80
W = total white population in all wards = 125
$|\;|$ = an absolute value. Anything between those bars means that we consider the number without regard to its sign. That is, any negative figures become positive. So if the result is -0.12, the absolute value would be 0.12.

Using the numbers above, the formula looks like this.

$$\textbf{Ward 1} = ((5 \div 115) - (80 \div 125)) = 0.60$$

Now we'll move onto the remaining wards.

$$\textbf{Ward 2} = ((10 \div 115) - (30 \div 125)) = 0.15$$
$$\textbf{Ward 3} = ((20 \div 115) - (10 \div 125)) = 0.09$$
$$\textbf{Ward 4} = ((80 \div 115) - (5 \div 125)) = 0.66$$

The next step is to add up all the wards, then multiply by 0.5.

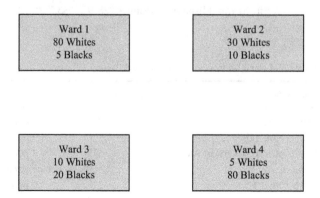

FIGURE 7.2 Population of Fictional Winston

$$D = 0.5 \; |(0.60) + (0.15) + (0.09) + (0.66)|$$
$$D = 0.5 \; |1.5|$$
$$D = 0.75$$

The scale for the index is 0–100, with 100 meaning that you'd have to move around 100 percent of the people to get racial evenness. In our example, we get a total of 0.75 x 100. So the index for Winston is 75, meaning that you'd have to move 75 percent of residents to get an even distribution of whites and blacks.

This is a very illuminating number, but again, the formula is a bit limited in that it only gives you an idea of how segregated a metropolitan area is across two racial groups. How do we measure a smaller geographic area and how do we account for the fact that many neighborhoods are not simply binary black/white, Asian/white, etc. Chris Bettinger, a professor of sociology at San Francisco State University, developed a formula that helps us accomplish both goals. He calls this "area dissimilarity." He also helped us invert this number. Instead of looking at the deficit of a neighborhood – the segregation of a neighborhood – we wanted to measure the gain or benefit of the community that is integrated. We'll call this "area integration." Area integration looks at proportionality of each of the racial and ethnic groups within one geographic area.

To get to area integration you'll need to collect the population of each group within your neighborhoods or census tracts. For Jackson Heights, the breakdown looks like this (see Table 7.3).

We will also need the breakdown for New York as a whole. It looks like this (see Table 7.4).

Here is the formula for area integration:

Area Integration = 100 − (0.5 (SUM | percentgroup$_i$ in neighborhood − percent group$_i$ in city|)

For Jackson Heights the calculation looks like this:

Latino/Hispanic = 53.2 − 29.2 = 24
White (Non-Hispanic) Alone = 28.9 − 33.7 = 4.8

TABLE 7.3 Neighborhood Racial Breakdown

Race/Ethnicity	Population A	Percent A
Latino/Hispanic	8,967	53.2 percent
White Non-Hispanic Alone	4,876	28.9 percent
Black/African American Alone	325	1.9 percent
Asian Alone	2,419	14.3 percent
Some Other Race Alone	278	1.6 percent
Total	16,865	100.0 percent

TABLE 7.4 Metro Area Racial Breakdown

Race/Ethnicity	Population B	Percent B
Latino/Hispanic	2,371,116	29.2 percent
White (Non-Hispanic) Alone	2,734,318	33.7 percent
Black or African American Alone	1,877,183	23.1 percent
Asian Alone	1,069,960	13.2 percent
Some Other Race Alone	66,078	0.8 percent
Total	8,118,655	100 percent

(Remember we're using the absolute number, so no negatives.)
Black or African American Alone = 1.9 − 23.1 = 21.2
Asian Alone = 14.3 − 13.2 = 1.1
Some Other Race Alone = 1.6 − 0.8 = 0.8
Area Integration = 100 − (0.5|24 + 4.8 + 21.1 + 1.1 + 0.8|)
Area Integration = 100 − (0.5|51.8|)
Area Integration = 100 − 25.9 = 74.1

Integration for Jackson Heights is 74 percent.

The Scale

Each one of these indicators must now be translated into a common scale that will allow us to add up the numbers and come to a final index number. To do this we must develop quintiles for each of the indicators. In this step, we divide each indicator into five groups, each representing 20 percent of the whole, making comparisons easier and forming the foundation of our scale. Some quintiles already have been calculated by think tanks that do these calculations all the time. For example, the Tax Policy Center calculates income distribution every year. You can find this table here: www.taxpolicy center.org/statistics/household-income-quintiles. Other indicators you'll have to calculate yourself. This is a very easy step. We'll use occupied housing as an example. To do this we need to get an idea of the range of the percent occupied housing by state plus Washington DC. Using the US Census we can gather the data easily (See Table 7.5).

On the low end we see that Maine has the lowest percentage of occupied housing units with 76.7 percent, while Iowa has the highest with 91.5 percent. To determine quintiles we have to examine the range of numbers and dived them into five parts – 20th, 40th, 60th, 80th, and 100th percentile. We determine quintiles using the following formula.

TABLE 7.5 Quintile for Occupied Housing Nationwide

Case Number	State	% Occupied Housing Units
1	Maine	76.7 percent
2	Florida	79.5 percent
3	Vermont	79.6 percent
4	Alaska	82.1 percent
5	Delaware	82.3 percent
6	Arizona	82.9 percent
7	South Carolina	83.1 percent
8	Montana	83.9 percent
9	New Hampshire	84.2 percent
10	West Virginia	84.2 percent
11	Alabama	84.4 percent
12	Michigan	84.4 percent
13	New Mexico	84.4 percent
14	Wyoming	84.7 percent
15	Nevada	84.8 percent
16	Mississippi	85.2 percent
17	North Carolina	85.4 percent
18	Arkansas	85.5 percent
19	Georgia	85.9 percent
20	Hawaii	86.1 percent
21	Idaho	86.5 percent
22	Louisiana	86.5 percent
23	Oklahoma	86.5 percent
24	Missouri	87.0 percent
25	Wisconsin	87.1 percent
26	Tennessee	87.7 percent
27	Kentucky	87.8 percent
28	Texas	88.2 percent
29	Washington, DC	88.4 percent
30	South Dakota	88.4 percent
31	North Dakota	88.5 percent
32	Indiana	88.6 percent
33	Rhode Island	88.7 percent
34	Ohio	88.9 percent
35	Colorado	89.0 percent
36	Pennsylvania	89.1 percent
37	New York	89.2 percent

(Continued)

TABLE 7.5 (Cont.)

Case Number	State	% Occupied Housing Units
38	New Jersey	89.4 percent
39	Virginia	89.4 percent
40	Minnesota	89.5 percent
41	Utah	89.7 percent
42	Kansas	89.9 percent
43	Maryland	89.9 percent
44	Massachusetts	90.1 percent
45	Illinois	90.2 percent
46	Oregon	90.4 percent
47	Nebraska	90.7 percent
48	Washington	90.7 percent
49	Connecticut	91.2 percent
50	California	91.4 percent
51	Iowa	91.5 percent

$$(n+1) \times \text{percentile}$$

Here, n is the number of cases we have – 50 states plus Washington, DC. We'll start with the 20th percentile.

$$(51+1) \times .20 = 10.4$$

We now want the divide line between the 10th and 11th case. In this instance we'll split the difference between 84.2 (West Virginia) and 84.4 (Alabama). The first quintile (or the 20th percentile) is 84.3.

Using the same formula for the remaining quintiles we get:

$$84.3$$
$$86.3$$
$$88.5$$
$$89.8$$

So the increments look like this.

First Quintile: 76.7–84.3
Second Quintile: 84.5–86.3
Third Quintile: 86.4–88.5
Fourth Quintile: 88.6–89.8
Fifth Quintile: 89.9–91.5

We're using a scale of 1 to 5 with five being the highest and best value (see Table 7.6).

TABLE 7.6 Five-Point Scale

Quintile	Scale
First	1
Second	2
Third	3
Fourth	4
Fifth	5

Follow this step for each of your indicators. To get a jump-start, you can also use the scales available in Appendix 7A at the end of this chapter.

After completing this process for each indicator, the scale for our final index number follows:

77–95: Great Opportunity (100th percentile)
58–76: Good Opportunity (80th percentile)
39–57: Some Opportunity (60th percentile)
20–38: Declining Opportunity (40th percentile)
19 and less: Negative Opportunity (20th percentile)

In this case the highest index number is 95 because we were unable to get the voting rate for New York at this time. If you have a problem getting any one number for your index remember you will use the highest possible score as your foundation. That means if 90 is your highest possible index score you divide the index score for your neighborhood by 90. Also see Appendix 7B.

Putting It All Together

Now that we have all the elements, we can create our index. Here is what it will look like (see Table 7.7).

Our results show that Jackson Heights, at the 63rd percentile, has good opportunity. If you were to create an index for several local neighborhoods, you could compare the level of opportunity that is available in each. There is great quantifying power in seeing these differences.

Recall that Jackson Heights has an integration score of 75. While segregation is not the only factor determining opportunity, it is a major factor. You will find, for example, that African Americans in many regions of the country live in highly segregated neighborhoods and that these neighborhoods tend to be poor. Even middle-class African Americans will often live in poorer neighborhoods than middle-class whites. Poorer neighborhoods have lower home values, which in turn influences families' ability to build

TABLE 7.7 Completed Table

	Figure	Percentile		Scale	Possible
WEALTH/INCOME/ EMPLOYMENT					
Employment (% of labor force)	93.92	80–100		4	5
Labor Force (%)	71.23	80–100		4	5
Median Family Income + Benefits	61,111	80–100		4	5
Homeownership (% of occupied homes)	37.50	20–40		2	5
Median Home Value	270,400	60–80		3	5
Banks per 1,000 Residents	0.29	80		4	5
TOTAL				21	30
COMMUNITY					
Median Gross Rent	1,149	80–100		5	5
Integration	74	80		4	5
Occupied Homes (%)	94	100		5	5
Owner-Occupied Homes (% of occupied)	37.50	40		2	5
Bachelor's or Graduate Degree	34.59	40		2	5
Crime Rates Per 100,000	550.78	80		4	5
Grocery Stores per 1,000 Residents	0.95	100		5	5
Liquor Stores per 10,000 Residents	1.80	60		3	5
TOTAL				30	40
VOICE					
Voting Rate (Last General Election)	NO NUMBER	n/a	n/a	n/a	n/a
Voter Registration Rate	39.57	20–40		2	5
TOTAL				2	5
SECOND CHANCES/SAFETY NET					
Incarceration Rates per 1,000 Residents	0.58	80		4	5
Prison Releases per 1,000 Residents	0.24	80		4	5
Youth Services per 1,000 Youth	0.07	20		1	5
Senior Services per 1,000 Seniors	0.12	20		1	5
TOTAL				10	20
		GOOD OPPORTUNITY		63	95

wealth. This is just one example of how residential segregation can influence opportunity.[14]

Residential segregation in many ways also drives school segregation, since school assignments are often based on residential addresses.[15] Researchers are also becoming more aware that racial segregation takes a toll on people's health.[16] Researchers have found a link between segregation and diseases such as high blood pressure, asthma, and diabetes.[17] Just determining the dissimilarity index, or in our case, area integration, for neighborhoods in a community could provide you with critical information that presents possible questions and lines of inquiry on a whole range of policies.

You may well wonder, how did these communities become so segregated in the first place? Too often the public thinks about segregation as an individual or group choice, folks deciding to live among those who look like them. But the reality is that both historical and current policies and practices in banking, housing, and real estate have driven most of the segregation we see today.[18] The legacy of those policies lives on.

When using the overall index to write about neighborhoods and compare opportunity with other areas of your community, make sure to discuss all the influencing and interconnected indicators. This should not be used as a label, rather it's the beginning of the exploration into your region.

While diving into the numbers may unnerve some of you, swallow your fear and take the plunge. These don't have to be numbers that you publish, though their publication may help the public understand how multiple disparities drive opportunities. At the very least, you can use these numbers to inform your reporting. Together they provide a snapshot of the pressures that influence people's everyday lives. In the end you may learn that disparities have less to do with community characteristics or individual decision-making, and more to do with the environmental pressures that drive one's choices.

Income Distribution

Source: Tax Policy Center	Percentile	Household Income	Scale
	20	$20,599	1
	40	$41,035	2
	60	$67,200	3
	80	$110,232	4
	100	$110,233 or more than	5

Employment Distribution

Source: Bureau of Labor Statistics	Percentile	Employment	Scale
	20	90 percent or less	1
Numbers may vary with quarterly reports	40	91 percent	2
	60	92 percent	3
	80	93 percent	4
	100	94 percent	5

Homeownership

Source: US Census	Percentile	Homeownership %	Scale
	20	20	1
	40	40	2
	60	60	3
	80	80	4
	100	100	5

Home Values

Source: US Census	Percentile	Median Home Value	Scale
	20	$122,600	1
	40	$149,100	2
	60	$205,600	3
	80	$254,200	4
	100	$537,400 or more	5

Labor Force

Source: US Census	Percentile	Labor Force %	Scale
	20	63	1
	40	65	2
	60	67	3
	80	69	4
	100	72	5

(Continued)

Occupied Housing Units

Source: US Census	Percentile	Occupied Homes %	Scale
	20	79 or less	1
	40	82	2
	60	86	3
	80	89	4
	100	92 or more	5

Gross Rents

Source: US Census	Percentile	Median Gross Rent	Scale
	20	$549	1
Will vary by region	40	$666	2
	60	$723	3
	80	$856	4
	100	$1,006 or more	5

Integration

Source: US Census	Percentile	Area Integration	Scale
	20	20	1
	40	40	2
	60	60	3
	80	80	4
	100	100	5

College Degrees

Source: US Census	Percentile	College Degree %	Scale
	20	20	1
	40	40	2
	60	60	3
	80	80	4
	100	100	5

Voting Rate

Source: Office of Elections (local or regional agency)	Percentile	Voting Rate	Scale
You might also try the Secretary of State of your state	20	20	1
The general election number will be the most robust	40	40	2
	60	60	3
	80	80	4
	100	100	5

(Continued)

APPENDIX 7A (Cont.)

Voter Registration Rate

Source: Office of Elections (local or regional agency)	Percentile	Voting Reg Rate	Scale
You might also try the Secretary of State of your state	20	20	1
	40	40	2
	60	60	3
	80	80	4
	100	100	5

Crime Rate (Violent Crime)

Source: US Department of Justice	Percentile	Rate per 100,000	Scale
	20	2,857 or more	1
	40	1,669	2
	60	647	3
	80	383	4
	100	95	5

Grocery Store Density

Source: US Census	Percentile	Per 1,000 Residents	Scale
Source: USDA Food Environment Atlas	20	0	1
	40	0.01–0.1	2
	60	0.11–0.2	3
	80	0.21–0.5	4
	100	0.51 or more	5

Liquor Store Density

Source: US Census	Percentile	Per 10,000 Residents	Scale
	20	3.6 – or more	1
	40	2.3–3.7	2
	60	1.7–2.2	3
	80	1–1.6	4
	100	0–0.9	5

Senior Services

Source: US Census	Percentile	Per 1,000 Seniors	Scale
	20	0–0.6	1
	40	0.7–1.3	2
	60	1.4–2.0	3
	80	2.1–2.7	4
	100	2.8 or more	5

(Continued)

Prison Releases

Source: Justice Atlas	Percentile	Per 1,000 Residents	Scale
	20	3.69 – or more	1
	40	1.3–3.68	2
	60	0.68–1.2	3
	80	0.17–0.67	4
	100	0–0.16	5

Prison Admissions

Source: Justice Atlas	Percentile	Per 1,000 Residents	Scale
	20	3.47 – or more	1
	40	1.83–3.46	2
	60	0.78–1.82	3
	80	0.27–0.77	4
	100	0–0.26	5

Banks

Source: US Census	Percentile	Per 1,000 Residents	Scale
	20	0	1
	40	0.01–0.1	2
	60	0.11–0.2	3
	80	0.21–0.5	4
	100	0.5 or more	5

Youth Services

Source: US Census	Percentile	Per 1,000 Youth	Scale
	20	0.07 or less	1
	40	0.08–0.18	2
	60	0.19–0.29	3
	80	0.30–0.40	4
	100	0.41 or more	5

Please note: This table is an example of the scales you need to make. Some scales and percentiles may vary based upon changing demographics and economic figures.

APPENDIX 7B Opportunity Index Scale

77–95 Great Opportunity
58–76 Good Opportunity
39–57 Some Opportunity
20–38 Declining Opportunity
19 and Less Negative Opportunity

Notes

1 Manny Fernandez. "Study Finds Disparities in Mortgages by Race." *New York Times*, October 15, 2007. Accessed June 26, 2018 from www.nytimes.com/2007/10/15/nyregion/15subprime.html.

2 Manny Fernandez. "Door to Door, Foreclosure Knocks Here." *New York Times*, October 19, 2008. Accessed June 26, 2018 from www.nytimes.com/2008/10/19/nyregion/19block.html.

3 This tool was created under a Knight Foundation Challenge Grant. Check such foundation sites to find new tools each year. CensusIRE also offers easy access to Census data. http://census.ire.org/.

4 US Census. Table B08013, "Aggregate Travel Time to Work (In Minutes) of Workers by Sex." Commute, Census Reporter. Accessed May 11, 2018 from https://censusreporter.org/topics/commute/.

5 Tyler Vigen. "Spurious Correlations." 2015. Accessed April 30, 2018 from http://tylervigen.com/spurious-correlations.

6 Marie Lynn Miranda, Lynne C. Messer, and Gretchen L. Kroeger. "Associations between the Quality of the Residential Built Environment and Pregnancy Outcomes among Women in North Carolina." *Environmental Health Perspectives* 120 (2012): 471–477. Accessed June 8, 2018 from https://ehp.niehs.nih.gov/1103578/#t4.

7 For a good discussion of the link between transportation and employment among African Americans, see Andre M. Perry. "Who Deserves Credit for Black Employment." The Brookings Institution, February 1, 2018. Accessed June 16, 2018 from www.brookings.edu/blog/the-avenue/2018/02/01/who-deserves-credit-for-african-american-employment/.

8 A 2018 rule change would require census-takers to ask about the immigration status of residents. Miriam Jordan. "If Census Asks About Citizenship, Some Already Have an Answer: No Comment." *New York Times*, March 27, 2018. Accessed June 16, 2018 from www.nytimes.com/2018/03/27/us/census-undocumented-immigrants.html.

9 For the proposed questions for 2020, see www.census.gov/library/publications/2018/dec/planned-questions-2020-acs.html.

10 You can also request special tabulations of data for a fee.

11 While the five-year ACS generally has lower margins of error, in areas of rapid change that reliability may break down. If rapid change happens in the five years data is collected, the dataset breaks down. As the reporter you'll know which areas of your community are in the midst of rapid change. In these cases, a one-year or three-year dataset may be better to use.

12 For a good analysis of when to use which dataset, see www.psc.isr.umich.edu/dis/acs/handouts/Compass_Appendix.pdf.

13 Matthew Desmond. "How Homeownership Became the Engine of American Inequality," *New York Times*, May 9, 2017. Accessed May 13, 2017 from www.nytimes.com/2017/05/09/magazine/how-homeownership-became-the-engine-of-american-inequality.html?hp&action=click&pgtype=Homepage&clickSource=story-heading&module=photo-spot-region&region=top-news&WT.nav=top-news.

14 John R. Logan and Brian Stults, US 2010 Project. "The Persistence of Segregation in the Metropolis: New Findings from the 2010 Census," March 24, 2011.

15 John R. Logan, US 2010 Project. "Whose Schools Are Failing." Russell Sage Foundation and Brown University, July 25, 2011. Accessed November 30, 2018 from https://s4.ad.brown.edu/Projects/Diversity/Data/Report/report5.pdf.

16 The Joint Center for Political and Economic Studies. "Segregated Spaces, Risky Places: The Effect of Segregation on Health Inequalities," September 2011.

17 Rob Stein. "Leaving Segregated Neighborhoods Lowers Blacks' Blood Pressure." National Public Radio. Aired May 15, 2017. Retrieved the same day from www. npr.org/sections/health-shots/2017/05/15/527966937/leaving-segregated-neighbor hoods-lowers-blacks-blood-pressure. Also see "Unnatural Causes," a documentary that makes a direct link between discrimination and poor health outcomes.
18 For more information about how policies fuel segregation read *American Apartheid* by Douglass Massey and Nancy Denton and *The Color of Law* by Richard Rothstein.

PART III
Best Practices

8

INTERVIEWING ACROSS DIFFERENCE

Omedi Ochieng

Omedi Ochieng, assistant professor at Denison University, is an expert on the ways in which one's own knowledge is modulated by class, gender, race, sexuality, disability, and other identities. Here he addresses the challenge reporters face when they assume their interview subjects use the same cultural cues as they do. This chapter offers a framework for understanding intercultural journalism and provides interview tips for situations when a source's cultural background is unfamiliar.

The Nuer and the Clash of Perspectives

Journalists setting out to interview people from marginalized communities and cultures may find striking lessons in the anthropologist E.E. Evans-Pritchard's frustrated efforts at interviewing the Nuer, an ethnic community in the Sudan. Evans-Pritchard traveled to Nuerland in 1930 in order to study the community's political institutions. There, he met a chilly reception. He recorded one of these encounters as follows:

> Nuer are expert at sabotaging an inquiry and until one has resided with them for some weeks they steadfastly stultify all efforts to elicit the simplest facts and to elucidate the most innocent practices ... The following specimen of Nuer methods is the commencement of a conversation on the Nyanding river, on a subject which admits of some obscurity but, with willingness to co-operate, can soon be elucidated.

I: Who are you?
Cuol: A man.
I: What is your name?

Cuol: Do you want to know my name?

I: Yes.

Cuol: You want to know my name?

I: Yes, you have come to visit me in my tent and I would like to know who you are.

Cuol: All right. I am Cuol. What is your name?

I: My name is Pritchard.

Cuol: What is your father's name?

I: My father's name is also Pritchard.

Cuol: No, that cannot be true. You cannot have the same name as your father.

I: It is the name of my lineage. What is the name of your lineage?

Cuol: Do you want to know the name of my lineage?

I: Yes.

Cuol: What will you do with it if I tell you? Will you take it to your country?

I: I don't want to do anything with it. I just want to know it since I am living at your camp.

Cuol: Oh well, we are Lou.

I: I did not ask you the name of your tribe. I know that. I am asking you the name of your lineage.

Cuol: Why do you want to know the name of my lineage?

I: I don't want to know it.

Cuol: Then why do you ask me for it? Give me some tobacco.

> I defy the most patient ethnologist to make headway against this kind of opposition. One is just driven crazy by it. Indeed, after a few weeks of associating solely with Nuer one displays, if the pun be allowed, the most evident symptoms of "Nuerosis."[1]

This encounter aptly captures the clash in perspective between Evans-Pritchard and the Nuer. Consider the manner in which Evans-Pritchard characterizes his motives for the interview. In this specific encounter, he states, his efforts were aimed at eliciting the "simplest facts" and elucidating "the most innocent practices." It is no wonder, then, that thinking himself patently guileless, Evans-Pritchard appears befuddled and bemused by the Nuer response. He states that the Nuer "country and character are alike intractable" and that they are "expert at sabotaging an inquiry." Indeed, Evans-Pritchard adds, such is their willful, even perverse, unresponsiveness, that they may well be able to drive even "the most patient ethnologist" crazy. Throwing up his hands, he proffers a diagnosis of the condition created by encounters with the Nuer, calling it "Nuerosis."[2]

The perspective of the Nuer, of course, likely stands in stark contrast to Evans-Pritchard's account. Consider that for the Nuer, Evans-Pritchard's entry into their lives came in the wake of punishing imperial raids that the British had been carrying out to subjugate the Sudan. Indeed, as anthropologist James Clifford has pointed out, the Nuer's chilly reception of Evans-Pritchard is far from the most remarkable thing about this encounter. The really intriguing question is why the Nuer did not kill Evans-Pritchard. Clifford has an explanation:

> Well, when white people go into situations of that sort – and this is true of many of the places anthropologists have worked – there's a prior history of pacification. The locals have understood the message: Don't harm white folks, because if you do many more of your own people will suffer. The anecdote points to a historical location, often based on white skin privilege that guarantees an important degree of safety.[3]

Evans-Pritchard is completely enmeshed in assumptions about his own innocence and good faith. It completely escapes him that his interviewees have reason to suspect him of compulsive dissimulation. Note, for example, the exchange that he has with his interviewee, Cuol:

I: [Pritchard] is the name of my lineage. What is the name of your lineage?
Cuol: Do you want to know the name of my lineage?
I: Yes.
Cuol: What will you do with it if I tell you? Will you take it to your country?
I: I don't want to do anything with it. I just want to know it since I am living at your camp.

Notwithstanding Evans-Pritchard's protestations, Nuer suspicions were well-founded. Evans-Pritchard's intellectual interest in Nuerland had been fueled and enabled in a cultural hothouse that promoted the production of "Oriental" and "Africanist" knowledge of the nonwhite "Other."[4] That cultural hothouse describes the historical era – roughly from the beginnings of the trans-Atlantic slave trade in the 15th century through to the end of settler colonialism in the 20th century – when white explorers, missionaries, travel writers, colonial administrators, journalists, and anthropologists constructed an image of Africa as, in the words of the Nigerian novelist and essayist Chinua Achebe, "a foil to Europe, as a place of negations at once remote and vaguely familiar, in comparison with which Europe's own state of spiritual grace will be manifest."[5]

Perhaps far more telling was the fact that the British colonial government had commissioned Evans-Pritchard's research. While Evans-Pritchard acted as if his research was motivated purely by curiosity, in actual fact the most likely goal of his research was to disseminate it to the British government, which would then use such knowledge to subjugate the Nuer.

Embodiedness and Embeddedness

Like Evans-Pritchard, journalists from dominant or majority demographic groups lean on a set of conventions that they claim renders their work innocent of being implicated in structures of dominance and oppression. Of these conventions, they cling with the most tenacity to the ethic of objectivity. University of Connecticut sociologist Gaye Tuchman refers to objectivity as a *strategic ritual*, a routine by which reporters attempt to prove that their work is systematic and transparent, and, consequently, that their stories are plain facts.[6]

What, however, the ethic of objectivity prevents journalists from recognizing is their own *embodiedness* – and, consequently, the extent to which their perspectives are necessarily partial and limited – and their *embeddedness* – the fact that their work is structured within institutions driven by particular interests. Embodiedness refers to the ways in which a person's perception, cognition, and behavior are deeply shaped by the habits and ideologies they have imbibed through acculturation and socialization. In other words, a person's identity – for example, a person's class, gender, race, sexuality, disability – structures his or her assumptions about what is plausible, what merits attention, and what is important. Embeddedness refers to the larger institutional and relational structures – such as family, schools, religious organizations, professional networks – that greatly determine the implicit and explicit rites, rituals, and rules that enable and constrain a person's worldview and behavior.

An acknowledgment of embeddedness and embodiedness ought to encourage journalists to thoroughly re-examine the conventions and concepts that they often take to be neutral. Take, for example, the notion of time. Much of the North Atlantic – Western European, Canadian and US – news media, prompted by the convention that the novelty or timeliness of an event determines newsworthiness, are apt to structure a news story by focusing on a recent event.[7] Such an orientation to time, as numerous media critics have argued, gives short shrift to historical events and the structural context from which the news of the day emerges.[8]

Fugitive Rhetoric

Sources and subjects from marginalized communities and cultures are unlikely to grant journalists the presumption of objectivity. They often see media practitioners as interested parties to the events and people they are reporting on and writing about. A journalist from the United States who is reporting on Kenya, for example, is likely to be seen as primarily interested in covering an event in ways that promote the national interests of the United States. Furthermore, members of these communities may likely regard this journalist as having a shallow and distorted picture of the complexities of the societies he or she is writing about.

In response, these communities may then employ what I call *fugitive rhetorics* and take on *protean personas* to thwart and elude what they view as journalism's interrogatory thrust. By protean personas, I mean the different sorts of identities, personalities, and voices that marginalized people construct, perform, and project in order to frustrate attempts by the powerful for control. Protean personas have ranged across many societies in the form of the trickster, the *femme fatale*, the outlaw, even the fool. The marginalized person uses for her defense "silence, exile, and cunning,"[9] a credo that Stephen Dedalus, the protagonist of James Joyce's novel, *A Portrait of the Artist as a Young Man*, vows to live by in response to what he regarded as the politically and culturally oppressive climate in Ireland. The escaped slave Harriet Jacobs referred in her autobiographic novel to the discourses and actions of the enslaved as the "weapon of the weak": "Who can blame slaves for being cunning? They are constantly compelled to resort to it. It is the only weapon of the weak and oppressed against the strength of their tyrants."[10]

New Approaches

The above discussion invites a fundamental revisioning of the interviewing protocols and practices that journalists often employ when engaging marginalized groups. Three implications are immediately apparent. First, journalists ought to acknowledge their own embeddedness in structures of power and privilege that shape their presuppositions, dispositions, and intuitions. By clinging to the myth of objectivity, journalists only deepen the suspicion with which they are often received. Moreover, they short-circuit other, richer modes of understanding. For example, journalists can emphasize their commitment to fairness without making the implausible claim that they are objective. This can occur, for instance, by their willingness to acknowledge their ignorance on certain topics and through efforts to build trust by owning up to their biases.

Second, journalists ought to be particularly attentive to the embodied and the unspoken forms of communication within the interview process. Oppressed people often communicate as much through silence, nonverbal forms of communication, and other indirect modes of rhetoric as they do through verbal utterances. Rather than pathologize such indirect forms of communication – as Evans-Pritchard does in coining the term "Nuerosis" – journalists may discover repertoires of communication just as intricate and complex as any natural language.

Third, by reckoning with the ways in which power and ideology inflects interviewing, a journalist opens up space for reimagining an interview as more than the gathering of "facts." Instead, journalists may look at each interview as an opportunity to not only learn about the "who, what, when, where, why and how," but also crucially as a site for enlarging their imagination about the counterfactual, the "what could have been" and what "may yet be." Attuned to the registers of the fugitive and the insurgent, journalists may yet find in the interview possibilities not just for knowledge of the "the other," but most crucially, an opportunity for understanding themselves.

Recommendations

In light of the above discussion, what are some practical tips that a journalist may use when interviewing people from different cultures? First, cultural knowledge is best acquired through "immersion journalism" – that is, the practice in which journalists embed themselves deep within the communities they are writing about. Through immersion journalism, reporters are likely to meet a greater diversity of interview subjects than the ones available in their Rolodexes. Moreover, immersion journalism enables journalists to interview subjects in the flow of everyday activity rather than in formal settings that may at times be forbidding or intimidating to subjects.

Second, journalists should seek to contextualize their interviews and news reports within the long sweep of history and the length and breadth of geography. This will often entail resisting the siren song of "breaking news" and "scoops." Journalists ought to aim for insight rather than settling for anecdotal facts or biographical vignettes.

Third, journalists ought to push beyond the "what is" to the "what may yet be." Such a task primarily involves visualizing interviewing as a dialogic encounter in the enlargement of the imagination. Journalists can enlarge their imagination by formulating questions that allow their interviewees room to reflect on counterfactual scenarios. For example, journalists may ask interviewees to imagine how things *could* have been different or how they *would* have been different had the circumstances been otherwise. Moreover, enlarging the imagination is as much an ethical task as it is a task of gathering knowledge. Thus, it behooves journalists to seek out multiple perspectives and to be self-critical of their biases and assumptions.

While these recommendations do not exhaust the possible steps journalists can take as they set out to interview subjects from unfamiliar cultures, they offer a start. In whatever direction journalists choose to proceed, it is vital that they pay greater attention to how culture shapes the process of interviewing and how they ought to plan and conduct their interviews in light of these cultural differences.

Notes

1 E.E. Evans-Pritchard. *The Nuer: A Description of the Modes of Livelihood and Political Institutions of a Nilotic People*. Oxford: Clarendon Press, 1940, pp. 12–13.
2 Ibid., p. 9.
3 See James Clifford. *On the Edges of Anthropology* (Interviews). Chicago: Prickly Paradigm Press, 2003.
4 On the production of knowledge of the Eastern Other, see Edward W. Said. *Orientalism*. New York: Random House, Inc., 1978. On the production of knowledge of the African Other, see V.Y. Mudimbe. *The Invention of Africa: Gnosis, Philosophy, and the Order of Knowledge*. Bloomington: Indiana University Press, 1988.
5 Chinua Achebe. *Hopes and Impediments: Selected Essays*. New York: Anchor Books, 1988, p. 3.

6 Gaye Tuchman. "Objectivity as Strategic Ritual: An Examination of Newsmen's Notions of Objectivity." *American Journal of Sociology* 77, no. 4 (January, 1972): 660–679.

7 See, for example, Michael Schudson. "When? Deadlines, Datelines, and History," in *Reading the News*, ed. Robert K. Manoff and Michael Schudson. New York: Pantheon Books, 1987.

8 See for example Shanto Iyengar. *Is Anyone Responsible? How Television Frames Political Issues*. Chicago: University of Chicago Press, 1991.

9 James Joyce. *A Portrait of the Artist as a Young Man*. New York: Penguin Books Ltd, 1964, p. 269.

10 Harriet Jacobs. *Incidents in the Life of a Slave Girl*. New York: The Modern Library, 2000, p. 234.

9

AVOIDING STEREOTYPES AND STIGMA

Sue Ellen Christian

When writing about racial disparity, journalists can unwittingly stigmatize a racial group or rely upon stereotypes. In this chapter, Sue Ellen Christian, professor of communication at Western Michigan University and former reporter for the Chicago Tribune, *offers reporters methods and tools for avoiding racial tropes that can advance discrimination rather than dismantle it. She is the author of* Overcoming Bias: A Journalist's Guide to Culture and Context.

How Stereotypes Work

The ever-efficient brain is all about categorizing people, places, things, and ideas. Our minds categorize in order to avoid constantly sorting through every piece of information we come across in any given day. Our minds categorize so we can be productive.[1] But our cognitive shortcuts can lead to trouble. Specifically, they can lead to stereotyping people unfairly and perpetuating societal stigmas.

Stereotypes are fixed ideas we have about a person, place, or thing that are simplified and standardized. Stereotypes are often held in common by members of one group about another. John T. Jost, a professor of psychology at New York University, and David L. Hamilton, a social psychologist from the University of California, Santa Barbara, in 2005 reviewed the research about the impact of stereotypes on our thinking.[2] They make several observations relevant to journalists.

Stereotypes direct our attention to certain information to the exclusion of others; for instance, a journalist reporting on a teen pregnancy clinic might mention that the population served is primarily Hispanic. Why is that important to note? Is the writer noting ethnicity because it is relevant to the story?

Stereotypes can color our interpretation of superficial information. A reporter may conclude that a Muslim woman who wears a head covering, or hijab, is acting in a subordinate manner when she repeatedly defers to her spouse in an interview. In fact, the woman may simply be a shy person.

Stereotypes play a role in eliciting the very behavior from others that actually *confirms* our biases. Say, for example, that our reporter holds the stereotype that people from a certain culture are always rude. Therefore, he may act accordingly, interacting with the same brusqueness that he anticipates receiving. The reporter's off-putting behavior, not surprisingly, elicits the very reaction that he anticipated. His stereotype is justified.

Stereotypes influence the way we remember information, prompting us to recall things better when they *don't* fit our stereotypes. If our reporter holds the stereotype that immigrant families are often ill-kempt and untidy, he will be particularly struck by the fastidious cleanliness of the apartment he visits to conduct his interview of the newly arrived refugee family. While he would expect an untidy apartment, a tidy one seems *especially* salient. He may be sure to remark on that in his coverage, for example, as if to note its unusual nature. As American psychologist Gordon Allport put it, "A stereotype is sustained by selective perception and selective forgetting."[3]

Also, stereotypes form the hypotheses we tend to favor when interpreting new information. Our reporter will filter information, particularly ambiguous information, through the lens of his hypothesis. If he holds the stereotype of Asians as the "model minority," he may well dismiss outright anecdotal evidence that a local Asian businessman is not running a stable or ethical business, rather than looking into it.

Consider how these habits of the mind may shape your reporting. And there's more. Are you partially discounting the information provided by a particular source because of his or her ethnic background? In 1991, Monica Biernat at the University of Kansas and Melvin Manis, then at the University of Michigan, conducted four studies that included 431 undergraduates and found that the students routinely adjusted their standards of judgment, based on differing standards of comparison, as they thought about members of different social groups.[4]

Do you opt for sources like yourself when you could easily opt for equally qualified people of a different race or ethnicity? Researchers have found that we are inclined to do so. John F. Dovidio, now a psychology professor at Yale, and Samuel L. Gaertner, at the University of Delaware, conducted a 2000 study in which white college students were asked to select from two evenly matched candidates, one black and one white, each with ambiguous credentials – not clearly qualified *or* unqualified. In these circumstances, students recommended the white candidate in substantially more instances.[5]

Conscious Interventions

If by now in this chapter you are feeling all is hopeless when it comes to mastering our brain's habit of stereotyping, take heart. Research on our implicit mental habits also suggests that we can reduce our biases long-term through conscious interventions. Patricia Devine, a social psychologist at the University of Wisconsin, described various tactics in a 2012 journal article with several of her colleagues. You can consciously replace a stereotypical response with one that is not based on stereotypes. Imagine or recall a specific person you know who is an example of someone who *breaks* the stereotypes you hold of a particular social group. You also can try on what you think may be the perspective of the person of a stereotyped group. You can take care to individualize and evaluate people on personal rather than group attributes. And you can work to increase your positive interactions with members of a social group with which you do not psychologically identify.[6]

Let's explore how you might employ these interventions as a journalist. Imagine that you are assigned a story on Iraqi citizens who are Muslim. Unless you have personal knowledge or lived experience with this group of people, you may well feel a bias against the people you'll be interviewing. "The Muslims in town claim that they value all religions and love America, but they don't talk to anyone and they all stick together. It feels secretive," you may think. As you travel to the first interview, you *identify the stereotype* you hold. You acknowledge that you have no personal knowledge about American Muslims. You reflect on why you hold this stereotype and think about how you might *replace your stereotype* with a less biased response, such as thinking about Muslims as fellow citizens instead of a foreign subgroup. With that in mind, you *take your sources' perspective* by imagining what it would be like to interview for a job at the local mall wearing a hijab. Approach the home of the source and notice that she has herbs growing in a flower box and no fewer than four bird feeders on her patio. Hmm, a birder? A gardener? Perhaps she enjoys cooking with fresh herbs? With this line of inquiry, you have begun evaluating the source on *individual personal attributes*, seeing her as a unique person and not as a representative of a group.

As journalists, "we're in the business of explaining people to each other," said Kevin Merida, former managing editor of the *Washington Post*, in a Nieman Reports article about why newsroom diversity works.[7] In that spirit of understanding and communication, I offer five strategies for mitigating biases that operate outside our awareness:

1.   Know your own worldview and how it shapes your perspectives.
2.   Immerse yourself in unfamiliar communities, in part by using the tools of "slow" listening, a practice modeled from anthropologists.
3.   Use the Maynard Institute's Fault Lines.
4.   Make yourself culturally competent by reading about the history, politics, religions, and conflicts of a community, and perhaps learning its language.

5. Evaluate your assumptions by talking with cultural experts and community leaders, and by reflecting on your work.

Know Your Own Worldview

The first step toward becoming an inclusive journalist is to acknowledge that your brain automatically works to be exclusive. It categorizes at a lightning-fast pace to allow you to do all you do on the job and elsewhere. Some categorizations are innocuous; how much does it matter if a transportation reporter believes left-handed people are creative? But, some categorizations are particularly conse-quential. If a state government reporter thinks women don't make savvy politi-cians, he may (knowingly or not) avoid interviewing female lawmakers for his stories. His reporting over time will maintain perceptions that women don't belong in politics, exclude important points of view, and short-change his audience. Furthermore, by not cultivating *all* his potential sources, he will miss out on story ideas and reporting leads.

The Implicit Association Test, which measures the strength of associations between concepts, is an indicator of our attitudes and beliefs, even those atti-tudes we don't know we have. Through a variety of studies and theories, psychology scholars have concluded that *explicit* attitudes affect deliberate, gen-erally non-prejudicial behaviors and *implicit* stereotyping attitudes affect spon-taneous behaviors.[8] Explicit attitudes formulate our responses when we have time to be deliberate and thoughtful about different approaches to a person or situation. Implicit stereotypes are those that occur outside our conscious awareness and control, and are ones that we often are unwilling or unable to report. The test reveals this type of reactive decision-making.

Experimental psychologist Anthony G. Greenwald of the University of Washington, who invented the test, has worked with Mahzarin R. Banaji, at Harvard University, and Brian Nosek, at the University of Virginia, to develop it further. "Implicit attitudes are introspectively unidentified (or inaccurately identified) traces of past experience that mediate favorable or unfavorable feel-ing, thought, or action toward social objects," Greenwald and Banaji wrote in a 1995 review article. Our past experience shapes present biases, which we often don't recognize we have. We also may not be aware of behavior that aligns with such biases. A white reporter, for instance, may not notice the awkward distance she puts between herself and black sources, or realize her inability to speak comfortably with those sources. She may wonder why her sources are less than eager to openly share opinions and information.

While there is no direct means to control our implicit biases – they are outside our conscious awareness – we can train ourselves to think more broadly and inclu-sively, and be more aware of our explicit attitudes and their influences on our behaviors. The aim is an overall state of mindfulness about our actions. A good starting strategy is working to know your own worldview.

A worldview is a framework of ideas and attitudes about the world. It is formed by our upbringing, background, education, and culture. "Worldview forms the building blocks of culture and guides individual perception, belief systems, appraisal, communication, and behavior," wrote a team led by psychologist Rheeda Walker, now at the University of Houston,[9] in a study that examined the influence of cultural worldview on suicide resilience.

Because we each have a worldview, a reporter who avoids having rigid opinions about topics she covers still cannot help but have a standpoint *in relation* to those topics. For example, a white heterosexual male journalist[10] raised by white heterosexual married parents will naturally assume his majority status in society. He will interpret events and issues from that vantage point. That male journalist, to be successful, will need to learn to actively appreciate others' vantage points on life and cultivate a depth of understanding of others' realities.

As you begin to understand your perspective on the world, you will see that the vantage point from which you access people, ideas, places, and situations is but one of many possibilities. Others have equally valid vantage points. Cultivate an open mind, such that you are curious and interested in others' perspectives. (The Tip Sheet below offers details on how to do this.) Thus, it is important to take time to think about the formative nature of your economic status, family composition and dynamics, schooling, moral upbringing, generational status, and race or ethnicity, among other major factors. Self-reflection is an essential starting point.

Another way of understanding one's worldview to acknowledge what is missing from the experiences that shape it. In other words, what do your own experiences limit you from knowing about? Recognizing these gaps allows you to find ways to fill them through research, education, and personal exchanges with people likely to have differing worldviews.

Immersion and Slow Listening

We can learn much about how to immerse ourselves in another's culture and situation through a particular group of experts – anthropologists. Anthropologists use the practice of ethnography to understand a culture, as anthropologist Clifford Geertz phrased it, "from the native's point of view."[11] Many disciplines, including social work and health care, have found value in adopting some of ethnography's main principles. Certainly journalism can benefit as well.

Geertz explored how and whether an outsider can accurately represent another culture. For our purposes, I'll substitute Geertz's "informants" and "anthropologists" with "sources" and "journalists." Geertz artfully describes how, in studying cultures in Java, Bali, and Morocco, he came to understand that getting an "accurate or even half-accurate" sense of a person or culture doesn't come from the *journalist's* experience of the situation. That's about the journalist, not the source. Rather, says Geertz, the source's point of view can be best articulated when the journalist works to discern a *culture's modes of expression:* Its words, images, institutions, and behaviors. How do people represent themselves to both themselves and to one another? How do they define themselves as persons? (By their ethnicity? Their occupation? Their family role?) What are the contexts in which they live and how do their definitions of "self" change given different contexts?

Placing yourself in the habitat and natural environment of people unlike yourself, where they are comfortable but you may not be, allows for what I've heard called "slow listening."[12] Listen deliberately, as one not in a hurry to get to the next question or figure a story angle, but as one sinking into the scene. Serene Thornton and Kendra J. Garrett, social work faculty at the University of St. Thomas in Minneapolis, emphasized in a 1995 article that researchers develop insights through observation, immersion in the details of daily life and analysis of the information they gather.

The details of daily life? Like what? Well, like the fact that a parent hollers at his or her teenager to stop staring into the refrigerator and shut the door in order to save on the electric bill. Or that no one starts to eat until everyone is seated at the dinner table. Or that the dinner table is a sofa in front of the television. In each case, guard against adding words that suggest judgment, as in: "*only* a sofa" or "*just* a sofa."

Sometimes, we as journalists are so hurried and harried that when we are given time to more thoroughly know a culture, we're at a loss about what to do. Quotes? Those we know how to get. But achieving a level of deep understanding? That is far harder – and scarier. Approach other cultures with a spirit of humility. Slow listening starts with a mindset that the listener has something to learn from the speaker. Trust that the story focus will come to you, and not the other way around, with you superimposing the news focus on a source's life story. Try out your story hypothesis on a source, and push for clarifications and examples.

Anthropologist Martin Gerard Forsey discusses the importance of "seeing voices."[13] He advocates for a "democracy of the senses" rather than relying on our highly visual, Westernized orientation to the world. To that end, listen for the ways in which culture and information are conveyed verbally: Through distinctive speech patterns (a source's pronunciations of English words that indicate ethnic or geographic heritage), habits of speech (interesting word choices, such as the Southern phrase, "sweatin' like a sinner in church"), language choices (blended languages such as Spanglish, or exclusively English spoken in an immigrant home), conversational styles (Does everyone get a nickname? Who is spoken to in a formal manner?) or, the use of silence and the hierarchy of who gets to talk and when (Only males? Or women when specifically addressed?).

If there's not much talk because a journalist is present, seek reporting opportunities in which you can melt into the background. Wonderful listening posts are family parties and celebrations, the weekly card game with friends, sports events featuring family members, coffee shop chit-chat, after-work beers, church or temple events.

Immersing yourself in the language can help you to understand a culture and the source's place in it; we tend to mirror the language of the social group with which we most closely identify at the moment. Be attuned to how a source adapts her speech to fit her audience. This "code switching" can mask the rich details of culture or the nuances of an issue because an outside reporter isn't privy to the dialogue that happens among friends and family. Reporters who spend a lot of time with a specific community and have the opportunity to build strong source relationships may find that sources no longer "code switch" with them.

Immersing ourselves in a community will help us to report *for* a community instead of *about* it. The first approach looks to represent and inform; the second approach objectifies and distances. A story about a women's store that features African-inspired fashions that is written for a community reads inclusively: "The new shop favorite is a bold yellow skirt of Ankara fabric that is appropriate for the workplace due to its chevron pattern." Versus: "Women who couldn't find clothes they liked at JC Penney are turning to a new store with such unusual prints that there's no danger that others will be wearing the same look."

Marginalized communities – whether due to ethnicity or race, gender or sexual orientation, poverty or religion – are especially weary of drive-by journalism fueled by single incidents. Your sources are more likely to share their lives with you once they realize you're there to listen and learn and that you aren't going away anytime soon. This technique is particularly challenging now that reporters often need to file online and immediately. Approach digital reporting in waves – the first dispatches should be factual and limited in scope. Qualify what you do know, and acknowledge what you haven't had time to learn. As you are able to spend more time reporting, the results can have more authority and scope.

Use the Fault Lines

Journalists tend to rely on the same old favorites – government officials, institutional spokespeople, and males in general – when it comes to sources. The Maynard Institute's Fault Lines are a simple but rich set of guideposts to help diversify your sources. Maynard believed that "the fault lines of race, class, gender, generation and geography are the most enduring forces shaping lives, experiences and social tension."[14] (For a full discussion on using Fault Lines in reporting, go to Chapter 10.)

Improve Your Cultural Competency

We can communicate more easily across cultures if we have some knowledge about the particular group of people with whom we're interacting. For journalists, this means developing a broad base of awareness about world religions, ethnic cultures, world history, the history of civil conflicts, and the history of protest. Make yourself culturally competent by reading about various communication styles and informal rules of interaction within communities outside of your own.

Seeking meaningful contact with people who identify differently than you do or are from a different culture will improve not only your cultural competency, but also perhaps alter your internal biases. To do this, you can attend local interest clubs (a community sports team or craft group) or nonprofit organizations (a racial equity group or cultural association) composed mainly of people from a specific cultural group other than your own.

This so-called intergroup contact has been found to have a positive effect on implicit bias, the unconscious attitudes we hold about one another.[15] Intergroup contact also helps to reduce anxiety about the threat of an unfamiliar group, and it increases one's empathy and ability to take the perspective of someone in that unfamiliar group.

If a sizable community in your reporting area relies on a language other than English, you may want to learn the language. Develop trusted translators who are not vested in the topic at hand, as stakeholders can have biases that may affect their interpretation of sources' statements. Also, younger family members often speak English, as do parents who attended college in their home countries.

A home interview is the richest source for learning. When you are reporting in someone's home, use all your senses: Take in the smells from the kitchen, the hangings on the walls, the type of music playing (or not), and even how tactile and physically affectionate family members are with one another. When you feel yourself moving toward judgment, move toward curiosity instead. Try on the neutral response of asking questions to understand and learn. This information will inform your word choice and behavior in future interview situations. The more appropriate you are, showing awareness of the cultural habits and mores of a group of people, the easier it is to develop rapport. Comfortable interviews yield more talkative sources. If in doubt, err on the side of formality.

Evaluate Your Assumptions

Debriefing published stories with select community sources will improve the inclusionary tone and focus of your work. Touch base with community leaders with the specific intent of checking on the cultural assumptions that you may have made. You're not asking permission from your source to report on their group as an outsider. You're not seeking their approval of your writing. You're asking for specific feedback: Did I accurately reflect these aspects of the culture? Do you notice any incorrect assumptions that I may have made? Am I inadvertently using euphemisms or loaded terms? Do you have suggestions of other sources of information (human or documents) that I should seek out?

Writing daily stories also can lead to what social scientist Donald Schön calls a "parochial narrowness of vision."[16] Schön advocates a reflective practice to guard against the assumptions we make as professionals skilled at our jobs.

The repetitive and formulaic nature of stories leaves us unsurprised by much of anything. We slot characters into set categories. We miss small but telling details. We overlook nuances of language. Yet such details and nuances are the makings of compelling portrayals of real people. With practice, we can all develop the habit of distancing ourselves from our work and reading it with a fresh eye to check for errors of omission.

Develop the habit of self-evaluation, be it after every story or every month or every quarter, but make it a practice. Look at the kinds of sources who pepper your stories – are they all experts and officials? Are you often casting one ethnic group in the role of victim or aggressor? What about the *origins* of your stories – are they typically emerging from neighborhoods and citizens, or from press releases and advocacy groups? Schön writes about reflecting-in-action, like a jazz musician who improvises on the spot or a pitcher who adjusts mid-game. Journalists, too, can adjust their game. In my book on culture and cognition, I suggest that for less complex stories, reporters do the "Two-Minute Brainstorm."[17] Think of alternative story angles *before* you complete your story. For 120 seconds, with no computer screen and just a paper and pen, let your mind go anywhere this topic leads. Focused, quiet attention like this can help you identify broader themes that you can allude to in the story, and highlight word choices that are biased. This is reflecting in action, mid-game.

Truly, our best and most accurate work will result from awareness of ourselves, knowledge of others, intergroup contact and honest self-appraisal.

Tip Sheet

- The Society of Professional Journalists urges reporters to ask sources two direct questions when reporting on people from different demographics than their own:

  o "Do you think your race or ethnicity (age, gender, religion, economic background, etc.) affects the way you think about this issue?"[18]
  o "As someone not of your community (race, ethnicity, gender, other) what do you think I might miss when reporting about this?"[19]

- Ways to begin connecting with different cultures include the following:

  o Go to the local eatery or coffee shop and pick up the local school newsletters, agency brochures, and free newspapers.
  o Track when the major holidays, festivals, or important anniversaries of the birthdays or deaths of cultural leaders are observed.
  o Watch community group calendars for picnics, meetings, or protests.
  o Follow community leaders on Twitter and other social media platforms, join Facebook pages, and sign up for a neighborhood or culturally-oriented email newsletter or listserv.

- Seek out documents, including private or informal documents such as letters, diaries, or personal voice and video recordings, to understand the heart of a community. Going beyond official documents such as business licenses, court filings, and police reports opens up an entirely new population of sources. Consider the Fault Lines as you do this because after all, someone with his or her own implicit biases created those documents.
- Evaluate the assumptions behind your 5Ws and the H. For a change, use these 5Ws and H: *Who* am I missing in this report? *What* is really happening here? *When* did this issue become important for this person and for the greater community? (Sometimes the disconnect between the importance of a particular issue to a cultural group versus the insignificance of that same issue to the larger community *is* the story.) *Where* have I seen this sort of behavior/attitude/argument before in history? *Why* am I sure this is true? *How* did things get this way?

Notes

1 Susan T. Fiske and Shelley E. Taylor. *Social Cognition: From Brains to Culture*. Los Angeles: Sage, 2013.
2 John T. Jost and David L. Hamilton. "Stereotypes in Our Culture," in *On the Nature of Prejudice: Fifty Years after Allport*, ed. John F. Dovidio, P. Glick, and L.A. Rudman. Oxford: Blackwell Publishing, 2005, Ch. 13.
3 Gordon W. Allport. *The Nature of Prejudice*. Cambridge, MA: Perseus Books, 1954, 1979, p. 196.
4 Monica Biernat and Melvin Manis. "Shifting Standards and Stereotype-based Judgments." *Journal of Personality and Social Psychology* 66, no. 1 (1991): 5–20.
5 John F. Dovidio and Samuel L. Gaertner. "Aversive Racism and Selection Decisions: 1989 and 1999." *Psychological Science* 11, no. 4 (2000): 315–319.
6 P.G. Devine, P.S. Forscher, A.J. Austin, and W.T. Cox. "Long-term Reduction in Implicit Race Bias: A Prejudice Habit-breaking Intervention." *Journal of Experimental Social Psychology* 48, no. 6 (2012): 1267–1278.
7 A. Stewart. "Why Newsroom Diversity Works: Effective Strategies for Making Newsrooms More Inclusive." Nieman Reports, June 2015. Accessed December 17, 2015 from http://niemanreports.org/articles/why-newsroom-diversity-works/.
8 Anthony G. Greenwald and Mahzarin R. Banaji. "Implicit Social Cognition: Attitudes, Self-esteem, and Stereotypes." *Psychological Review* 102 (1995): 4–27. And, John F. Dovidio, K. Kawakami, and Samuel L. Gaertner. "Reducing Contemporary Prejudice: Combating Explicit and Implicit Bias at the Individual and Intergroup Level," in *Reducing Prejudice and Discrimination*. The Claremont Symposium on Applied Social Psychology, ed. S. Oskamp. Mahwah, NJ: Erlbaum, 2000, pp. 137–163.
9 Rheeda L. Walker, David Alabi, Jessica Roberts, and Ezemenari M. Obasi. "Ethnic Group Differences in Reasons for Living and the Moderating Role of Cultural Worldview." *Cultural Diversity & Ethnic Minority Psychology* 16, no. 3 (2010): 372–378.
10 This is by far the most common demographic in newsrooms, according to the 2016 American Society of News Editors' annual diversity survey. http://asne.org/newsroom_census.
11 Clifford Geertz. "'From the Native's Point of View': On the Nature of Anthropological Understanding." *Bulletin of the American Academy of Arts and Sciences* 28, no. 1 (1974): 26–45.

12 Media Education Summit. Boston. Emerson College, October 2015.

13 Martin G. Forsey. "Ethnography as Participant Listening." *Ethnography* 11, no. 4 (2010): 558–572.

14 Maynard Institute for Journalism Education, *Reality Checks. Content Analysis Kit.* Accessed February 19, 2018 from http://media-diversity.org/en/additional-files/documents/Z%20Current%20MDI%20Resources/How%20inclusive%20is%20your%20coverage%20%5BEN%5D.pdf.

15 T.F. Pettigrew. "Intergroup Contact Theory." *Annual Review of Psychology* 49 (1998): 65–85. And, T.F. Pettigrew and L.R. Tropp. "How Does Intergroup Contact Reduce Prejudice? Meta-analytic Tests of Three Mediators." *European Journal of Social Psychology* 38 (2008): 922–934.

16 Donald A. Schön. *The Reflective Practitioner: How Professionals Think in Action.* New York, NY: Basic Books, 1983.

17 Sue Ellen Christian. *Overcoming Bias: A Journalist's Guide to Culture and Context.* New York, NY: Taylor & Francis, 2012.

18 The Society of Professional Journalists. "The Whole Story: Diversity Tips and Tools. Build Some Background." Accessed February 19, 2018 from www.spj.org/divws3.asp.

19 Ibid.

10

USING FAULT LINES IN REPORTING

Marquita S. Smith

Journalists cannot help but see any story through the lens of their own experience. In this chapter, Marquita S. Smith, associate professor at John Brown University and former editor and reporter in many newsrooms, explains an important conceptual tool called the Fault Lines, which was developed by the Maynard Institute for Journalism Education. By using the Fault Lines of race, class, gender, geography, and generation, journalists can better understand the limits to their own perception of events, people, and policies, and how to widen the lens.

Introduction

Growing up I was always amazed that local news, which highlighted crimes and mayhem in our low-income neighborhood, rarely mentioned the interesting, colorful personalities that dwelled in our apartments. As a result, I wanted to give voice to and tell the stories of minorities and underrepresented groups. That desire sparked my passion for journalism. After graduating from college and beginning a career as a reporter and editor, I quickly learned that the perspectives of minorities and low-income families were not just left out of my hometown newspaper – there was a national void. Today, news media across the nation continue to struggle to be more inclusive and to be more accurate.

Indeed, ask journalists to define diversity, and too often their response is silence. Then, they may come up with race, ethnicity, and gender. And, with all the talk about Millennials, Gen Xers, Gen Yers, and retiring Baby Boomers, generational diversity is becoming a more common conversation. Much is missing in this simple outline of categories, however. The late Robert C. Maynard created a framework that better captures the complexity of diversity in America, giving journalists, leaders, and employers a more effective common language. Maynard co-founded the Institute for Journalism Education, which was renamed the Robert C. Maynard

Institute for Journalism Education after his death in 1993. Maynard, a former reporter and columnist for the *Washington Post*, was the first African American to own a major metropolitan daily, the *Oakland Tribune*. Maynard said, "This country cannot be the country we want it to be if its story is told by only one group of citizens. Our goal is to give all Americans front-door access to the truth."[1]

Truth-seeking should be the primary business of journalism. In this chapter, I'll discuss the use of Fault Lines as a way to think about news stories. I'll examine coverage of a few news stories and use Fault Lines to explore possible vantage points from which to look at these news events differently. Finally, I'll show how Fault Lines can also be used to make individual journalists more aware of their own blind spots in regard to truly achieving diverse coverage.

The Five Fault Lines

While working as an editor for the *Virginian-Pilot* in Norfolk, Virginia, I had the opportunity to learn a great deal about the public's concerns regarding the credibility of the news. Our readers told us they wanted us to hire more minorities and deliver diverse content. They wanted to see more people of color in high-profile political stories and in everyday feature and business stories. Readers also requested more stories that accurately depicted their daily lives. An audit of our coverage supported the complaints, revealing that as a newsroom we did a poor job of including multiple voices in our reports.

To help us solve this problem, the late Dori J. Maynard introduced me and the *Pilot* to her father's work. Dori, who loved to talk diversity, explained the motivation for her father's model. After years of covering riots and social upheavals in the 1960s, Robert Maynard identified five fault lines of race, class, gender, generation, and geography as key differences that influence the ways in which Americans see their world. He shaped the model after the places where cracks deep within the Earth's crust cut the surface. Robert believed that by understanding the Fault Lines, we could build bridges across our diverse perspectives and discover better ways both to frame news stories and to help people to connect. This model continues to evolve, with the Fault Lines expanding to include religion, political views, social hierarchies, immigration status, and other factors. Dori often referred to such subcategories as "fissures."

The Fault Lines are:

- **Race and Ethnicity:** African American, Asian, Hispanic/Latino, Native American/American Indian and Native Islander, multiracial, biracial, white. Some international reporters might be tempted to say such categories aren't relevant – consider instead the ways in which the population you are covering divides itself.

- **Gender, Gender Identity, and Sexual Orientation:** Male, female, transgender, genderqueer, agender, gay, lesbian, bisexual, questioning.
- **Generation:** Youth, 20s, 30s, 40s, 50s, 60s+; Baby Boomer (born 1946–1964), Generation X (born 1965–1976), Generation Y or Millennial (born 1977–2002), Generation Z or iGeneration (born 2003–present). While age itself can create a point of view, that same point of view often is defined by generational experiences. For instance, Generation X didn't watch Richard Nixon resign as president. The Baby Boomers did not live through the Great Depression.
- **Class or Social Economics:** Rich, upper middle class or wealthy, middle class, working class, working poor, poor.
- **Geography:** Urban, suburban, rural; plus region – as in Midwestern or on the coasts.

Please keep in mind that identity terms change over time and it's important to keep up with them. Often it's best to ask your source what term they prefer.

Fault Lines at Work

If you walked around the *Pilot* newsroom after we learned about the Fault Lines, you would have likely noticed small round mirrors strategically placed at several cubicles. The mirrors were a reminder to writers and editors that we all have some blind spots.

Imagine with me that you are a reporter covering the North Dakota Access Pipeline, the Orlando mass shooting, the terrorist attacks in Europe, California, and Florida, or the church shooting that killed nine African Americans in South Carolina. Based on the Fault Lines model, what blind spots might you anticipate? What sources would you seek out? How might you frame your reports?

The Missing Fault Lines: North Dakota Access Pipeline

In 2016, Native Americans from the Standing Rock Sioux reservation began protesting the North Dakota Access Pipeline's construction on their sacred land.[2] The pipeline would span four states and produce some 570,000 barrels of oil per day. The Environmental Protection Agency asked to re-evaluate the environmental impact, but the US Army Corps of Engineers continued with its plans. Despite protests and lawsuits, oil began flowing through the pipeline in the summer of 2017. Supporters now say the pipeline has lowered energy transportation costs, improved safety, provided jobs, and benefited state coffers. Opponents say the project violates sacred lands and that public health remains at risk.

In the beginning, as the heat of protests rose around the nation, the news media framed the story as Native Americans hoping to protect sacred lands, then shifted to Native Americans as villains destroying property and endangering communities. The protestors were reported to have set construction equipment on fire in Iowa, which led to increased police presence at protests. Police officers began using brute force such as pepper spray and concussion grenades.

Many Fault Lines surfaced. Many Native Americans saw the protests as a peaceful, respectful, and pivotal struggle. They described their aim as protecting the Standing Rock tribe's sole water source.[3] Additionally, the protestors fought to preserve what they considered sacred, a place for their artifacts and burial grounds. Many news articles focused on the spiritual aspect of their effort, taking a racial Fault Line perspective and emphasizing cultural pride. Also, under the Fault Line of geography, they explored the impact on the protests by people who showed up from outside of the region, and the perspectives they brought to the situation. Another not so obvious Fault Line to consider would have been class, combined with geography. Forty percent of those living near the project were impoverished. In the event of an oil spill, would those residents recover? Often news coverage focused on the chaotic and troublesome nature of the protests rather than the group's attempts to keep the protests safe and nonviolent.[4] Both characteristics should have been included. Few media reports talked about the indigenous vision of sacred water, land, and air.

Choosing the Appropriate Fault Lines: Orlando Mass Shooting

Omar Mateen of Fort Pierce, Florida, gunned down 49 people on June 12, 2016, at a gay nightclub in Orlando. Authorities reported the attack as the deadliest mass shooting in the United States and the nation's worst terrorist attack since September 11, 2001. Mateen was American-born, but had pledged allegiance to ISIS (an Islamic State militant group). Major news outlets covered the unfolding of the event, Mateen's background and his radicalization. Several focused on a side story of the importance of gay nightclubs as a community gathering space in Orlando.

Reporting on this event revealed to the straight and cisgender[5] public that despite social gains in the last 50 years, the LGBTQ+ community still felt safer being themselves behind closed doors. The absence of gay voices and perspectives in daily news coverage up to that moment, combined with the dominant theme of safety in the breaking news, also conveyed an implicit, unintentional message: The invisibility of LGBTQ+ people also protects the rest of society. Using the Fault Lines of gender, race and ethnicity, or class, what other angles might have offered insights into the incident? How could journalists have more fully and accurately captured the community most deeply affected? Socio-economic challenges affect every community, including this one. What insights might have been brought to the story through this lens? As a place to start, consider that 42 percent to 68 percent of LGBTQ+ individuals report experiencing employment discrimination.[6]

Intersectionality: White Supremacy, Dylann Roof, and Charlottesville

Each of these news events shows that if journalists want to capture the full complexity of a story, they should go deeper than a single Fault Line and see what other forces are at play. Too often, issues are covered from only the most obvious perspective. The Fault Lines often run deep beneath the surface, contributing to volatile situations. More often than not, Fault Lines also intersect. Let's consider the massacre that killed nine people at an African American church in Charleston, South Carolina, and the protests over Confederate monuments in Charlottesville, Virginia.

On June 17, 2015, a white gunman opened fire at the Emanuel African Methodist Episcopal Church in Charleston, South Carolina, during its weekly prayer gathering and Bible study. Nine black Americans were killed. Media pundits and some in the black community criticized conservative media, particularly the Fox News network, for avoiding the race angle when covering the tragedy. Critics also called out CNN for being slow to respond and running international feeds about other news instead. People debated whether the news media showed unwarranted sympathy to the then-alleged white gunman by portraying him as mentally incapacitated.

But the repercussions of the incident went beyond the Fault Line of race. Consider geography. Both white and black residents of the South can be wary of justice systems and the news media. They recognize the oft-overlooked historical context that shades criminal justice and the politics of local communities. Law enforcement was often complicit in the thousands of lynchings that took place from the 1880s to 1960s, a vast majority of which took place in the South.[7] Local authorities participated in white Southerners' massacre of black citizens and destruction of their homes and businesses in incidents like the Tulsa 1921 "Race Riot."[8] News media often played a role in inciting violence with inflammatory reporting. And for generations, Southern media organizations and publications have refused to give voice to nonwhite groups. This painful past reverberated in the aftermath of the horrific shootings.

We can go deeper still by looking at generation and perhaps the intersection of race and generation. Some people think that younger Americans are overcoming the problem of racism and creating a "colorblind" society. Yet Dylann Roof, 21, who pleaded guilty, was convicted and sentenced to the death penalty for the shooting as a federal hate crime in 2017. He showed no regret and said he "had to do it." He held strong ideas about white racial superiority and used social media to promote them. He posted the South African apartheid flag and other hate speech on Facebook. How pervasive is this thinking among Southerners his age? Are members of the younger white generation looking for purpose in the South's racially charged past?[9]

That same year, the tumultuous events in Charlottesville, Virginia, sparked actions and ongoing debates about Confederate monuments in public spaces. In August 2017, the *Daily Progress* in Charlottesville reported on a series of protests by white nationalists who objected to a city decision to remove a statue of Confederate General Robert E. Lee. The white nationalists marched on the University of Virginia campus and in the town center. Students and others showed up in force to oppose their actions.[10] The clashes culminated on Saturday, August 11, 2017, when a white nationalist rammed his car into a crowd of counter-protestors, killing Heather Heyer, a 32-year-old paralegal.

Using the Fault Lines, let's analyze a news story from the Charlottesville *Daily Progress*, which described the run-up of events that led to confrontations between white nationalists marching on campus with Tiki torches and the mostly white student body that counter-protested. At first glance, the piece speaks to obvious race and ethnicity Fault Lines. In the story, students denounced white supremacists and their hatred of African Americans, Jews, and others they do not consider white. They expressed concern that the university allowed the value of free speech to supersede community comfort and safety.

Today many would describe the University of Virginia as a moderately liberal institution. However, few stories explored political fissures, which would have acknowledged the various political layers at play in the story. The story also failed to offer any details about students' socio-economic backgrounds, another important Fault Line. Many of the white supremacists argued that "others" were taking away opportunities from them. If many were working class, their feeling of loss may indeed be acute. They may have resented the white student body along with the "others" they malign. The story was about the removal of Confederate statutes in public spaces, but there were other important aspects to the white nationalists' viewpoints that could have been revealing.

Additionally, the Fault Line gender (sexual orientation) emerges as an important avenue to pursue. The article quotes a source responding to President Donald Trump's statement that some of those in the white supremacist group were "very nice people": "A person doesn't say, 'Die, *faggot*,' to my face. That's not a good person, and anyone who thinks that is either a white supremacist themselves or completely deranged." But the article doesn't explore that statement any further. Major themes of white solidarity are often focused on masculinity and heteronormative nuclear family values.

A subtler Fault Line of geography surfaces in Virginia history. A slave-owning territory, the Commonwealth of Virginia was a prominent part of the Confederacy. Here, local history – and US history overall – is filled with examples of oppression and subjugation spanning an array of social locations, including across class, gender, race and ethnicity, and sexual orientation. And here, in this story, there is the potential for showing the cross connections – or intersectionality – of the Fault Lines. Sometimes more than one Fault Line is in play and when journalists can probe how each one informs the other, they can help the public understand the depth and complexity of an issue. Many of these intersections in Fault Lines were lost in coverage because the primary focus was solely on race and the conflict between white nationalists and their opposition.

Revealing Power Dynamics: Coverage of Mexican American Studies Ban in Arizona

In 2010, news outlets across the nation reported on the Arizona law that banned ethnic studies courses in public schools. Conservative lawmakers and educators had decided that courses in the curriculum were promoting anti-white sentiment, even sedition, among Mexican American and Chicano students. In this case, race and ethnicity was the dominant Fault Line. But the fissure of the immigration status of students and others in the community also emerged, even though it was barely discussed.

The original coverage of the ban included few diverse sources.[11] In fact, most of the initial stories featured officials and politicians who were heavily involved in the issue – skewing coverage toward the official version of events. Where were the other stakeholders? Few students' quotes or viewpoints were included in reports. This missing generational Fault Line made the power dynamics of generation and social status more difficult for the public to notice.

Coverage of the issue, even as it evolved in 2017, failed to explore the students' perceived status as foreigners and immigrants, and the associated view that they were demanding something to which they were not entitled. There was also little reflection on the role of identity in healthy adolescent development,[12] or examination of the actual history curricula for high schools and whether these included Mexican Americans as central players. When stories described what students were learning in the classroom or the ways such lessons may have applied to their lives, it helped audiences understand why and how students' ethnicity affected their engagement with learning.

In late 2017, federal Judge Wallace Tashima blocked the ethnic studies ban, ruling it unconstitutional and "not for a legitimate educational purpose, but for an invidious discriminatory racial purpose and a politically partisan purpose."[13] Wallace concluded lawmakers had been motivated by racial animus when they eliminated the program, and that they violated students' constitutional rights in doing so.[14]

Fault Lines Reveal Your Blind Spots

In addition to enhancing reporting and sourcing, contemplating the Fault Lines can assist in your personal and professional journey toward more inclusive thinking. Recently, I attended a conference on multiculturalism in higher education. During a seminar, several participants introduced themselves using their gender pronouns. For instance, "Hello, I am Kate. My pronouns are she/her/hers. My major is Communication." This was the first time I had encountered a declaration of gender pronouns, even though it has become common on college campuses. I was perplexed and uncomfortable. Should I state my pronouns? What does it really say about me? Although I consider myself open to trans and non-binary people, my discomfort was real.

After reflecting, I realized that within the gender and sexual orientation Fault Line I had some blind spots. As an editor, I had struggled with finding creative ways to encourage reporters to be inclusive and respectful of the LGBTQ+ community. A decade of experience as a Fault Lines trainer and diversity practitioner had not made me culturally competent with LGBTQ+ people, let alone with those with varying gender identities. My experience as an African American woman added another layer, due to interactions between some parts of the black community and the white LGBTQ+ community. But my race/ethnicity did not make me especially good at understanding and resolving LGBTQ+ concerns. This is a lesson we must all learn. Even though we may have expertise about one Fault Line doesn't mean we will understand the nuance in the others.

Upon further thought, I realized that my uncomfortableness was not just about the pronouns. I had honestly assumed that everyone is the gender they were assigned at birth and used pronouns that match their physical features. Admitting that I have a blind spot came more easily with the help of Fault Lines.

After reviewing a few national stories, I realized that others are struggling with a similar blind spot in the gender Fault Line. In a *New York Times* story, "The Fire on the 57 Bus in Oakland," for instance, the author did an excellent job telling the story of Sasha, a white 16-year-old who identified as genderqueer and agender, and who used the pronoun "they."[15] While riding the 57 bus home from school, Sasha, who was wearing a skirt, fell asleep, and an African American teenager flicked a lighter at the skirt and it quickly went up in flames. Without demonizing anyone, the author brought forth the intersection of several Fault Lines, including race, class, and gender, and the clashes across them. While well-written, however, the story wrongly assumed readers understand gender identities, and beyond Sasha, no other voices from LGBTQ+ community were provided.

To understand my own blind spot more thoroughly, I sought counsel from a long-time friend and colleague who understood the rainbow-hued community. In 2003, she came out at age 35 as a lesbian, and her growth facilitated my growth. She told me that coverage of her community often has been distilled to the question of gay rights. While important, if this focus dominates coverage, such stories can fuel a narrative that LGBTQ+ members threaten traditional communities in society. Journalists often frame gay rights stories as a battle between civil rights and religious rights, as we see in coverage of the transgender bathroom legislation and in the coverage of the legal debate over refusing service to LGBTQ+ people on religious grounds.

Conclusion

Fault Lines can help journalists willing to take the risk to reflect on their blind spots and challenge them. The conversation with my lesbian colleague prompted me to evaluate media coverage of the LGBTQ+ community, and also to think about my unique position as someone who educates future journalists and professionals.

Whether journalists are brainstorming story ideas, designing a story plan or planning an in-depth project, it is important to think through the Fault Lines model. We should consider what lens or perspective may be missing from our news reports and strive to tell a more complete story. We should remember that readers and viewers consider diversity a credibility issue. All journalists should strive to present the whole truth.

Tip Sheet

Below is a list of best practices for applying the Fault Lines in news reports and media organizations. For more information on Fault Lines go to: www.mije.org/.

- Move beyond just covering crime, violence, poverty, or drugs in minority communities. Explore topics on health and wellness, finances, and unsung heroes.
- Become culturally competent and understand the historical and environmental contexts and issues that affect groups and communities. Worship services and community neighborhood events are good ways to begin.
- Develop a diverse source list with experts who can speak on news developments.
- Cultivate multiple sources from minority communities. Don't deputize minority community leaders and assume that they speak for the whole community. Remember, each community contains a range of viewpoints.
- Editors, reporters, photographers, and other staffers should all spend time away from the office engaging with minority communities.
- Create "listening posts," or opportunities to observe and learn about issues and concerns. Ethnic restaurants, beauty salons, community centers and social media hangouts are places journalists can connect. (See more detail in Chapter 11.)
- Leverage the differences among your colleagues and conduct brainstorming sessions to discuss the Fault Lines relevant in *future* story ideas and projects.[16]
- Check in with colleagues and others to explore your own blind spots.

Notes

1 "Robert C. Maynard: Life and Legacy." The Maynard Institute for Journalism Education. Accessed February 2, 2017 from http://mije.org/robertmaynard. The Robert C. Maynard Institute for Journalism Education is the nation's oldest organization dedicated to helping news media accurately portray all segments of society, particularly those often overlooked, such as communities of color.
2 Rebecca Hersher. "Key Moments in the Dakota Access Pipeline Fight." National Public Radio, February 22, 2017. Accessed March 9, 2018 from www.npr.org/sections/thetwo-way/2017/02/22/514988040/key-moments-in-the-dakota-access-pipeline-fight.
3 Various news reports contribute to this section on the North Dakota Pipeline, including Ryan W. Miller. "How the Dakota Access Pipeline Battle Unfolded." *USA Today*, December 2, 2016. Accessed January 24, 2018 from www.usatoday.com/story/news/nation/2016/12/02/timeline-dakota-access-pipeline-and-protests/94800796/.
4 Associated Press and Kelly McLaughlin. "Violent Scenes at North Dakota Oil Pipeline as Native American Protesters Claim Sacred Burial Grounds Were Destroyed by Construction Crew." Daily Mail.com, September 4, 2016. Accessed February 13, 2018 from www.dailymail.co.uk/news/article-3772859/Native-American-protesters-confronted-security-demonstration-against-work-Dakota-Access-oil-pipeline.html.
5 The term cisgender means people whose gender identity aligns with the biological sex they were assigned at birth.
6 Mary Virginia Lee Badgett. "Employment and Sexual Orientation: Disclosure and Discrimination in the Workplace." *Journal of Gay and Lesbian Social Services* 4, no. 4 (1996): 29–52. doi: 10.1300/J041v04n04_03; Mary Virginia Lee Badgett, Holning Lau, Brad Sears, and Deborah Ho. "Bias in the Workplace: Consistent Evidence of Sexual Orientation and Gender Identity Discrimination." The Williams Institute, June 2007. Accessed March 8, 2018 from https://escholarship.org/uc/item/5h3731xr.
7 John Hammontree. "New Memorial Ends the 'Silence' on a History of Lynching." AL.com, April 26, 2018. Accessed April 27, 2018 from www.al.com/opinion/index.ssf/2018/04/new_memorial_ends_the_silence.html. See also "History of Lynchings." NAACP, 2018. Accessed April 27, 2018 from www.naacp.org/history-of-lynchings/.
8 "1921 Tulsa Race Riot." Tulsa Historical Society & Museum, 2018. Accessed April 27, 2018 from https://tulsahistory.org/learn/online-exhibits/the-tulsa-race-riot/.
9 Various news reports contribute to this section on Dylan Roof, including *USA Today* and MSN websites: Tonya Maxwell and Tim Smith. "Dylann Roof Guilty in Charleston Church Shooting." *USA Today*, December 15, 2016, Accessed February 4, 2017 from www.usatoday.com/story/news/nation-now/2016/12/15/jury-deliberating-fate-charleston-church-shooter/95474302/; "Dylann Roof Laughs in Video Confession of Church Shooting." MSN Video, December 10, 2016. Accessed February 4, 2017 from www.msn.com/en-us/video/news/dylann-roof-laughs-in-video-confession-of-church-shooting/vi-AAloCbe; Meg Kinnard. "Charleston Church Shooter Dylann Roof Pleads Guilty, Awaits Execution." *Chicago Tribune*, via Associated Press, April 10, 2017. Accessed March 9, 2018 from www.chicagotribune.com/news/nation world/ct-charleston-church-shooter-pleads-guilty-20170410-story.html.
10 Michael Bragg. "Students Who Confronted Torch-Bearers Demand UVa Take Action." *The Daily Progress*, August 19, 2017. Accessed September 16, 2017 from www.dailyprogress.com/news/local/students-who-confronted-torch-bearers-demand-uva-take-action/article_f56a4e02-8531-11e7-a55d-c33d43b75ef4.html.
11 Robert Mackey. "Arizona Law Curbs Ethnic Studies Class." *New York Times*, May 13, 2010. Accessed March 8, 2018 from https://thelede.blogs.nytimes.com/2010/05/13/arizona-law-curbs-ethnic-studies-classes/; Andy Barr. "Arizona Bans 'Ethnic Studies'."

Politico, May 12, 2010. Accessed March 8, 2018 from www.politico.com/story/2010/ 05/arizona-bans-ethnic-studies-037131.

12 Beverly Daniel Tatum. *Why Are All the Black Kids Sitting together in the Cafeteria: And Other Conversations about Race.* New York, NY: Basic Books, 1997.

13 Jaweed Kaleem. "Federal Judge Blocks Arizona from Banning Mexican American Studies Classes." *Los Angeles Times*, December 27, 2017. Accessed January 27, 2018 from www.latimes.com/nation/la-na-mexican-american-studies-20171227-story.html.

14 Maggie Astor. "Tucson's Mexican Studies Program Was a Victim of 'Racial Animus,' Judge Says." *New York Times*, August 23, 2017. Accessed January 16, 2018 from www. nytimes.com/2017/08/23/us/arizona-mexican-american-ruling.html.

15 Dashka Slater. "The Fire on the 57 Bus in Oakland." *New York Times Magazine*, January 29, 2015. Accessed January 25, 2018 from www.nytimes.com/2015/02/ 01/magazine/the-fire-on-the-57-bus-in-oakland.html.

16 This list is compiled from professional experience, newspaper industry reports from the Freedom Forum, and the American Society of Newspaper Editors.

11

BUILDING RELATIONSHIPS IN UNDER-COVERED COMMUNITIES

Keith Woods

Sometimes the most difficult step for journalists is the very first: to enter a community that on its face appears foreign and even hostile. Here Keith Woods, NPR's vice president for Newsroom Training and Diversity, explains why and how to build rapport and trust with unfamiliar communities.

The Link between Staff Demographics and Coverage

In the late 1990s, my colleague Aly Colón and I did an experiment. We were both on the faculty of The Poynter Institute in St. Petersburg, Florida, the nation's premier school for working journalists. The profession was struggling, as it always had, with the task of telling the full stories of people historically left out of the news: poor communities; people of color; those who lived outside of the geographic and economic centers of the nation's cities.

The problem had persisted despite the best intentions of some journalists, the professed commitments of others, and inconsistent, but decades-long efforts of leading industry organizations. The American Society of Newspaper Editors (now the American Society of *News* Editors) had conceded that its "Goals 2000" plan to have the diversity of newspaper staffs match the demographics of their communities by the turn of the century wouldn't happen. Not even close. In 2000, nearly 25 percent of the US population was people of color. Racial/ethnic minorities accounted for fewer than 12 percent of journalists that year.[1]

We knew that there was a strong relationship between staff demographics and the depth of coverage of people of color and issues affecting them. We knew the coverage gaps we were seeing weren't merely intentional exclusion or apathy – although these were once rampant in US journalism. We suspected it was a deep-seated but unacknowledged ignorance and a cultural estrangement that wouldn't fix itself.

Our experiment at Poynter would test the notion that if journalists knew more about their communities, if they met more people from places poorly represented in the news – sat with them, ate with them, talked with them – the media would do smarter journalism and these new relationships would prove valuable down the road.

We called our experiment *Making Connections*.[2] We brought together 16 journalists from the six major news organizations in Tampa Bay. We launched the effort by making the arguments for inclusion – from the fuller truth that diversity provides to the new and interesting stories it can reveal, and we asked the journalists to help us put those arguments to the test. Our project provided much of the wisdom that underlies this chapter.

We began our experiment with this core message: To build relationships in under-covered communities, journalists need to act against three powerful obstacles standing in the way of a change – *individual* biases and blind spots, *organizational* roadblocks, and *societal* structures still serving to divide and exclude.

Why Build Relationships?

Journalism, were it guided only by the values that lie at the root of the profession, wouldn't need the efforts that fall under the umbrella term "diversity." If we routinely attended to the core principles of the craft – accuracy, completeness, fairness, giving voice to the voiceless, for example – that ought to ensure that everybody's story gets told.

Why, then, is it necessary to seek out communities, people, or perspectives in this way? One way to better understand the "why" behind diversity is to look at three forces arrayed against journalism's nobler goals. Start with yourself.

Our Individual Blinders

As *individuals*, journalists come to the work with limitations and biases. Your upbringing, education, connections, life experiences, habits all combine with your prejudices and biases – both conscious and unconscious – to create the lens through which you see some stories. These can become blinders that block your view or understanding of others. (See Chapter 4 on implicit bias for an elaboration of this point.)

In an internal study of on-air sources we conducted at National Public Radio between 2013 and 2015, we found what most advocates of media diversity had always suspected: The race, ethnicity, and gender of reporters correlated profoundly with the race, ethnicity, and gender of their sources. Three of every four sources used by NPR's male reporters in the 2015 fiscal year, for example, were men. And, we found that journalists who were Latino, white, black, and Asian had substantially higher percentages of sources of their own race and ethnicity than did others. The results alone argued the case for diversity in hiring and in reporting. Left to our own devices, journalists are drawn to people they know, people like them.

In dozens of workshops I've run with journalism students, professors, and professionals, fear emerges as an obstacle to diversity in sourcing. People express concerns ranging from physical safety to simple comfort. These anxieties deter the news media from learning more about other people, other communities, and other experiences beyond their own lives.

"I'm reasonably comfortable talking about all these differences except race," a professor at one of the country's leading journalism schools wrote in a 2015 email to me. The subject, the professor said, is "still the most sensitive subject in our society (in my view) and the hardest to address with students. We are all so careful and so nervous, afraid of offending. I don't feel on solid ground there."

Unless we make specific efforts to address our own discomfort, fears, and natural inclinations to gravitate toward the familiar, our *individual* boundaries will limit the truths journalists are able to tell, and under-covered communities will remain so. (See Chapter 9 on stereotypes and Chapter 10 on Fault Lines for ideas about how to address fear and discomfort.)

Organizational Barriers

News organizations, whether we're talking about a three-person startup or the industry's long-established giants, have constraints of their own that make this work necessary. How might beat structures, staffing levels, technological deployment, or even the physical location of the organization limit which communities get covered?

In the NPR sourcing analysis, we found that coverage of national politics, general news and business combined to account for more than half of all stories in 2015. Coverage of education, religion, and health together accounted for only 12 percent of the coverage. Those three latter categories also were home to the highest proportions of sources that were female and racial and ethnic minorities.

An organizational bent toward analysis, when combined with those coverage preferences, drove the news division to lean heavily upon college professors, other journalists, and people with expertise in politics and governance as sources. This predilection for experts and analysts, on the surface unrelated to race, ethnicity, or gender, predisposed journalists toward having an overwhelmingly white and male source base.

Why? Because in 2015, three-fourths of all professors in the United States were men, and 84 percent of all full-time professors were white.[3] And, for reasons related to the history of discrimination in the United States, the higher up you go in industry and politics, the fewer people of color or women you'll find.

Organizational coverage patterns and individual habits together, then, can conspire to keep people out of the news. They make conscious efforts to diversify coverage and sourcing necessary. And, to further bolster the diversity of your story-telling, you can expand your coverage of topics that, by their nature, touch more people across the country. Faith and education; schools and parenting; small businesses and neighborhoods – these all are threads that run through every demographic slice of the country; they all are beats that will take you into under-covered communities for stories beyond crime and other social pathologies. You can bring in more voices from the general public in stories that invariably affect them.

Consider who you rely upon as experts. Covering leaders within institutions like the state legislature or city council is important if you hope to be of service to your community. But those institutions represent people in cities, towns, and neighborhoods who are affected by the decisions at the state capitol or city hall. They are "experts" when it comes to their lives and their communities, and in seeking them out, you almost certainly will find a greater diversity of sources by race/ethnicity, class, geography, and ideology.

Societal Barriers

Finally, *society* itself stacks the deck against complete coverage. Many of our communities are segregated by class, by race and ethnicity, by faith, ideology, and other dimensions of difference. So journalists have to work harder to find and authentically tell the stories of under-covered communities. In such a geographically divided society, the school you choose to cover on the first day of class, the mall you visit for the day-after-Thanksgiving retail story, or the church, mosque, or synagogue you use as the backdrop for a piece on trends in faith can determine the race, ethnicity, class, or sometimes the sexual orientation of your sources. This, in turn, can affect the framing of the story itself.

An individual journalist or her organization may embrace the ideals of diversity and still be thwarted by the habits, limitations, and biases of the larger society. Reporter Sonari Glinton of NPR, in covering the automotive industry, found that public relations officials, men and women, tended to pitch stories and sources to him that were overwhelmingly male. They did this despite strong evidence that women are the primary decision-makers when it comes to buying cars.[4]

Glinton took on this problem in several ways: He often asked PR officials whether there was a woman who could speak with expertise on the subject. He looked for automotive stories that focused on the things women seek in cars (beyond better consoles to store purses and other bags; outlets for kids to plug in electronic devices, for example). Over time, companies were pitching those stories and touting those sources without being prompted by Glinton.

Without Glinton's conscious effort, stories about the industry would exclude the voices of those central to the purchasing power that propels the industry forward.

These three factors – *individual, organizational,* and *societal* – have been omnipresent and persistent in blocking diversity throughout the history of journalism. They must be routinely and repeatedly counteracted if journalists are to give an accurate, complete, and fair account of what's happening in their communities, especially communities routinely left out of the daily report.

Why Cover the Under-Covered?

The best answer is contained in one word, "truth." If we hope to fulfill the top tenet of ethical journalism, "Seek truth and report it,"[5] then it follows that the next task is to seek out truth wherever it can be found. That means we're forever expanding the breadth and depth of reporting to discover stories yet untold. Like the mythical goal of "objectivity," we aspire to "truth" with a lower-case "t," aware that the pictures we paint of our communities are forever incomplete. So covering those typically left out of the news is no mere act of benevolence. Seeking out untold stories and unheard voices brings us closer to the heart and soul of ethical journalism. (Also see Chapter 5 on the colorblind conundrum for more discussion about seeking stories on racial communities.)

There's more. One definition of journalism's purpose is "to provide citizens with the information they need to make the best possible decisions about their lives, their communities, their societies and their governments."[6] We can do that only if our reporting delivers on that promise.

Over the decades, traditional news organizations have been late to many stories that might have helped citizens better understand what was happening around them. In my home state of Louisiana, for example, news organizations reported almost exclusively on the controversy that encircled former Ku Klux Klan Grand Wizard David Duke as he rose to prominence in politics. They did not sufficiently investigate the groundswell behind his popularity.

In 1991, he took 60 percent of the white vote and exposed a stunning racial chasm across the state. The story of disaffected poor and blue-collar white people, many economically devastated by the oil bust of the late 1980s, at odds with social liberals in larger cities, and harboring unexpressed racial prejudices, had eluded news organizations for years. These residents felt their political and economic power slipping away and proved willing to cast their lot with a white supremacist.

Twenty-five years later, journalists found themselves again out of touch with that demographic slice of the electorate as businessman Donald Trump rose to capture the Republican nomination for president and, ultimately, the presidency.

In 2008, the steady increase in middle-class Puerto Ricans migrating to central Florida would change the politics of the state and swing a critical chunk of the nation's Electoral College votes toward Democrats and then-Sen. Barack Obama. The Latino power base moved from the Cubans of South Florida to the Puerto Ricans of the Interstate-4 corridor. For news organizations not tapped into this burgeoning community, the political shift came as a surprise. As a result, it was a surprise to many readers, listeners, and viewers.

Many news organizations across the country missed the early signs that attitudes among straight Americans toward those who are lesbian, gay, bisexual, and transgender were undergoing a profound shift. They were late to discover and understand the roiling angst that gave rise to the Occupy movement in late 2009 or the Black Lives Matter phenomenon that more recently came to define the protests in cities across the country over the deaths of young black men at the hands of police.

Though national in scope, each of those stories and many more had roots in local, poorly covered communities.

It falls to journalists to master the reporting and interviewing skills necessary to get to that greater truth. That was our thinking at Poynter when we launched our *Making Connections* project, and the lessons we learned then remain relevant today.

Telling Untold Stories: Three Easy Lessons

It was the late *St. Petersburg Times* columnist Peggy Peterman who introduced me to the notion of the "Listening Post," which in turn became the cornerstone of *Making Connections*. Peterman was a vocal, untiring advocate of diversity in newsrooms and news coverage, weaving her message into so much of the award-winning work she did as a columnist. She took our Poynter group on a tour of south St. Petersburg, home to the bulk of the city's black middle class and nearly all of those who were black and poor, communities rarely visited by mainstream media.

The first stop on the tour was a tree. It was a large, sprawling oak that provided shade to a gathering of middle-aged and older black men who met regularly to play checkers and swap stories. It was, Peterman said, the perfect *listening post* — a place to sit, meet people in a relaxed way, soak up their stories, and build relationships with those who might later become sources. In a 1991 column, she showed how she'd approached this slice of an under-covered community:

> I want to write about The Tree and the people who enjoy fellowship under it, I say, nervously hoping they will agree.

> "You need to wait for Mr. Willie," one young man says, resting leisurely against the picnic table, peering through his sunglasses . . .

> At 4:30 p.m., I return. "Here she is, Mr. Willie," someone says . . .

> A slender man of average height steps forward. Mr. Willie's hands say he works hard. His eyes are tender; face, compassionate. He seems embarrassed that he's getting so much attention. With his hands clasped behind his back, he greets me:

> "Yes, I'm Mr. Willie," he says. "Can I help you, ma'am?"

A protective quietness falls over those sheltered beneath the tree's branches. Men and women lower their voices to listen. With a quick smile, Mr. Willie, whose full name and age are Willie Collier, 55, not only agrees to be interviewed but thinks his friends also will be cooperative. The tree and its occupants seem to breathe a sigh of relief, and the fellowship resumes.[7]

The patience, observation, and listening packed into that passage say much about what we learned from Peterman about reporting in under-covered communities. By putting the notebook away, paying deep attention to details, and listening not just to what people say, but what they convey beyond words, journalists can get to fuller, more authentic stories. As a discipline, there's value in starting every reporting assignment with a closed notebook and open mind.

Peterman took our 16 journalists on a tour of south St. Petersburg, launching our year-long experiment. When we were done, she had provided some distinct lessons that go to the heart of building a meaningful, productive rapport with the people journalists too often misunderstand and overlook. The most important of those lessons was the one Peterman taught first:

Lesson 1: Go There

Award-winning photojournalist Jamie Francis, who made a name for himself in Florida and Oregon by telling the stories of people journalism usually missed, once told me that sometime the hardest thing was to get out of his car and meet and talk to people.

With all of the communications technology available and emerging – mobile, instant, networked, video-enabled, and GPS-supported – it's easy to do a lot of arm's-length reporting and lose the value of being present. For journalists like Francis, it can be challenging to overcome the discomfort and awkwardness of starting from scratch with strangers. Technology becomes all the more tempting. Yet connecting face-to-face is always the best way to build relationships. It's critical in communities where journalists have historically been absent.

The best approach, as former reporter Angie Chuang shows in the accompanying case study, is to go into communities at a time when there's no story and no agenda. Francis said he overcame the awkwardness by allowing himself to be driven by curiosity and bolstered by a single assumption: There was something he had in common with every source. If he could discover what it was, he and his source would relax enough for their story to reveal itself.

Over the course of our experimental year, the *Making Connections* team visited a mosque and Islamic school, a daycare center, a funeral home, a recreation center, and the central gathering place of the county's Asian Americans and Asian immigrants.

At the Islamic Center of Tampa Bay, we got an inside perspective from women who wear the traditional hijab and live in a society that sometimes equates this act of faith with misogyny. In greeting the group, Imam Dr. Mohamad Sultan made a simple point about journalism's relative estrangement from Muslim communities: "I'm glad you're here," he began, "when there is no killing, no war."

At a small funeral home on Tampa's west side, where the city's poorest black citizens live, the owners outlined the things you might learn about a community during one of the worst times in the lives of its people. Like Sultan, they described how journalists were not around to tell the full story of the neighborhood. The last time they'd seen a reporter around was after a shooting near the funeral parlor. The husband and wife team described what they could tell journalists if they'd only ask.

"For sure, we get all the bad news," one said, including insights into the financial struggles of the people around them and the devastation they see in families who lost relatives to gun violence. But they also told journalists about the "Old Timers" group of community elders who met regularly at a local diner. They tipped the group off to a story about how cremation trends among black people was threatening the existence of the black funeral home, one of the pillars of black communities from the nation's earliest days.

During a year of visiting such listening posts, we discovered that there is something qualitatively better about starting a source relationship while breaking bread. We ate with Latino professionals at an historic Cuban restaurant and with Asian professionals at a prominent Chinese restaurant.

In the years since that Poynter experiment, much has changed about journalism and the way we in the profession conduct our business. What hasn't changed, what makes the enduring lessons of *Making Connections* relevant well into a new millennium, is the fundamental value of walking a community's streets and meeting its people in person.

Lesson 2: Read the Walls

Social media and a society saturated with cameras have combined to give journalists an easy and direct pipeline to community information. Technology allows you to tap into communities of interest that live only online and provide a window into actual places through their digital pages. Tapping into these quick-access networks is an essential tool for any journalist.

Many people, though, are either not plugged in or aren't very active in the digital space, so *reading the walls* is more than just a metaphor. Our *Making Connections* team found that this piece of advice could be taken literally.

When we visited the Islamic Center, a bulletin board held a flier that was also stapled to utility poles around the neighborhood, calling people to a protest. The focus was *The Siege*, a movie starring Denzel Washington and Bruce Willis in which Muslims were portrayed as rabid terrorists. One of the team's reporters ran with the story and brought to the surface a simmering concern among US Muslims that would soon become a national issue.

On a visit to the Asian Family and Community Empowerment Center, known locally then as the FACE center, we met with the director. The FACE center helped keep cultural traditions alive with dance classes, after-school homework help for school children, and help for immigrants making their way through the bureaucratic maze of a new country. On the wall behind the director's desk was a mural depicting the "killing fields" of Cambodia. Someone asked about it.

The director told the group his story of escaping Cambodia as a child; of seeing relatives murdered by Khmer Rouge soldiers or starved to death in the regime's drive to purge the country of anyone deemed a threat to the power of its leader, Pol Pot. Later that year, and a world away, Pol Pot died. Because they had read the walls (and asked questions), the journalists were able to bring an international story home and show its resonance in the face and words of a St. Petersburg neighbor.

Reading the walls in the virtual world is as easy as using search tools to find groups, languages, organizations, or individuals whose worlds you can tap into with a keyword or hashtag. Search the profiles of people using LinkedIn, Facebook, Twitter, or any of the established and emergent social media sites to discover new sources and new trailheads to stories.

Lesson 3: Find Guides

People like Peggy Peterman and "Mr. Willie" Collier, or the funeral directors, each had high credibility in the communities they represented. A phone call, email or in-person introduction from one of them could go a long way toward opening pathways along which you could meet new people and find more stories. At its core, this is wisdom deeply rooted in reporting, no matter what the beat.

Award-winning *Sacramento Bee* journalist Stephen Magagnini has made a living telling the stories of people in under-covered communities. In some cases, he has had to work through a gulf of cultural and language differences that made it difficult to even begin a conversation. In others, he has had to overcome deep distrust of media that was years in the making. More than many journalists, he understood how to find guides.

When he wrote the 2000 series "Orphans of History" about Hmong families adjusting to a new life in northern California, a series that earned an ASNE distinguished writing award, Magagnini started his reporting with guides.

"I didn't know any Hmong to begin with," he wrote for the web supplement to the textbook *The Authentic Voice: The Best Reporting on Race and Ethnicity*,

> so I started gradually by finding the society's gatekeepers: a savvy Hmong court interpreter, a Hmong social service agency, and a feminist

and community activist who was the daughter of a Hmong woman my wife had met at a farmers' market. I took the time to get to know them, talking about their lives and the issues confronting their families and community. I also read a few books on the secret war in Laos. Laying such groundwork – even before you have specific stories in mind – is a great way to build trust, open doors, and develop story ideas.[8]

In places where trust may be an issue, whether that's a local police department, an immigrant community, or a sovereign Indian nation, having a guide – someone to speak for you and connect you with others – is essential. You can borrow the credibility and deep roots these guides have cultivated and build your own source network from there.

Conclusion

Every tip you'll ever find for building relationships in under-covered communities will work for you in any other journalistic endeavor. It is, after all, just good reporting. But the antidote for estrangement, isolation, and distrust requires more.

Meeting people where they live, eating with them, listening and observing – those are the tools for relationship building. Journalists need to go into under-covered communities with an open mind and closed notebook, listening deeply and reading the walls, tapping seldom-heard sources and taking the hands of guides who can provide entry into places journalists too seldom go.

The wisdom of countless journalists over decades suggests that, for journalists who can overcome fear, overrule biases, and expand what they know about their communities, a world of untold stories await.

The Chicken and the Listening Post

Angie Chuang

The first day I reported to my new editor at *The Oregonian* in Portland to launch a beat on Race and Ethnicity Issues, she had some unusual instructions for me.

It was January 2000. My editor, Michele McLellan, handed me a map of the city created by the newsroom data expert, specially coded to highlight the areas of greatest change in race and ethnicity in the last decade. Go to these places, she said. Don't do formal interviews or ask for story ideas. Instead, observe, eavesdrop, and converse with regular people.

"And I don't want you to file a story for at least a month," she said.

Either my editor is crazy, or I have the easiest job in the world, I thought, as I went straight to the brightest spot on the map. It turned out to be a subsidized apartment complex in the heart of northeast Portland. Until recently, it had been home to working-class whites. Now it was a first stop of choice for resettled refugees from Southeast Asia, China, Somalia, Iraq, and elsewhere.

As I chatted with the apartment manager, he told me he had recently been talking to health officials and animal rights groups about an unusual complaint: Because so many of the complex's newer residents were accustomed to buying and slaughtering chickens in their home countries for food and ceremonial purposes, a nearby poultry farm had begun driving a truckload in once a week. Business was brisk, but longer-term residents and neighbors had been calling the authorities.

Of course, I had to return, with a photographer, the next time the chicken truck was at the complex. I talked to Hmong, Chinese, Mien, and Lao residents amid a cacophony of clucking and feathers as they told me about their favorite recipes for the upcoming Lunar New Year. When the county health department confirmed that the truck did not violate any laws, I had a story. I wrote about the ways in which refugees and immigrants adapt familiar traditions to new places, and how businesses and neighbors respond by capitalizing, accommodating, or resisting.

Michele McLellan, who had been inspired by a Poynter Institute lesson on using the "Listening Post" method of reporting, had played an editor trick on me. She knew that the approach, which emphasized observation and listening to "regular" people, would produce stories. But removing the pressure for immediate results made me more open to letting ideas develop organically from the ordinary, everyday lives of people in under-covered communities, rather than the editor or reporter's preconceived ideas.

Notes

1 American Society of Newspaper Editors Newsroom Diversity Survey, 2000 Census. Accessed March 14, 2017 from http://asne.org/content.asp?contentid=172.
2 Keith Woods and Aly Colón. "Making Connections." *The Poynter Report*, Spring, 2000.
3 Richard Van Noorden. "U.S. Women Progress to PhD at Same Rate as Men." *Nature*, February 17, 2015. Accessed March 14, 2017 from www.nature.com/news/us-women-progress-to-phd-at-same-rate-as-men-1.16939; Caroline Sotello Viernes Turner, Juan Carlos Gonzalez, and J. Luke Wood. "Faculty of Color in Academe: What 20 Years of Literature Tells Us." *Journal of Diversity in Higher Education* 1 no. 3 (September, 2008): 139–168. doi: 10.1037/a0012837.
4 Sue Mead. "Women Flex Their Car Buying Muscles." boston.com, August 24, 2013. Accessed March 14, 2017 from www.boston.com/cars/news-and-reviews/2013/08/24/women-flex-their-car-buying-muscles.
5 Society of Professional Journalists Code of Ethics. Accessed March 14, 2017 from www.spj.org/pdf/spj-code-of-ethics.pdf.

6 American Press Institute. "What Is the Purpose of Journalism?" Accessed March 14, 2017 from www.americanpressinstitute.org/journalism-essentials/what-is-journalism/purpose-journalism/.

7 Peggy Peterman. "A Community Branches Out." *The St. Petersburg Times* The Floridian Section, January 15, 1991, p. D-1.

8 Steve Magagnini. "Reporter's Journal: Orphans of History." *The Authentic Voice.* Accessed March 14, 2017 from http://theauthenticvoice.org/mainstories/orphansofhistory/essay_orphansofhistory/.

PART IV

Case Studies

12

CASE STUDIES

Introduction to Case Studies

Sometimes the best way to learn something new is to deconstruct examples. In this section, we have asked senior reporters to describe their experiences covering health, education, wealth, housing, immigration, and a safety net program, the foster care system. Most of the case studies presented here start from a reported story. Journalists discuss their reporting strategies, challenges they faced, and how they overcame those barriers. At the end of each case study is a tip sheet that you can apply to your own reporting. These tips suggest questions to ask your sources and data to gather in order to uncover the roots of structural disparities. Consider how you might build a "B-roll" of background material and knowledge that you can call into play anytime you must quickly produce a piece. Finally, while it is instructive to examine how each reporter applied the structural framework to his or her individual beat, we encourage you to extend their experiences across beat structures to maximize the impact of your coverage.

CASE STUDY A

Reporting Opportunity in Health

Sally Lehrman

While news media have begun reporting more often on health disparities by race, the implicit message can be one of biological determinism or behavioral failures. In this case study, science and health reporter Sally Lehrman explains the public health theory of social determinants of health and how to show the connections between a policy or practice and a specific health outcome.

As a medical science and health reporter, I've covered remarkable genetic research and medical breakthroughs. It's a world that moves at lightning speed, with discoveries promising to enhance human health dramatically. I've had a chance to write about scientists identifying the genetic variations that underlie breast cancer, discovering families of tuberculosis that are surprisingly virulent, and achieving the first gene therapy approval, for the purpose of treating cancer.

Yet even this fairly technical field can fall into the personal responsibility trap. In recent years, for example, genomics has investigated the ways in which an individual's personal experiences and environment can influence the way her genes work, even change them. Scientists call this field "epigenetics." "We're beginning to understand that the choices we make can have a long-term impact on our health and can cause genetic level change, which could even impact future generations," writes one genetic testing company in an online history of DNA. Then it makes a moral assertion: "Individual responsibility for our lifestyle choices is therefore more important than ever before."[1]

Now we're responsible for our very genetic code – and those of our grandchildren?

Beyond Personal Responsibility

In health and medical reporting, it's easy to drop right into personal responsibility and behavior to explain unequal health outcomes. The stubbornly discouraging figures about higher rates of asthma, diabetes, heart disease, HIV – you name it – among nonwhite populations often become motivational tools in narratives about how to make better choices in food, exercise, and sexual health. Health writers cover interesting programs designed to get people eating better, walking more, or addressing stress through yoga or meditation. Medical writers offer insight into new treatments should we fall ill. And now, even reports on the latest genomics research can become part of the refrain.

Promoting healthy choices is always a good idea, of course, but it only gets to the symptoms of health inequities, not their root causes. While we all make decisions every day that influence our physical and emotional well-being – and indeed, perhaps even affect our genes – factors well beyond our control shape those decisions. If we break it down by the numbers, about one-third of health outcomes can be attributed to behavior, says Julia Caplan, a public health expert at the Public Health Institute in Oakland, California. But one-half is deeply influenced by our social and physical environment. Even the remaining one-fifth, which is clinical care – the purview of medical writers like me – relies greatly on our economic status and has been documented to differ radically by race.[2]

Environments Shape Behavior

Furthermore, "all the behavioral inputs are shaped by the environment, too," Caplan adds. While day-to-day choices about health do matter tremendously, those choices are expanded or limited based on the environment that surrounds us. This includes who we know, where we live, where we work or go to school, and the resources we have available in our lives, from time to transportation. Even policy can be considered part of our environment. It shapes our physical, economic, and social surroundings. Consider the impact of seatbelt laws, no-smoking rules, and broadened health care coverage. Seatbelt use has cut injuries and deaths from traffic accidents by about half, according to the National Highway Traffic Safety Administration.[3] Dozens of studies have found a significant association between public smoking bans and a reduction in both heart attacks and strokes.[4] And the Affordable Care Act increased use of some types of health care and expanded diagnosis – and thus treatment – of chronic health conditions in low-income adults.[5]

Journalists and communication specialists can produce powerful stories with long-term impact by getting at the heart of compromised health – that is, the factors behind the choices people make. Fortunately, public health researchers and practitioners have made great advances in recognizing these forces and developing ways to address them. As we described in Chapter 6, we can think about unequal health outcomes as the result of toxic debris washed downstream from hidden sources further up the river. We know that behavior has an immediate effect on health. But further upstream, neighborhood and living conditions play an important role in shaping those behaviors and either polluting the stream or keeping it clean. Structural policies, and the institutions that create these and carry them out, shape those living conditions. At the top, social hierarchies and privileges shape institutions, their policies, and their operations. Journalists can adapt this "social determinants of health" model as a framework to report and flesh out the details.

Neighborhood Differences

Let's look at Alameda County, California, as an example. In the 1990s, this diverse county of 1.5 million had a greater life expectancy than anywhere else in the state or across the United States, at 80.5 years. The public health department, however, was growing increasingly concerned that some population groups in some areas were faring much better than others. A unit to assess the problem found a whopping 24-year difference in life expectancy across census tracts. At one end, people living in the low-income, majority black area known as West Oakland could look forward to a life expectancy of only 67 years. That's similar to North Korea and Kazakhstan. And at the opposite end, in the leafy district of Lower Hills, residents could expect to live to 91.

"Differences in neighborhood conditions powerfully predict who is sick, who is healthy, and who lives longer," their report summarized.[6] Economic conditions, the built environment, crime, and education levels, they concluded, explained more than half of the variability in lifespan. But why did those conditions exist, and how did they affect health? All these factors, even crime and education, tie back to policies and power relations that afford the wealthier, whiter areas of the county more resources and support. Some studies suggest, for instance, that government and corporations deliberately site toxic facilities in nonwhite, economically disadvantaged communities because residents lack the political capital to fight them.[7] The same might be said for less desirable businesses such as liquor stores, a high density of which in turn is associated with higher levels of violent crime.[8]

Over time in Alameda County, resources for good health had accumulated in higher income, whiter neighborhoods, while they decayed in lower income, nonwhite areas.[9] Housing prices and availability, pay and benefit levels, transportation, air quality, crime laws, and access to insurance all influence health and interact. They may build supportive conditions like the compounding interest of a bank account for health or, on the other hand, create health costs that can never quite be paid off and eat away at a person's underlying reserves. And rather than resulting from poor choices by people who happen to live in the same neighborhood, these conditions come into being as a result of institutional decisions and structural forces.

The health department consulted the public on what should be done. "We wanted to do something upstream, based on the data and the literature," said Sandi

Galvez, director of health equity, policy, and planning for the Alameda County Health Department. "We worked with community partners to focus on each area, and what policy changes were needed." Transportation, housing, and the cumulative trauma of discrimination were all areas that residents wished to address.

Transportation

First, they tackled transportation. The department conducted a health impact assessment of bus funding and identified ways in which fare increases and service cuts had harmed health,[10] for example:

- Stress caused by long waits, getting passed by the bus, safety concerns while waiting, and longer travel times.
- Forced economic tradeoffs such as cutting back on food, social activities, and doctor visits because of higher transportation costs.
- Missed school and reduced work hours, lost job opportunities, late arrivals to school and work, and longer commutes.
- Social isolation due to poor transit options.

Their report recommended a discounted transit pass program and other improvements that could lessen waits, crowding, and travel time. Eventually, no-idling signs helped clear motor vehicle exhaust from areas with high asthma rates. Free shuttles gave rides from the local rapid transit system to facilities such as a hospital and a juvenile justice center.

Housing

Housing was also a major concern,[11] Galvez said – in particular, the impact of the foreclosure crisis that began in 2006. Over four years, one in four mortgages in the city of Oakland entered into foreclosure. In low-income communities of color, bank auction signs could be found on every other block. Foreclosures were rampant in communities of color throughout the United States because banks had targeted black and Latino borrowers with high-interest loans even when they qualified for lower-interest offerings.[12] The health department teamed up with a community group, Causa Justa :: Just Cause, to identify the hardest hit neighborhoods and survey residents about their health. Before the financial crisis, they found, many of these neighborhoods already had struggled with the highest premature mortality rates in the county. Uncertain futures, forced moves, and abandoned properties worsened the toll.

Researchers discovered that when banks took over apartment buildings in foreclosure, they often did not maintain the property and stopped paying utility bills. Tenants would find themselves without water and stuck with mold, rodents, or cockroaches that landlords refused to address. People who owned homes in foreclosure faced anxiety and stress,[13] loss of their wealth, overcrowded living conditions, and hard choices about whether to pay for food, utilities, or medicines. Disrupted schedules made it a challenge to maintain healthy diets, get exercise, and visit the doctor or pharmacy. Their neighbors suffered too, with their property values also declining as neighborhood vandalism and crime rose. When long-time residents were forced to move, these families lost health-promoting community ties, including access to friends, schools, and churches.

Causa Justa :: Just Cause and the health department developed ideas to mitigate the impact and began advocating for policy change. They involved residents in lobbying for ordinances that required banks to register vacant and foreclosed properties with the city and maintain them until a sale. They pushed for a state law to ensure that utilities would continue delivering water to foreclosed buildings. Through such legislative advocacy, Alameda County's health department aimed to address both power relations and the upstream causes of health conditions directly affected by landlord neglect and housing instability: asthma, depression, anxiety, and poorly controlled diabetes and heart disease.

The influx of technology workers throughout the county also has pressured rents and home prices in the area, forcing displacement, overcrowding, and ever-higher proportions of monthly income spent on housing. Over one two-year period, residents who paid more than a third of their income on rent were twice as likely as others to land in the hospital for hypertension or mental illness, and children packed into overcrowded homes filled up emergency rooms with urgent asthma needs.[14] Technology companies, whose extensive growth helped create the crisis, have built "company towns" for incoming workers, developments that in turn produce their own structural repercussions.[15] While these companies often contribute funds for recreation facilities, buses, immigration, education, and even policing, they also benefit from major state and local subsidies and tax benefits. The tax credits they collect can drain resources that normally go to transportation, schools, and parks for the whole community.

You can find important stories at each level of the structural equity ladder. Show the differences in health opportunity across two neighborhoods by tracing the direct effect on individual lives. Or go further up the ladder and show why those neighborhood conditions exist. What is the history behind settlement patterns and the distribution of resources that led to long-standing community characteristics? What are the institutional pressures now in force, such as banking practices, investor ownership of properties, or the loss of neighborhood infrastructure such as family-oriented stores? What polices and power relations led to recent neighborhood changes? Do tax incentives steer particular types of development? Do subsidies upset the balance of big companies and smaller businesses that supports a diverse economy?

Trauma and Toxic Stress

As journalists look into the physical conditions in neighborhoods that shape both health behaviors and outcomes, it's important to investigate the social environment as well. Chronic stress, the result of living in an unsafe, loud, noisy, and potentially violent neighborhood, or living under the threat of being deported at any moment, or living in fear of police authorities despite their motto to "to protect and to serve,"[16] is the unspoken reality of many people's lives.

"That insidious energy has a negative effect on our health," points out Fred Ferrer, former chief executive of the Health Trust, a nonprofit that promotes health equity. Chronic stress produces constant surveillance and reactivity by the heart, nervous system, and brain. An unrelieved alertness and heightened response state increases one's vulnerability to disease and ability to overcome it.

Chronic stress isn't just an urban problem. Rural communities throughout the United States struggle with the nation's highest levels of poverty and the stark, depressing omnipresence of boarded-up stores and gas stations along main streets.[17] The effects are both physical and psychosocial. No matter the geography, poor communities contend with hazardous waste, dilapidated housing, air and water pollution, poor sanitation, and more. Families struggle with high levels of turmoil, separation, violence, and day-to-day uncertainty and lack of routine. Very early, children show the biological effects.[18]

These conditions weren't created by families themselves. External institutional factors such as a supervisor's habits in scheduling shifts, a multi-unit landlord's policies about smoking and garbage, or an employer's decisions about cooperating with immigration raids all contribute. Even health matters that an individual can control, such as choosing to limit drinking and smoking, can become hostage to a loss of self-efficacy and a sense that life is captive to powerful external forces.

While toxic stress may seem difficult to address in health reporting, attention to the need for culturally responsive, trauma-informed policies and services is growing nationwide. Reporters can investigate the extent of awareness of trauma in schools, health departments, criminal justice facilities, and other institutions. Are schools addressing trauma from experiences such as violence, poverty, and neglect? Can residents access trauma-sensitive arts, mental health services, and opportunities for civic engagement?

Discrimination and subtle, day-to-day racism also are forms of toxic stress. "It's a proven fact that racism and other forms of discrimination make people sick," says Caplan of the Public Health Institute. "It gets under the skin." When going upstream to understand the origins of health inequities, Galvez advises journalists to probe inequities in power. "We talk about making healthy choices. But the whole world helps you make healthy choices or not." Reporters can look at policies, enforcement, and access to decision-makers. Do the responsible agencies enforce housing and sanitation codes equally across low-income or racially segregated areas? Do public investment and agency budgets favor some communities over others? Who has access to city council members or county supervisors? How open are decision-making processes? How do private investors and corporations wield power, and how do the results impact communities of color?

Tying the Pieces Together

When reporting on these social determinants of health, it's important to follow through and show the links between social conditions and individual behavior. I-News, an investigative reporting team in Colorado, examined the widening disparity between their state's low infant mortality rate for whites and its high rate for Latinos and blacks. The story mentioned access to care, and also what it termed "a catchall that experts call the social determinants of health." Poverty and lack of education influence health, the story mentioned, continuing with a list: "Where you live. Whether you buckle your seat belt. What you eat and drink. How much you exercise. Even which school you attend."

The next paragraph gave an example:

> Black and Latino children were much less likely than white children to wear seat belts or bike helmets and reported significantly lower levels of physical activity … As a physician, Schuster regularly talks about the importance of seat belts and bike helmets with his patients. But he can't make them comply.

The story was on the right track but went awry. By placing behavior on equal footing with external factors such as schools and neighborhoods in describing the infant (and child) mortality gap, the story muddled the causal relationship between the two. The central example – the choice to wear seatbelts – failed to unpack the reasons behind children's choices and put the blame squarely on them. The reader can only assume that a weakness in culture, values, or appropriate discipline is at root. Some questions that might have led the reporter to a clearer example: Are Colorado neighborhoods and schools generally segregated? Do the schools that serve white children have better bike safety programs and rules that require wearing helmets on campus? Do the white children tend to live in neighborhoods with sidewalks and green parks, where it's safe, easy, and fun to get out and play?

Understanding the living conditions that shape health "is hard," says Caplan, of the Public Health Institute. "It's messy." But it's both possible and powerful.

Tip Sheet

• *Ask, "Why?"*: One simple question offers a straightforward way to begin unpacking high rates of disease and identifying underlying causes. It is, "Why?" Why is a parent not exercising? Perhaps because he isn't making it a priority. Why? Perhaps because it's unpleasant to exercise. Why? Perhaps because it's too hot outside. Why? Perhaps the heat is exacerbated by asphalt all around, with no trees for shade or grass to cool the air. And so on.

- *Use HIAs for leads*: Some cities and counties have begun to use studies called Health Impact Assessments to investigate the health repercussions of transportation, land use, agriculture, or other institutional plans and policies. HIA reports lay out health impacts across population segments and make mitigation proposals. These documents can provide fodder for reporting on the intersection between development policies and health equity. In San Francisco, for example, an HIA studied residential energy efficiency programs and advised features and subsidies that would support health in high-risk areas by addressing indoor air quality and reducing outdoor noise.[19] Reporters can use HIAs to identify where resources are being directed and to hold developers and other actors accountable. Also, HIAs from other locales can serve as guides to investigate projects and proposals in your own region.

- *Look for unintended consequences*: News about infrastructure or transportation plans provide a great opportunity to check whether the changes may favor some neighborhoods over others, and what impact this may have on health. Notice, too, that policies that seem to benefit everyone sometimes do hidden harm. Consider public transit and roadways. When routes are expanded, where do they go? Are maintenance and operations included? Older diesel buses spew fumes that affect air quality, and bus depots are often located in low-income and non-white communities.[20] In what neighborhoods do local officials place health-promoting features such as new traffic-calming measures, walking and bicycling paths, and cleaner bus fleets?

- *Probe housing and health*: Investigate the many relationships between health outcomes and housing issues including gentrification, soaring rents and home prices, and foreclosures.[21,22] Relocation to either low-opportunity areas or suburbs distant from jobs makes it more difficult to schedule doctor's appointments, pick up medicines, and participate in exercise classes or other self-care. Wheelchair users may not find housing on the ground floor or with elevators. Children often fall behind in language development, physical dexterity, and social skills because their families are struggling with simply keeping a roof over their heads.[23,24]

- *Show community members in action*: We tend to focus on the "downtrodden," but by doing so, we undermine a community's self-efficacy and can unwittingly reinforce stereotypes. Look for community members who are leaders and who are working with local health departments to make change. Focus on solutions, not just the problem.

- *Make the connections*: When you learn about policy or program changes in an area such as education, employment, or transportation, look into the health implications. You can ask agency representatives about the potential health impact, or call the public health officer and ask them. Ask for an example of a local community or group whose health may be affected, why, and how.

Notes

1 DNA Worldwide. *The History of DNA Timeline*. Accessed April 14, 2018 from www.dna-worldwide.com/resource/160/history-dna-timeline.

2 Institute of Medicine. *Unequal Treatment: Confronting Racial and Ethnic Disparities in Health Care (Full Printed Version)*. Washington, DC: The National Academies Press, 2003. doi: 10.17226/10260.

3 Centers for Disease Control and Prevention. *Seat Belts: Get the Facts*. Accessed April 14, 2018 from www.cdc.gov/motorvehiclesafety/seatbelts/facts.html.

4 Kate Frazer, Joanne E. Callinan, Jack McHugh, Susan van Baarsel, Anna Clarke, Kirsten Doherty, and Cecily Kelleher. "Legislative Smoking Bans for Reducing Harms from Secondhand Smoke Exposure, Smoking Prevalence and Tobacco Consumption." *Cochrane Database of Systematic Reviews* 2, art. no. CD005992 (2016). doi: 10.1002/14651858.CD005992.pub3.

5 Laura R. Wherry and Sarah Miller. "Early Coverage, Access, Utilization, and Health Effects Associated with the Affordable Care Act Medicaid Expansions: A Quasi-Experimental Study." *Annals of Internal Medicine* 164, no. 12 (2016): 795–803. doi: 10.7326/M15-2234.

6 Joint Center for Political and Economic Studies. *Place Matters for Health in Alameda County: Ensuring Opportunities for Good Health for All*, November 2012. Accessed April 12, 2018 from www.nationalcollaborative.org/wp-content/uploads/2016/02/PLACE-MATTERS-for-Health-in-Alameda-County-2.pdf.

7 Robert J. Brulle and David N. Pellow. "Environmental Justice: Human Health and Environmental Inequalities." *Annual Review of Public Health* 27 (2006): 103–124. doi: 10.1146/annurev.publhealth.27.021405.102124; Also, Robert D. Bullard. "Confronting Environmental Racism in the 21st Century." *Global Dialogue* 4, no. 1 (2002): 34–48.

8 Ethan M. Berke, Susanne E. Tanski, Eugene Demidenko, Jennifer Alford-Teaster, Xun Shi, and James D. Sargent. "Alcohol Retail Density and Demographic Predictors of Health Disparities: A Geographic Analysis." *American Journal of Public Health* 100, no. 10 (October 2010): 1967–1971. doi: 10.2105/AJPH.2009.170464.

9 Alameda County Public Health Department. *Life and Death from Unnatural Causes, Executive Summary*, p. vii. Accessed April 14, 2018 from www.acphd.org/media/144757/lduc-execsum.pdf.

10 Alameda County Public Health Department. *Getting on Board for Health: A Health Impact Assessment of Bus Funding and Access*, May 2013. Accessed March 17, 2018 from www.acphd.org/media/309841/transithia_es.pdf.

11 Dawn Phillips, Robbie Clark, Tammy Lee, and Alexandra Desautels. *Rebuilding Neighborhoods, Restoring Health: A Report on the Impact of Foreclosures on Public Health*, 2010. Accessed March 7, 2018 from www.acphd.org/media/53643/foreclose2.pdf.

12 Dan Immergluck and Geoff Smith. "The External Costs of Foreclosure: The Impact of Single-Family Mortgage Foreclosures on Property Values." *Housing Policy Debate* 17, no. 1 (2006): 57–80.

13 See also Alexander C. Tsai. "Home Foreclosure, Health, and Mental Health: A Systematic Review of Individual, Aggregate, and Contextual Associations." *PLoS ONE* 10, no. 4 (2015): 1–21.

14 The *San Francisco Chronicle* reported, "Between 2012 and 2014, Alameda County residents who spent 35 percent of their income on rent were twice as likely to be hospitalized for hypertension or mental illness as residents who spent less than 25 percent of their income on rent. Children living in homes packed with 10 to 12 extra people were six times more likely to go to the emergency room for asthma than children living in homes that were not overcrowded." Rachel Swan. "Public Health Problems in Oakland Linked to Housing Crisis." *San Francisco Chronicle*,

September 1, 2016. Accessed March 17, 2018 from www.sfgate.com/bayarea/art icle/Housing-crisis-linked-to-public-health-problems-9193855.php.

15 David Streitfeld. "Welcome to Zucktown. Where Everything Is Just Zucky." *New York Times*, March 21, 2018. Accessed March 25, 2018 from www.nytimes.com /2018/03/21/technology/facebook-zucktown-willow-village.html.

16 Los Angeles Police Department. *The Origin of the LAPD Motto*. (Reprinted from BEAT magazine, December, 1963.) Accessed April 14, 2018 from www.lapdonline. org/history_of_the_lapd/content_basic_view/1128.

17 "6 Charts That Illustrate the Divide between Rural and Urban America." PBS News Hour, March 17, 2017. Accessed March 25, 2018 from www.pbs.org/news hour/nation/six-charts-illustrate-divide-rural-urban-america.

18 Gary W. Evans, Jeanne Brooks-Gunn, and Pamela Kato Klebanov. *Stressing Out the Poor: Chronic Physiological Stress and the Income-Achievement Gap*. Stanford Center on Poverty & Inequality, Winter, 2011. Accessed March 25, 2018 from https://inequal ity.stanford.edu/sites/default/files/media/_media/pdf/pathways/winter_2011/ PathwaysWinter11_Evans.pdf.

19 Centers for Disease Control and Prevention. "Healthy Places, Funded Health Impact Assessments: San Francisco Department of Public Health." Accessed April 14, 2018 from www.cdc.gov/healthyplaces/fundedhias/sanfrancisco.htm.

20 PolicyLink and Prevention Institute. "The Transportation Prescription: Bold New Ideas for Transportation Reform in America." Accessed April 14, 2018 from www. convergencepartnership.org/TransportationHealthandEquity.

21 Sandro Galea. "Housing and the Health of the Public." Boston University School of Public Health, February 12, 2017. Accessed on July 16, 2018 from www.bu. edu/sph/2017/02/12/housing-and-the-health-of-the-public/.

22 James Krieger and Donna L. Higgins. "Housing and Health: Time Again for Public Health Action." *American Journal of Public Health* 92, no. 5 (2002): 758–768.

23 Alameda County Public Health Department and Behavioral Health Services. *Improving Housing and Health for All in Alameda County: The Opportunity Is Now*, June 2016. Accessed March 23, 2018 from www.acphd.org/media/425883/hous ing-brief-june-2016.pdf.

24 Bay Area Regional Health Inequities Initiative. *BARHII Displacement Brief*. Accessed April 7, 2018 from http://barhii.org/wp-content/uploads/2016/03/BARHII_Hou sing_Displacement_Brief_short.pdf.

CASE STUDY B

Sometimes School Segregation Comes from Race Neutral Policies

Venise Wagner

Emerging social science research suggests that some "race neutral" education policies have racialized outcomes. In this case study, former education reporter Venise Wagner shows ways to incorporate the latest findings in your reporting through an examination of educational policies.

Labeled Emotionally Disturbed

As an education reporter with the Hearst-owned *San Francisco Examiner* in the mid 1990s, I learned that the San Francisco Unified School District was struggling to address the overrepresentation of African American students placed in special education because they had been deemed emotionally disturbed. In 1995, black students were 35 percent of those assigned to special education even though they made up 18 percent of the student population in the district. Outraged with the disproportion, the brash, newly appointed superintendent, Bill Rojas, created a committee of psychologists, teachers, and administrators called the Superintendent's Intervention Prevention Committee (SIPC) to review individual cases of students who were thought to be at risk of being wrongly assigned to special education. His goal was to reduce the overrepresentation of black students in special education.

I tracked the story of one African American boy at Rooftop Elementary School, located in one of San Francisco's white, affluent neighborhoods. He was in second grade at the time, and had been acting out and disturbing class. He had shown no signs of being able to read. A school psychologist, brought in to observe him and administer a battery of tests, concluded he was emotionally disturbed. But his mother believed this assessment was cursory at best. She also feared that a special education designation would stigmatize her son.

She quickly had her son transferred into another school, John Muir Elementary, which was seen as an urban school with primarily black kids. It was also a school that served as a training ground for up-and-coming teachers. There her son was assigned to a young teacher, Robin Davis, who had a reputation for knowing how to handle discipline in the classroom. The boy flourished under her tutelage and he was soon reading close to grade level. The boy's mother took matters into her own hands to get this outcome, but she regretted having to move her child away from Rooftop, a school with rich resources. Rooftop was known for its enriched arts program.

District administrators believed the superintendent's committee, SIPC, could have provided an important intervention in a case such as this. Rojas and other administrators were concerned that the disproportionate labeling of black students as "emotionally disturbed" correlated with low educational demands on students and thus low achievement, higher suspensions, lower on-time graduation rates, and increased involvement with the juvenile justice system.[1] It was a sure pathway to the schools-to-prison pipeline for minority students and also proved to be a form of racial segregation.

De Facto Segregation in Schools

In 1954 the landmark US Supreme Court decision, *Brown* v. *Board of Education*, seemed to guarantee the dismantling of laws that segregated public schools on the basis of race. Yet more than six decades later, separate and unequal as a rule and practice has calcified in school districts throughout the country. Nonwhite enrollment in public schools systems has climbed by two-thirds from 1990 to 2013, while white enrollment has dropped by one-third in the same time period, according to the UCLA Civil Rights Project.[2] As white students leave the public school system, blacks and Latinos have become more racially isolated in schools. Michigan, New York, Illinois, Maryland, and California are at the top of the list of states with severe segregation of Latino and black students.[3]

The UCLA Civil Rights Project attributes this trend in part to a series of federal court decisions that have rolled back desegregation plans. Continued residential segregation and white flight to private schools also contribute. Most racially isolated schools experience economic isolation as well, suffering from fewer resources, higher teacher turnover, and a higher percentage of inexperienced teachers.

While some journalists have begun to dig deep into policies – district mapping and open enrollment, as examples – that drive school segregation, there is much more work to be done in this area. Additionally, segregation *within* schools deserves public scrutiny. Racial isolation within schools can be just as damaging and often equates to an unequal distribution of resources and poor outcomes for students of color.[4] Budgets for special education programs vary considerably across the country but are notoriously under-resourced.[5] When students of color are assigned to special education programs they are often relegated to substandard curricula and services, sometimes in a separate physical area.

Journalists have a lot of possibilities to explore in examining how district and school policies and practices may be driving racialized outcomes such as the disproportionate number of blacks in special education. Reporters should examine the trends in their district and make connections between the outcomes and the policy choices of the district.

In the last decade, social psychology research has informed our understanding of the many invisible levers and gears at work, often indirectly or unconsciously informing policy decisions and teaching practices. Even though many of these policies and practices are seemingly race neutral, they result in devastating outcomes for students of color but beneficial outcomes for white students. Here, education reporters have a deep well of issues to dive into.

New Federal and State Guidelines

At San Francisco Unified, some parents, special education advocates, and teachers pushed back against Rojas' committee, believing it blocked students with special needs from getting the right services. At the same time, despite the SIPC's efforts, the number of black students assigned to special education continued to rise in the district. The committee died when Rojas left the district in 1999.

The US Department of Education grew more concerned with the national trend of racial disproportionality in special education programs, however, and in 2006, began mandating that state departments of education track and reduce the disproportionate number of black students assigned to special education. Six years later the California Department of Education notified San Francisco Unified School District that it had a significant problem with disproportionality that had continued for more than four years and demanded a plan to reduce it. This plan, called the Coordinated Early Intervening Services (CEIS) plan, is a great place for any education reporter to start when delving into this issue. If a district has a problem with disproportionality, they will be required to develop a CEIS plan, which provides intervention strategies, district data, and perhaps some data for individual schools.

In the case of San Francisco Unified, little had changed since the dissolution of the SIPC and the emergence of the CEIS plan. There were now fewer black students in the public schools as the black population fell in San Francisco to 5 percent, but the disproportion was still there. In 2015, black students made up 9 percent of the district, but represented 17 percent of special education students, according to the district. The most common special education label for African Americans students is emotionally disturbed, and that year, African American students made up 29 percent of special education students with that label.

The District's Search for Root Causes

The US Department of Education requires school districts to use 15 percent of their special education budgets to fund the development and implementation of CEIS plans.[6] For San Francisco Unified in 2016 that amounted to about $1.8 million. The required CEIS plan includes a deep dive analysis of root causes behind disproportionality and an action plan to address those root causes. The intervention strategies may include direct services to general education students or the plan may recommend training and professional development. San Francisco identified five root causes in 2012, including an inability to teach a diverse group of students and low academic expectations of students of color; an inability to create positive cultures in the classroom and inconsistent positive school cultures across the district; a lack of teacher training and inability to support students who have experienced violence and trauma at home and in their neighborhoods; poor community outreach to parents of struggling students; and a district-level inability to coordinate and sustain individual initiatives that aim to address disproportionality.

Education Policies and Practices and Today's Social Psychology

Underlying all of these specific causes is implicit bias, the unconscious thread that runs through the daily practices of teaching and the decision-making behind most district and school policies. Social psychologists have unearthed the various ways implicit bias affects a range of disciplines, and in education we now have a framework that can help people better understand how social status impacts the way people and groups interact.

For example, a Yale study found that many preschool teachers unconsciously focus their disciplinary attention on black children (boys especially), expecting bad behavior.[7] This means that as early as preschool, black students are already more likely than their white peers to be labeled as having emotional problems in the school. It also means that white students as early as preschool are given the message that if they misbehave it will likely go unremarked.

Implicit bias also fuels expectations of academic performance. We know that ideas of intelligence are often linked to race. Expectation states theory helps explain the symbolic capital that many teachers attach to white students over students of color. Unconsciously, teachers may give greater value to the work of white students over that of black students even though the two may be comparable. Additionally, status characteristics such as race influence everyday interactions and inform performance expectations.[8] When teachers expect more of white students than they do of students of color, it means students of color will expect less of themselves and will be less prepared for the demands of college. The former George W. Bush administration called this the soft bigotry of low expectations.

Stereotype threat, which is a situational phenomenon in which people are at risk of conforming to the stereotype that is expected of them, is an especially troubling factor for students of color, who are often associated with negative stereotypes.[9] Anxiety about fulfilling these negative stereotypes can lead to reduced performance in the classroom and on tests. When black students were given a test and told it was a test of their cognitive ability, they performed worse than their white peers, even though the two groups were matched by ability. The anxiety of not wanting their performance to fulfill the negative stereotype that black students are less intelligent was so great that black students often unwittingly fulfilled the stereotype.

The various forms of implicit bias provide journalists with several lines of inquiry: What are districts doing to ameliorate the impact of implicit bias among teachers and principals? Are they training teachers in classroom management and instructional practices that can turn the tide of racially disproportionate outcomes? What are districts doing to reverse the effects of stereotype threat and the subtle messaging of low expectations?

Cultural competence is also a factor. How well prepared are teachers, administrators, and other staffers to address the needs of a diverse group of students with a wide range of cultural backgrounds and attitudes? As an example, Elizabeth Blanco, San Francisco Unified's former chief of special education,[10] said that many behaviorists who are hired to determine the emotional stability of students often lack cultural competence and fail to account for cultural norms outside of white middle-class behavior.

Hoarding Resources

Opportunity hoarding, the consolidation of resources by those who already have the resources, is also prevalent in schools. Even when the school staff states it wants to improve racial disparity in education, white parents can sometimes thwart efforts to redistribute resources in an equitable way if they feel their children will be denied what they believe is rightfully theirs. Amanda Lewis and John Diamond explore this phenomenon in their book *Despite the Best Intentions*. Looking at a high school in a Midwestern suburb, they found that white parents expected their white children to be enrolled in higher-tracked courses and, when they weren't, exerted pressure on administrators to place them there. As a result, school employees often placed white children in these courses in anticipation of complaints. Black children, on the other hand, were not afforded these advantages.

In San Francisco, the large Asian American population changes this dynamic some. Asian American and white students dominate higher-tracked courses, which may be the case for other districts on the Pacific Coast. Also in San Francisco, Chinese American families won a settlement with the school district after they filed suit in 1995 saying the district's desegregation plan interfered with their right to send their kids to neighborhood schools. The settlement in effect meant schools continued to mirror San Francisco's segregated neighborhoods and allowed affluent neighborhoods to maintain the best resources in their geographic areas.

When reporting on disparity, it's crucial for journalists to show more than the harm done to one particular group. Reporters must also demonstrate who benefits from the systems in place and why they benefit from them. Sometimes this is a difficult subject to address. In the case of the story I followed in 1995, I highlighted the experience of the black student who had been designated emotionally disturbed, but I also provided context that Rooftop was a school primarily attended by affluent white students, with a bevy of resources that allowed students to flourish, particularly in the arts. The "troubled" black student would not have had access to those enriching resources had he been assigned to special education. And because he left the school, he was still denied that access.

Too often the racial disparities in education are attributed to cultural attributes of groups. The most recent debate is about the importance of resilience and grit. Amy Chua and Jed Rubenfeld talk about the "triple package": superiority complex, insecurity, and impulse control.[11] Immigrant groups are cited as carrying this trifecta of cultural characteristics. But what is missing from this national debate on the role of cultural traits is the role played by institutions and physical and social environments. Yes, culture plays a role, but only within this larger context. In fact, sometimes the broader contextual elements drive the development of cultural characteristics.[12] Journalists must include the full picture to help the public have a more robust dialogue on disparities in education.

Epilogue

In a conversation after the story ran, a white parent told me how important diversity was to her and her children. She prided herself on keeping her kids in public school when many parents in her social circle had abandoned public school and sent their kids to private school. She never complained about the story, but she believed Rooftop Elementary had done all it could for the "disturbed" boy and therefore deserved kudos for trying and for its attempts at diversifying its student body. It was difficult for her to see that Rooftop's inability to teach and manage the black child who had been giving them trouble was an impediment to diversity in the classroom. Readers need to understand how policies, behaviors, implicit beliefs, and attitudes often betray the high principles that we in society say we hold.

Social psychologists have helped reveal invisible gears at work, deeply embedded in the ways many teachers interact with students and in the various ways policies are administered. Educators are becoming ever more mindful of these gears and it is up to journalists to help the public know whether and how well educators are incorporating this new knowledge.

Tip Sheet

- Education reporters can deepen their coverage of racial disparity by asking the following questions:

- Are schools or districts addressing implicit bias in the classroom? If so, how, and is it working?
- How do teachers view and treat parents, especially parents of color and working-class or poor parents? What steps are they taking to reach out to these parents?
- What are district measures and criteria for assessing emotional disturbance?
- Are schools creating a schools-to-prison pipeline? Check the policies that dictate suspensions and expulsions. Then square those with practices. What are the numbers by race? In what way does race play a role in how decisions are made?
- Are university education programs properly preparing teachers to handle a variety of learning styles and discipline scenarios? What training do districts offer in this area?

- Big data can play an important role in understanding racial trends in schools. Reporters who are working on deadline can do a quick-turnaround story just by looking at numbers such as suspensions/expulsions, gifted and talented assignments, special education assignments, resources of schools primarily filled with students of color vs. resources of schools primarily filled with white students. Reporters can then follow up with a more detailed story that examines the "why" behind the numbers.
- Sometimes it's helpful for reporters to keep a database of important facts about disparity – to serve as B matter or B roll for future stories. For example, a reporter can get a district's CEIS plan, pull out the root causes identified in the plan and place them in the database. Many news organizations follow test score results every year, and the racial disparity in these results might be related to root causes identified in the CEIS plan. It's important for reporters to help connect these dots.
- There may be opportunities for collaboration between reporters covering education and those covering the foster care system and other social service agencies. As an example, about half of foster care youth are engaged with the special education program in their schools because they have been identified as having a special need. This results from the constant moving, which leads to a loss of learning and instruction time. Additionally, these young people have experienced many layers of trauma – from family separation to feelings of abandonment among others – and often need counseling. Reporters can examine the strategies school districts have in place to help foster care youth navigate these issues.

Notes

1 Daniel J. Losen, *San Francisco District Profile*, San Francisco Unified School District report, February 19, 2012.

2 Gary Orfield, Jonyeong Ee, Erica Frankenberg, and Genevieve Siegel-Hawley "Brown at 62: School Segregation by Race, Poverty and State." Civil Rights Project, UCLA. Accessed February 15, 2018 from www.civilrightsproject.ucla.edu/research/k-12-education/integration-and-diversity/brown-at-62-school-segregation-by-race-poverty-and-state/Brown-at-62-final-corrected-2.pdf.

3 Ibid.

4 Jeannie Oakes. *Keeping Track: How Schools Structure Inequality*, second edition. New Haven: Yale University, 2005. Also, Beth A. Ferri and David J. Connor. "Tools of Exclusion: Race, Disability and (Re)segregated Education," *Teachers College Record* 107, no. 3 (March 2005): 453–474.

5 Jay G. Chambers, Thomas B. Parrish, Joanne C. Lieberman, and Jean M. Wolman. "What Are We Spending on Special Education." Center for Special Education Finance, Brief No. 8 (February 1998). Also, Daniel J. Losen and Gary Orfield. *Racial Inequity in Special Education*. Cambridge, MA: Harvard Education Press, 2002.

6 Funds from the special education budget rather than the district's general fund cover expenses for CEIS plans and programs. This means that special education programs are deprived of these resources.

7 Walter S. Gilliam, Angela N. Maupin, Chin R. Reyes, Maria Accavitti, Frederick Shic. "Do Early Educators' Implicit Biases Regarding Sex and Race Relate to Behavior Expectations, Recommendations of Preschool Expulsions, and Suspensions?" Yale University Child Study Center, September 28, 2016. Accessed February 15, 2018 from http://ziglercenter.yale.edu/publications/Preschool%20Implicit%20Bias%20Policy%20Brief_final_9_26_276766_5379.pdf.

8 Amanda E. Lewis and John B. Diamond. *Despite the Best Intentions: How Racial Inequality Thrives in Good Schools*. New York, NY: Oxford University Press, 2015.

9 Claude Steele. *Whistling Vivaldi: And Other Clues to How Stereotypes Affect Us*. New York, NY: W.W. Norton & Company, 2010.

10 Elizabeth Blanco left San Francisco Unified School District July 1, 2017 to work in Pasadena Unified School District. She was interviewed for this case study in December 2016.

11 Amy Chua and Jed Rubenfeld. *The Triple Package: How Three Unlikely Traits Explain the Rise and Fall of Cultural Groups in America*. New York: Penguin Books, 2014.

12 Erin B. Godfrey, Carlos E. Santos, and Esther Burson. "For Better or Worse: System-Justifying Beliefs in Sixth Grade Predict Trajectories of Self-Esteem and Behavior across Early Adolescence." *Child Development*, June 19, 2017. doi: 10.1111/cdev.12854.

CASE STUDY C

Exploring the Wealth/Income Gap

Jeff Kelly Lowenstein

In this case study, investigative reporter Jeff Kelly Lowenstein uses the example of school funding to show how journalists can combine observation, interviews, and database reporting to expose structural wealth and income disparities and the deep repercussions in individual lives. Kelly Lowenstein is an assistant professor at Grand Valley State University's School of Communications.

Same Scores, Different Experiences

It began with a one-building schoolhouse in one of Illinois' wealthiest communities and an elementary school in one of the state's poorest. It ended with a revelation about entrenched disparities in funding one of the most critical tasks any society undertakes: the education of its young people.

It was 2006 and I had just started working for the *Chicago Reporter*, an investigative nonprofit that focuses on race and poverty issues in Chicago, Illinois, and across the nation. Founded in 1972 in the aftermath of the civil rights movement in the city, the *Reporter* sought to use data to hold elected officials and city leaders accountable to their promises of equal treatment for all. My assignment was to examine the issue of school funding in Illinois. Like the majority of states across the country, Illinois relies on local property tax as the primary source for funding public schools. The inequities in per pupil expenditures that result from this policy decision have been well documented. We set out to see if we could identify other ways this tax policy affected students' educational experiences.

I started with school districts' test scores and discovered something that seemed out of the ordinary. Fourth grade students in one of two schools in the Ford Heights District, a poor, former company town south of Chicago, performed as well as those who attended the single school in the Rondout School District in

Lake Forest, a white and affluent community north of Chicago that annually has the highest annual per pupil expenditure in the state. Ford Heights, a black suburb, only spent about $12,500 per student per year, while Rondout doled out more than $22,000 annually for each child.

I visited both schools to find out what was happening in the classroom. Even though the scores were identical, the educational experience offered by each school was dramatically different. The differences I found could affect students' readiness for college, ability to get there, and opportunities to thrive once they arrived.[1] Not surprisingly, much rested on how administrators spent their funds. And that, I learned, tied closely to community health and how schools raised their dollars.

Wealthier districts like Rondout not only spent more per pupil, they generated nearly all of that money from local property taxes, even though the communities they served almost always enjoyed a substantially lower tax rate than others in the state. As a result, school administrators in richer towns were able to have far more control over academic decisions than their counterparts in places like Ford Heights. In Ford Heights and other impoverished communities, property taxes could not raise enough to fund schools adequately, so school administrators relied on federal funding sources. These monies – such as Title I funding for low-income students – were non-discretionary, tied to specific activities, and could not be counted upon for renewal year after year.

In our interviews, Ford Heights administrators told us that their uncertainty about reliable funding made it hard to forge long-term plans. There was no time or money for world language or arts programs at the school, both of which could enrich learning, boost critical thinking, and put students on track for college.

Instead, teachers drilled their students to prepare for the battery of tests mandated through the No Child Left Behind Act of 2002. The law required states to test students in reading and math each year in grades three through eight, as well as once in high school. By the 2013–2014 school year, all students had to reach proficient levels on state tests.

Teachers at Ford Heights spent much of the school day preparing students for state-defined testing goals. Schools that did not meet the standard for two years or more faced an escalating set of consequences. Students in poorly performing schools, for instance, could choose to transfer to another school in the same district. Over time the school could ultimately face state intervention, shutdown, or the loss of federal dollars.

Rondout stood in sharp contrast. There, teachers assumed that the affluent homes their students came from had the resources to provide strong academic support, and therefore students were expected to perform well on the exams without daily test preparation at school. As a result, teachers could gear education much more toward each student's individual interests.

Classes included heavy doses of enrichment, including foreign languages, fine arts, physical education, technology, and life skills. The teachers worked with students on understanding and appreciating racial, ethnic, and economic diversity. Children were grouped for reading and math in multi-grade clusters in order to meet their particular needs. While watching the children play happily on the green grass outside Rondout's quaint single building during recess, I noticed another striking distinction. Industrial parks surrounded the affluent school on all four sides. Intrigued, I called Alden Loury, my editor, and described what I had seen.

It Was All about the Property Tax Base

In Ford Heights, I told Loury, there were about ten businesses in the entire community. I saw a liquor store, grocery, fast food restaurant, currency exchange, beauty supply, and a used car lot.

But Rondout was literally enveloped by five industrial parks and large office buildings. Less than a quarter-mile south, more than 50 businesses stood in the Bradley Business Park.

We're going to find out if this is the story of two unequal school districts or if it says something larger about the nature of school funding in Illinois, Loury said.

The latter turned out to be true.

Illinois relies on local residential and business property taxes to provide the majority of funding for education. Residents often support this policy under the banner of local control, but it dramatically favors wealthy communities over poorer ones in a series of related ways.

To understand the impact, we requested 20 years of school funding data from the Illinois State Board of Education, including annual per pupil spending and the percentage that came from local, state, and federal sources. We also secured data from the Illinois Department of Revenue about property tax rates and property tax amounts billed to residential, commercial, industrial, and farm properties for 2003. We then linked the school spending and property tax billing datasets for more than 640, or about 70 percent, of the state's school districts. Once we started digging into the data, we made some revealing discoveries.

First, property-rich districts like Rondout taxed themselves at rates that were far lower than those of their poorer counterparts. Close to 70 districts, including some of the school districts in Chicago's northern suburbs with the highest property values, for instance, had a local property tax rate that was less than 2 percent. Rondout's property tax rate was about 1.5 percent.

On the other hand, in close to 100 poorer districts with less property wealth, such as Ford Heights, the property tax rate was at least 5 percent. Ford Heights' tax rate was more than five times higher than Rondout's. But because the property wealth was so much lower in poorer areas, this higher level of taxation generated less than half the amount of money for students than in Rondout and other districts in affluent North Shore suburbs such as Kenilworth, Wilmette, and Winnetka. "[Poorer] areas end up trying to squeeze blood out of a turnip," said Bindu Batchu, then campaign manager for A+ Illinois, a coalition working to boost school funding and improve the quality of education throughout the state, in the story. "This makes it hard for communities to attract business and jobs. All things being equal, [businesses] will want to go in communities that have lower property taxes and [good] municipal services, including schools."[2]

More Businesses Means More Money

Wealthy districts could far more easily attract businesses because of their lower property tax rate. In the case of Rondout, businesses were considering a community that was located near a major highway, that had an educated workforce and that had a tax rate that was one of the lowest in the state. Businesses weighing if they should settle in a place like Ford Heights were looking at a less-educated workforce and a tax rate that was many times higher.

Communities that taxed themselves at high rates in a commitment to their children's future not only generated insufficient funds for education, but they also nearly guaranteed that businesses would not invest there.

In an effort to attract businesses, some Illinois communities created Tax Increment Financing, or TIF, zones. Established in economically distressed areas, TIFs offer businesses willing to stay and invest in the community a property tax rate guarantee for as many as 20 years. Boosters say that TIFs can help revitalize a downtown area or former industrial site, or raise the area's property value through new industrial parks or manufacturing facilities. But based on a number of studies, it's difficult to determine whether the strategy is successful.

As we investigated these trends, we found that downstate districts in more rural areas faced the same dilemmas and followed much the same pattern as the poorer urban or suburban communities.

The structural nature of the funding inequities led us to call our story, "The Never-Ending Cycle." We determined that there was very little, if any, means to make school funding truly equal as long as the state continued to rely on local property tax revenue for education funding. In fact, the situation had worsened as the percentage of state and federal revenue had decreased over the several years before we did the analysis. Nine years later, the state of Illinois still relies on local property tax to fund schools.

After our series ran there was a concerted push to guarantee per-pupil funding and change the underlying tax structure that funds schools. A lawsuit filed on behalf of children of color in poor districts in Illinois cited our work. Yet the system remains intact. Clearly, there is more work to be done.

Tip Sheet

For others looking into similar structural concerns, I recommend the following:

- *Remember Alden's insight: Use the individual to identify the structural.* Pay attention to your assumptions and to items that surprise you. Always look to see how an individual instance contributes to, or differs from, a larger structure that can reveal something meaningful about the state or nation.

- *Keep digging and you can often find new and revealing conclusions.* School funding discussions, especially about how students perform, can often bleed into talking about parents' and teachers' supposed level of commitment to their students. Our analysis helped shift the conversation from individual or cultural habits – and the implicit idea that people get what they deserve – to a broader discussion about collective responsibility.

- *Bring in different data sets to answer your evolving questions.* Asking questions to better understand your findings or come up with alternate explanations can lead you to explore new sources of data. Of course, these new data can often generate more questions.

- *Connect the dots.* Once you have taken the time to report such an in-depth story, you can incorporate some patterns you learned about in your breaking news or daily stories. For example, in a future story about small businesses in low-income districts, you can explain how commercial property taxes fund education. In a news story about high unemployment in a particular district, you can connect the dots to lagging educational funding. Help your reader see the patterns.

- *Strike a balance between affected people, experts, and findings from the data.* It can be easy to either fall in love with data or get totally immersed in telling another person's difficult story. The best work integrates both. It also reveals the policies behind the data and personal stories that have reduced or increased inequality.

- *Read what else has been done on the topic.* This may seem obvious, but it is something that can be easy to overlook. In our case, we dug and didn't find anyone making the same point we identified. This led us to believe that we had an opportunity to bring something new and original to public attention.

- *Don't overstate what your data says.* This can be tempting, especially when you care strongly about an issue and have been working on it for months. Don't do it. You ultimately do a disservice to the issue and can work your way straight out of journalism. Defining the data you have, how you did your analysis, and sharing these with the reader builds greater trust and credibility. In the school funding project, for example, we identified the number of districts for which we found property tax billed data so that the reader understood we did not have that information for all of them.

Notes

1 David T. Conley. "The Challenge of College Readiness." *Educational Leadership* 64, no.
   7 (2007): 23–29. Accessed February 2, 2017 from www.researchgate.net/profile/David_
   Conley2/publication/237305729_The_Challenge_of_College_Readiness_Research_
   shows_a_mismatch_between_high_school_preparation_and_college_expectations_How_
   can_high_schools_prepare_students_for_college_success/links/564b677908ae4ae893
   b7c7a8.pdf.
2 Jeff Kelly Lowenstein. "The Never-Ending Cycle." *The Chicago Reporter*, September 25,
   2007. Accessed August 25, 2018. www.chicagoreporter.com/never-ending-cycle/.

CASE STUDY D

When Housing Separates Us

Nikole Hannah-Jones

Nikole Hannah-Jones, an investigative reporter and winner of the Tobenkin Award and the MacArthur Fellowship award, covers racial justice for the New York Times Magazine. *Here she offers readers best practices in reporting on the institutional and historical causes of housing discrimination and segregation. She urges journalists to dig into policy decisions and their consequences, including whether or not government agencies enforce anti-discrimination laws that are on the books.*

It Started with a Daily Beat Story

In 2011, I was a beat reporter covering local government for the *Oregonian* in Portland, Oregon, when a press release from the city of Portland came across my desk. It said that the city had contracted with an agency to test for housing discrimination and had found pervasive illegal discrimination against black and Latino renters. It seemed like an interesting and important daily story, so I picked up the phone and called the office that did the testing. I asked what I thought was a simple question: Now that the city had found landlords violating the 1968 Fair Housing Act, how did it intend to hold them accountable for breaking the law and denying residents housing because of their race or ethnicity?

The answer surprised me. City officials planned to do nothing – they told me they were not going to seek to prosecute or otherwise punish the landlords who had violated the law. The testing, they said, had been designed to gauge the level of housing discrimination renters faced in the Portland market, but they never had intended to actually hold anyone accountable. They'd merely done the testing in order to comply with a federal mandate that communities study obstacles to fair housing in order to get large federal community development grants.

Now, that was a story. I wrote it up for the front-page of the *Oregonian*.[1] But the daily story piqued my deeper interest. I knew that housing segregation was pervasive in Portland and across the country, and that it was at the root of nearly every other racial disparity nationwide. Housing segregation has been linked to school segregation, to the location of environmental toxicants and waste sites, to crime, to access to jobs, transportation and city services, to health problems, and to premature death. Yet, here were landlords caught in blatant violation of a 40-year-old law intended to give people of all races the freedom to move to any neighborhood, and a governmental body had no desire to enforce it. Why was that? Why did the city feel it could avoid enforcing the law and still get federal money tied to eliminating housing segregation? And what did that tell us about the continuing entrenchment of segregation, decades after discrimination in housing had become illegal?

Deeper Revelations

My gut told me there was a bigger story there. But like many journalists, I knew very little about fair housing law and its protections. So I spent the next few days reading everything I could on fair housing, the law, its history, and the role of the government – from federal down to local – in enforcing it. Quickly I realized there was a much, much bigger story than the one about local officials deciding to let discriminatory landlords slide.

I spent the next year reporting both the local and national angles, showing that cities like Portland were simply taking their cues from the federal government – they did not take their duty to enforce fair housing law seriously because the federal government did not.

I continued to investigate this story when I left the *Oregonian* for a job at Pro-Publica. The next year, ProPublica published the 2012 series "Living Apart: How the Government Betrayed a Landmark Civil Rights Law."[2] I used archival research; US Census data; extensive interviews with officials at the US Department of Housing and Urban Development (HUD), civil rights attorneys and researchers; and documents and data accessed through public records requests. The Fair Housing Act, I found, was a complete failure in fulfilling its civil rights mandate.

Segregation Maintained, Not Addressed

Within a few years of passing the 1968 Fair Housing Act, the federal government, helmed by President Richard Nixon, decided not to aggressively enforce the anti-discrimination provisions of the law, the series documented. This allowed segregation to grow and fester. In turn, federal officials continued to ignore the provision in the law that mandated they take active steps to break down the very segregation they in fact had helped create.

My reporting established that over the course of four decades, the federal government had largely refused to enforce fair housing law. Since the early 1970s, HUD, the agency charged with enforcing the Fair Housing Act, had only twice used its most powerful tool – the ability to withhold federal funds from communities that were not complying with the law – even when federal courts found these communities had intentionally segregated black residents.

The ProPublica series showed that HUD was often at war with itself over how vigorously to enforce the law, and that its fair housing division was the smallest, least funded and least respected within the agency. Further, HUD itself operated and funded some of the most segregated housing in the country and had been sued over and over again through the years for violating the very law it was supposed to uphold.

Collusion across the Country

The piece also established how cities such as Portland often failed to comply with even menial requirements for receiving federal development dollars. Yet the federal government kept rubber-stamping their grant applications as they had done year after year, funneling hundreds of millions of dollars into some of the most segregated cities in the country.

The series demonstrated how the federal government repeatedly refused to use the biggest tool for fighting housing discrimination – audit testing of the real estate market – and instead provided a small amount of funding to a patchwork of nonprofits that checked if landlords, real estate agents, and home sellers were discriminating.

National audit tests performed by HUD would have sent trained testers – white, black, and Latino – methodically into the housing market to see if landlords discriminate. But instead, HUD relied on these underfunded nonprofits, which typically test by investigating specific complaints about discrimination. The problem with this approach is that often people don't realize they are being discriminated against in the process of looking for a home. This has meant that housing discrimination largely was and continues to go unchecked, with landlords having little fear of ever being caught.

The series, using real people, showed the actual harm of these government practices on communities.

Taking an investigative eye to fair housing was critical because we tend to see, and reporters tend to report on, housing segregation as if it were inevitable and natural. In fact, residential segregation is often the product of decades of official actions and decisions, and it is maintained in the present day through official action and decision-making. Instead of just reporting on the fact of residential segregation, this series showed how it was sanctioned, and often, entrenched, by government policies and behavior.

Strategies for Structural Reporting

Most reporters cannot spend a month on a single project – and certainly not a year. But do not be intimidated. It is important to remember that this project began as a series of beat stories.

Every community that receives federal community development block grants (CDBG) is required to do an assessment of barriers to fair housing and submit it to HUD. This includes nearly all communities of significant size. In the assessment, the communities must list the barriers and then their plans for addressing them. A good place to start understanding segregation in your community is to find out how much CDBG funding it receives and request the assessments. If the community hasn't done one recently, that's a story. If it has, read it. Is it thorough? Does it have measurable goals? Has the city made progress on the goals, and if not, why not? Often, cities do fair housing testing similar to that performed by Portland as part of the assessment. Check to see if your city or county has done this testing, and if so, what the results were. What, if any, enforcement action did the municipality take?

Another easy story is to find out who is charged with fair housing enforcement in your town. How are they funded? How aggressively are they enforcing the law? What are they finding? If fair housing is not a priority, why not?

Study Patterns

A more ambitious project would look at where the city or county has placed its affordable and public housing. Does it have a pattern of concentrating this housing in lower-income black and Latino communities? How are these decisions made? What is the impact of these housing policies on residential segregation?

Reporters can also request housing voucher data from HUD and see whether or not families using housing vouchers are able to move into higher-opportunity areas. Do landlords who accept these vouchers only do so in areas that are poor and black and Latino?

Look for fair housing lawsuits and settlements in your area. Which landlords are repeat offenders? Has your city or town been sued, or settled a lawsuit or HUD complaint? These lawsuits can be treasure troves of data and information on official policies that have caused segregation. For instance, following the protests that erupted after Freddie Gray died in the back of a police van while in the custody of the Baltimore Police Department, it went largely unreported that the federal government had recently settled a long-running fair housing lawsuit in the Baltimore region.[3] The plaintiffs, which included several families who lived in public housing, accused local administrations and HUD of helping to maintain and create segregation by concentrating low-income housing in the city and away from much whiter Baltimore County.

Reporting on the government's role in establishing the severe segregation that Freddie Gray lived in would have gone a long way toward helping the nation understand how his community came to be the way it is, and why the city exploded.

In another vital but under-covered story, states and cities are applying the federal housing program, called the Low Income Housing Tax Credit program, in a manner that maintains racial segregation. LIHTC is the largest producer of affordable housing in the nation, as it gives private builders tax credits for this purpose. But most of this housing is constructed in neighborhoods that are already poor and black and Latino, and many fair housing advocates argue that state and local officials are administering the program in a way that illegally maintains segregation. A look at this program in your own community and state could make for great accountability reporting.

Intent Is beside the Point

Reporters covering racial inequality often feel they need to prove intent in order to show discrimination. When it comes to race, we get caught up in the intentions of people in a way we seldom do in other reporting. Race discrimination has been banned in most parts of US life since the 1960s. So the odds that officials will openly show bias are extremely low. And officials, business people, and others do not have to have any particular racial animus in order to take actions that produce discriminatory results.

Consider the lending discrimination lawsuits that the US Department of Justice brought against banks in recent years. These actions alleged that banks targeted segregated black communities because they were vulnerable and had few banking options, not necessarily because they wanted to harm black homebuyers.

With that in mind, this type of reporting must show that an official, or agency, took actions that unfairly or disproportionately hurt a group of people and that the harm was predictable. Once you establish those two things, the reporting speaks for itself. While the ability to show that a policy or action is intentionally discriminatory is a bonus, it is unnecessary.

Key Questions and Resources

For instance, using the Baltimore example, let's say a reporter used federal data and found that HUD built all of its public housing in poor black neighborhoods and built none in affluent white ones.

Some important questions to ask are:

1. How did HUD and the local housing authorities that HUD funds and empowers site their public and affordable housing?
2. Why did these agencies place housing in X community and not in Y community?

3.   Were HUD and the local housing authorities aware of the extensive research on racial isolation and concentrated poverty? If so, why would they choose to build housing that has been found to be harmful to communities? If not, why are federal officials charged with siting public housing not aware of this research?

4.   Federal law mandates that the government not take steps that increase housing segregation. How did HUD and the local housing authorities justify building this housing in a way that maintains segregation?

5.   What efforts, if any, did HUD and the local housing agency make to site the housing in whiter, more affluent communities?

A reporter is unlikely to find a document or federal official admitting to placing affordable housing in black communities because white residents will not tolerate it. But one can show that HUD supported housing that increased and maintained segregation when it is supposed to be doing the opposite, possibly in violation of the Fair Housing Act.

To report on housing, it is essential that reporters read the Fair Housing Act in its entirety and also have a good grasp of the case law around it. Some important cases are *Shelley* v. *Kraemer, Jones* v. *Mayer; Village of Arlington Heights* v. *Metropolitan Housing Development Corp; U.S.* v. *Westchester County; South Burlington County NAACP* v. *Township of Mt. Laurel; Texas Department of Housing and Community Affairs* v. *The Inclusive Communities Project, Inc.; NAACP* v. *HUD*; and *Trafficante* v. *Metropolitan Life Insurance*.

Reporters who need quick access to data on residential segregation in their own communities and other research in this topic area should go to Brown University's Census 2010 project, which is a massive repository of US Census data, mapping, and other reports that are searchable by city and metro area. www.s4.brown.edu/us2010/

Housing remains at the nexus of all other opportunity, even though its effects can often operate invisibly. That is why it is so critical for reporters to tackle these stories in depth, getting at the very policies that allow segregation to continue.

Tip Sheet

•   Take the time to read the Fair Housing Act in its entirety. A copy can be found here: www.justice.gov/crt/fair-housing-act-2.

•   You don't have to report this story as a monster package. Take pieces of the story to write as a daily or beat story.

•   Become grounded in the history of segregation in the United States and the policies that reinforced it. A critical background read is *American Apartheid*, by Douglas Massey and Nancy Denton – it is central to understanding the history of officially created segregation of black Americans in this country.

- Spend time becoming acquainted with case law surrounding Fair Housing.
- Follow the outcomes of policies and decisions made by housing agencies.

Notes

1 Nikole Hannah-Jones. "Portland Housing Audit Finds Discrimination in 64 Percent of Tests; City has Yet to Act against Landlords." *The Oregonian*, May 9, 2011. Accessed February 21, 2017 from www.oregonlive.com/portland/index.ssf/2011/05/a_portland_housing_audit_finds.html.

2 Nikole Hannah-Jones. "Living Apart: How the Government Betrayed a Landmark Civil Rights Law." ProPublica updated June 25, 2015. Accessed February 21, 2017 from www.propublica.org/article/living-apart-how-the-government-betrayed-a-landmark-civil-rights-law. *The Oregonian* also published its own series in 2012, with reporter Brad Schmidt conducting all interviews and analysis. Brad Schmidt. "Locked Out: The Failure of Portland-Area Fair Housing." *The Oregonian*, June 2, 2012. Accessed May 27, 2017 from projects.oregonlive.com/housing/.

3 Christine Serlin. "Settlement to Increase Affordable Housing in Baltimore County." *Affordable Housing Finance*. March 17, 2016. Accessed February 21, 2017 from www.housingfinance.com/policy-legislation/settlement-to-increase-affordable-housing-in-baltimore-county_o; "Baltimore Public Housing Families Applaud Court Approval of Fair Housing Lawsuit Settlement." ACLU Press Release November 20, 2012. Accessed February 21, 2017 from https://www.aclu-md.org/en/press-releases/baltimore-public-housing-families-applaud-court-approval-fair-housing-lawsuit; "Baltimore Public Housing Families Win Settlement in Fair Housing Law." NAACP Legal Defense Fund, August 24, 2012. Accessed February 21, 2017 from www.naacpldf.org/press-release/baltimore-public-housing-families-win-settlement-fair-housing-lawsuit.

CASE STUDY E

Gaps in the Social Safety Net

Karen de Sá

In this case study, San Francisco Chronicle *investigative reporter Karen de Sá uses the example of dependency courts to show how journalists can examine the policies and practices that make safety net programs difficult to access and negotiate – and as a result, create deep inequities in outcomes by race and income. De Sá has won numerous journalism awards, and her work has led to corrective legislation and overhauled institutions.*

In 2007, working as an investigative reporter for the *San Jose Mercury News*, I set out to examine the quality of justice in foster-care courts in California. Despite dependency court's power over the lives and the well-being of more than 400,000 children nationwide, it remains a little-known branch of the legal system. In much of the country, hearings are held in secret to protect the family's privacy.[1] In California, participants can be charged with a misdemeanor for revealing information from dependency court files.[2] Our inquiry focused on legal decisions made after social workers remove children from their homes, and whether those decisions are the result of a fair legal process. Our examination of the system exposed deep flaws.

Understanding the System

The authority of social workers to remove children from their homes when maltreatment is suspected is among the most invasive of all government powers. Following allegations of abuse or neglect, kids can be whisked off in the back of county-issued sedans or police cars – headed for a bewildering network of shelters, residential facilities, or temporary foster homes. Even if life had been scary or painful at home for these kids, being separated from parents and dropped into an uncertain future filled with strangers is an additional trauma.

As a safeguard against government overreach and flawed judgment on the part of emergency response workers, civil courts quickly step in. Within days a hearing is held to determine whether it's safe for a child to return to the family. In California, home to the nation's largest foster care system, parents and their children are each appointed attorneys to represent their interests. Unless parents can afford legal help on their own, court-appointed panels of private attorneys, public defenders, or contracted firms of varying skill and resources represent them. The opposing side – the child welfare agency – typically has a seasoned attorney arguing the social worker's case for removal.

Initially, a judicial officer decides whether children should remain temporarily separated from parents believed to have harmed them until the facts of the case can be more thoroughly weighed. At subsequent hearings, families can be legally separated for life.

Families in this system are overwhelmingly low-income, census and child welfare data show. They are disproportionately black families. American Indian and Alaska Native children also are overrepresented at 2.4 times their rate in the general population. According to ongoing tracking by the National Council of Juvenile and Family Court Judges, in broad demographic strokes, white, Asian and Pacific Islander children are the least likely to enter foster care. Latino youth as a whole are overrepresented in foster care in just a few states.[3]

Studies of racial disparities in the child welfare system point to many contributing factors, including a child's socio-economic condition at birth; each group's historical advantages or disadvantages in American society; and the possible presence of racial bias among those who report and handle abuse allegations. Differences between the children of US-born and foreign-born mothers may contribute to lower overall averages for Latinos, suggests research by Emily Putnam-Hornstein at the University of Southern California's School of Social Work.[4] New immigrants may arrive with social and cultural protective factors such as strong family bonds, community networks, and religion that they may lose in subsequent generations.

Journalists must examine each of these factors in reporting the policies and the structural factors that lead to unequal outcomes. It's vital when covering historically marginalized groups. Otherwise, bias, assumptions, and discrimination can creep into your work – consciously or not – perpetuating myths such as the supposed "welfare queens" that drove massive reductions in cash assistance for poor families, and the juvenile "superpredator" panic that fueled the excessive criminalization of youth.

Contrary to popular belief, children who enter foster care mostly are not the victims of physical or sexual abuse. Spend a day in any dependency court and you will quickly learn that families usually come to the attention of the child welfare authorities due to poverty, untreated addiction, mental illness, and domestic violence. Roughly three-quarters of parents are accused of neglect.[5] Working multiple jobs, inebriated, homeless, or resorting to desperate survival measures, parents leave children home alone or with incompetent caregivers. They leave the refrigerator empty, get arrested, or give birth with drugs in their system. Children are often removed from mothers who are themselves victims of violent abuse.

In my reporting on foster care over decades, I have consistently heard from judges, social workers, and the children themselves: Once removed, many if not most kids are desperate to return to their families – no matter how troubled and in need of social services their homes may be. Although there are certainly clear-cut cases where children are actively abused and face imminent danger, in many others, research suggests the risks of removal may outweigh the harm.

Joseph Doyle, an economist at the Massachusetts Institute of Technology, studied 23,000 Illinois foster youth.[6] After excluding the most severe cases of maltreatment that unambiguously warranted removal, he found that as adults, former foster youth faced arrest, conviction, and imprisonment rates three times more often than children left with their families.

Researchers at the University of Chicago have been tracking the progress of hundreds of former foster youth for years across several states, documenting a pattern of incarceration, homelessness, failed schooling, and unemployment.[7]

These outcomes, and the circumstances of struggle among families who lose their children, provide a rich source of inquiry for social science researchers and reporters. Could greater investments in public health nursing and non-punitive drug treatment drive down rates of child endangerment? Does racism within child welfare agencies influence the decision to pull a child from home? Are domestic violence victims losing their kids for failing to protect them from an abuser, when they themselves are victims?

Diving In

This is the backdrop to the 2008 *San Jose Mercury News* series "Broken Families, Broken Courts," which I reported over a year's time under negotiated deals with four juvenile courts in northern California. The agreements allowed me to sit in on otherwise confidential proceedings on the condition that I would not reveal the identities of any clients or approach them outside of court.

In my investigation I found widespread evidence of a system overwhelmed by problems that invited poor judgment. I found that legal professionals in dependency court struggled to meet even minimal standards of ethical representation. Individual courtrooms raced through as many as 135 cases in a single day. Hearings to permanently sever children from their families lasted mere minutes. While polished legal teams from county counsels' offices represented social workers, inexperienced – and poorly paid – young attorneys represented parents. The parents' lawyers conferred with their clients immediately prior to hearings in harried hallway encounters. They rarely sought outside experts or investigated the facts of social workers' allegations. Such efforts would have required greater financial resources.

Lawyers for kids were equally overwhelmed, carrying crushing caseloads of as many as 1,000 children at a time. One attorney conceded that she seldom met her child clients in person – unless they were hospitalized after suicide attempts.

Dependency courts in California determine the futures of tens of thousands of children each year, but decisions often fall on commissioners and referees otherwise assigned to handle minor traffic infractions. In the hierarchy of most California Superior Courts, I quickly learned, dependency court was near the bottom. Given the heavy dockets, gut-wrenching cases, and closed proceedings that offer little professional visibility for career advancement, judges rarely stick around juvenile divisions for more than a couple of years.

It's about Relationships

After observing confidential hearings in Santa Clara, Sacramento, San Francisco, and San Mateo counties, I realized that their value in telling the foster care story was substantial but limited. The series needed identifiable foster youth and parents who had lost their children to serve as an anchor. People's lives provide insight and allow readers to understand stories that numbers, reports, and talking-heads can rarely inspire. Yet finding these sources is undeniably one of the greatest challenges of reporting on the foster care system. A journalist must not only identify people to interview, film, and photograph, but also stay in touch over time. Regular contact is vital in order to earn trust and prepare an in-depth report.

I looked for sources inside nonprofit service agencies and advocacy groups for foster youth – those most invested in the reporting. They see the systemic flaws in dependency courts every day and generally understand that it takes human stories to move policymakers. Such connections will lead you to the greatest rewards of reporting on social justice issues: The people who will share their life stories with you, and the somewhat awesome responsibility of telling those stories. While the experiences of children and families in the foster care system can be crushing and sad and overwhelming, they also can also become undeniable and unforgettable agents for change.

People Were Willing to Talk

Our dependency court series featured Marquita Jackson, a first-time mother who grew up in foster care herself. Marquita, then 20, lost all legal rights to her son at a hearing in San Jose, California, with an attorney she had only just met by her side. I met Marquita through a source that ran foster care group homes, including one where her boyfriend had grown up. Although the baby's father was suspected of shaking the infant while Marquita was at work, social workers alleged that she was responsible for failing to protect him. A succession of ill-equipped lawyers failed to successfully challenge the Department of Family and Children's Services' case. Over numerous interviews, Marquita described to me just how it felt to lose parental rights at that final court hearing in 2006, after years of fighting to get her baby boy back: "It was like getting my heart ripped out," she said in tears.[8]

Zairon Fraizer, 20, was another central source in the "Broken Families, Broken Courts" series. Zairon and I met through the advocacy group California Youth Connection. Zairon had spent five years in foster care in Alameda County beginning in 2002. Over five years, he traveled by bus and train to make sure he attended all his court hearings, even though his social workers advised him not to bother. As he moved through eight San Francisco Bay Area shelters and group homes, three middle schools, and three high schools, Zairon's life in foster care cried out for zealous advocacy. Sometimes there wasn't enough hot water; often he struggled to avoid the drug use around him. Frightened and alone, his circumstances were often so unbearable that he simply ran away from court-ordered placements and slept in the streets.

Other than in Los Angeles, youth voices were typically absent from hearings in California courts at the time, even though child welfare experts and many judges say their presence in court is vital. Many dependency court parties – from advocates to social workers and foster parents – actively discouraged kids from attending hearings. They told youth that transportation was too difficult, or that they shouldn't miss school.

Zairon made it a point to show up. He never knew who would appear to represent him before the judge. A stranger would act as his stand-in parent when it came time to discuss such critical matters as sibling visits, his latest move in foster care, or his progress in school. "They'd say, 'Hi, I'm your attorney. Here are your case notes, look them over,'" Zairon recalled. "And that was about it."[9]

These Stories Have Impact

The experiences of Marquita and Zairon – and the system that failed to serve them – did not go unnoticed. The state legislature and local courts enacted key structural changes that may make their experiences less likely for others to endure. The owner of the private law firm that had represented thousands of parents in the Santa Clara County dependency court over the previous decade resigned just two days after the *Mercury News* published "Broken Families, Broken Courts."

Within months, the court hired a new, nonprofit firm that substantially raised attorneys' salaries to deter turnover; gave bonuses to lawyers who filed appeals; and devoted new funding to hire experts and investigators. Zairon's story inspired California State Assembly Bill 3051, which became law in 2008 and strengthened children's rights to attend their own court hearings. When then-Gov. Arnold Schwarzenegger signed the bill, Zairon was 21 and working three jobs to attend the University of Hawaii. "I did not know the entire state senate would be voting on a story about what happened to me in foster care. I consider it an honor, it's very exciting," he told me seven years ago. "But I also consider it a duty. If something went wrong with you, change it so that it won't happen to anybody else."[10]

Tip Sheet

While gathering many such stories, I repeatedly asked myself how the courts' larger dysfunction played out in the lives of disadvantaged children and families. I also questioned my reporting process. As journalists who push society to be more just and equitable, our information-gathering methods must mirror that justice standard. Whether you're working on deadline stories or enterprise projects, I suggest this personal checklist:

- Have I paid attention to my own biases and assumptions based on the race, class, gender, geographic origin, or age of people I am interviewing or observing?
- Have I consciously sought out, interviewed, and quoted experts who are nonwhite and not often in the news – academics, researchers, or policy analysts, for instance?
- Have I interviewed and quoted both men and women?
- And, perhaps most importantly, have I included in my story the voices of those whose lives are most at stake?

Interviewing foster youth, their parents, and survivors of trauma more generally requires self-awareness. Here are some suggestions:

- Above all else, be human. Consider the experiences people have gone through before you approach them. How easy would it be for any of us to discuss trauma, abuse, and our most personal and difficult experiences with a stranger, especially one who intended to publish our story?
- Be gentle. Stop and acknowledge people's pain during interviews. And don't rush. Reporting on vulnerable populations involves some hanging-out time, sometimes simple meals together.
- Be aware that if foster youth are not yet 18, it can be difficult to get permission from their attorney or caregiver. But in my experience, older teens and young adults want to talk. They want to share their experiences to help others like them. Make sure, if possible, that there is a supportive adult with whom you can confer. I allow foster children to decline to answer any questions that make them feel uncomfortable and walk them through the material from our interviews I plan on using. With young people who have suffered trauma, there should be no surprises.
- Be transparent. Describe in detail what your story is about and specifically what you will need – do not assume your source understands your reporting process. And while it's unfair to make promises that your source's personal story will make a difference, you can discuss how it could contribute to helping others understand a major social problem.

Notes

1 The privacy being protected is both the child and the parents'. See Child Welfare Information Gateway. "Disclosure of Confidential Child Abuse and Neglect Records." June 2013. Accessed January 31, 2017 from www.childwelfare.gov/pubPDFs/confide.pdf.

2 Welfare and Institutions Code Section 827(b)(2) states it is a misdemeanor to reveal information in the juvenile file. Section 827 is long and defines the juvenile file broadly to include information in the child protective services file and the district attorney file concerning a juvenile. In *In re Tiffany G.* (1994) 29 Cal.App.4th 443, 450, the juvenile court made a specific order to the parent that revealing information in the social worker reports could be charged as a misdemeanor.

3 Fiscal Year 2013 data from the National Council on Juvenile and Family Court Judges. "Disproportionality Rates For Children of Color in Foster Care." June 2015. Accessed January 31, 2017 from www.ncjfcj.org/sites/default/files/NCJFCJ%202013%20Dispro%20TAB%20Final.pdf.

4 Emily Putnam-Hornstein, Barbara Needell, Bryn King, and Michelle Johnson-Motoyama. "Racial and Ethnic Disparities: A Population-Based Examination of Risk Factors for Involvement with Child Protective Services." *Child Abuse & Neglect Journal* 37, no. 1 (January 2013): 33–46.

5 The neglect rates are roughly 75 percent of all confirmed maltreatment cases. See Kids Count Data Center. "Children Who are Confirmed by Child Protective Services as Victims of Maltreatment by Maltreatment Type, 2008–2012." Accessed January 31, 2017 from http://datacenter.kidscount.org/data/tables/6222-children-who-are-confirmed-by-child-protective-services-as-victims-of-maltreatment-by-maltreatment-type?loc=1&loct=1#detailed/1/any/false/868,867,133,38,35/3885,3886,3887,3888,3889,3890,872/12951,12950.

6 Joseph J. Doyle Jr. "Child Protection and Adult Crime: Using Investigator Assignment to Estimate Causal Effects of Foster Care." *Journal of Political Economy* 116, no. 4 (2008): 746–770. Accessed January 31, 2017 from www.mit.edu/~jjdoyle/doyle_jpe_aug08.pdf.

7 Mark E. Courtney, Amy Dworsky, Jennifer Hook, Adam Brown, Colleen Cary, Kara Love, Vanessa Vorhies, JoAnn S. Lee, Melissa Raap, Gretchen Ruth Cusick, Thomas Keller, Judy Havlicek, Alfred Perez, Sherri Terao, and Noel Bost. "Midwest Evaluation of the Adult Functioning of Former Foster Youth." Report from Chapin Hall, University of Chicago, 2011. Accessed January 31, 2017 from www.chapinhall.org/research/report/midwest-evaluation-adult-functioning-former-foster-youth.

8 Karen de Sá. "A Timid Advocate for Parents' Rights." *San Jose Mercury News*, February 10, 2008. Accessed September 3, 2018 from www.mercurynews.com/2008/02/10/part-ii-a-timid-advocate-for-parents-rights/.

9 Karen de Sá. "If It Was About Me, Why Didn't They Ask Me?" *San Jose Mercury News*, February 12, 2008. Accessed September 3, 2018 from www.mercurynews.com/2008/02/11/part-iii-if-it-was-about-me-why-didnt-they-ask-me/.

10 Karen de Sá. "Governor Signs Bill to Improve Rights for Foster Children in Court." *San Jose Mercury News*, July 22, 2008. Accessed September 3, 2018 from www.mercurynews.com/2008/07/22/governor-signs-bill-to-improve-rights-for-foster-children-in-court/.

CASE STUDY F

The Path to Legal Status Isn't so Clear Cut

Susan Ferriss

Susan Ferriss, an investigative reporter with the Center for Public Integrity and a former foreign correspondent, offers guidance on covering immigration policies and best practices for reporting their impact. In this case study, the Tobenkin award winner examines one policy that affects families with mixed legal status and may prevent immigrants from assimilating.

The Impact of Immigration Reform Can Create Crisis Rather than Solution

The accusations can get shrill when it comes to the undocumented. They're accused of stealing jobs. They're accused of being lazy and using welfare. They're accused of refusing to assimilate and become Americans.

This is the debate we largely see covered in the news. But is it possible the country is systematically preventing immigrants from assimilating? Even those married to American citizens?

In the mid 2000s, I was stunned to discover that Congress had approved obscure mandates that were deliberately doing exactly this – and affecting hundreds of thousands of US citizens. These laws can upend the lives of immigrants along with their US-born children and American spouses.

Stories on immigration often fail to dig beyond reporting individual anecdotes or summarizing conflicting opinions. They leave the public unaware of deeper forces that shape immigration outcomes. Instead, journalists can offer more informative stories that look at current laws and policies, how well they work, and how they may at times create immigration crises rather than solving them.

Without journalism's spotlight, these policies don't have much meaning to the average American who is generations away from the immigrant experience – until suddenly a policy they had no idea existed involves them in intimate ways.

A Policy that Hurts American Families

In talks with immigration attorneys and their clients, I came to learn about new provisions tucked into a sweeping federal overhaul of immigration laws in 1996. The reform was called the Illegal Immigration Reform and Immigration Responsibility Act. I discovered that little-known rules were beginning to shatter American families. Immigrant spouses who originally entered the country "without inspection" – meaning illegally – now face banning from the United States for prolonged periods.

Sometimes forever.

Immigration-restriction lobbyists promoted this policy idea as a tool that would deter illegal immigration. By harshly punishing this group of people, they argued, fewer foreigners would attempt to enter unlawfully in the future. The theory was that word would spread abroad that there is a much steeper price to pay now if an undocumented person happens to meet an American, marry, and try to then seek legal status.

The rules were put into action in the early 2000s. They impose immigration bars of five, 10, 20 years, even permanent prohibitions on spouses. Until the bars imposed on them expire, which not all do, these spouses are blocked from again applying for a green card or from re-entering the United States in any legal fashion, including on a temporary visa.

The length of a bar depends on the applicant's history. And while these bars can apply to other foreigners seeking legal status through sponsorship – through an employer or another relative, for example – they fall mainly on spouses. That's because marriage is one of the chief reasons immigrants seek to become legal permanent residents, not because the bars were designed for that purpose. Provisions to reduce marriage fraud were already in place before the bars.

Does the Policy Do What It's Designed to Do?

In promoting the bars to members of Congress, immigration restriction activists argued that it was simply too easy for an undocumented immigrant to marry, apply for a green card, perhaps pay a fine or pass a criminal background check, and thus legalize his or her status.

But there is no evidence that these bars have played any role at all in deterring unlawful immigration. In general, the estimated number of migrants has ebbed and flowed along with the US economy. After officials began applying bars, the estimated flow of migrants trying to enter the United States has increased at times. Meanwhile, security along the US–Mexico border has slowed the flow in certain areas and pushed people into tougher areas to attempt to cross.

What the penalty bars have most certainly done, though, is throw families into years of uncertainty and chaos.

US citizens who entered into legitimate marriages with undocumented people have received the shock of a lifetime. After thinking it was their right as citizens to legalize a spouse, they discover a catch. If immigrant spouses originally entered the country "without inspection," they must leave the United States and return to their country of origin for an interview with US visa officials. Once the spouse is outside the country, the bars are triggered. Officials who conduct interviews must tell the spouses that they are ineligible to apply for a green card for five years if they resided in the United States for more than six months without documents. More than a year on US soil elicits a 10-year bar. Other offenses in the past – such as a deportation – can pile on more years. An accusation by a border agent or another official that a spouse made a false claim to US citizenship at one time to try to enter can result in a lifetime bar.

The Impact on Family Ties

Once a bar is imposed, it's up to the couples to decide how to shape their family life. Foreign spouses don't have to reside in their country of origin. But most do. The US spouse or children don't have to pick up and join the foreign spouse, either. But many do. Or they must patch together a family life across long distances and borders.

There is a system for waivers, but the criteria are extremely narrow. Having children, a marriage of many years, or strong community or job ties is no foundation for a waiver.

Now that word has spread inside the United States about these provisions, some couples have made the choice to try to hunker down and not come forward to seek green cards at all.

The bars, whether imposed or avoided, have impoverished entire families by preventing immigrants' ability to assimilate and thrive. Some families have to maintain two households in two countries. They've forfeited houses and drained savings. Children are shuttled back and forth, their educational opportunities limited. Americans with advanced degrees and skills – including medical professionals, computer scientists, professors, and business owners – have had to abandon careers to move abroad. Some spouses living alone in dangerous parts of Mexico or Central America have been extorted or threatened by gangs – even killed – in countries where the rule of law is weak.

Digging into the Details of Immigration Policy

When journalism focuses only on the debate about immigration, its impact and broad-stroke policies, it overlooks some of the most important legal and political decisions that shape the lives of immigrants and the people around them. The best stories highlight not only the human impact of a little-known policy like these bars, but reveal the roots of the law and investigate its original purposes. They hold those who sponsored the policy accountable to the law's original purpose. Stories of pain humanize individuals, to be sure. But tracing the origins and execution of a policy provides context to help the public judge a policy's intentions and true impact beyond the individual.

In 2007, at the *Sacramento Bee* newspaper, I reported an anecdote-driven story – with a basic explainer about the policy – that focused on several families I had discovered through a network of outraged American citizens. They had been unable to legalize spouses and some had been forced into exile. Most of these families filled out their own papers for the green card application and were shocked when, during the interview abroad, they learned for the very first time that the spouse would be denied and their re-entry barred.

One person I interviewed was a former CIA station chief in Latin America whose daughter had married a Mexican man she met in Arkansas. They met at a plant nursery where they both worked. She, along with a young child, was forced to move to Mexico with him in order to keep their marriage intact.

Another exceptional character I found for the story was a US Marine combat veteran in California whose Mexican-born, US-raised, and undocumented wife was banished for 10 years after they both unwittingly showed up for an interview in Mexico, as required. They had two children by then.

Years after our story, the former Marine's wife was able to return after a lawyer helped the couple navigate through a complex waiver request process. This allowance – the most common one – can be pursued only if the US citizen spouse successfully argues that he or she is suffering from an exceptional medical or other condition that is worsened due to separation. Emotional suffering is not enough, nor is the suffering of children living in divided families. The Marine got mental health support from a veterans' group. He also sought special help from representatives in Congress to try to exert pressure – help many spouses have been denied. In the meantime, the family's coffers had been drained as they tried to support two homes.

The System Doesn't Have a Brain

In 2011, as an investigative reporter with the nonprofit Center for Public Integrity, I pursued a deeper radio and written narrative built around three families. Each family was coping with terrible choices due to forced separation. Each represented the rigid consequences of the punitive bars.[1]

The three US spouses illustrated to readers and listeners how draconian this policy truly can be.

US citizen Chris Xitco was stunned to hear about the law after he thought he could simply go to a federal office and fill out paperwork to legalize his wife. After the couple took the plunge and applied for a green card based on the advice of an attorney, Xitco's wife emerged from her interview in Mexico and told him she'd been denied. By law, Xitco wasn't allowed to attend the interview. He had to relocate his wife and infant daughter to Mexico on the spot and then return to the United States to his job. "They don't seem to think, well, what about the daughter?" Xitco said. "She doesn't count? The system doesn't have a heart. And it doesn't have a brain."[2]

Despite compelling anecdotes of family suffering, loss of income and career dreams, we wanted to assess and quantify the larger human impact. We looked into the existing work and immigrant visa system, and why both employers and immigrants argue that it has failed. At bottom, the system has been designed to inflict minimal pain on US employers. They are required only to record ID information, not verify legal status, which can be painstaking and also lead to unequal application of efforts. Yet employers complain that visas designed to fill worker shortages remain far too narrowly drawn, with too few opportunities to sponsor workers for jobs that citizens historically avoid due to the physical demand and low pay – such as farm labor, dairy work, and other tasks. Over time, employers have taken advantage of a continuing flow of workers desperate to work and who've been assured – in some cases by employers, smugglers, or by word of mouth – that they can use fake Social Security numbers.

Policy Encourages More Undocumentation, Not Less

Over decades, as the border has become more secure, people have settled down and integrated into families and communities. As lawyers began to advise clients of the risk of the immigration bars, they say, a significant number of couples decided not to try to legalize the foreign spouse. But that decision comes with hardship because of the risk of an encounter with immigration officials. Children old enough to realize one of their parents could be deported can suffer anxiety. Couples suffer financially because a spouse's continuing undocumented status hinders advancement in jobs and involvement in schools and communities.

In interviews, immigration lawyers characterized the bars as the primary reason why so many people remain undocumented in the United States. Oklahoma lawyer Douglas Strump, a former president of the American Immigration Lawyers Association, estimated that for every 100 people who approached him to try to petition for legal status for a family member, half would face harsh bars that would keep their spouse out of the country for many years.[3]

While many foreign spouses are Latin American, people originating elsewhere have also faced bars for violating immigration law. But the bars – intentionally or not – have a harsher structural impact on nonwhite immigrants. Those who overstay visas and usually escape the harsh bars are often people from Canada and Europe, from which it's easier for nationals to enter on visas. People who overstay a legal visa can often adjust their status to permanent residency more easily than an undocumented spouse, who generally has a more restricted path to legal status.

Numbers are Hard to Nail Down, but Try Anyway

We tried for hard numbers on who had been barred, filing Freedom of Information Act requests with the Department of State to obtain visa rejections and sort out which ones had resulted from the bars. We were told that such precise information wasn't available. What we did obtain suggested that thousands of rejections had been handed down since the policy began. We inferred that most were spouses because spouses were the single biggest category of applicants.

Over the period between 2000 and 2011, about 89,000 applicants were able to overcome a visa disqualification due to illegal presence in the United States for more than one year – which carries a 10-year bar. But over the same period, visas were denied more than 68,000 times because applicants were unable to get their disqualification waived. There were almost 19,000 disqualifications of visa applications for the offense of being "unlawfully present after previous immigration violations," which means a migrant was caught crossing, deported, and then re-entered – a very typical scenario. Only five such disqualification cases were reversed. The penalty for being deported and then re-entering is a lifetime bar, with the possibility of being able to seek a pardon, but frequently only after 10 years.

The visa records also showed us that there were thousands of rejections during that period for other immigration-related offenses, including "misrepresentation of facts" during the application process. A government official can simply decide that an immigrant spouse is not telling the truth – and the result may be a lifetime visa ban. We spoke with an American nurse who was gainfully employed but whose husband received a lifetime ban because officials deemed his facts as misrepresentations. She now lives with him and three children in Mexico, piecing together a living and aching to return home.

Pushed to the Shadows

We filled out our story and subsequent stories with examples of people, some speaking anonymously, describing how they live day by day in fear, worried their spouses will be discovered – perhaps on the job, perhaps at a traffic stop that leads to police calling immigration officials.

One family – the Barbours – were separated because the Mexican wife, Maythe, was stopped for driving too slowly in San Diego. A police officer turned the mother of two over to immigration officials. She was placed in detention for six months while her American husband, a tech professional, attempted to fight her deportation in court. She had been caught crossing the border once years before, and that resulted in a court order of a 20-year bar. She told us of becoming suicidal while living in a tiny apartment south of Tijuana, fearing what she felt was imminent violence and waiting for weekend visits from her family, including the couple's bewildered 10-year-old son.

T.J. Barbour, the US citizen spouse, said the mandatory bars clearly don't fit the offense. While serious medical conditions are sometimes a waivable factor, as referenced above, depression or financial ruin are not. And the law has stripped immigration judges and other officials of the discretion to consider the entirety of a person's life and family situation.

"I want people to know that, hey, we US citizens are really hurting here, and our children are," T.J. said. "The family ramifications of this have to be taken into account. We need to deal with the fact that people have become a part of the fabric of our society."[4]

Not a Deterrent

The story wouldn't be complete without a response from those who support these measures. We interviewed Jessica Vaughan, policy studies director at the Center for Immigration Studies, a Washington, DC, group favoring less immigration, who called the bars "proportionate to the offense." But she also suggested that they may not have the broad deterrent power that was advertised at the time. She said: "It is most definitely time to take a good, hard look at this section of the law."[5]

President Barack Obama issued a narrow executive tweak to the law as we were doing our report. We explained the origins of the law and Obama's tweak in a sidebar, which was an organizational choice that can help readers make sense of complex policies. Obama's change, we explained, allows couples to seek green cards and hardship waivers without the immigrant spouse first having to leave the country for a basic interview and risk letting the exile bar fall on them. None of the couples we interviewed would benefit, however. Bars had already been imposed on some. And many spouses were ineligible for waivers because they had either been caught crossing the border illegally or had been accused of making false claims.

Immigration hardliners in Congress attacked Obama for what they considered was the president siding with illegal immigrants once again. Rep. Lamar Smith, R-Texas, the chairman of the House of Representatives Judiciary Committee, said: "Who is the President batting for – illegal immigrants or the American people?"[6]

Our story found that there are Americans who feel very differently. The record shows that bars have met a goal of inflicting punishment on individual undocumented people. But American citizens argue that they, too, are being deprived of basic rights. They suffer disproportionately because of a policy with no proven deterrent impact on illegal immigration, despite the policy's intended goals.

Tip Sheet

The Trump administration is taking a different approach to immigration and as new policies are developed, journalists must examine their success in attaining their stated goals.

- Remember that people you interview often can't explain in detail the legal barriers they face in attempting to emigrate legally or to alter their status. Immigration attorneys are the best sources to detail these barriers.
- Don't rely on quotes that condemn undocumented people for not getting legal status without also examining the barriers to gaining legal status. If you fail to investigate, you add to the notion that people have the agency to correct their status even when they don't.
- Get a quick briefing from an immigration attorney at a national organization and check reliable agency websites to learn about the laws and regulations that may explain why people you've interviewed are in a predicament.
- Here are some websites that are helpful. They can provide details about laws and regulations, and may offer briefing papers that explain the visa system, which is very narrowly drawn and confusing.
  - American Families United: americanfamiliesunited.org.
  - American Immigration Council: www.americanimmigrationcouncil. org/research/three-and-ten-year-bars.
  - Migration Policy Institute:www.migrationpolicy.org/research/going-back-line-primer-lines-visa-categories-and-wait-times.

Notes

1 Susan Ferriss and Amy Isackson. "Separated by Law: Families Torn Apart by 1996 Immigration Measure: American Dream becomes Nightmare as Immigrant Spouses are Barred for Years." Center for Public Integrity, October 19, 2012. Accessed April 3, 2017 from www.publicintegrity.org/2012/10/19/11563/separated-law-families-torn-apart-1996-immigration-measure.
2 Ibid.
3 Ibid.
4 Ibid.
5 Ibid.
6 Ibid.

CONCLUSION

Sally Lehrman and Venise Wagner

As we complete this book, we are contemplating the violence that erupted in Charlottesville, Virginia,[1] during a 2017 white nationalist rally to oppose the city's decision to remove confederate monuments. Participants carried Neo-Nazi flags and shouted racist and anti-Semitic slogans while residents, anti-fascist, and anti-racist groups counter-protested.[2] During the clashes, a man drove a Dodge Challenger into a crowd of counter protestors, killing 32-year-old Heather Heyer. Police arrested and charged a 20-year-old who had expressed white supremacist views since at least high school.

Incidents such as these remind us that overt racism persists in many corners of our society, perhaps less in the shadows than we once thought. Yet we feel journalists offer little when they focus attention on marginal extremists while overlooking the everyday, invisible gears of structural racism. "White supremacy" exists in many forms, some intentional and confrontational, others, unintended but not benign.

In this book, we have attempted to show the ways in which journalists can shed light on the root causes of racial disparity in our country. Some may accuse us of promoting a liberal perspective because we begin by acknowledging that racial inequity exists. As we have shown, the data back us up. We also have shown why it's inaccurate and incomplete to rely solely on personal responsibility or cultural explanations for this inequity. Some may believe that active pursuit of racial angles in stories is in and of itself an activist position, not a journalistic one. We argue that this approach is the only way to tell the full and complete story of America.

What is the impact, for example, of the delay of a Department of Education regulation that allows loan forgiveness if a student was defrauded or misled by their college? The delay will likely do the most harm to poor students of color, who disproportionately enroll in for-profit colleges. Such colleges have a poor record of delivering on their stated educational goals.[3] Or how will Native American nations experience President Donald J. Trump's decision to shrink the size of Bears Ears National Monument by 85 percent and Grand Staircase-Escalante by half?[4] His action will open up these areas to commercial activity, challenging the culture and economy of tribes who rely on the lands. Our tools can enable you to reach beyond liberal vs. conservative, he said vs. she said coverage of these topics. When journalists explore such stories more fully, the public can come to informed conclusions about the best way forward.

Addressing Resistance

Uncovering structural inequity and showing its racial impact may put you in an uncomfortable position with your audiences. Specifically, you may encounter resistance from white people, including those who consider themselves racially aware. Addressing race head-on is often considered impolite in white society, except in situations when racism already is an agreed-upon topic or white people want to express interracial support. In a class one term taught by co-editor Sally Lehrman called "Race, Gender and Public Health in the News," for instance, students were mostly white and at first resisted any discussion of racism. Despite the title of the course, they felt that the topic should be avoided. It was divisive and in itself racist, they said.

Robin DiAngelo, a consultant and trainer on racism and social justice, invented the term "white fragility" to describe the anger, fear, and guilt that white people often exhibit when confronted with racial realities. Whites generally have grown up surrounded by people that look like them – starting with their neighbors and fellow students all the way to the business leaders and politicians they encounter in the news. Even God is often understood to be white. White people have very little experience talking or thinking about race, DiAngelo writes, and so may resist the topic, avoid it or grow emotional. Even you may feel these emotions as you take our challenge to go deeper on race.[5]

White fragility is on full display at the bottom of many news stories about race in the comment thread – often a gathering spot for hostile voices. Along with a smattering of thoughtful commentary and the obligatory white nationalist polemic, you'll see various diversion techniques – an attack on political correctness, a tirade on people of color's supposed self-inflicted "victimhood," protests that white people aren't monolithic, an argument that class should really be the issue, or a litany of evidence that white people suffer from economic and social distress too.[6]

As journalists, we want to avoid the trap of appeasing white audiences and stepping gingerly around race. We also must avoid the temptation to lean on another common strategy, which is to exceptionalize the nonwhite racial experience as a sort of unfortunate handicap in life that must be over-come. As we've shown, when character-driven stories about inequity leave out structural and institutional forces, they point audiences toward the latter perspective. Racial inequity is understood as essentially happenstance – or the result of poor choices by those most affected. Sure, a white person may consequently be moved to want to "help less fortunate people," as we often hear. But that just leaves power structures unaddressed and, in fact, cements them further in place. Confronting the structures that give fortune to ourselves over others is harder, yet ultimately, far more affirming and powerful.

White people generally don't have the opportunity to see inequity in action because of continuing segregation in neighborhoods, schools, and many types of jobs. Despite the passage of the Fair Housing Act in 1968 and a resulting increase in integration, in the largest, most populated areas of the United States segregation remains about the same. It's high in all types of areas where large groups of racial and ethnic minorities live, driven by America's segregated social structure and our legacy of physical separation.[7]

As a result, many white people seem to have little awareness of the world experienced by others. There is a tremendous racial and partisan gap between those who say racism is a "big problem" in the United States and those who disagree, for instance, even though the proportion of white people that say so has roughly doubled since 2011.[8] Researchers at the University of Illinois in Chicago studied racial attitudes and found disinterest among whites. They dis-covered a waning belief in structural explanations for racial inequality, with white people nearly equally endorsing a lack of motivation and a low chance for education as the cause.[9]

By using the practices described in this book, you can reveal not just the unequal opportunity rampant in education, health, criminal justice, and other areas of US life and the resulting unequal outcomes, but also the machinery behind these. You can build the stamina of white people to understand, talk about, and, ultimately, address social inequality. As Dr. Martin Luther King Jr. said to proponents of segregation in a 1965 speech in Selma, Alabama, "You are making slaves out of white children also ... They are not being prepared to live in the modern world." So, too, do journalists make "slaves" out of white people when we avoid uncomfortable racial topics.

Even though we have centered on whites in this portion of our discussion, we do not mean to suggest in any way that your reporting should do so. The best journalism keeps diverse audiences at heart and also helps introduce the perspectives and experiences of one sector to another. Furthermore, as several theorists have pointed out, while people of color may understand race and racism at a visceral level, they too may lack a framework for understanding its systemic workings.[10]

Class and Race

Historically, journalists have failed to recognize the ways in which powerful interests often place a wedge between people of color and poor whites. Consider the desegregation of schools, which unfolded in the South during the civil rights movement of the late 1950s. Recall the iconic photo of Elizabeth Eckford holding her notebook tightly as she walked toward Central High School in Little Rock, Arkansas, while a crowd of white students jeered her. The photojournalist turned the lens toward one white student, Hazel Bryan, who shows hatred on her face as she yells something at Eckford.

What was (and remains) not widely known is that Hazel, her family, and most of the kids in the school were working-class or poor. In *White Trash: The 400-Year Untold History of Class in America*, Nancy Isenberg explains the backstory behind city leaders' choice of Central High, which served mainly poor and working-class white families, for desegregation. There were three high schools in Little Rock at the time: Horace Mann High for blacks, R.C. Hall High for wealthy families on the west side of town, and Central High. The selection deliberately stoked class resentment. A local white citizens' league fanned class flames by declaring that the only race-mixing that would happen in Little Rock would be among poor whites.[11]

White elites exploited desegregation rulings to pit poor and working-class white people against African Americans. These tensions have lingered and are arising with new force throughout the country, with poor or working-class whites fearful of losing resources to people of color – including Latinos, Asian Americans, African immigrants, Arabs, American Indians, and blacks. Such racial resentment drives a decline in white people's support for the social safety net, for instance, due to anxieties about their own declining social and financial status. Yet whites benefit far more than other groups from such programs.[12] And as the social safety net degrades, of course, it affects everyone.

Many white people see their own very real wants and needs being overlooked by journalists and policymakers. Economic and social disadvantage does grip white communities. Non-Hispanic whites suffer disproportionately from the opioid epidemic by far, with 79 percent of deaths by overdose among this population.[13] The Center on Budget and Policy Priorities found that nearly one-quarter of white people would live below the poverty line were it not for government programs. (Such aid reduces white poverty to 14 percent.)[14] About the same proportion of white and black people must contend with disability, which limits opportunities across multiple dimensions, although Native Americans and Alaskan Natives experience the highest rates of all.[15]

And yes, there is a widening economic divide between the richest and everyone else in the United States.[16] Yet racial inequality persists. Even low-income whites have access to structurally powered advantages and gains. Along with government aid, other benefits have accrued and compounded invisibly over generations in a system that was originally designed to protect white land-owner interests. And, as DiAngelo adds, whites do not bear the burden of an ever-present emotional and social assault due to implicit and overt racism.

Inequity Touches Everyone

Class and race have had an intertwined relationship since race was invented in our country. It was the white elites of the South who convinced poor whites that preserving the institution of slavery was in their economic best interest, when in reality, it was not.[17] In the urban North, industrialists used people of color as pawns to challenge the rise of unions.[18] Yet, in our history there have been times when poor whites and people of color have come together to fight against powerful interests.[19]

Showing the workings of inequity, done well, points to opportunities for constructive engagement across race and class, rather than sowing further division. Journalists can offer an impartial view that shines light on our American legacy of racial preferences for whites. We can also show the ways in which the persistence of institutional and structural racism hurts everyone. Intercultural working groups work smarter and more creatively – inequity in hiring and unequal pay makes them more difficult to achieve. Diverse schools help children develop skills to interact with all types of people and ensure that all children get a fair chance to go to college or pursue other dreams. High-quality health care in early life and later propels the economy by, among other benefits, strengthening the workforce and extending productive lives. On the other hand, the costs of supplying remedial education, cleaning up neglected neighborhoods, and maintaining prisons are the high price of inequity that we all must pay.

Eventually, if left unaddressed, the impoverished social, environmental, and institutional conditions caused by diversion of resources away from communities of color begin to affect white communities, too. Polluted air wanders away from nonwhite neighborhoods. Neglected public transit results in congested roadways and stressful commutes throughout a region. Toxic law enforcement–community relations leak out from communities of color to white neighborhoods nearby and beyond. Reporters using our method can clarify such realities, which are often misunderstood or overlooked.

The opioid epidemic is a good case in point. While drug addiction affects people across income and race, black and brown neighborhoods have for years borne the stereotype of being ravaged by crack addiction. Legislators treated the problem as a law enforcement issue, placing harsh sentences on people of color convicted of nonviolent drug crimes.[20] In contrast, when opioid use reached unprecedented proportions in white middle-class communities, the initial response was to call for a humane approach, with both legislators and the public applying a public health framework to the problem.

Now we are beginning to see more punitive measures emerge. A growing number of prosecutors across the country are filing homicide charges against people who may have been present with drug overdose victims or shared drugs with the person who died. The cases are called "murder by overdose."[21] The law enforcement approach to drug dependency, which gained acceptance when applied in black and brown communities, is now spreading to white middle-class communities.

We are all connected – laws, perceptions, and even physical surroundings do not remain isolated to one population. When journalists reflect these inter-sectionalities in reporting, we all benefit. We also encourage reporters to open their eyes to the assets of race in American life, not just the challenges we face. The rich and layered complexities of this nation's various communities truly make America great. Many public school districts enroll students who speak hundreds of languages other than English, talent that can be harnessed and translated into global strength. The wide range of cultural experiences in towns and cities provide a rich source of ideas that fuel our economy. It isn't an accident that the United States is known for its innovation. Even in our differences, we have shared values.

Key Themes of This Book

In Europe and the United States today, some individuals are taking advantage of financial and social insecurity to promote white nationalist and supremacist ideas. Many observers and scholars have argued that news media coverage of such extremist views simply gives them more weight than warranted, providing a veneer of legitimacy and power.[22] In our view, they might even be understood as a diversion from wide-reaching, structurally embedded white supremacy of a more mundane, everyday variety. "White supremacy" is a strong, perhaps shocking, label for policies and practices that give an advantage to white neighborhoods, white workers, and white families needing health care. Yet it reminds us of the collective impact of these structural forces and why journalists have a responsibility to uncover them.

We hope this book will give you the theoretical framework to understand how structural racism came into being and why it persists, often unseen. In our individualistic culture, journalists tend to go immediately to individual choices and cultural context to unpack the reasons behind a person or group's struggles or successes. We rely on the personal responsibility frame, often with the goal of building a compelling narrative, to the detriment of offering a more accurate picture of the forces at play. In our first chapter, social psychologist Hazel Markus helps us understand the ways in which socio-cultural context constrains individual agency, even limiting journalists' ability to interpret the potential for individual agency. Other chapters offer in-depth examinations of structural and systemic racism, including a case study in the city of Chicago. To help the public understand the inequities we see today, journalists must include the historical context that underlies them. How is it that we got to where we are now? When we help the public see the legacy of policies and laws that lead to racial inequity, we show the intransigent nature of inequity unaddressed, replicated, and passed on through generations.

The ethics guidelines of the Society of Professional Journalists and other journalism organizations establish a foundation of journalistic principles that call for full representation of communities of color. To that end, our book offers a bevy of best practices including interviewing techniques and strategies for sourcing and conceptualizing stories about racial disparity. Our case studies offer a model for conceiving and developing your own strategies for telling these stories.

Through our theoretical chapters, case studies, and Opportunity Index, we hope we have shown how reporting on inequality requires a holistic view. Every beat – cops, health, environment, education, even sports – offers great opportunities to report on inequality. And often policies and practices in one area will shape outcomes in another.

Structural Racism within Journalism

For coverage of disparities to improve we must also recognize the structural racism that exists within our own field, journalism. While our book doesn't focus on this, we encourage others to pursue questions about the complicity of journalism in perpetuating structural racism. Policies and practices within the institution of journalism, like most American institutions, normalize racial inequity. For example, editors often assign the best reporting stories to white reporters. It is not uncommon for elite investigative teams in newsrooms to be mostly white men.[23] This is most evident when attending the Investigative Reporters and Editors yearly conference. There you will see only a smattering of journalists of color. While we see some change in this area, more can be done.

Unwittingly, journalists tend to replicate the social order in our reporting, too. For an authoritative source, we turn to people at high levels of business, government, and universities. We rely on the documents they produce. This book has shown the forces that make those high levels harder to reach for people of color. Of course we should carefully evaluate a source's knowledge. But titles and other institutional recognition cannot be our only signposts. Furthermore, journalists readily recognize that we should take into account a source's social, political, or economic position relative to a topic, yet we rarely consider how race or gender may influence what we accept to be common knowledge.

What We Can Learn from #Metoo

The #metoo movement provides an object lesson on the social dynamics that may keep inequalities from surfacing or being recognized as important to address. Women in every field have come forward with examples of sexual harassment, often commonplace, that date back decades and are nearly as persistent today. For many, they had seemed too small or distinct to mention, but when taken together, we discover a disempowering and hostile system that cuts across educational institutions and workplaces. It was reporting by the *New Yorker* and the *New York Times* on the extensive allegations against film producer Harvey Weinstein that triggered an outcry in 2017, followed by a flood of similar stories. Social media propelled awareness and debate.

We hope our book can help journalists raise awareness of harmful, racialized structures that also remain stubbornly in place, and the reasons behind their persistence. Instead of dismissing racial micro-aggressions, for instance, we might think of them as symptoms of a larger dysfunction. They can be seen as individual acts that are replicated within institutions, enshrined in policies and practices, and tolerated even though they limit individual opportunity and our collective health as a society.

The News Media's Role in a Splintered Society

The news media have been suffering from a decline in public trust since the late 1990s, with distrust and hostility against national media reaching a peak in 2016.[24] A deep partisan divide has since arisen, with Democrats far more confident in the news than Republicans.[25] Journalists questioned themselves, too, when they so poorly predicted the outcome of the 2016 presidential election.

In today's digital environment, we all suffer from an increasingly splintered and specialized information diet. People can easily choose news that confirms what they believe they already know – and they do.[26] At the same time, the internet has become an active forum for the public to engage in debate, even as social media and personalization channel us into like-minded spaces. News organizations must do a better job of facilitating the exchange of views that the Hutchins Commission described as our duty in 1947. Our weakness in this area, well-described when it comes to racial and religious minorities, became apparent in fresh ways after Trump's surprise win of the presidential election revealed a large white population overlooked by journalists. Journalists didn't notice the fear and loss many whites were feeling due to economic disruption and changing demographics. Using our method, journalists may have identified the invisible gears at work that were spreading structural disadvantage beyond communities of color.

In a 2018 Gallup poll, more than 80 percent of Americans rated the news media as "very important" to "critical" to our democracy. But most didn't feel we do enough to support democracy well by issuing nonpartisan reports that highlight vital issues, hold leaders accountable, and connect residents to their communities and their country.[27] This book is an attempt to help reporters rebuild trust through more effectively fulfilling journalism's essential role in society – including telling more representative stories and revealing the underlying forces that shape this country in all its frailty, power, and potential.

Notes

1 Maggie Astor, Christina Caron, and Daniel Victor. "A Guide to the Charlottesville Aftermath." *New York Times*, August 13, 2017. Accessed July 9, 2018 from www.nytimes.com/2017/08/13/us/charlottesville-virginia-overview.html.
2 Farah Stockman. "Who Were the Counterprotesters in Charlottesville?" *New York Times*, August 24, 2017. Accessed July 7, 2018 from www.nytimes.com/2017/08/14/us/who-were-the-counterprotesters-in-charlottesville.html.
3 Mamie Lynch, Jennifer Engle, and José L. Cruz. "Subprime Opportunity: The Unfulfilled Promise of for-Profit Colleges and Universities." The Education Trust, 2010.
4 Eric Lipton and Danielle Ivory. "Trump Says His Regulatory Rollback Already Is the 'Most Far-Reaching'." *New York Times*, December 14, 2017. Accessed December 29, 2017 from www.nytimes.com/2017/12/14/us/politics/trump-federal-regulations.html.
5 Robin DiAngelo. "White Fragility." *International Journal of Critical Pedagogy* 3, no. 3 (2011). Accessed July 6, 2018 from https://robindiangelo.com/2018site/wp-content/uploads/2016/01/White-Fragility-Published.-1.pdf.
6 For an example of all these reactions, see the discussion on Quora, "Why Are So Many White People in America Unaware of Their White Privilege? Why Is It So Difficult to See That Conformity, Wealth, Class, and Gender Can Also Intersect With Race?" www.quora.com/Why-are-so-many-white-people-in-America-unaware-of-their-white-privilege-Why-is-it-so-difficult-to-see-that-conformity-wealth-class-and-gender-can-also-intersect-with-race.
7 Maria Krysan and Kyle Crowder. *Cycle of Segregation: Social Processes and Residential Stratification*. New York, NY: Russell Sage Foundation, 2017.
8 While 80 percent of black people told the Pew Research Center in 2017 that racism was a big problem, just over half of whites said so. Samantha Neal. "Views of Racism as a Major Problem Increase Sharply, Especially among Democrats." Pew Research Center, August 29, 2017. Accessed July 3, 2018 from www.pewresearch.org/fact-tank/2017/08/29/views-of-racism-as-a-major-problem-increase-sharply-especially-among-democrats/.
9 Maria Krysan and Sarah Patton Moberg. "Trends in Racial Attitudes." Institute of Government and Public Affairs, University of Illinois, 2016. Accessed July 3, 2018 from https://igpa.uillinois.edu/programs/racial-attitudes#section-0.
10 DiAngelo. "White Fragility."
11 Nancy Isenberg. *White Trash: The 400-Year Untold History of Class in America*. New York, NY: Viking Press, 2016, pp. 247–250.
12 Kat Chow. "Why More White Americans Are Opposing Government Welfare Programs." National Public Radio, June 8, 2018. Accessed July 7, 2018 from www.npr.org/sections/codeswitch/2018/06/08/616684259/why-more-white-americans-are-opposing-government-welfare-programs.
13 Henry J. Kaiser Family Foundation. "Opioid Overdose Rates by Race and Ethnicity, 2016." State Health Facts, 2018. Accessed July 6, 2018 from www.kff.org/other/state-indicator/opioid-overdose-deaths-by-raceethnicity/?dataView=1&currentTimeframe=0&sortModel=%7B%22colId%22:%22Location%22,%22sort%22:%22asc%22%7D.
14 Without government aid, 43 percent of blacks and 36 percent of Hispanics would live in poverty. Taking into account government programs, poverty rates were: 13 percent among whites; 24 percent among black people; and 26 percent among Hispanics. Isaac Shapiro, Danilo Trisi, and Raheem Chaudhry. "Poverty Reduction

Programs Help Adults Lacking College Degrees the Most." Center on Budget Policies and Priorities, February 16, 2017. Accessed July 6, 2018 from www.cbpp.org/research/poverty-and-inequality/poverty-reduction-programs-help-adults-lacking-college-degrees-the. See also Tracy Jan. "The Biggest Beneficiaries of the Government Safety Net: Working Class Whites." *Washington Post*, February 16, 2017. Accessed July 6, 2018 from www.washingtonpost.com/news/wonk/wp/2017/02/16/the-biggest-beneficiaries-of-the-government-safety-net-working-class-whites/?utm_term=.85aef7235b3c.

15 Henry J. Kaiser Family Foundation. "Percentage of Non-Institutionalized Population Who Reported a Disability, by Race/Ethnicity." State Health Facts, 2015. Accessed July 6, 2018 from www.kff.org/other/state-indicator/percentage-of-non-institutionalized-population-who-reported-a-disability-by-raceethnicity/?currentTimeframe=0&sortModel=%7B%22colId%22:%22Location%22,%22sort%22:%22asc%22%7D.

16 Allianz. *Allianz Global Wealth Map*, 2018. Accessed July 14, 2018 from www.allianz.com/en/economic_research/research_data/interactive-wealth-map/.

17 David R. Roediger. *The Wages of Whiteness: Race and the Making of the American Working Class*. New York, NY: Verso, 2007.

18 Bruce Nelson. *Divided We Stand: American Workers and the Struggle for Black Equality*. Princeton, NJ: Princeton University Press, 2000, pp. 145–184.

19 Ibid., pp. 185–218. Here Nelson details the brief collaboration between blacks and whites in the union movement of the mid 1930s and the dissolution of that collaboration at the advent of World War II.

20 Michelle Alexander. *The New Jim Crow: Mass Incarceration in the Age of Colorblindness*. New York, NY: The New Press, 2012.

21 Rosa Goldensohn. "They Shared Drugs. Someone Died. Does That Make Them Killers?" *New York Times*, May 25, 2018. Accessed July 14, 2018 from www.nytimes.com/2018/05/25/us/drug-overdose-prosecution-crime.html.

22 Whitney Phillips. "The Oxygen of Amplification: Better Practices for Reporting on Extremists, Antagonists and Manipulators Online." *Data & Society*, May 22, 2018, pp. 10–12. Accessed July 7, 2018 from https://datasociety.net/pubs/oh/1_PART_1_Oxygen_of_Amplification_DS.pdf.

23 Susannah Nesmith. "Investigative Reporting 'Is Still a Very White Male Business.' How the Online News Association and The Georgia News Lab Are Working to Diversify Journalism." *Columbia Journalism Review*, September 18, 2015. Accessed February 9, 2018 from https://archives.cjr.org/united_states_project/georgia_news_lab_bring_diversity_to_investigative_reporting.php. Also, Sonia Paul. "The State of Investigative Reporting: Highlights from IRE 2017." Mediashift, June 28, 2017. Accessed February 9, 2018 from http://mediashift.org/2017/06/highlights-annual-investigative-reporters-editors-conference-show-state-investigative-reporting/.

24 Art Swift. "In U.S., Confidence in Newspapers Still Low but Rising." Gallup, June 28, 2017. Accessed July 7, 2018 from https://news.gallup.com/poll/212852/confidence-newspapers-low-rising.aspx.

25 Michael Barthel and Amy Mitchell. "Americans' Attitudes about the News Media Deeply Divided Along Partisan Lines." Pew Research Center, May 10, 2017. Accessed July 7, 2018 from www.journalism.org/2017/05/10/americans-attitudes-about-the-news-media-deeply-divided-along-partisan-lines/.

26 George Sylvie. "The Call and Challenge for Diversity," in *Changing the News: The Forces Shaping Journalism in Uncertain Times*, ed. Wilson Lowrey and Peter J. Gade. New York, NY: Routledge, 2011.

27 Zacc Ritter and Jeffrey M. Jones. "Media Seen as Key to Democracy but Not Supporting It Well." Gallup, January 16, 2018. Accessed July 7, 2018 from https://news.gallup.com/poll/225470/media-seen-key-democracy-not-supporting.aspx.

BIBLIOGRAPHY

American Press Institute. "What is the Purpose of Journalism?" Accessed March 14, 2017 from www.americanpressinstitute.org/journalism-essentials/what-is-journalism/pur pose-journalism/.

#BlackLivesMatter. "Black Lives Matter: Freedom and Justice for all Black Lives," April 2017. Accessed September 21, 2017 from http://blacklivesmatter.com/.

"1921 Tulsa Race Riot." Tulsa Historical Society & Museum, 2018. Accessed April 27, 2018 from https://tulsahistory.org/learn/online-exhibits/the-tulsa-race-riot/.

Aberson, Christopher L., Carl Shoemaker, and Christina Tomolillo. "Implicit Bias and Contact: The Role of Interethnic Friendships." *The Journal of Social Psychology* 144, no. 3 (2004): 335–347. doi: 10.3200/SOCP.144.3.335-347.

Achebe, Chinua. *Hopes and Impediments: Selected Essays.* New York, NY: Anchor Books, 1988.

Acs, Gregory, Rolf Pendall, Mark Treskon, and Amy Khare. "The Cost of Segregation: National Trends and the Case of Chicago, 1990–2010." Metropolitan Housing and Communities Policy Center, March 2017.

Alameda County Public Health Department. *Getting on Board for Health: A Health Impact Assessment of Bus Funding and Access,* May 2013. Accessed March 17, 2018 from www.acphd.org/media/309841/transithia_es.pdf.

Alameda County Public Health Department. *Life and Death from Unnatural Causes, Executive Summary,* p. vii Accessed April 14, 2018 from www.acphd.org/media/144757/lduc-execsum.pdf.

Alameda County Public Health Department and Behavioral Health Services. *Improving Housing and Health for all in Alameda County: The Opportunity Is Now,* June 2016. Accessed March 23, 2018 from www.acphd.org/media/425883/housing-brief-june-2016.pdf.

Albarracín, Dolores and Patrick Vargas. *Attitudes and Persuasion: From Biology to Social Responses to Persuasive Intent.* Hoboken, NJ: John Wiley & Sons, 2010.

Alcindor, Yamiche. "Baltimore Police Say Freddie Gray Protest Turns Destructive." *USA Today,* April 25, 2015. Accessed February 3, 2018 from www.usatoday.com/story/news/nation/2015/04/25/baltimore-protests-freddie-gray/26354515/.

Alexander, Michelle. *The New Jim Crow: Mass Incarceration in the Age of Colorblindness.* Revised Edition. New York, NY: The New Press, 2012.

Allen, Reniqua. "Our 21ˢᵗ Century Segregation: We're Still Divided by Race." *Guardian*, April 3, 2013. Accessed July 7, 2018 from www.theguardian.com/commentisfree/2013/apr/03/21st-century-segregation-divided-race.

Allen, Thomas J., Jeffrey W. Sherman, and Karl Christoph Klauer. "Social Context and the Self-Regulation of Implicit Bias." *Group Processes & Intergroup Relations* 13, no. 2 (2010): 137–149. doi: 10.1177/1368430209353635.

Allport, Gordon W. *The Nature of Prejudice.* Cambridge, MA: Perseus Books, 1954, 1979.

Alvarez, Lizette. "A Florida Law Gets Scrutiny After a teenager's Killing." *New York Times*, March 20, 2012. Accessed February 22, 2018 from www.nytimes.com/2012/03/21/us/justice-department-opens-inquiry-in-killing-of-trayvon-martin.html.

Annie E. Casey Foundation. "Kids Count Data Center, Children in Poverty by Race and Ethnicity, 2012 to 2016." Accessed February 3, 2018 from http://datacenter.kidscount.org/data/tables/44-children-in-poverty-by-race-and-ethnicity#detailed/1/any/false/870,573,869,36,868/10,11,9,12,1,185,13/323.

Aspen Institute Roundtable on Community Change. *Structural Racism and Community Building*, 2004. Accessed July 7, 2018 from https://assets.aspeninstitute.org/content/uploads/files/content/docs/rcc/aspen_structural_racism2.pdf.

Associated Press and Kelly McLaughlin. "Violent Scenes at North Dakota Oil Pipeline as Native American Protesters Claim Sacred Burial Grounds were Destroyed by Construction Crew." Daily Mail.com, September 4, 2016. Accessed February 13, 2018 from www.dailymail.co.uk/news/article-3772859/Native-American-protesters-confronted-security-demonstration-against-work-Dakota-Access-oil-pipeline.html.

Astor, Maggie. "Tucson's Mexican Studies Program was a Victim of 'Racial Animus,' Judge Says." *New York Times*, August 23, 2017. Accessed January 16, 2018 from www.nytimes.com/2017/08/23/us/arizona-mexican-american-ruling.html.

Astor, Maggie, Christina Caron, and Daniel Victor. "A Guide to the Charlottesville Aftermath." *New York Times*, August 13, 2017. Accessed July 9, 2018 from www.nytimes.com/2017/08/13/us/charlottesville-virginia-overview.html.

Badgett, Mary Virginia Lee. "Employment and Sexual Orientation: Disclosure and Discrimination in the Workplace." *Journal of Gay and Lesbian Social Services* 4, no. 4 (1996): 29–52. doi: 10.1300/J041v04n04_03.

Badgett, Mary Virginia Lee, Holning Lau, Brad Sears, and Deborah Ho. "Bias in the Workplace: Consistent Evidence of Sexual Orientation and Gender Identity Discrimination." The Williams Institute, June 2007. Accessed March 8, 2018 from https://escholarship.org/uc/item/5h3731xr.

Bailey, Stanley R. and Edward E. Telles. "Multiracial versus Collective Black Categories: Examining Census Classification Debates in Brazil." *Ethnicities* 6, no. 1 (2006): 74–101. doi: 10.1177/1468796806061080.

Balfanz, Robert and Nettie Legters. "Graduation Rate Crisis: We Know What Can be Done about It," *Education Week*, July 12, 2006.

Balfanz, Robert, Liza Herzog, and Douglas J. Mac Iver. "Preventing Student Disengagement and Keeping Students on the Graduation Path in Urban Middle-Grade Schools: Early Identification and Effective Interventions." *Educational Psychologist* 42, no. 4 (2007): 223–235.

"Baltimore Public Housing Families Applaud Court Approval of Fair Housing Lawsuit Settlement." ACLU Press Release, November 20, 2012. Accessed February 21, 2017 from https://www.aclu-md.org/en/press-releases/baltimore-public-housing-families-applaud-court-approval-fair-housing-lawsuit.

"Baltimore Public Housing Families Win Settlement in Fair Housing Law." NAACP Legal Defense Fund, August 24, 2012. Accessed February 21, 2017 from www.naacpldf.org/press-release/baltimore-public-housing-families-win-settlement-fair-housing-lawsuit.

Barr, Andy. "Arizona Bans 'Ethnic Studies'." *Politico*, May 12, 2010. Accessed March 8, 2018 from www.politico.com/story/2010/05/arizona-bans-ethnic-studies-037131.

Barry, Dan and John Eligon. "'Trump, Trump, Trump!' How a President's Name became a Racial Jeer." *New York Times*, December 16, 2017. Accessed December 29, 2017 from www.nytimes.com/2017/12/16/us/trump-racial-jeers.html?_r=0.

Barthel, Michael and Amy Mitchell. "Americans' Attitudes about the News Media Deeply Divided along Partisan Lines." Pew Research Center, May 10, 2017. Accessed July 7, 2018 from www.journalism.org/2017/05/10/americans-attitudes-about-the-news-media-deeply-divided-along-partisan-lines/.

Bay Area Regional Health Inequities Initiative. *BARHII Displacement Brief*. Accessed April 7, 2018 from http://barhii.org/wp-content/uploads/2016/03/BARHII_Housing_Displacement_Brief_short.pdf.

Benavides-Vaello, Sandra and Sharon A. Brown. "Sociocultural Construction of Food Ways in Low-Income Mexican-American Women with Diabetes: A Qualitative Study." *Journal of Clinical Nursing* 25, no. 15–16 (2016): 2367–2377. doi: 10.1111/jocn.13291/full.

Benegal, Salil D. "The Spillover of Race and Racial Attitudes into Public Opinion about Climate Change." *Environmental Politics* 27, no. 4 (2018): 733–756. doi: 10.1080/09644016.2018.1457287.

Berke, Ethan M., Susanne E. Tanski, Eugene Demidenko, Jennifer Alford-Teaster, Xun Shi, and James D. Sargent. "Alcohol Retail Density and Demographic Predictors of Health Disparities: A Geographic Analysis." *American Journal of Public Health* 100, no. 10 (October 2010): 1967–1971. doi: 10.2105/AJPH.2009.170464.

Bernstein, Irving. *Promises Kept: John F. Kennedy's New Frontier*. New York, NY: Oxford University Press, 1991.

Bertocchi, Graziella and Arcangelo Dimico. "Slavery, Education, and Inequality." *European Economic Review* 70 (August 2014): 197–209. doi: 10.1016/j.euroecorev.2014.04.007.

Bertrand, Marianne and Sendhil Mullainathan. "Are Emily and Greg more Employable than Lakisha and Jamal? A Field Experiment on Labor Market Discrimination." *American Economic Review* 94, no. 4 (September 2004): 991–1013.

Biernat, Monica and Melvin Manis. "Shifting Standards and Stereotype-Based Judgments." *Journal of Personality and Social Psychology* 66 (1991): 5–20.

Blair, Irene V., Edward P. Havranek, David. W. Price, Rebecca Hanratty, Diane L. Fairclough, Tillman Farley, ... John F. Steiner. "Assessment of Biases against Latinos and African Americans among Primary Care Providers and Community Members." *American Journal of Public Health* 103, no. 1 (2013a): 92–98.

Blair, Irene V., Edward P. Havranek, David. W. Price, Rebecca Hanratty, Diane L. Fairclough, Tillman Farley, ... John F. Steiner. "Clinicians Implicit Ethnic/Racial Bias and Perceptions of Care among Black and Latino Patients." *Annals of Family Medicine* 11, no. 1 (2013b): 43–52. doi: 10.1370/afm.1442.

Blank, Rebecca M., Marilyn Dabady, and Constance F. Citro, eds. *Measuring Racial Discrimination*. Panel on Methods for Assessing Discrimination. Committee on National

Statistics, Division of Behavioral and Social Sciences and Education. National Research Council. Washington, DC: The National Academies Press, 2004.

Bragg, Michael. "Students Who Confronted Torch-Bearers Demand UVa Take Action." *The Daily Progress*, August 19, 2017. Accessed September 16, 2017 from www.daily progress.com/news/local/students-who-confronted-torch-bearers-demand-uva-take-action/article_f56a4e02-8531-11e7-a55d-c33d43b75ef4.html.

Brauer, Markus, Abdelatif Er-Rafiy, Kerry Kawakami, and Curtis E. Phills. "Describing a Group in Positive Terms Reduces Prejudice Less Effectively than Describing it in Positive and Negative Terms." *Journal of Experimental Social Psychology* 48, no. 3 (2012): 757–761. doi: 10.1016/j.jesp.2011.11.002.

Brooks-Gunn, Jeanne and Lisa B. Markman. "The Contribution of Parenting to Ethnic and Racial Gaps in School Readiness." *The Future of Children* 15, no. 1 (2005): 139–168.

Brown, Emma. " 'Giving up wasn't an option': How One Man Beat the Odds to Graduate from College." *Washington Post*, July 25, 2017. Accessed February 4, 2018 from www.washingtonpost.com/local/education/giving-up-wasnt-an-option-how-one-man-beat-the-odds-to-graduate-from-college/2017/07/25/3495b6b2-6e4d-11e7-9c15-177740 635e83_story.html?utm_term=.526f46cd34f5.

Brown, Michael K. *Race, Money, and the American Welfare State*. Ithaca, NY: Cornell University Press, 1999.

Brulle, Robert J. and David N. Pellow. "Environmental Justice: Human Health and Environmental Inequalities." *Annual Review of Public Health* 27 (2006): 103–124. doi: 10.1146/annurev.publhealth.27.021405.102124.

Bullard, Robert D. "Confronting Environmental Racism in the Twenty-First Century." *Global Dialogue* 4, no. 1 (2002): 34–48.

Byrd, W. Michael and Linda A. Clayton. *An American Health Dilemma, Vol. 1, A Medical History of African Americans and the Problem of Race: Beginnings to 1900*. New York, NY: Routledge, 2000.

Calanchini, Jimmy, Karen Gonsalkorale, Jeffrey W. Sherman, and Karl Christoph Klauer. "Counter-Prejudicial Training Reduces Activation of Biased Associations and Enhances Response Monitoring." *European Journal of Social Psychology* 43, no. 5 (2013): 321–325.

Carson, Clayborne, ed. *The Papers of Martin Luther King, Jr. Vol. III: Birth of a New Age, December 1955 – December 1956*. Berkeley, CA: University of California Press, 1997.

Chambers, Jay G., Thomas B. Parrish, Joanne C. Lieberman, and Jean M. Wolman. "What Are We Spending on Special Education." Center for Special Education Finance, Brief No. 8 (February 1998).

Chaney, John, Amanda Burke, and Edward Burkley. "Do American Indian Mascots = American Indian People? Examining Implicit Bias towards American Indian People and American Indian Mascots." *American Indian and Alaska Native Mental Health Research: the Journal of the National Center* 18, no. 1 (2011): 42–62.

Chang, Ailsa. "For City Teens, Stop-and-Frisk is Black and White." WNYC News, May 29, 2012. Accessed March 7, 2017 from www.wnyc.org/story/212460-city-teen agers-say-stop-and-frisk-all-about-race-and-class/.

Chermak, Steven and Nicole M. Chapman. "Predicting Crime Story Salience: A Replication." *Journal of Criminal Justice* 35, no. 4 (2007): 351–363. doi: 10.1016/j.jcrimjus. 2007.05.001.

Cholo, Ana Beatriz. "Latino Dropout Rate Called 'Crisis.'" *Chicago Tribune*, January 8, 2004. Accessed March 17, 2018 from http://articles.chicagotribune.com/2004-01-08/news/0401080381_1_dropout-rate-dropout-problem-hispanic-dropout.

Chow, Kat. "Why More White Americans are Opposing Government Welfare Programs." National Public Radio, June 8, 2018. Accessed July 7, 2018 from www.npr.org/sections/codeswitch/2018/06/08/616684259/why-more-white-americans-are-opposing-government-welfare-programs.

Christian, Sue Ellen. *Overcoming Bias: A Journalist's Guide to Culture and Context.* New York, NY: Taylor & Francis, 2012.

Clifford, James. *On the Edges of Anthropology (Interviews).* Chicago, IL: Prickly Paradigm Press, 2003.

Cohen, Deborah A. et al. "The Paradox of Parks in Low-Income Areas: Park Use and Perceived Threats." *Environmental Behavior* 48, no. 1 (January 2016): 230–245.

Coleman, Jennifer A., Kathleen M. Ingram, Annalucia Bays, Jennifer A. Joy-Gaba, and Edward L. Boone. "Disability and Assistance Dog Implicit Association Test: A Novel IAT." *Rehabilitation Psychology* 60, no. 1 (2015): 17–26. doi: 10.1037/rep0000025.

Collins, Jr., James W., Richard J. David, Arden Handler, Stephen Wall, and Steven Andes. "Very Low Birthweight in African American Infants: The Role of Maternal Exposure to Interpersonal Racial Discrimination." *American Journal of Public Health* 94, no. 12 (2004): 2132–2138.

Conley, Dalton. *Being Black, Living in the Red.* Berkeley, CA: University of California Press, 1999.

Conley, David T. "The Challenge of College Readiness." *Educational Leadership* 64, no. 7 (2007): 23–29. Accessed February 2, 2017 from www.researchgate.net/profile/David_Conley2/publication/237305729_The_Challenge_of_College_Readiness_Research_shows_a_mismatch_between_high_school_preparation_and_college_expectations_How_can_high_schools_prepare_students_for_college_success/links/564b677908ae4ae893b7c7a8.pdf.

Courtney, Mark E., Amy Dworsky, Jennifer Hook, Adam Brown, Colleen Cary, Kara Love, Vanessa Vorhies, JoAnn S. Lee, Melissa Raap, Gretchen Ruth Cusick, Thomas Keller, Judy Havlicek, Alfred Perez, Sherri Terao, and Noel Bost. "Midwest Evaluation of the Adult Functioning of Former Foster Youth." Report from Chapin Hall, University of Chicago, 2011. Accessed January 31, 2017 from www.chapinhall.org/research/report/midwest-evaluation-adult-functioning-former-foster-youth.

Cunningham, William A., Kristopher J. Preacher, and Mahzarin R. Banaji. "Implicit Attitude Measures: Consistency, Stability, and Convergent Validity." *Psychological Science* 12, no. 2 (2001): 163–170. doi: 10.1111/1467-9280.00328.

D'Souza, Dinesh. *The End of Racism: Principles for a Multiracial Society.* New York, NY: The Free Press, 1995.

Danziger, Sheldon and Peter Gottschalk. *America Unequal.* New York, NY: Russell Sage Foundation, 1995.

Darity, Jr., William. "What's Left of the Economic Theory of Discrimination." In Steven Shulman and William Darity, Jr (eds.). *The Question of Discrimination.* Middletown, CT: Wesleyan University Press, 1989, pp. 335–374.

Darity, Jr., William A. and Patrick L. Mason. "Evidence on Discrimination in Employment: Codes of Color, Codes of Gender." *Journal of Economic Perspectives* 12 (1998): 63–90.

Darity, Jr., William and Samuel Myers, Jr. *Persistent Disparity: Race and Economic Inequality in the United States since 1945*. Northhampton, MA: Edward Elgar, 1998.

Deaton, Jeremy. "Racial Resentment may be Fueling Climate Denial: New Research Finds a Link between Racial Prejudice and Climate Change Denial." NexusMedia, May 24, 2018. Accessed July 14, 2018 from https://nexusmedianews.com/racial-resentment-could-be-fueling-climate-denial-65d32fbeaa8e.

Degregory, Lane. "The Retreat." *Tampa Bay Times*, March 25, 2012, p. 1A.

Delaney, Arthur and Julia Craven. "Police, Protestors Clash in Baltimore after Freddie Gray Funeral." Huffington Post, April 28, 2015. Accessed February 3, 2018 from www.huffingtonpost.com/2015/04/27/freddie-gray-protest-mall_n_7154708.html.

Delpit, Lisa. *Other People's Children: Cultural Conflict in the Classroom*. New York, NY: The New Press, 2006.

"Demographic Trends and Well-Being." In *On Views of Race and Inequality, Blacks and Whites are Worlds Apart*. Pew Research Center, July 27, 2016. Accessed July 14, 2018 from www.pewsocialtrends.org/2016/06/27/1-demographic-trends-and-economic-well-being/.

Desmond, Matthew. "How Homeownership became the Engine of American Inequality." *New York Times*, May 9, 2017. Accessed May 13, 2017 from www.nytimes.com/2017/05/09/magazine/how-homeownership-became-the-engine-of-american-inequality.html?hp&action=click&pgtype=Homepage&clickSource=story-heading&module=photo-spot-region&region=top-news&WT.nav=top-news.

Devine, Patricia G., Patrick S. Forscher, Anthony J. Austin, and William T.L. Cox. "Long-Term Reduction in Implicit Race Bias: A Prejudice Habit-Breaking Intervention." *Journal of Experimental Social Psychology* 48, no. 6 (2012): 1267–1278. doi: 10.1016/j.jesp.2012.06.003.

DiAngelo, Robin. "White Fragility." *International Journal of Critical Pedagogy* 3, no. 3 (2011). Accessed July 6, 2018 from https://robindiangelo.com/2018site/wp-content/uploads/2016/01/White-Fragility-Published.-1.pdf.

Dixon, Travis L. "Black Criminals and White Officers: The Effects of Racially Misrepresenting Law Breakers and Law Defenders on Television News." *Media Psychology* 10, no. 2 (2009): 270–291. doi: 10.1080/15213260701375660.

Dixon, Travis L. "A Dangerous Distortion of Our Families: Representations, by Race, of Families in News and Opinion Media." Co-commissioned by Family Story and Color of Change, December 2017. Accessed December 31, 2017 from https://s3.amazo naws.com/coc-dangerousdisruption/full-report.pdf.

Dixon, Travis L. "Good Guys are Still Always in White? Positive Change and Continued Misrepresentation of Race and Crime on Local Television News." *Communication Research* 44, no. 6 (2015): 775–792. doi: 10.1177/0093650215579223.

Dixon, Travis L. "Psychological Reactions to Crime News Portrayals of Black Criminals: Understanding the Moderating Roles of Prior News Viewing and Stereotype Endorsement." *Communication Monographs* 73, no. 2 (2006): 162–187. doi: 10.1080/03637750600690643.

Dixon, Travis L. and Charlotte L. Williams. "The Changing Misrepresentation of Race and Crime on Network and Cable News." *Journal of Communication* 65, no. 1 (February 2015): 24–39. doi: 10.1111/jcom.12133.

"Don't Shoot." *The Economist*, December 11, 2014. Accessed August 2, 2017 from www.economist.com/news/united-states/21636044-americas-police-kill-too-many-people-some-forces-are-showing-how-smarter-less.

Dovidio, John F. and Samuel L. Gaertner. "Aversive Racism and Selection Decisions: 1989 and 1999." *Psychological Science* 11, no. 4 (2000): 315–319.

Dovidio, John F., K. Kawakami, and Samuel L. Gaertner. "Reducing Contemporary Prejudice: Combating Explicit and Implicit Bias at the Individual and Intergroup Level." In S. Oskamp (ed.). *Reducing Prejudice and Discrimination.* The Claremont Symposium on Applied Social Psychology. Mahwah, NJ: Erlbaum, 2000, pp. 137–163.

Doyle, Jr., Joseph J. "Child Protection and Adult Crime: Using Investigator Assignment to Estimate Causal Effects of Foster Care." *Journal of Political Economy* 116, no. 4 (2008): 746–770. Accessed January 31, 2017 from www.mit.edu/~jjdoyle/doyle_j pe_aug08.pdf.

Dragović, Milan, Johanna C. Badcock, Milenković Sanja, Margareta Gregurović, and Zlatko Šram. "Social Stereotyping of Left-Handers in Serbia." *Laterality: Asymmetries of Body, Brain and Cognition* 18, no. 6 (2013): 719–729. doi: 10.1080/1357650X.2012.755993.

Dresser, Michael. "State Designates Five 'Health Enterprise Zones'." *The Baltimore Sun,* January 24, 2013. Accessed February 25, 2018 from www.baltimoresun.com/health/bs-md-health-enterprise-20130124-story.html.

Du Bois, W.E.B. *The Souls of Black Folk.* New York, NY: Penguin Books, 1969.

Duhé, Lester. "Local College Graduate Beats the Odds, Wants to Inspire Others." KLFY. com, December 15, 2017. Accessed February 4, 2018 from www.klfy.com/news/local/local-college-graduate-beats-the-odds-wants-to-inspire-others/933636805.

"Dylann Roof Laughs in Video Confession of Church Shooting." MSN.com video, December 10, 2016. Accessed February 4, 2017 from www.msn.com/en-us/video/news/dylann-roof-laughs-in-video-confession-of-church-shooting/vi-AAloCbe.

Eberhardt, Jennifer L., Phillip A. Goff, Valerie J. Purdie, and Paul G. Davies. "Seeing Black: Race, Crime, and Visual Processing." *Journal of Personality and Social Psychology* 87, no. 6 (2004): 876–893. doi: 10.1037/0022-3514.87.6.876.

Edsall, Thomas B. "The Persistence of Racial Resentment." *New York Times,* February 6, 2013. Accessed July 14, 2018 from https://opinionator.blogs.nytimes.com/2013/02/06/the-persistence-of-racial-resentment/.

El-Sayed, Abdulrahman M., Magdalena Paczkowski, Caroline G. Rutherford, Katherine M. Keyes, and Sandro Galea. "Social Environments, Genetics and Black-White Disparities in Infant Mortality." *Paediatric & Perinatal Epidemiology* 29, no. 6 (2015): 546–551. doi: 10.1111/ppe.12227.

Entman, Robert M. and Andrew Rojecki. *The Black Image in the White Mind.* Chicago, IL: University of Chicago Press, 2000.

Epstein, Richard. *Forbidden Grounds: The Case against Employment Discrimination Laws.* Cambridge, MA: Harvard University Press, 1992.

Espinoza, Martin. "New Report Details Life Expectancy, Leading Causes of Death in Sonoma County." *The Press Democrat,* February 16, 2018. Accessed February 19, 2018 from www.pressdemocrat.com/news/7997819-181/new-report-details-life-expectancy.

Evans, Gary W., Jeanne Brooks-Gunn, and Pamela Kato Klebanov. *Stressing Out the Poor: Chronic Physiological Stress and the Income-Achievement Gap.* Stanford Center on Poverty & Inequality (Winter, 2011). Accessed March 25, 2018 from https://inequality.stanford.edu/sites/default/files/media/_media/pdf/pathways/winter_2011/PathwaysWinter11_Evans.pdf.

Evans-Pritchard, E.E. *The Nuer: A Description of the Modes of Livelihood and Political Institutions of a Nilotic People.* Oxford: Clarendon Press, 1940.

Farley, Reynolds and Walter Allen. *The Color Line and the Quality of Life in America.* New York, NY: Oxford University Press, 1989.

Ferguson, Ronald. "Toward Skilled Parenting & Transformed Schools: Inside a National Movement for Excellence with Equity." Wiener Center for Social Policy, John F. Kennedy School of Government, Harvard University, 2005.

Fernandez, Manny. "Door to Door, Foreclosure Knocks Here." *New York Times*, October 19, 2008. Accessed June 26, 2018 from www.nytimes.com/2008/10/19/nyregion/19block.html.

Fernandez, Manny. "Study Finds Disparities in Mortgages by Race." *New York Times*, October 15, 2007. Accessed June 26, 2018 from www.nytimes.com/2007/10/15/nyregion/15subprime.html.

Ferriss, Susan and Amy Isackson. "Separated by Law: Families Torn Apart by 1996 Immigration Measure: American Dream becomes Nightmare as Immigrant Spouses are Barred for Years." Center for Public Integrity, October 19, 2012. Accessed April 3, 2017 from www.publicintegrity.org/2012/10/19/11563/separated-law-families-torn-apart-1996-immigration-measure.

Fields, Liz. "Police Have Killed at Least 1,083 Americans since Michael Brown's Death." *Vice News*, August 9, 2015. Accessed August 2, 2017 from https://news.vice.com/article/police-have-killed-at-least-1083-americans-since-michael-browns-death.

Fiske, Susan T. and Shelley E. Taylor. *Social Cognition: From Brains to Culture.* Los Angeles, CA: Sage Publications, 2013.

"Florida Police Question whether the Shooting of a 17-Year-Old was Self-Defense or Unjustified Over-Reaction." *NBC Nightly News.* March 17, 2012. Accessed February 22, 2018 from https://archive.org/details/WBAL_20120317_223000_NBC_Nightly_News/start/1260/end/1320.

Forsey, Martin G. "Ethnography as Participant Listening." *Ethnography* 11, no. 4 (2010): 558–572.

Frazer, Kate, Joanne E. Callinan, Jack McHugh, Susan van Baarsel, Anna Clarke, Kirsten Doherty, and Cecily Kelleher. "Legislative Smoking Bans for Reducing Harms from Secondhand Smoke Exposure, Smoking Prevalence and Tobacco Consumption." *Cochrane Database of Systematic Reviews* 2 art. no. CD005992 (2016). doi: 10.1002/14651858.CD005992.pub3.

Fredrickson, George. *The Arrogance of Race.* Middletown, CT: Wesleyan University Press, 1988.

Fredrickson, George. *White Supremacy.* New York, NY: Oxford University Press, 1981.

Galea, Sandro. "Housing and the Health of the Public." Boston University School of Public Health, February 12, 2017. Accessed July 16, 2018 from www.bu.edu/sph/2017/02/12/housing-and-the-health-of-the-public/.

Gallespie, Patrick. "Black Unemployment Hits All-Time Low." CNN Money, January 5, 2018. Accessed July 9, 2018 from http://money.cnn.com/2018/01/05/news/economy/black-unemployment/index.html.

Gandy, Oscar and Zhan Li. "Framing Comparative Risk: A Preliminary Analysis." *Howard Journal of Communications* 16, no. 2 (2005): 71–86.

Gans, Herbert. *Democracy and the News.* New York, NY: Oxford University Press, 2003.

Gawronski, Bertram, Daniel Geschke, and Rainer Banse. "Implicit Bias in Impression Formation: Associations Influence the Construal of Individuating Information." *European Journal of Social Psychology* 33, no. 5 (2003): 573–589. doi: 10.1002/ejsp.166.

Geertz, Clifford. " 'From the Native's Point of View': On the Nature of Anthropological Understanding." *Bulletin of the American Academy of Arts and Sciences* 28, no. 1 (1974): 26–45.

George, Cherian. "Journalism and the Politics of Hate: Charting Ethical Responses to Religious Intolerance." *Journal of Mass Media Ethics* 29, no. 2 (2014): 74–90. doi: 10.1080/08900523.2014.893771.

Gilliam, Frank D. and Shanto S. Iyengar. "Prime Suspects: The Influence of Local Television News on the Viewing Public." *American Journal of Political Science* 44, no. 3 (July 1 2000): 560–573.

Gilliam, Walter S., Angela N. Maupin, Chin R. Reyes, Maria Accavitti, and Frederick Shic. "Do Early Educators' Implicit Biases Regarding Sex and Race Relate to Behavior Expectations and Recommendations of Preschool Expulsions and Suspensions?" Yale Child Study Center, September 28, 2016. Accessed March 4, 2018 from http://ziglercenter.yale.edu/publications/Preschool%20Implicit%20Bias%20Policy%20Brief_final_9_26_276766_5379_v1.pdf.

Glantz, Aaron. "Struggle for Black and Latino Mortgage Applicants Suggests Modern-Day Redlining." *PBS News Hour*, February 15, 2018. Accessed February 21, 2018 from www.pbs.org/newshour/show/struggle-for-black-and-latino-mortgage-applicants-suggests-modern-day-redlining.

Godfrey, Erin B., Carlos E. Santos, and Esther Burson. "For Better or Worse: System-Justifying Beliefs in Sixth Grade Predict Trajectories of Self-Esteem and Behavior across Early Adolescence." *Child Development* (June 19, 2017). doi: 10.1111/cdev.12854.

Goldensohn, Rosa. "They Shared Drugs. Someone Died. Does That Make Them Killers?" *New York Times*, May 25, 2018. Accessed July 14, 2018 from www.nytimes.com/2018/05/25/us/drug-overdose-prosecution-crime.html.

Goldman, Russell. "Trayvon Martin Drug Photos Can't be Mentioned, Says Judge." *ABC News*. May 28, 2013. Accessed February 11, 2017 from http://abcnews.go.com/US/trayvon-martin-drug-photos-mentioned-judge/story?id=19271093.

Goldmann, Emily, Allison Aiello, Monica Uddin, Jorge Delva, Karestan Koenen, Larry M. Gant, and Sandro Galea. "Pervasive Exposure to Violence and Posttraumatic Stress Disorder in a Predominantly African American Urban Community: The Detroit Neighborhood Health Study." *Journal of Traumatic Stress* 24, no. 6 (December 2011): 747–751. doi: 10.1002/jts.20705.

Gonzalez, Juan and Joseph Torres. *News for All the People*. London, UK: Verso, 2011.

Graves, Bill. "Portland-Area Native Americans Burdened Health Hurdles Generation after Generation." *The Oregonian*. May 2, 2013. Accessed February 28, 2017 from www.oregonlive.com/health/index.ssf/2012/05/portlands_native_americans_wag.html.

Greenwald, Anthony G. and Mahzarin R. Banaji. "Implicit Social Cognition: Attitudes, Self-Esteem, and Stereotypes." *Psychological Review* 102 (1995): 4–27.

Greenwald, Anthony G., Debbie E. McGhee, and Jordan L.K. Schwartz. "Measuring Individual Differences in Implicit Cognition: The Implicit Association Test." *Journal of Personality and Social Psychology* 74, no. 6 (1998): 1464–1480. doi: 10.1037/0022-3514.74.6.1464.

Gruenewald, Jeff, Jesenia Pizarro, and Steven M. Chermak. "Race, Gender, and the Newsworthiness of Homicide Incidents." *Journal of Criminal Justice* 37, no. 3 (2009): 262–272. doi: 10.1016/j.jcrimjus.2009.04.006.

Guo, Jeff. "Police are Searching Black Drivers More Often, but Finding More Illegal Stuff with White Drivers." *Washington Post*, October 27, 2015. Accessed July 9, 2018 from www.washingtonpost.com/news/wonk/wp/2015/10/27/police-are-searching-black-drivers-more-often-but-finding-more-illegal-stuff-with-white-drivers-2/? noredirect=on&utm_term=.86b12e13bc13.

Gutierrez, Belinda, Anna Kaatz, Sarah Chu, Denis Ramirez, Clem Samson-Samuel, and Molly Carnes. " 'Fair Play': A Videogame Designed to Address Implicit Race Bias through Active Perspective Taking." *Games for Health* 3, no. 6 (2014): 371–378. doi: 10.1089/g4h.2013.0071.

Hacker, Andrew. *Two Nations*. New York, NY: Ballantine Books, 1992.

Hagiwara, Nao, Louis A. Penner, Richard Gonzalez, Susan Eggly, John F. Dovidio, Samuel L. Gaertner, … Terrance L. Albrecht. "Racial Attitudes, Physician–Patient Talk Time Ratio, and Adherence in Racially Discordant Medical Interactions." *Social Science & Medicine* 87 (2013): 123–131. doi: 10.1016/j.socscimed.2013.03.016.

Hall, Natalie R., Richard J. Crisp, and Mein-woei Suen. "Reducing Implicit Prejudice by Blurring Intergroup Boundaries." *Basic and Applied Social Psychology* 31, no. 3 (2009): 244–254. doi: 10.1080/01973530903058474.

Hammontree, John. "New Memorial Ends the 'Silence' on a History of Lynching." AL. com, April 26, 2018. Accessed April 27, 2018 from www.al.com/opinion/index.ssf/2018/04/new_memorial_ends_the_silence.html.

Hanchard, Michael. "You Shall Have the Body: On Trayvon Martin's Slaughter." *Theory & Event* 15, no. 3 (2012).

Hannah-Jones, Nikole. "Living Apart: How the Government Betrayed a Landmark Civil Rights Law." ProPublica, June 25, 2015. Accessed February 21, 2017 from www.propublica.org/article/living-apart-how-the-government-betrayed-a-landmark-civil-rights-law.

Hannah-Jones, Nikole. "Portland Housing Audit Finds Discrimination in 64 Percent of Tests; City Has Yet to Act Against Landlords." *The Oregonian*, May 9, 2011. Accessed February 21, 2017 from www.oregonlive.com/portland/index.ssf/2011/05/a_portland_housing_audit_finds.html.

Hannon, Lance. "Hispanic Respondent Intelligence Level and Skin Tone: Interviewer Perceptions from the American National Election Study." *Hispanic Journal of Behavioral Sciences* 36, no. 3 (2014): 265–283.

Harris, Rebecca. "Suburban Chicago Schools Lag as Bilingual Needs Grow." *Chicago News Cooperative, New York Times*, February 9, 2012. Accessed July 8, 2018 from www.nytimes.com/2012/02/10/education/suburban-chicago-schools-lag-as-bilingual-needs-grow.html.

Harry, Beth and Janette Klingner. "Discarding the Deficit Model." *Educational Leadership* 64, no. 5 (February 2007): 16–21.

Harvey, Thomas, John McAnnar, Michael-John Voss, Megan Conn, Sean Janda, and Sophie Keskey. "Arch City Defenders Municipal Courts White Paper." Accessed August 2, 2017 from http://s3.documentcloud.org/documents/1279541/archcity-defenders-report-on-st-louis-county.pdf.

Hauser, Christine. "Florida Woman whose 'Stand Your Ground' Defense was Rejected is Released." *New York Times*, February 7, 2017. Accessed February 11, 2017 from www.nytimes.com/2017/02/07/us/marissa-alexander-released-stand-your-ground.html?_r=0.

Hayasaki, Erika. " 'It's like you're climbing Everest'; Eleven Boys Thought They'd Leave High School as They Entered It – Together – On Graduation Day. It Wasn't That Simple." Series: The Vanishing Class, Third of Four Parts. *Los Angeles Times*, February

3, 2006. Accessed March 13, 2018 from http://articles.latimes.com/2006/feb/03/local/me-dropout3.

Hayes, Stephanie. "The Hoodie's Many Personas." *The Tampa Bay Times.* March 25, 2012, p. 1P. Accessed February 22, 2018 from www.tampabay.com/opinion/essays/hoodies-have-a-complicated-fashion-story/1221529.

Heckman, James A. "Detecting Discrimination." *Journal of Economic Perspectives* 12 (1998): 101–116.

Helfand, Duke. "A Formula for Failure in L.A. Public Schools." Series: The Vanishing Class, Fourth of Four Parts. *Los Angeles Times*, January 30, 2006. Accessed March 13, 2018 from www.latimes.com/local/la-me-dropout30jan30-story.html.

Henley, William Ernest. "Invictus." Accessed August 8, 2017 from www.poetryfoundation.org/poems/51642/invictus#poem.

Hersher, Rebecca. "Key Moments in the Dakota Access Pipeline Fight." National Public Radio, February 22, 2017. Accessed March 9, 2018 from www.npr.org/sections/thetwo-way/2017/02/22/514988040/key-moments-in-the-dakota-access-pipeline-fight.

Higginbotham, Leon A. *In the Matter of Color: Race and the American Legal Process.* New York, NY: Oxford University Press, 1978.

Hill, Herbert. *Black Labor and the American Legal System.* Madison, WI: University of Wisconsin Press, 1985.

Hill, Jane H. *The Everyday Language of White Racism.* West Sussex: Wiley-Blackwell, 2008.

Hill, Kashmir. " 'Sexism' Public-Shaming via Twitter Leads to Two People Getting Fired (Including the Shamer)." *Forbes*, March 21, 2013. Accessed February 11, 2017 from www.forbes.com/sites/kashmirhill/2013/03/21/sexism-public-shaming-via-twitter-leads-to-two-people-getting-fired-including-the-shamer/#359c27bb3eb3.

Hirsch, Arnold R. *Making the Second Ghetto: Race & Housing in Chicago 1940–1960.* Chicago, IL: University of Chicago Press, 1983.

"History of Lynchings." NAACP, 2018. Accessed April 27, 2018 from www.naacp.org/history-of-lynchings/.

Hofrichter, Richard and Rajiv Bhatia, eds. *Tackling Health Inequities through Public Health Practice: Theory to Action.* New York, NY: Oxford University Press, 2010.

"How Blogs, Twitter and the Mainstream Media Have Handled the Trayvon Martin Case." Pew Research Center, March 30, 2012. Accessed February 18, 2018 from www.journalism.org/2012/03/30/special-report-how-blogs-twitter-and-mainstream-media-have-handled-trayvon-m/.

Howard, Simon and Samuel R. Sommers. "Exploring the Enigmatic Link between Religion and Anti-Black Attitudes." *Social and Personality Psychology Compass* 9, no. 9 (2015): 495–510. doi: 10.1111/spc3.12195.

Howard, Simon and Samuel R. Sommers. "Exposure to White Religious Iconography Influences Black Individuals' Intragroup and Intergroup Attitudes." *Cultural Diversity and Ethnic Minority Psychology* (April 10, 2017). doi: 10.1037/cdp0000152.

Hugenberg, Kurt and Galen V. Bodenhausen. "Ambiguity in Social Categorization: The Role of Prejudice and Facial Affect in Race Categorization." *Psychological Science* 15, no. 5 (2004): 342–345. doi: 10.1111/j.0956-7976.2004.00680.x.

Hutchins, Robert M., et al. *A Free and Responsible Press.* Report by the Commission on the Freedom of the Press. Chicago, IL: University of Chicago Press, 1947. Accessed February 11, 2017 from www.archive.org/stream/freeandresponsib029216mbp#page/n5/mode/1up.

Immergluck, Dan and Geoff Smith. "The External Costs of Foreclosure: The Impact of Single-Family Mortgage Foreclosures on Property Values." *Housing Policy Debate* 17, no. 1 (2006): 57–80.

Institute of Medicine. *Unequal Treatment: Confronting Racial and Ethnic Disparities in Health Care (Full Printed Version)*. Washington, DC: The National Academies Press, 2003. doi: 10.17226/10260.

Isenberg, Nancy. *White Trash: The 400-Year Untold History of Class in America*. New York, NY: Viking Press, 2016.

Iyengar, Shanto. *Is Anyone Responsible? How Television Frames Political Issues*. Chicago, IL: University of Chicago Press, 1991.

Jacobs, Harriet. *Incidents in the Life of a Slave Girl*. New York, NY: The Modern Library, 2000.

Jacoby, Tamar. *Someone Else's House: America's Unfinished Struggle for Integration*. New York, NY: The Free Press, 1998.

Jan, Tracy. "The Biggest Beneficiaries of the Government Safety Net: Working Class Whites." *Washington Post*, February 16, 2017. Accessed July 6, 2018 from www. washingtonpost.com/news/wonk/wp/2017/02/16/the-biggest-beneficiaries-of-the-government-safety-net-working-class-whites/?utm_term=.85aef7235b3c.

Jaschik, Scott. "Anger Over Stereotypes in Textbook." *Inside Higher Ed*, October 23, 2017. Accessed February 7, 2018 from www.insidehighered.com/news/2017/10/23/nursing-textbook-pulled-over-stereotypes.

Jensen, Robert. *The Heart of Whiteness: Confronting Race, Racism, and White Privilege*. San Francisco, CA: City Lights, 2005.

The Joint Center for Political and Economic Studies. *Place Matters for Health in Alameda County: Ensuring Opportunities for Good Health for All*. November 2012. Accessed April 12, 2018 from www.nationalcollaborative.org/wp-content/uploads/2016/02/PLACE-MATTERS-for-Health-in-Alameda-County-2.pdf.

The Joint Center for Political and Economic Studies. "Segregated Spaces, Risky Places: The Effect of Segregation on Health Inequalities." September 2011.

Jordan, Miriam. "If Census Asks about Citizenship, Some Already Have an Answer: No Comment." *New York Times*, March 27, 2018. Accessed June 16, 2018 from www.nytimes.com/2018/03/27/us/census-undocumented-immigrants.html.

Jost, John T. and David L. Hamilton. "Stereotypes in Our Culture." In John F. Dovidio, P. Glick, and L.A. Rudman (eds). *On the Nature of Prejudice: Fifty Years after Allport*. Oxford: Blackwell Publishing, 2005, Ch. 13.

Joyce, James. *A Portrait of the Artist as A Young Man*. New York, NY: Penguin Books, 1964.

Kaleem, Jaweed. "Federal Judge Blocks Arizona from Banning Mexican American Studies Classes." *Los Angeles Times*, December 27, 2017. Accessed January 27, 2018 from www.latimes.com/nation/la-na-mexican-american-studies-20171227-story.html.

Kam, Cindy D. and Carl L. Palmer. "Reconsidering the Effects of Education on Political Participation." *The Journal of Politics* 70, no. 3 (2008): 612–631.

Kasinitz, Philip and Jay Rosenberg. "Missing the Connection: Social Isolation and Employment on the Brooklyn Waterfront." *Social Problems* 43 (1996): 180–196.

Kearns, Erin, Allison Betus, and Anthony Lemieux. "Why Do Some Terrorist Attacks Receive More Media Attention Than Others?" Social Science Research Network (March 5, 2017). Accessed February 23, 2018 from https://ssrn.com/abstract=2928138.

Kerner, Otto et al. *Report of the National Advisory Committee on Civil Disorders*. The New York Times edition. New York, NY: E.P. Dutton & Co., 1968.

Khimm, Suzy. "Will the Government Stop Using the Poor as a Piggy Bank?" MSNBC, September 9, 2014. Accessed August 2, 2017 from www.msnbc.com/msnbc/will-the-government-stop-using-the-poor-piggy-bank.

Kiely, Eugene. "Terrorism and Trump's Travel Ban." FactCheck.org, February 26, 2017. Accessed April 21, 2017 from www.factcheck.org/2017/02/terrorism-and-trumps-travel-ban/.

King, Ryan D., Steven F. Messner, and Robert D. Baller. "Contemporary Hate Crimes, Law Enforcement, and the Legacy of Racial Violence." *American Sociological Review* 72, no. 2 (April 2009): 291–315.

Kinnard, Meg. "Charleston Church Shooter Dylann Roof Pleads Guilty, Awaits Execution." *Chicago Tribune*, via Associated Press, April 10, 2017. Accessed March 9, 2017 from www.chicagotribune.com/news/nationworld/ct-charleston-church-shooter-pleads-guilty-20170410-story.html.

Kivisto, Peter and Johanna Leinonen. 2011. "Representing Race: Ongoing Uncertainties about Finnish American Racial Identity." *Journal of American Ethnic History* 31, no. 1 (2011): 11–33.

Kochhar, Rakesh and Anthony Cilluffo. "Key Findings on the Rise in Income Inequality within America's Racial and Ethnic Groups." Pew Research Center, July 12, 2018. Accessed July 15, 2018 from http://www.pewresearch.org/fact-tank/2018/07/12/key-findings-on-the-rise-in-income-inequality-within-americas-racial-and-ethnic-groups/.

Kozol, Jonathan. *The Shame of the Nation: The Restoration of Apartheid Schooling in America.* New York, NY: Crown Publishing, 2005.

Krieger, James and Donna L. Higgins. "Housing and Health: Time again for Public Health Action." *American Journal of Public Health* 92, no. 5 (2002): 758–768.

Krysan, Maria and Kyle Crowder. *Cycle of Segregation: Social Processes and Residential Stratification.* New York, NY: Russell Sage Foundation, 2017.

Krysan, Maria and Sarah Patton Moberg. "Trends in Racial Attitudes," Institute of Government and Public Affairs, University of Illinois, 2016. Accessed July 3, 2018 from https://igpa.uillinois.edu/programs/racial-attitudes#section-0.

Kubota, Jennifer T. and Tiffany A. Ito. "The Role of Expression and Race in Weapons Identification." *Emotion* 14, no. 6 (2014): 1115–1124. doi: 10.1037/a0038214.

Ladson-Billings, Gloria. "Just What Is Critical Race Theory and What's It Doing in a Nice Field like Education?." In Edward Taylor, David Gillborn, and Gloria Ladson-Billings (eds.). *Foundations of Critical Race Theory in Education.* New York, NY: Routledge, 2009, Vol. 2016, pp. 15–30.

Lareau, Annette. *Unequal Childhoods: Class, Race, and Family Life.* Berkeley and Los Angeles, CA: University of California Press, 2011.

Leonardo, Zeus. "The Color of Supremacy: Beyond the Discourse of 'White Privilege'." *Educational Philosophy and Theory* 36, no. 2 (2004): 137–152.

Leonardo, Zeus. *Race, Whiteness, and Education.* New York, NY: Routledge, 2009.

Leovy, Jill. *Ghettoside: A True Story of Murder in America.* New York, NY: Spiegel & Grau, 2015.

Leslie, Derek. *An Investigation of Racial Disadvantage.* Manchester: Manchester University Press, 1998.

Lewan, Todd and Delores Barcaly. "Torn from the Land: AP Documents Land Taken from Blacks through Trickery, Violence and Murder." Associated Press, December 2001. Accessed September 17, 2017 from http://nuweb9.neu.edu/civilrights/wp-content/uploads/AP-Investigation-Article.pdf.

Lewis, Amanda E. and John B. Diamond. *Despite the Best Intentions: How Racial Inequality Thrives in Good Schools.* New York, NY: Oxford University Press, 2015.

Lewis, Sukey. "New Bill Aims to Stop Charging Parents of Incarcerated Kids." KQED Radio, March 8, 2017. Accessed March 9, 2017 from https://ww2.kqed.org/news/2017/03/09/new-bill-aims-to-stop-charging-parents-of-incarcerated-kids/.

Lieberman, Robert. *Shifting the Color Line: Race and the American Welfare State.* Cambridge, MA: Harvard University Press, 1998.

Lieberson, Stanley. *A Piece of the Pie: Blacks and White Immigrants since 1880.* Berkeley and Los Angeles, CA: University of California Press, 1980.

Lippmann, Walter. "The Habits of Our Eyes: Toward a Critique of Public Opinion." *The Century Magazine*, December 1921, pp. 243–252. Accessed February 11, 2017 from www.unz.org/Pub/Century-1921dec-00243.

Lipsitz, George. *The Possessive Investment in Whiteness: How White People Profit from Identity Politics.* Philadelphia, PA: Temple University Press, 1998.

Liptak, Adam. "Pulled Over in a Rental Car, with Heroin in the Trunk." *New York Times*, January 1, 2018. Accessed February 21, 2018 from www.nytimes.com/2018/01/01/us/politics/rental-car-privacy-supreme-court.html.

Lipton, Eric and Danielle Ivory. "Trump Says His Regulatory Rollback Already Is the 'Most Far Reaching.'" *New York Times*, December 14, 2017. Accessed December 29, 2017 from www.nytimes.com/2017/12/14/us/politics/trump-federal-regulations.html.

Logan, John. "Whose Schools are Failing?" Russell Sage Foundation and Brown University, July 25, 2011. Accessed March 17, 2018 from https://s4.ad.brown.edu/Projects/Diversity/Data/Report/report5.pdf.

Logan, John R. and Brian Stults. "The Persistence of Segregation in the Metropolis: New Findings from the 2010 Census." US2010Project, March 24, 2011. Accessed March 4, 2018 from https://s4.ad.brown.edu/Projects/Diversity/Data/Report/report2.pdf.

Logan, Tim and Molly Hennessy-Fiske. "Ferguson's Mounting Racial and Economic Stress Set the Stage for Turmoil." *Los Angeles Times*, August 16, 2014. Accessed August 2, 2017 from www.latimes.com/nation/la-na-ferguson-economy-20140817-story.html.

Lopes, German, ed. "Police Shootings and Brutality in the US: 9 Things You Should Know." *Vox*, May 6, 2017. Accessed August 2, 2017 from www.vox.com/cards/police-brutality-shootings-us/community-police-accountability.

Los Angeles Police Department. *The Origin of the LAPD Motto.* (Reprinted from *BEAT* magazine, December 1963). Accessed April 14, 2018 from www.lapdonline.org/history_of_the_lapd/content_basic_view/1128.

Losen, Daniel J. *San Francisco District Profile.* San Francisco Unified School District report. February 19, 2012.

Losen, Daniel J. and Gary Orfield. *Racial Inequity in Special Education.* Cambridge, MA: Harvard Education Press, 2002.

Loury, Alden. "Data Points: Chicago's Segregation Isn't Just in the City." Metropolitan Planning Council. 2016. Accessed July 8, 2018 from www.metroplanning.org/news/7324/Data-Points-Chicagos-segregation-isnt-just-in-the-city.

Loury, Alden. "The Persistent Problem of Segregation in Chicago's Public Schools." Metropolitan Planning Council, 2017. Accessed July 8, 2018 from www.metroplanning.org/costofsegregation/roadmap.aspx.

Lueke, Adam and Bryan Gibson. "Mindfulness Meditation Reduces Implicit Age and Race Bias: The Role of Reduced Automaticity of Responding." *Social Psychological and Personality Science* 6, no. 3 (2015): 284–291. doi: 10.1177/1948550 614559651.

Lujan, Antonio. "Rise in Latino Dropout Rate." ABC News Salt Lake City, November 15, 2011.

Lundman, Richard J. "The Newsworthiness and Selection Bias in News about Murder: Comparative and Relative Effects of Novelty and Race and Gender Typifications on Newspaper Coverage of Homicide." *Sociological Forum* 18, no. 3 (2003): 357–386. doi: 10.1023/A:1025713518156.

Lynch, Grace Hwang. "Breast Cancer Rates Rise among Asian-American Women as Others Stay Stable." NBC News, April 21, 2017. Accessed February 24, 2017 from www.nbcnews.com/news/asian-america/breast-cancer-rates-rise-among-asian-ameri can-women-others-stay-n749366.

Lynch, Mamie, Jennifer Engle, and José L. Cruz. *Subprime Opportunity: The Unfulfilled Promise of For-Profit Colleges and Universities.* The Education Trust, 2010.

McIntosh, Peggy. "White Privilege: Unpacking the Invisible Knapsack." National SEED Project on Inclusive Curriculum, 1989. Accessed February 11, 2017 from www.nationalseedproject.org/white-privilege-unpacking-the-invisible-knapsack.

Mackey, Robert. "Arizona Law Curbs Ethnic Studies Class." *New York Times*, May 13, 2010. Accessed March 8, 2018 from https://thelede.blogs.nytimes.com/2010/05/13/ arizona-law-curbs-ethnic-studies-classes/.

McWhorter, John. "Rachel Jeantel Explained, Linguistically: Trayvon Martin's Friend and a Key Witness in the Trial of George Zimmerman Made a Lot More Sense Than You Think." *Time*, June 28, 2013. Accessed February 23, 2018 from http://ideas. time.com/2013/06/28/rachel-jeantel-explained-linguistically/.

Magagnini, Steve. "Reporter's Journal: Orphans of History." The Authentic Voice. Accessed March 14, 2017 from http://theauthenticvoice.org/mainstories/orphansof history/essay_orphansofhistory/.

Majumder, Maimuna. "An Intriguing Link between Police Shootings and Black Voter Registration." *Wired*, September 29, 2016. Accessed August 2, 2017 from www.wired.com/2016/09/intriguing-link-police-shootings-black-voter-regis tration/.

"Mark Cuban on Secret to His Success and the Lure of Politics." Fox News, November 5, 2017. Accessed February 4, 2018 from http://video.foxnews.com/v/5636067861001/? #sp=show-clips.

Marsden, Peter V. "The Hiring Process: Recruitment Methods." *American Behavioral Scientist* 7 (1994): 979–991.

Massey, Douglas S. and Nancy A. Denton. *American Apartheid: Segregation and the Making of the Underclass.* Cambridge, MA: Harvard University Press, 1993.

Mathews, T.J. and Anne K. Driscoll. "Data Brief 279: Trends in Infant Mortality in the United States, 2005–2014." National Center for Health Statistics, Centers for Disease Control and Prevention. Accessed February 19, 2018 from www.cdc.gov/nchs/data/ databriefs/db279_table.pdf#1.

Maxwell, Tonya and Tim Smith. "Dylann Roof Guilty in Charleston Church Shooting." *USA Today*, December 15, 2016, Accessed February 4, 2017 from www.usatoday.com/ story/news/nation-now/2016/12/15/jury-deliberating-fate-charleston-church-shooter/ 95474302/.

Mead, Sue. "Women Flex Their Car Buying Muscles." boston.com, August 24, 2013. Accessed March 14, 2017 from www.boston.com/cars/news-and-reviews/2013/08/24/women-flex-their-car-buying-muscles.

Milkman, Ruth and Eleanor Townsend. "Gender and the Economy." In Neil J. Smelser and Richard Swedberg (eds.). *Handbook of Economic Sociology*. Princeton, NJ: Princeton University Press, 1994.

Miller, Ryan W. "How the Dakota Access Pipeline Battle Unfolded." *USA Today*, December 2, 2016. Accessed January 24, 2018 from www.usatoday.com/story/news/nation/2016/12/02/timeline-dakota-access-pipeline-and-protests/94800796/.

Miller, Shazia R. and James E. Rosenbaum. "Hiring in a Hobbesian World." *Work and Occupations* 24 (1997): 498–523.

Miranda, Marie Lynn, Lynne C. Messer and Gretchen L. Kroeger. "Associations between the Quality of the Residential Built Environment and Pregnancy Outcomes among Women in North Carolina." *Environmental Health Perspectives* 120 (2012): 471–477. Accessed June 8, 2018 from https://ehp.niehs.nih.gov/1103578/#t4.

Mitchell, Daphne Koinis. "Asthma and School Functioning in Children: Still More Work to Do." Brown University Child and Adolescent Behavior Letter, September 1, 2015.

Mock, Brentin. "The Meaning of Blight." City Lab, February 16, 2017. Accessed March 4, 2018 from www.citylab.com/equity/2017/02/the-meaning-of-blight/516801/.

Morgan, Ivy and Ary Amerikaner. "Funding Gaps 2018: An Analysis of School Funding Equity across the U.S. and within each State." The Education Trust, February 27, 2018. Accessed July 14, 2018 from https://edtrust.org/resource/funding-gaps-2018/.

Moskowitz, Gordon B., Irmak Olcaysoy Okten, and Cynthia M. Gooch. "On Race and Time." *Psychological Science* 26, no. 11 (2015): 1783–1794. doi: 10.1177/095679761 5599547.

Mudimbe, V.Y. *The Invention of Africa: Gnosis, Philosophy, and the Order of Knowledge.* Bloomington, IN: Indiana University Press, 1988.

Nagata, Donna K. "Intergenerational Effects of the Japanese American Internment." In Danieli Y. and Yael Danieli (eds.). *International Handbook of Multigenerational Legacies of Trauma.* Boston, MA: Springer. The Plenum Series on Stress and Coping, 1998, pp. 125–139.

National Fair Housing Alliance. *The Case for Fair Housing*, 2017 Fair Housing Trends Report. Accessed September 18, 2017 from http://nationalfairhousing.org/wp-content/uploads/2017/07/TRENDS-REPORT-2017-FINAL.pdf.

Neal, Samantha. "Views of Racism as a Major Problem Increase Sharply, Especially among Democrats." Pew Research Center, August 29, 2017. Accessed July 3, 2018 from www.pewresearch.org/fact-tank/2017/08/29/views-of-racism-as-a-major-problem-increase-sharply-especially-among-democrats/.

Nehisi-Coates, Ta. "How Stand Your Ground Relates to George Zimmerman." *The Atlantic*, July 16, 2013. Accessed February 11, 2018 from www.theatlantic.com/national/archive/2013/07/how-stand-your-ground-relates-to-george-zimmerman/277829/.

Neiwert, David. "Trump's Fixation on Demonizing Islam Hides True Homegrown US Terror Threat." Revealnews.org, June 21, 2017. Accessed January 22, 2018 from www.revealnews.org/article/home-is-where-the-hate-is/

Nelson, Bruce. *Divided We Stand: American Workers and the Struggle for Black Equality.* Princeton, NJ: Princeton University Press, 2000.

Nesmith, Susannah. "Investigative Reporting 'is still a very white male business': How the Online News Association and Georgia News Labs are Working to Diversify

Journalism." *Columbia Journalism Review,* September 18, 2015. Accessed February 9, 2018 from https://archives.cjr.org/united_states_project/georgia_news_lab_bring_di versity_to_investigative_reporting.php.

Nisbett, Richard E. *Intelligence and How to Get It: Why Schools and Culture Count.* New York, NY: W.W. Norton & Company, 2009.

Nolen, Stephanie. "Brazil's Colour Bind." *The Globe and Mail,* July 31, 2015. Accessed January 5, 2018 from www.theglobeandmail.com/news/world/brazils-colour-bind/ article25779474/.

Nosek, Brian A., Frederick L. Smyth, Jeffrey J. Hansen, Thierry Devos, Nicole M. Lind-ner, Kate A. Ranganath, ... Mahzarin R. Banaji. "Pervasiveness and Correlates of Implicit Attitudes and Stereotypes." *European Review of Social Psychology* 18 (2007): 36–88. doi: 10.1080/10463280701489053.

Oakes, Jeannie. *Keeping Track: How Schools Structure Inequality,* Second Edition. New Haven, CT: Yale University Press, 2005.

Obasogie, Osagie K. *Blinded by Sight: Seeing Race through the Eyes of the Blind.* Stanford, CA: Stanford University Press, 2013.

Okonofua, Jason A. and Jennifer L. Eberhardt. "Two Strikes: Race and the Disciplining of Young Students." *Psychological Science* 26, no. 5 (2015): 617–624. doi: 10.1177/ 0956797615570365.

Oliver, Mary Beth, Ronald L. Jackson, Ndidi N. Moses, and Celnisha L. Dangerfield. "The Face of Crime: Viewers' Memory of Race-Related Facial Features of Individ-uals Pictured in the News." *Journal of Communication* 54, no. 1 (2004): 88–104. doi: 10.1111/j.1460-2466.2004.tb02615.x.

Omi, Michael and Howard Winant. *Racial Formation in the United States from the 1960s to the 1990s.* Second Edition. New York, NY: Routledge, 1994.

Orfield, Gary and John T. Yun and Civil Rights Project (Harvard University). *Rese-gregation in American Schools.* Cambridge, MA: Civil Rights Project. Harvard Uni-versity, 1999.

Orfield, Gary, Jonyeong Ee, Erica Frankenberg, and Genevieve Siegel-Hawley "Brown at 62: School Segregation by Race, Poverty and State." Civil Rights Project, UCLAAc-cessed February 15, 2018 from www.civilrightsproject.ucla.edu/research/k-12-educa tion/integration-and-diversity/brown-at-62-school-segregation-by-race-poverty-and-state/Brown-at-62-final-corrected-2.pdf.

Pager, Devah. "Mark of a Criminal Record." *American Journal of Sociology* 108, no. 5 (March 2003): 937–975. Accessed July 9, 2018 from http://s3.amazonaws.com/fiel dexperiments-papers2/papers/00319.pdf.

Pappas, Gregory et al. "The Increasing Disparity in Mortality between Socioeconomic Groups in the United States, 1960 and 1986." *New England Journal of Medicine* 329 (1987): 103–109.

Paul, Sonia. "The State of Investigative Reporting: Highlights from IRE 2017." Media-shift, June 28, 2017. Accessed February 9, 2018 from http://mediashift.org/2017/06/ highlights-annual-investigative-reporters-editors-conference-show-state-investigative-reporting/.

Pearson, Michael and David Mattingly. "Gun, Drug Texts Feature in New Trayvon Martin Shooting Evidence." CNN, May 26, 2013. Accessed February 11, 2017 from www.cnn.com/2013/05/23/justice/florida-zimmerman-defense/.

Penner, Louis A., John F. Dovidio, Tessa V. West, Samuel L. Gaertner, Terrance L. Albrecht, Rhonda K. Dailey, and Tsveti Markova. "Aversive Racism and Medical

Interactions with Black Patients: A Field Study." *Journal of Experimental Social Psychology* 46, no. 2 (2010): 436–440. doi: 10.1016/j.jesp.2009.11.004.

Pepin, Joanna R. "Nobody's Business? White Male Privilege in Media Coverage of Intimate Partner Violence." *Sociological Spectrum* 36, no. 3 (2016): 123–141. doi: 10.1080/02732173.2015.1108886.

Perry, Andre M. "Who Deserves Credit for Black Employment." The Brookings Institution, February 1, 2018. Accessed June 16, 2018 from www.brookings.edu/blog/the-avenue/2018/02/01/who-deserves-credit-for-african-american-employment/.

Peterman, Peggy. "A Community Branches Out." *The St. Petersburg Times* The Floridian Section, January 15, 1991, p. D-1.

Peterson, Elizabeth R., C. Rubie-Davies, Danny Osborne, and C. Sibley. "Teachers' Explicit Expectations and Implicit Prejudiced Attitudes to Educational Achievement: Relations with Student Achievement and the Ethnic Achievement Gap." *Learning and Instruction* 42 (2016): 123–140. doi: 10.1016/j.learninstruc.2016.01.010.

Pettigrew, T. and L.R. Tropp. "How Does Intergroup Contact Reduce Prejudice? Meta-Analytic Tests of Three Mediators." *European Journal of Social Psychology* 38 (2008): 922–934.

Pettigrew, T.F. "Intergroup Contact Theory." *Annual Review of Psychology* 49 (1998): 65–85.

Phillips, Dawn, Robbie Clark, Tammy Lee, and Alexandra Desautels. *Rebuilding Neighborhoods, Restoring Health: A Report on the Impact of Foreclosures on Public Health*, 2010. Accessed March 7, 2018 from www.acphd.org/media/53643/foreclose2.pdf.

Phillips, Whitney. "The Oxygen of Amplification: Better Practices for Reporting on Extremists, Antagonists and Manipulators Online." *Data & Society*, May 22, 2018, pp. 10–12. Accessed July 7, 2018 from https://datasociety.net/pubs/oh/1_PART_1_Oxygen_of_Amplification_DS.pdf.

Plaisance, Patrick Lee. *Media Ethics: Key Principles for Responsible Practice*. Los Angeles, CA: Sage Publications, 2009.

PolicyLink and Prevention Institute. "The Transportation Prescription: Bold New Ideas for Transportation Reform in America." Accessed April 14, 2018 from www.convergencepartnership.org/TransportationHealthandEquity.

"Pollution, Poverty, and People of Color." A nine-part series with various authors. *Environmental Health News*. June 4, 2012 – June 20, 2012. Accessed February 28, 2017 from www.environmentalhealthnews.org/ehs/news/2012/pollution-poverty-people-of-color-series-summary.

Putnam-Hornstein, Emily, Barbara Needell, Bryn King, and Michelle Johnson-Motoyama. "Racial and Ethnic Disparities: A Population-Based Examination of Risk Factors for Involvement with Child Protective Services." *Child Abuse & Neglect Journal* 37, no. 1 (January 2013): 33–46.

Quadagno, Jill. *The Color of Welfare*. New York, NY: Oxford University Press, 1994.

Ramirez, Kelsey. "Freddie Mac Breaks Down Homeownership Gap in Hispanic Population." HousingWire, June 27, 2017. Accessed August 2, 2017 from www.housingwire.com/articles/40543-freddie-mac-breaks-down-homeownership-gap-in-hispanic-population.

Reinberg, Steven. "Babies Face Higher SIDS Risk in Certain States." *U.S. News & World Report*, February 12, 2018. Accessed February 19, 2018 from https://health.usnews.com/health-care/articles/2018-02-12/babies-face-higher-sids-risk-in-certain-states.

Richeson, Jennifer A. and Samuel R. Sommers. "Toward a Social Psychology of Race and Race Relations for the 21st Century." *Annual Review of Psychology* 67 (2016): 439–463.

Ritter, Zacc and Jeffrey M. Jones. "Media Seen as Key to Democracy but Not Support-ing It Well." Gallup, January 16, 2018. Accessed July 7, 2018 from https://news.gallup.com/poll/225470/media-seen-key-democracy-not-supporting.aspx.

"Robert C. Maynard: Life and Legacy." The Maynard Institute for Journalism Education. Accessed February 2, 2017 from http://mije.org/robertmaynard.

Robles, Frances. "Mistrust Lingers as Ferguson Takes New Tack on Fines." *New York Times*, September 12, 2014. Accessed August 2, 2017 from www.nytimes.com/2014/09/13/us/mistrust-lingers-as-ferguson-takes-new-tack-on-fines.html.

Rodriguez, Daniel, Heather A. Carlos, Anna M. Adachi-Mejia, Ethan M. Burke, and James D. Sargent. "Predictors of Tobacco Outlet Density Nationwide: A Geographic Analysis." *Tobacco Control* 22 (2013): 34–355.

Roediger, David R. *The Wages of Whiteness: Race and the Making of the American Working Class*. New York, NY: Verso, 2007.

Rose, Tricia. "How Structural Racism Works." Presentation for the Center on the Study of Race and Ethnicity in America, Brown University. Published December 21, 2015. Accessed August 8, 2017 from www.youtube.com/watch?v=T5b3DJMBmic.

Rothstein, Richard. *The Color of Law: A Forgotten History of How Our Government Segre-gated America*. New York, NY: Liveright Publishing Corporation, 2017.

Rudman, Laurie A. "Social Justice in Our Minds, Homes, and Society: The Nature, Causes, and Consequences of Implicit Bias." *Social Justice Research* 17, no. 2 (2004): 129–142. doi: 10.1023/B:SORE.0000027406.32604.f6.

Ruef, Lauren. "Sheryl Sandberg's Response to Life's Crushing Blows is Grit and Resili-ence: Here are 5 Ways to Build Both." *Entrepreneur*, September 20, 2017. Accessed February 4, 2018 from www.entrepreneur.com/article/300568.

Russell, Jesse and Alicia Summers. "Reflective Decision-Making and Foster Care Placements." *Psychology, Public Policy, and Law* 19, no. 2 (2013): 127–136. doi: 10.1037/a0031582.

Said, Edward W. *Orientalism*. New York, NY: Random House, 1978.

Salem, Tala. "Are Schools Measuring the Progress of English-Language Learners all Wrong?" *U.S. News & World Report*, June 12, 2018. Accessed July 8, 2018 from www.usnews.com/news/education-news/articles/2018-06-12/are-schools-measur ing-the-progress-of-english-language-learners-all-wrong.

Savani, Krishna, Nicole M. Stephens, and Hazel Markus. "The Unanticipated Interper-sonal and Societal Consequences of Choice: Victim Blaming and Reduced Support for the Public Good." *Psychological Science* 22, no. 6 (2011): 795–802.

Schimdt, Brad. "Locked Out: The Failure of Portland-Area Fair Housing." *The Oregon-ian*, June 2, 2012. Accessed February 21, 2017 from http://projects.oregonlive.com/housing/.

Schleicher, Nina C. et al. "Tobacco Outlet Density near Home and School: Associations with Smoking and Norms among U.S. Teens." *Preventive Medicine* 91 (2016): 287–293.

Schön, Donald A. *The Reflective Practitioner: How Professionals Think in Action*. New York, NY: Basic Books, 1983.

Schudson, Michael. "When? Deadlines, Datelines, and History." In Robert K. Manoff and Michael Schudson (eds.). *Reading the News*. New York, NY: Pantheon Books, 1987.

Scroggins, W. Anthony, Diane M. Mackie, Thomas J. Allen, and Jeffrey W. Sherman. "Reducing Prejudice with Labels: Shared Group Memberships Attenuate Implicit Bias and Expand Implicit Group Boundaries." *Personality and Social Psychology Bulletin* 42, no. 2 (2016): 219–229. doi: 10.1177/0146167215621048.

Seipel, Tracy. "Breast Cancer on the Rise among Asian Americans." *Chicago Tribune*, April 27, 2017. Accessed February 19, 2018 from www.chicagotribune.com/life styles/health/ct-breast-cancer-rise-among-asian-americans-20170427-story.html.

Serlin, Christine. "Settlement to Increase Affordable Housing in Baltimore County." *Affordable Housing Finance*, March 17, 2016. Accessed February 21, 2017 from www. housingfinance.com/policy-legislation/settlement-to-increase-affordable-housing-in-bal timore-county_o.

Shapiro, Issac, Danilo Trisi, and Raheem Chaudhry. "Poverty Reduction Programs Help Adults Lacking College Degrees the Most." Center on Budget Policies and Priorities, February 16, 2017. Accessed July 6, 2018 from www.cbpp.org/research/ poverty-and-inequality/poverty-reduction-programs-help-adults-lacking-college-degrees-the.

Shapiro, Joseph. "As Court Fees Rise, the Poor are Paying the Price." National Public Radio, May 19, 2014. Accessed August 2, 2017 from www.npr.org/2014/05/19/ 312158516/increasing-court-fees-punish-the-poor.

Shapiro, Joseph. "In Ferguson, Court Fines and Fees Fuel Anger." National Public Radio, August 25, 2014. Accessed August 2, 2017 from www.npr.org/2014/08/25/ 343143937/in-ferguson-court-fines-and-fees-fuel-anger.

Shih, Margaret J., Rebecca Stotzer, and Angélica S. Gutiérrez. "Perspective-Taking and Empathy: Generalizing the Reduction of Group Bias towards Asian Americans to General Outgroups." *Asian American Journal of Psychology* 4, no. 2 (2013): 79–83. doi: 10.1037/a0029790.

Simmons, Ann M. "For Antelope Valley African Americans, a Lower Life Expectancy." *Los Angeles Times*, May 29, 2012. Accessed February 28, 2017 from http://articles. latimes.com/2012/may/29/local/la-me-av-black-health-20120529.

Slater, Dashka. "The Fire on the 57 Bus in Oakland." *New York Times Magazine*, January 29, 2015. Accessed January 25, 2018 from www.nytimes.com/2015/02/01/maga zine/the-fire-on-the-57-bus-in-oakland.html.

Sleeper, Jim. *Liberal Racism*. New York, NY: Penguin Books, 1997.

Smedley, Audrey and Brian D. Smedley. *Race in North America: Origin and Evolution of a Worldview, Third Edition*. Boulder, CO: Westview Press, 2011.

Smelser, Neil J. and Richard Swedberg, eds. *Handbook of Economic Sociology*. Princeton, NJ: Princeton University Press, 1994.

Smith, David Barton. *Health Care Divided: Race and Healing a Nation*. Ann Arbor, MI: University of Michigan Press, 1999.

Smith, James and Finis Welch. *Closing the Gap: Forty Years of Economic Progress for Blacks*. Santa Monica, CA: Rand Corporation, 1986.

Smitherman-Donaldson, Geneva and Teun Van Dijk, eds. *Discourse and Discrimination*. Detroit, MI: Wayne State University Press, 1988.

Snibbe, Alana Conner and Hazel Rose Markus. "You Can't Always Get What You Want: Educational Attainment, Agency, and Choice." *Journal of Personality and Social Psychology* 88, no. 4 (2005): 703–720. doi: 10.1037/0022-3514.88.4.703.

The Society of Professional Journalists. "Build Some Background." In: The Whole Story: Diversity Tips and Tools, 2015. Accessed February 19, 2018 from www.spj.org/ divws3.asp.

Solorzano, Daniel G. and Tara J. Yosso. "From Racial Stereotyping and Deficit Discourse toward a Critical Race Theory in Education." *Multicultural Education* 9, no. 1 (Fall 2001): 2–8.

Sommers, Samuel R. and Satia A. Marotta. "Racial Disparities in Legal Outcomes: On Policing, Charging Decisions, and Criminal Trial Proceedings." *Policy Insights from the Behavioral and Brain Sciences* 1, no. 1 (2014): 103–111.

Sommers, Zach. "Missing White Woman Syndrome: An Empirical Analysis of Race and Gender Disparities in Online News Coverage of Missing Persons." *Journal of Criminal Law and Criminology* 106, no. 2 (Spring 2016): 275–314.

Song Richardson, L. and Phillip A. Goff. "Self-Defense and the Suspicion Heuristic." *Iowa Law Review* 98, no. 1 (2012): 293–336.

Stanley, Damian A., Peter Sokol-Hessner, Mahzarin R. Banaji, and Elizabeth A. Phelps. "Implicit Race Attitudes Predict Trustworthiness Judgments and Economic Trust Decisions." *PNAS Proceedings of the National Academy of Sciences of the United States of America* 108, no. 19 (2011): 7710–7775. doi: 10.1073/pnas.10 14345108.

Steele, Claude. *Whistling Vivaldi: And Other Clues to How Stereotypes Affect Us.* New York, NY: W.W. Norton & Company, 2010.

Steele, Shelby. *A Dream Deferred.* New York, NY: Harper Perennial, 1999.

Stein, Rob. "Leaving Segregated Neighborhoods Lowers Blacks' Blood Pressure." National Public Radio, May 15, 2017. Retrieved the same day from www.npr.org/sections/health-shots/2017/05/15/527966937/leaving-segregated-neighborhoods-lowers-blacks-blood-pressure.

Stewart, A. "Why Newsroom Diversity Works: Effective Strategies for Making Newsrooms More Inclusive." Nieman Reports, June 2015. Accessed December 17, 2015 from http://niemanreports.org/articles/why-newsroom-diversity-works/.

Stivers, Tanya and Asifa Majid. "Questioning Children: Interactional Evidence of Implicit Bias in Medical Interviews." *Social Psychology Quarterly* 70, no. 4 (2007): 424–441. doi: 10.1177/019027250707000410.

Stockman, Farah. "Who Were the Counterprotesters in Charlottesville?" *New York Times*, August 24, 2017. Accessed July 7, 2018 from www.nytimes.com/2017/08/14/us/who-were-the-counterprotesters-in-charlottesville.html.

Stolberg, Sheryl Gay and Stephen Babcock. "Scenes of Chaos in Baltimore as Thousands Protest Freddie Gray's Death." *New York Times*, April 25, 2015. Accessed February 3, 2018 from www.nytimes.com/2015/04/26/us/baltimore-crowd-swells-in-protest-of-freddie-grays-death.html.

Streitfeld, David. "Welcome to Zucktown: Where Everything Is Just Zucky." *New York Times*, March 21, 2018. Accessed March 25, 2018 from www.nytimes.com/2018/03/21/technology/facebook-zucktown-willow-village.html.

Struthers, Silvia. "Hispanic Dropout Rate Raises Concern in Houston." *Houston Chronicle*, May 26, 2012. Accessed March 2, 2017 from www.chron.com/news/houston-texas/article/Houston-s-Hispanics-dropping-out-of-school-at-3587972.php.

Sugrue, Thomas. *The Origins of the Urban Crisis.* Princeton, NJ: Princeton University Press, 1996.

Sullivan, Laura. "Behind the Bail Bond System." National Public Radio. Three-part series. January 21–22, 2010. Accessed March 8, 2017 from www.npr.org/series/122954677/behind-the-bail-bond-system.

Swan, Rachel. "Public Health Problems in Oakland Linked to Housing Crisis." *San Francisco Chronicle*, September 1, 2016. Accessed March 17, 2018 from www.sfgate.com/bayarea/article/Housing-crisis-linked-to-public-health-problems-919 3855.php.

Swift, Art. "In U.S., Confidence in Newspapers Still Low but Rising." Gallup, June 28, 2017. Accessed July 7, 2018 from https://news.gallup.com/poll/212852/confidence-newspapers-low-rising.aspx.

Sylvie, George. "The Call and Challenge for Diversity." In Wilson Lowrey and Peter J. Gade (eds.). *Changing the News: The Forces Shaping Journalism in Uncertain Times.* New York, NY: Routledge, 2011.

Takaki, Ronald. *A Different Mirror: A History of Multicultural America.* New York, NY: Little, Brown and Company, 1993.

Tatum, Beverly Daniel. *Why are All the Black Kids Sitting Together in the Cafeteria: And Other Conversations about Race.* New York, NY: Basic Books, 1997.

Tavernise, Sabrina. "Health Problems Take Root in a West Baltimore Neighborhood that is Sick of Neglect." *New York Times,* April 29, 2015. Accessed February 28, 2017 from www.nytimes.com/2015/04/30/us/health-problems-take-root-in-a-west-balti more-neighborhood-that-is-sick-of-neglect.html?hp&action=click&pgtype=Homepa ge&module=b-lede-package-region&region=top-news&WT.nav=top-news&_r=0.

Teachman, Bethany A., Kathrine D. Gapinski, Kelly D. Brownell, Melissa Rawlins, and Subathra Jeyaram. "Demonstrations of Implicit Anti-Fat Bias: The Impact of Providing Causal Information and Evoking Empathy." *Health Psychology* 22, no. 1 (2003): 68–78. doi: 10.1037/0278-6133.22.1.68.

Tesler, Michael. *Post-Racial or Most-Racial? Race and Politics in the Obama Era.* Chicago, IL: University of Chicago Press, 2016.

Thernstrom, Stephen and Abigail Thernstrom. *America in Black and White: One Nation, Indivisible.* New York, NY: Simon & Schuster, 1997.

Tilly, Charles. *Durable Inequality.* Berkeley, CA: University of California Press, 1998.

Tow, Charlene. *The Effects of School Funding on Student Academic Achievement: A Study of California School Districts 2000–2004.* Undergraduate Economic Honors Thesis, University of California, Berkeley. Spring 2006. Accessed July 8, 2018 from https://pdfs.semanticscholar.org/c5ac/56ccc2f172cdcee48ec468f3041bb5c91794.pdf.

Tsai, Alexander C. 2015. "Home Foreclosure, Health, and Mental Health: A Systematic Review of Individual, Aggregate, and Contextual Associations." *Plos ONE* 10, no. 4 (2015): 1–21.

Tuchman, Gaye. "Objectivity as Strategic Ritual: An Examination of Newsmen's Notions of Objectivity." *American Journal of Sociology* 77, no. 4 (January 1972): 660–679.

Tukachinsky, Riva, Dana Mastro, and Moran Yarchi. "Documenting Portrayals of Race/ Ethnicity on Primetime Television Over a 20-Year Span and Their Association with National-Level Racial/Ethnic Attitudes." *Journal of Social Issues* 71, no. 1 (2015): 17–38. doi: 10.1111/josi.12094.

Turkewitz, Julie. "For Native Americans, Historic Moment on the Path to Power at the Ballot Box." *New York Times,* January 4, 2018. Accessed January 4, 2017 from www.nytimes.com/2018/01/04/us/native-american-voting-rights.html?rref=collection% 2Ftimestopic%2FNative%20Americans&action=click&contentCollection=timesto pics&region=stream&module=stream_unit&version=latest&contentPlacement=1&pg type=collection&_r=0.

Turner, Caroline Sotello Viernes, Juan Carlos Gonzalez, and J. Luke Wood. "Faculty of Color in Academe: What 20 Years of Literature Tells Us." *Journal of Diversity in Higher Education* 1, no. 3 (September 2008): 139–168. doi: 10.1037/a0012837.

U.S. Department of Health and Human Services Office of Minority Health. "Profile: Asian Americans." https://minorityhealth.hhs.gov/omh/browse.aspx?lvl=3&lvlid=63.

Van Dijk, Teun. "Critical Discourse Studies: A Sociocognitive Approach." In Ruth Wodak and Michael Meyer (eds.). *Methods of Critical Discourse Analysis*, Second Edition. London: Sage Publications, 2010, p. 63.

Van Noorden, Richard. "U.S. Women Progress to PhD at Same Rate as Men." *Nature*, February 17, 2015. Accessed March 14, 2017 from www.nature.com/news/us-women-progress-to-phd-at-same-rate-as-men-1.16939.

Vicens, A.J. "Native Americans Get Shot by Cops at an Astonishing Rate." *Mother Jones*, July 15, 2015. Accessed July 9, 2018 from www.motherjones.com/politics/2015/07/native-americans-getting-shot-police/.

Vigen, Tyler. Spurious Correlations. 2015. Accessed April 30, 2018 from http://tylervi gen.com/spurious-correlations.

W. Haywood Burns Institute. "Stemming the Rising Tide: Racial & Ethnic Disparities in Youth Incarceration & Strategies for Change." May 2016. Accessed February 10, 2018 from www.burnsinstitute.org/wp-content/uploads/2016/05/Stemming-the-Rising-Tide_FINAL.pdf.

Wagner, Venise. "The Dream Today: Economic Equality." *San Francisco Examiner*, January 17, 2000. Accessed March 23, 2017 from www.sfgate.com/news/article/The-dream-today-Economic-equality-3079184.php.

Walker, Renee, Christopher R. Keane, and Jessica G. Burke. "Disparities and Access to Healthy Foods in the United States: A Review of Food Deserts Literature." *Health and Place* 16, no. 5 (2010): 876–884.

Walker, Rheeda L., David Alabi, Jessica Roberts, and Ezemenari M. Obasi. "Ethnic Group Differences in Reasons for Living and the Moderating Role of Cultural Worldview." *Cultural Diversity & Ethnic Minority Psychology* 16, no. 3 (2010): 372–378.

"Was Trayvon Martin Targeted for Being Black?" NPR's Tell Me More program. March 20, 2012. Accessed February 22, 2018 from http://wamc.org/post/was-tray von-martin-targeted-being-black.

Welch, Ashley. "Surprising Discovery on Racial Disparities in Health Care." CBS News, September 25, 2015. Accessed February 19, 2018 from www.cbsnews.com/news/when-health-care-is-equal-blacks-fare-better-than-whites/.

Weston Phippen, J. "How One Law Banning Ethnic Studies Led to Its Rise." *The Atlan-tic*, July 19, 2015. Accessed March 8, 2018 from www.theatlantic.com/education/arch ive/2015/07/how-one-law-banning-ethnic-studies-led-to-rise/398885/.

Wherry, Laura R. and Sarah Miller. "Early Coverage, Access, Utilization, and Health Effects Associated with the Affordable Care Act Medicaid Expansions: A Quasi-Experimental Study." *Annals of Internal Medicine* 164, no. 12 (2016): 795–803. doi: 10.7326/M15-2234.

Widner, Daniel and Stephen Chicoine. "It's All in the Name: Employment Discrimination against Arab Americans." *Sociological Forum* 26, no. 4 (2011): 806–823. doi: 10.1111/j.1573-7861.2011.01285.x.

Willard, Greg, Kyonne-Joy Isaac, and Dana R. Carney. "Some Evidence for the Nonver-bal Contagion of Racial Bias." *Organizational Behavior and Human Decision Processes* 128 (2015): 96–107. doi: 10.1016/j.obhdp.2015.04.002.

Wing, Nick. "When the Media Treats White Suspects Better than Black Victims." The Huffington Post, August 14, 2014. Accessed February 23, 2018 from www.huffington post.com/2014/08/14/media-black-victims_n_5673291.html.

Wolf, Richard. "From Heroin in Rental Car Trunk to Stolen Motorcycle, Supreme Court Defends Privacy Rights." *USA Today*, June 1, 2018. Accessed July 15, 2018 from www.usatoday.com/story/news/politics/2018/06/01/heroin-motorcycle-supreme-court-privacy-rights/660586002/.

Wolfe, Alan. "Enough Blame to Go Around." *New York Times Book Review*, June 21, 1998, p. 12.

Woodard, Stephanie. "The Police Killings No One Is Talking About." *In These Times*, October 17, 2016. Accessed July 9, 2018 from http://inthesetimes.com/features/native_american_police_killings_native_lives_matter.html.

Woodcock, Anna and Margo J. Monteith. "Forging Links with the Self to Combat Implicit Bias." *Group Processes & Intergroup Relations* 16, no. 4 (2013): 445–461.

Woods, Keith and Aly Colón. "Making Connections." *The Poynter Report*, Spring 2000.

Wozniak, Abigail. "Discrimination and the Effects of Drug Testing on Black Employment." *Review Of Economics And Statistics* 97, no. 3 (2015): 548–566. doi: 10.1162/REST_a_00482.

Yan, Holly and Dana Ford. "Baltimore Riots: Looting, Fires Engulf City after Freddie Gray's Funeral." CNN, April 28, 2015. Accessed February 3, 2018 from www.cnn.com/2015/04/27/us/baltimore-unrest/index.html.

Yeung, Bernice and Grace Rubenstein. "Female Workers Face Rape, Harassment in U.S. Agricultural Industry." Center for Investigative Reporting, June 25, 2013. Accessed August 8, 2017 from http://cironline.org/reports/female-workers-face-rape-harassment-us-agriculture-industry-4798.

CONTRIBUTORS

The Editors

Sally Lehrman is an award-winning reporter on medicine and science policy with an emphasis on race, gender, and social diversity. She is founder and CEO of the Trust Project (http://www.thetrustproject.org), a network of newsrooms around the world that is implementing the Trust Indicators for news, a standard of transparency that helps both audiences and search engines recognize ethical, honest journalism out of the hubbub online. Lehrman's byline credits include *Scientific American, Nature, Health*, the *Boston Globe*, the *New York Times*, Salon.com and *The DNA Files*, several public documentary series distributed by NPR. Before going independent, she was a reporter and editor at the Hearst-owned *San Francisco Examiner* for more than a decade. Her book, *News in a New America*, argues for an inclusive news media and her teaching has emphasized community-based reporting on the structures that influence health equity. Her honors include a Peabody Award, a duPont-Columbia Award, and the JSK Fellowship at Stanford University. Lehrman is Science and Justice Professor at the UC-Santa Cruz Center for Science and Justice.

Venise Wagner is a professor of journalism at San Francisco State University, where she has taught since 2001. She has a 12-year career as a reporter for several California dailies, including the *Orange County Register*, the *San Francisco Examiner* and *Chronicle*. She has covered border issues, religion and ethics, schools and education, urban issues, and issues in the Bay Area's various black communities. She holds a BS in chemistry from the University of Illinois, Champaign-Urbana and an MA in international policy studies, with an emphasis in Latin America, from the Monterey Institute of International Studies, now known as the Middlebury

Institute of International Studies. Wagner integrates cultural proficiency and intercultural communication in the journalism curriculum as a way to enhance students' ability to write across a variety of cultures and experiences outside of their own.

The Contributors

Michael K. Brown is Professor Emeritus of Politics at UC Santa Cruz and the author of *Race, Money, and the American Welfare State* and co-author of *Whitewashing Race: The Myth of a Color-Blind Society*. His current research focuses on race and equality of opportunity during three moments of madness – Reconstruction, the New Deal, and the Great Society – in six Southern states.

Martin Carnoy is the Vida Jacks Professor of Education at Stanford University School of Education. He is a labor economist with a special interest in the relation between the economy and the educational system. To this end, he studies the US labor market, including the role in the relation of race, ethnicity, and gender, the US educational system, and systems in many other countries. He uses comparative analysis to understand how education influences productivity and economic growth, and, in turn, how and why educational systems change over time, and why some countries' educational systems are marked by better student performance than others.

Sue Ellen Christian is a professor of communication at Western Michigan University, which in 2014–2015 awarded her the university's highest teaching award. She is the author of *Overcoming Bias: A Journalist's Guide to Culture and Context* (Holcomb Hathaway Publishers, 2012). Christian was an award-winning reporter for the *Chicago Tribune* and has also served on the reporting staffs of the *Detroit News* and the *Los Angeles Times*.

Angie Chuang is an associate professor of journalism in the College of Media, Communication and Information at the University of Colorado, Boulder. She is a former reporter with an 11-year career as a reporter for a variety of daily newspapers including *The Oregonian* and *The Hartford Courant*. Her research focus is on American otherness and on race and identity construction in the news media.

Elliott Currie is Professor of Criminology, Law, and Society at the University of California, Irvine. He has also taught in the Legal Studies Program at the University of California, Berkeley, and in the Board of Studies in Sociology at the University of California, Santa Cruz. Professor Currie is the author of many works on crime, juvenile delinquency, drug abuse, and social policy, including *Confronting Crime* (1985), *Dope and Trouble: Portraits of Delinquent Youth* (1991), *Reckoning: Drugs, the Cities, and the American Future* (1993), and *Crime and Punishment in*

America (1998), which was a finalist for the 1999 Pulitzer Prize in General Nonfiction. He is a coauthor of *Whitewashing Race: The Myth of a Colorblind America* (2003), a finalist for the C. Wright Mills award of the Society for the Study of Social Problems in 2004 and winner of the 2004 Book Award from the Benjamin L. Hooks Institute for Social Change.

Karen de Sá is an investigative reporter for *The San Francisco Chronicle* whose work has focused on child welfare, juvenile justice, and social services. Over a 25-year career, her projects have exposed injustice in youth prisons, courts, and the foster care system, including the excessive use of psychotropic drugs and unnecessary arrests at children's shelters. A 2006 Knight Fellow at Stanford University and finalist for the Goldsmith Award for Investigative Reporting, de Sá has won numerous journalism honors, including Investigative Reporters and Editors Awards, the American Bar Association's Silver Gavel Award, and the Heywood Broun and National Headliners awards. Her work has led to nine laws and improved public contracts with the nation's most vulnerable populations.

Troy Duster is one of seven authors of *Whitewashing Race: The Myth of a Color-Blind Society*. Duster is a sociologist with research interests in the sociology of science, public policy, race and ethnicity, and deviance. He is a Chancellor's Professor of Sociology at UC Berkeley and professor of sociology and director of the Institute for the History of the Production of Knowledge at New York University. Duster is the grandson of civil rights activist Ida B. Wells-Barnett. In 1970, he wrote *The Legislation of Morality*, in which he showed how the moral indignation regarding addiction at the time of the Harrison Narcotic Law (1914) pointed fingers not at the middle- and upper-class users of drugs but at the lower classes of Americans.

Susan Ferriss is a prize-winning investigative reporter at the Center for Public Integrity and a former foreign correspondent. She has investigated the treatment of children by the US justice and immigration system, law enforcement, and the school-discipline process. She won a first-place investigative prize from the national Education Writers Association for her 2012 series revealing how thousands of Los Angeles school police citations were pushing mostly Latino and black kids into courts for minor infractions. In 2014, she won Columbia University's Tobenkin national journalism award for reporting on institutionalized discrimination against Latino farmworker children. As a reporter at the *Sacramento Bee*, Susan produced prize-winning immigration stories and covered state government and politics. And as a Latin America correspondent with Cox Newspapers, Susan covered everything from indigenous rights movements and death squads in Colombia to transnational migration and drug trafficking. She was a JSK fellow at Stanford University and is a graduate of the University of California, Santa Cruz, and UC Berkeley.

Nikole Hannah-Jones is an award-winning investigative reporter covering racial injustice for *The New York Times Magazine*. Her most recent investigation documents the resegregation of Southern schools through an intensive look at Tuscaloosa, Alabama, one of the most rapidly resegregating districts in the country. The investigation shows the backroom dealing, political compromises, and intentional decision-making that has led to resegregation, while also laying out the devastating personal consequences. Hannah-Jones has also written extensively about the decades-long failure of the federal government to enforce the landmark 1968 Fair Housing Act and analyses of the racial implications of the controversial *Fisher* v. *University of Texas* affirmative action and other civil rights cases before the Supreme Court. Her reporting has been featured in *Pro-Publica, The Atlantic Magazine, Essence Magazine, Grist, Politico Magazine*, and on Face the Nation, This American Life, NPR, the Tom Joyner Morning Show, MSNBC, C-SPAN, among others. She is also a 2017 recipient of the MacArthur Fellowship.

Simon Howard is Assistant Professor of Psychology at Marquette University. His research focuses on the social psychological underpinnings of racial disparities, and individual and institutional manifestations of racial bias.

Alden Loury is director of research and evaluation at the Metropolitan Planning Council in Chicago. Before that, he served as investigative reporter and policy analyst at the Better Government Association. During his time there, Loury provided research, data analyses and lobbying for reform efforts to address inefficient and unethical practices in government. He also wrote several stories analyzing campaign finance data, redistricting changes and government spending.

Loury also spent 12 years at *The Chicago Reporter* serving as a reporter, an editor, and publisher. During his time there, Loury won several journalism awards for stories highlighting the experiences of young black men and documenting racial disparities in drug sentencing, jury selection, and jury verdicts. As an editor, he led and analyzed data for more than 50 investigative projects examining the impact of race and poverty in lottery ticket sales, fatal police shootings of civilians, retail leakage in black neighborhoods, residential development surrounding demolished public housing, and subprime home mortgage lending, among others. As publisher, he shared *The Chicago Reporter*'s findings in numerous media appearances and meetings with elected officials.

Jeff Kelly Lowenstein is an assistant professor at Grand Valley State University in Grand Rapids, Michigan. Before he began his academic career he served as database and investigative editor at *Hoy Chicago*, the Chicago Tribune company's Spanish-language newspaper. He has won numerous awards and honors including an appointment as a Fulbright Scholar and as a Laventhol visiting professor at Columbia University. He is also past president of the Ochberg Society for

Trauma Journalism, an international organization of journalists who cover issues of trauma and violence with sensitivity and compassion. His work has been published in *The New Yorker* and the *Center for Public Integrity*, among many publications, and has earned local, regional, national, and international recognition from organizations like the National Press Club, Investigative Reporters and Editors, the Society for News Design, and the National Association of Black Journalists. He has written two books and currently blogs for the Huffington Post.

Satia A. Marotta is a doctoral candidate in the psychology department at Tufts University. Her research focuses on how social psychology can inform law and public policy, especially with regard to issues of diversity and equality.

Omedi Ochieng is an assistant professor of communication at Denison University, in Granville, Ohio. His areas of expertise include rhetorical theory and criticism; the rhetoric of philosophy and the philosophy of rhetoric; social normativity; and the intersection of culture and media studies. Among other topics, he is exploring how knowledge is inflected by class, gender, race, sexuality, disability, and so on. He has published articles in the *International Philosophical Quarterly, Radical Philosophy*, and the *Western Journal of Communication*. He teaches courses on rhetorical criticism, public address, communication theory, and philosophies of the good life.

David B. Oppenheimer is a clinical professor of law at UC Berkeley Law. Following his graduation from Harvard Law School, Professor Oppenheimer clerked for California Chief Justice Rose Bird. He then worked as a staff attorney for the California Department of Fair Employment and Housing, prosecuting discrimination cases, and was the founding director of the Boalt Hall Employment Discrimination Clinic. He is co-author of *Whitewashing Race: The Myth of a Color-Blind Society* (with M. Brown et al.) (University of California Press, 2003).

Majorie M. Shultz is Professor Emerita at UC Berkeley Law. After graduating from Berkeley Law, Shultz joined the school's faculty in 1976. She has authored numerous articles on medical research, informed consent, and health care law, as well as commentaries on the intersection of contracts, feminism, and family issues. Shultz is a co-author of *Whitewashing Race: The Myth of A Color-Blind Society* (2003). Other recent publications include "Conflict of Interest and the Law's Role in Medical Research Ethics," published as part of a collection by the University of Lausanne.

Marquita S. Smith, associate professor of communication at John Brown University, worked in various newsrooms over 16 years. Her most recent role was as the Virginia Beach bureau chief at *The Virginian-Pilot*, which she joined as a local government editor in 2001 and left in 2010. At *The Pilot*, Smith championed diversity efforts and served as a diversity trainer and facilitator. In 2008, Smith went on leave from *The Pilot* to complete a Knight International Journalism Fellowship in Liberia. During her year in West Africa, she created a judicial and justice reporting network and continues to help journalists develop skills to cover the post-war nation's poverty reduction efforts. Ghanaians elected a new president in 2008, and she created several training models to help reporters and editors prepare for covering the event. In 2016 she returned to Ghana on a Fulbright teaching and research position to enhance media development across several platforms. Before moving to Virginia, she worked as an assistant metro editor at the Montgomery (Alabama) *Advertiser.* She also has worked as a reporter at the *Lexington-Herald Leader*, the (Biloxi) *Sun Herald* and in Knight Ridder's Washington bureau. Smith was named one of the Top 50 Journalism Professors as published on journalismdegree.org. Besides teaching, Smith serves as coordinator for diversity relations at John Brown University.

Samuel R. Sommers is professor in the Department of Psychology at Tufts University in Medford, Massachusetts. He is a social psychologist whose research focuses on issues related to intergroup relations, diversity, and how a group's composition affects its dynamics and performance.

David Wellman, a co-author and lead editor in *Whitewashing Race*, is professor emeritus in community studies and the sociology department of UC-Santa Cruz. His research focuses on working class culture, American ethnic and racial diversity, critical race theory, interrogations of whiteness, and social documentary studies. He is author of *"You Understand?" Portraits of White Racism*, which advanced a sociological theory of racism in the late 1970s.

Keith Woods is Vice President, Newsroom Training & Diversity at NPR. He leads NPR's team that works with journalists in the NPR newsroom and those at more than 260-member stations across the country, training them in leadership, story-telling, editing, audio engineering, digital strategy, and diversity. He is member of the corporate and newsroom leadership teams, working on organizational strategy and key initiatives. Keith joined *NPR* in 2010 to lead the organization's diversity programs. He was Dean of Faculty of The Poynter Institute, a school for journalists in St. Petersburg, Florida, and taught for 15 years in courses ranging from reporting on race relations, to diversity, ethics, and newspaper writing. He is co-author of *The Authentic Voice: The Best Reporting on Race and Ethnicity*, a text still used in some of the nation's top journalism schools. While at Poynter, Keith chaired two Pulitzer Prize juries. He has worked to help professionals, faculty, and students better understand and handle matters of diversity and race relations through workshops at dozens of journalism schools and major radio stations, newspapers, and television stations across the country.

He is a native of New Orleans and a graduate of Dillard University and the Tulane University graduate school of social work. He is a former sports writer, news reporter, city editor, editorial writer, and columnist, working his way through those jobs in 16 years at the New Orleans *Times-Picayune*.

INDEX